EXTREME MUSIC

FROM SILENCE TO NOISE AND EVERYTHING IN BETWEEN
by MICHAEL TAU

EXTREME MUSIC
FROM SILENCE TO NOISE AND EVERYTHING IN BETWEEN

©2022 Michael Tau

Designed by Ron Kretsch

ISBN: 9781627311243

Feral House
1240 W Sims Way #124
Port Townsend WA 98368

www.feralhouse.com

10 9 8 7 6 5 4 3 2 1

TABLE OF CONTENTS

INTRODUCTION

In 2007, a noise music duo from Italy released an album on CD-R that came in a box filled with cooked spaghetti and pesto. When it arrived in the mail, it was caked in mold. In 1989, a Dutch musician named Freek Kinkelaar put out a 12" single on an American label that was nothing more than a wad of vinyl with directions to heat it up and flatten it into a record, then play it on one's home stereo. In 2010, an experimental music group from Denver put out an album that was 5.7 years long. It was made available to download for free—but required over a terabyte of memory to store.

The purpose of this book is to look at musical and quasi-musical moments such as these and to try to understand them. I conducted over one hundred interviews to identify strains of conceptually extreme music, ranging from the edges of the mainstream to the deepest recesses of the underground.

In section one, I look at several music scenes marked by their extremeness, exploring music that is extremely loud, quiet, fast, vulgar, and candid. A sub-sub-subgenre of experimental music called Harsh Noise Wall consists of producers who create long, unchanging blocks of pure noise. An unusual offshoot of electronic music, speedcore, includes beats that are so fast, they stop sounding like beats and instead become tones. Goregrind is a variant of extreme metal that revels in detailed descriptions of human viscera. In the process of uncovering these scenes, I explore how a genre can become an arms race toward extremeness and will also touch on the *zone of fruitless intensification*.

In section two, I look at the extremes of duration: very long compositions and very short ones. In this area of highly conceptual music, I explore the very different reasons people are drawn to these peculiarly impractical compositions. One producer tells me about fitting eighty-three tracks into two seconds. A PhD-trained composer, meanwhile, explains that his million-years-long tape composition is a tribute to Mark Rothko's paintings.

In section three, I focus on the physical format of vinyl records. I start by exploring records that are unusually small and large—anywhere from one inch to twenty inches in diameter. I then explore the obscure history of picture discs, examine records that come in strange shapes, and delve into the intriguing world of hand-produced, lathe-cut records. I conclude with records that transcend the limits of vinyl, including discs adulterated with hair and blood and records made entirely of chocolate or ice.

In section four, I look at some unusual music formats. I examine the aesthetic of being willfully archaic, telling the history of chiptune (or 8-bit) music and looking at labels that put out music at extremely low bitrates. I then speak with members of communities devoted to outdated methods of sound reproduction, who cannibalize dusty 8-track cartridges for parts and scour eBay for blank microcassettes.

In section five, I touch on gimmicks like scented records before examining some truly unusual packaging concepts from underground music scenes. I speak with John Olson, who has run American Tapes since the early nineties, crafting elaborate handmade cassette packages from detritus from an antiques store. Fabrizio De Bon talks about his record label, Toxic Industries, which has released music sealed inside broken hard drives. I then look at releases with deliriously grotesque cover art and profile several releases that incorporate real body fluids into their cover art. And finally, I look at packaging that is perishable—rotting covers that challenge record collectors to hang on to progressively putrefying objects.

In section six, I explore records that challenge our very concept of music. These include records that are silent, records that are intentionally damaged, and records that are fundamentally unplayable. An entrepreneur named Jerry Cammarata tells me about how he pressed a silent record in the seventies, bandying it as a tool for self-reflection. The experimental artist GX Jupitter-Larsen details the story of a record that came accompanied by a handful of dirt. Ron Lessard, who runs RRRecords, takes me through several unplayable releases he has unleashed upon the world. I relate these releases to the Dadaist concept of anti-art.

In section seven, I conclude the tour by looking at a handful of phenomena that have emerged in the digital age, including online music subcultures focused on hyper-specific concepts—for example, evoking the sensation of walking through an abandoned mall. Finally, I detail how the world of outsider music has survived and thrived with the advent of online music distribution.

In examining these music phenomena, I showcase the diverse reasons people have created these unusual works, while also highlighting their commonalities. I am indebted to the many artists, producers, and record label owners who have told me their stories. Over the course of this book, their words bring these tales alive, revealing the strange and very human motivations that underlie the world of extreme music.

SECTION I

EXTREME SCENES

1.1 LOUD

"I'm a family man with two children. I currently work in administration. But I'm also a noise artist and a music fan. All these different levels make up my personality. I also feel it's important to dissolve my personality into noise from time to time. My family understands that and knows that it is a real necessity for me to do that."

— Romain Perrot a.k.a. Vomir, August 20, 2014[1]

There are several music scenes that emphasize loudness. Countless breeds of metal, several species of punk, multiple shades of electronic music, and even older styles like rock 'n' roll and funk have worshiped at the altar of *loud*. When it comes to recorded music, the listener ultimately controls the volume knob—but that hasn't stopped many a rapper, singer, and grindcore growler from commanding you to "turn it up!"

In my mind, post-hardcore bands like Unsane and Helmet are among the most impressive purveyors of viscerally loud music. But they traffic in a very subjective loudness that is difficult to disentangle from the far more nebulous concept of *heaviness*. I might find a Jawbox song loud, whereas someone else might feel the same way about a Skrillex bass drop or an orchestral hit.

1.1.1 The Loudness War

The *loudness war* offers one objective example of loudness in recorded music. This is the name given to a phenomenon in which recording engineers manipulate the sonic parameters of a recording to make it sound louder. These tweaks allow the music to compete for listeners' attention against other songs on the radio, or to enable songs to separate themselves from the din—for example, to sound crisp and clear while listened to through earbuds in a noisy subway car. Sound engineers accomplish this using a method called *dynamic range compression*. To understand how this works, it's helpful to visualize the effect on a diagram of the sound spectrum.

For example, take a recording that looks like this:

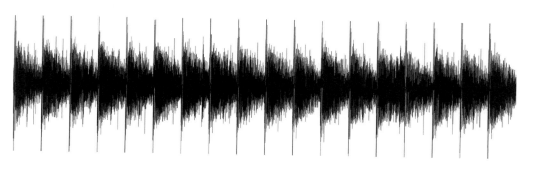

---

1   Russell Williams, 'Anti-Musicality: An Interview With Romain Perrot Of VOMIR,' *The Quietus*, 2014 <thequietus.com/articles/16050-romain-perrot-vomir-interview-harsh-noise-wall> [accessed 27 July 2020].

EXTREME MUSIC

At any given point, the taller the audio spectrum is, the louder that part sounds. Those tall spikes are the sounds of the drums, which are the loudest elements of a song in a traditional recording.

Sounds cannot get louder than the height of the audio spectrum. This is because the top boundary of the spectrum is the standardized maximum, as set by compact disc technology. Anything that transgresses the top boundary will sound distorted, which is what people mean when they refer to something being "in the red." Therefore, the maximum loudness of a recording is a relative value, since the listener can just turn up their stereo to increase the absolute loudness.

These principles are important, because they explain how dynamic range compression can be used to change how music is perceived. Using audio processing software, engineers will flatten the entire sound spectrum, like so, and compress everything together. The peaks where the drums used to be are pushed down to the same volume as the rest of the instruments.

Then the whole thing is stretched out, like so, to make it loud:

As you can see, once compressed, the drums no longer pop out. Instead, all parts of the piece are nestled just below the upper maximum threshold of sound. As a result, the entire recording sounds much louder when played at the same volume as an uncompressed song. The drums don't pop as much; instead, *everything* blares.

The loudness war emerged as a strategy to sell more music by commandeering the listener's attention. Dynamic range compression allows songs to sound clear in a real-world setting—for example, when piped out of ceiling speakers at a supermarket.

In the early 2000s, engineers and old-school artists like Bob Dylan began to complain that dynamic range compression stripped music of its natural dynamics. "You listen to these modern records, they're atrocious, they have sound all over them," Dylan said in a 2006 interview with Jonathan Lethem for *Rolling Stone* magazine. "There's no definition of nothing, no vocal, no nothing, just like—static."[2]

---

2 Jonathan Lethem, 'The Genius and Modern Times of Bob Dylan,' *Rolling Stone*, 2006 <www.rollingstone.com/music/music-news/the-genius-and-modern-times-of-bob-

Audiophiles then complained that dynamically compressed music led to "ear fatigue." Critics demonized certain egregious recordings, for example Metallica's *Death Magnetic*, claiming that its use of compression was so wanton that the whole album sounded distorted and unnatural. The Red Hot Chili Peppers' album *Californication* was also shellacked for its heavy use of compression. Nick Southall, in his seminal loudness war article for *Stylus* magazine, "Imperfect Sound Forever,"[3] noted that even non-audiophiles complained about its loudness and clipping.

Amid the hubbub about loudness, it was only a matter of time before an artist used dynamic range compression as a pointed aesthetic choice. In 2010, the Brooklyn band Sleigh Bells designed their debut album, *Treats*, to exploit compression, using it gratuitously as its own form of artistic expression. In an interview with Valerie Siebert for *The Quietus*,[4] Sleigh Bells member Alexis Krauss acknowledges their use of the digital processing technique, which started off as a way of enhancing their lo-fi recordings. "All the beats were being made on really shitty drum stations, so kind of freaking it out and pushing everything into the red was one of the only ways it sounded good and was exciting to our ears," she explains.

Once they started recording in a professional studio, they decided to stick with the production tactic, noting it gave their music more punch. "Sleigh Bells is meant to be listened to over loud speakers in a live setting or club setting, and that is a trait that we're proud of, and it's intentional," she explains. "I think the dynamic and the loudness is something that works in our favor."

"Infinity Guitars," one of the most ubiquitous songs on *Treats*, is the summation of their obsession with compression. The guitars, drums, and vocals are pushed up to the point that they're constantly clipping. Each tone or drum hit is kind of scratchy, as though the original sound has been blowtorched, leaving a scorched husk.

Recent research has suggested that the loudness war, thought to be a contemporary phenomenon, is merely the latest chapter in a long-running debate. In an academic paper published in *Popular Music*, musicologist Kyle Devine argues that the current obsession with dynamic range compression is merely the latest iteration in a longstanding tension between loudness and fidelity.[5] The first marketed product to reproduce sound was the Edison cylinder, and these were only capable of playing at low volume, often necessitating an "ear tube" to amplify the audio. Then phonograph records arrived on the scene, and a big part of their appeal was their increased volume. But an echelon of early audiophiles often criticized the technology, claiming that records' increased amplitude came at the expense of sonic fidelity. Devine quotes a 1901 editorial from trade magazine *The Phonoscope*, comparing the gramophone's "blasty, whang-doodle noises" to "the braying of a wild ass."

This same tension between volume and fidelity would arise at significant turns in playback technology—for example, with the advent of electrical amplification, another evolution bemoaned by snobs but pushed into ubiquity by the mainstream. The

dylan-237203/> [accessed 27 July 2020].

3 Nick Southall, 'Imperfect Sound Forever,' *Stylus Magazine*, 2006 <web.archive.org/web/20130326021421/http://www.stylusmagazine.com/articles/weekly_article/imperfect-sound-forever.htm> [accessed 27 July 2020].

4 Valerie Siebert, 'Treats On Display: Sleigh Bells Interviewed,' *The Quietus*, 2010 <thequietus.com/articles/04778-sleigh-bells-interview-treats> [accessed 27 July 2020].

5 Kyle Devine, 'Imperfect Sound Forever: Loudness Wars, Listening Formations and the History of Sound Reproduction,' *Popular Music*, 2013, 159–76.

populist appeal of loud music has been continually derided by the audiophile clan, eager to disdain the public's musical hedonism as a rampant corruption of good sound.

Devine advocates that we move past the ideal of improved fidelity as the marker of achievement in audio technology. "The trade-offs between ideals of sound and practices of audition," he writes, "point to a need for histories and theories of sound reproduction that orbit less exclusively in the problem space of fidelity, and which are more attentive to the pragmatics and irreducible ontological pluralism of the audible past."[6]

Interestingly, some researchers have challenged the dogma of the loudness war, arguing that while music has indeed gotten louder, in most circumstances, this has not actually altered the dynamic range of today's music. In a dense technical article, audio engineers Emmanuel Deruty and Damien Tardieu use quantitative evidence from popular songs' sound spectrums to demonstrate that the "macrodynamics" in recorded music have not significantly changed over the past few decades. In other words, they argue the functional highs and lows that Bob Dylan considers endangered have not disappeared over time.

It's difficult to know what to make of all this. In the past few years, the outrage surrounding loudness seems to have cooled off a little. And most people don't get bogged down in the technical details. If something sounds good, why *not* listen to it?

On music's outer fringes, however, there exists a whole world of people who take loudness to a whole new extreme.

1.1.2 Noise Music

"The main idea was to take music as we know it and strip it entirely of what we know music to be. Its rhythm, musical tone, production quality, and construction, i.e. verse-chorus, verse-chorus nonsense."

—Knurl, circa 2008[7]

"This release was made using circular saw blades mounted on a length of threaded rod. The instrument had two contact mics on it, and each mic was hooked up to a separate bank of effects. Thereby giving the sound a stereo effect. It is probably my favourite recording to date. It's got a very intense wall of sound."

—Knurl, circa 2008[8]

For me, the aesthetic of loudness reaches its epitome in noise music, one of the rare music genres that truly lives up to its name. Imagine an entire scene of producers composing lengthy passages of abrasive white noise, usually by turning the dials on their equipment up so far that all that remains is feedback.

Paris-based producer Romain Perrot, a leading figure in noise music, captures the noise aesthetic in an interview with *Quietus*:

---

6   Devine.
7   'Knurl,' *Terror*, 2008 <www.terror.lt/news/31/61/Knurl.html> [accessed 27 July 2020].
8   'Knurl.'

"I'd encourage anyone who is interested in finding out more about noise who hasn't listened to it before just to take a radio, tune it to between two stations, and turn up the volume. If you can see the appeal, then perhaps it is time to investigate harsh noise in a little more detail."[9]

In fact, in 2014, a minor uproar surfaced in Cleveland after a DJ at Case Western University's campus radio station, WRUW, was told by his station manager to stop playing Perrot's music for fear that listeners were confusing it with radio static and tuning out.[10]

Noise as a concept is nothing new, and it has been a feature of experimental music dating back to the early twentieth century, from the recordings of Futurist artist Luigi Russolo through to the work of John Cage and the musique concrète composers. But many consider Lou Reed's 1975 double album *Metal Machine Music,* to be a seminal event in noise. Like much noise music to come, even that first album was shrouded in controversy. It's been rumored that Reed recorded it as a cynical gesture to fulfill his label's contractual obligations, or that it was a joke directed at his fans. In the liner notes, he claims that he didn't even listen to the whole thing before its release. A groundbreaking alternative music reference book, the *Trouser Press Record Guide,* had a lukewarm take on the record: "If he was simply looking to goad people and puncture perceptions, *Metal Machine Music* was a rousing success."[11] Elsewhere, *Rolling Stone* magazine described it as "the tubular groaning of a galactic refrigerator."[12]

Despite mainstream revulsion, *MMM*'s sound was an influential one. Today, it is seen as a key progenitor to a noise scene that developed in the late seventies and early eighties. Around then, a subculture of Japanese musicians started putting out cassettes filled with harsh noise, primarily using electric guitar reduced to feedback by effects units.

Several big names emerged from this Japanoise scene, many with exotic names that hinted at noise's cold industrial overtones (MSBR, short for Molten Salt Breeder Reactor) and curious relationship to the vulgarity of the human body (The Gerogerigegege, a Japanese onomatopoeia for vomiting and expelling diarrhea at the same time). Their noise often reveled in debasement and excess. The Gerogerigegege, a duo particularly fond of extremes, had a member named Gero 30, whose sole responsibility was to masturbate on stage, most famously by using a vacuum cleaner. Reportedly, both members of The Gerogerigegege would sometimes play with, and even eat, feces onstage.

But no noise act was as big as Merzbow, the pseudonym of Masami Akita, whose career has spanned five decades since his 1980 debut tape, *Fuckexercize.* An oft-cited noise music quotation is attributed to him: "If by noise, you mean uncomfortable sound, then pop music is noise to me."

---

9   Williams.

10   Doug Brown, 'WRUW's "Harsh Noise" Problem | Scene and Heard: Scene's News Blog,' *Cleveland Scene,* 2014 <www.clevescene.com/scene-and-heard/archives/2014/02/13/wruws-harsh-noise-problem> [accessed 27 July 2020].

11   Ira A. Robbins, *The Trouser Press Record Guide* (Collier Books, 1991).

12   James Wolcott, 'Metal Machine Music,' *Rolling Stone,* 1975 <www.rollingstone.com/music/music-album-reviews/metal-machine-music-99547/> [accessed 27 July 2020].

Merzbow's discography is unquantifiable, given the many lost releases along the way, but the website Discogs lists 374 official standalone releases, not including compilation appearances. The pièce de résistance is 2000's *Merzbox* boxed set, an elaborately designed stalwart on the Extreme label that entails fifty CDs of harsh noise. One thousand copies of this impenetrable bombshell were produced, selling at $450 USD apiece. A couple decades later, Extreme Records' Roger Richards estimates that fewer than 120 copies remain unsold.

Lou Reed's *Metal Machine Music* LP.

Many people argue that noise is a rejection of everything that makes music appealing as a commodity. And yet the massive noise pantheon, with its enormity of ultra-limited-edition releases, has produced a gigantic collectors' market. Obscure Japanoise tapes and records routinely sell for hundreds of dollars, and opportunistic record dealers have been known to monitor the release dates for recordings on labels like Hospital Productions and then buy up copies to immediately sell at multiples of their original price.

I asked Richards whether he thought the *Merzbox*, a slick item in a fancy case with various collectible odds and ends, was incompatible with noise as an anti-consumerist enterprise. He doesn't doubt that it's been fetishized by some, but he thinks that's a price worth paying. "I'm sure that some people do buy the *Merzbox* as a collector's item and never listen to the music. No doubt! The soft rubber Merzcase is a playful hint to this. But I also know that some have ventured into the many dimensions of noise music through the *Merzbox*—be it listening to other noise musicians or creating noise music themselves."

He points out that, like noise, many genres started out with an anti-consumerist message. "Punk, rock, and industrial to name a few." And while noise "has stood the test of anti-consumerism for many years for some would say obvious reasons," there have begun to be "fragments of noise entering pop music which is certainly a commodified music form."

But noise is also interesting because it's been written about quite prolifically from the standpoint of theory. Several papers and books have been published on the subject, most notably *Japanoise: Music at the Edge of Circulation* by David Novak and *Noise/Music* by Paul Hegarty. Reading Hegarty's musings on noise can be intense, as he parses concept after concept, becoming exponentially more abstract. I admire his love for the obscure details of the Japanese noise scene, although I somewhat resent his writing style, which amounts to reading sentence after sentence of this:

> *"This double failure—not being noise, not being music—is the only fleeting success noise can have. This is not negative, except at the level of noise being a negativity—i.e., noise*

The *Merzbox* boxed set, complete with extensive paraphernalia. Image courtesy of Roger Richards of Extreme Records

does not positively inhere in a specific piece or style of music, it occurs in a relation."[13]

You might be wondering what there is about static noise that warrants this sort of dense theorizing. Consider that *noise*, whose etymological origins stem from the Greek word *nausea*, refers to something broader than the phenomenon of geeks in non-prescription glasses rubbing contact mics through their pubic hair. Noise refers to stimuli that are gut-churning or aversive. Many define noise by what it is not—whereas music is "organized sound," noise is everything else. But what does that mean for those who prefer to listen to noise instead of "organized sound," or those who organize harsh noise into sound sculptures?

Hegarty summarizes several different theories of noise in his essay "Noise Music."[14] One theory sees noise as a triumph of the physical over the rational, a cathartic experience that can bring people together—the rave scene in the nineties being an example. Another sees noise as a form of "pure expression," for example the abstract spatters of paint in Jackson Pollock's work, which could be the visual analog of noise. Yet another interpretation sees noise as the "absence of meaning," though this becomes a bit of a paradox, since meaninglessness is, in fact, a form of meaning itself.

Most noise theory eventually references Theodor Adorno, a German philosopher who argued that all elements of culture essentially end up as commodities, including art. A connoisseur of classical music, he believed that popular culture essentially collapsed music, and all art, into subtle variations upon a theme, designed to entertain an easily placated public to serve the ends of industry. In Adorno's eyes, the avant-garde suffers the same fate, its lofty ideas similarly reduced to a product to be sold. In an article titled "Why Hardcore Goes Soft," writer Nicholas J. Smith reflects on Adorno as he laments the experience of buying a noise album, which he equates to "paying twenty dollars for an hour of noise."[15] He points out how rapidly noise and experimental music get typecast as oddball:

"...[T]he standard track for modernists' works is to be perceived as strange and dissonant, then to be appreciated as somehow artistically meaningful, and then to slip into cliché. When these stages are conflated and the strange and dissonant is immediately taken for the cliché, then art never hints at anything beyond one-dimensional instrumental culture."

13 Paul Hegarty, 'Noise Music,' *The Semiotic Review of Books*, 16 (2006).
14 Hegarty.
15 Nicholas J. Smith, 'Why Hardcore Goes Soft: Adorno, Japanese Noise, and the Extirpation of Dissonance,' *Cultural Logic*, 4.2 (2001), 2–4.

EXTREME MUSIC

The *Merzbox* is both enactment and satire of that concept. It's a consumer product that nods at its own collectability while simultaneously straining the limits of what can be considered consumable by the sheer fact that it comprises fifty CDs' worth of feedback noise. It is just about as close as you can get to an unlistenable work of music, but it looks great on a shelf.

1.1.3 Harsh Noise Wall (HNW)

"I have thought for a while that HNW is the endpoint of audio creation. there cannot be anything more extreme than a continuous barrage of static noise."
— Distorted Souls Within A Corrupt Vision, Oct. 6, 2016

Believe it or not, there exists a scene even noisier than noise music.

How to push harsh noise even further toward the extreme? The answer is harsh noise wall, a subgenre of noise music restricted to the purest of purists. A harsh noise wall, often abbreviated to HNW, is a noise composition that maintains an unchanging stretch of harsh noise throughout its duration, often for an hour or more. The sole event is the block of constant noise. If you start playing a track at the start, then skip ahead to the middle, there will be no change—at all points, the track will sound the same. This will often go on for an hour or more.

Pragmatically, an HNW is easy to make. An artist fires up a white noise generator, then channels the signal through one or more effects pedals or other devices. Once they find a specific set of parameters that appeal to them, they allow the equipment to run undisturbed, so that a constant noise is produced. Then they hit the record button and let the equipment do the work with no further human intervention, for however long they feel inclined. While artists will often expand by adding gradual shifts in texture throughout their compositions, the consensus is that true HNW is committed to an inflexible aesthetic: "no dynamics, no change, no development, no ideas." Those are the words of the subgenre's kingpin, Romain Perrot, who records HNW music as Vomir.[16]

One articulate HNW maestro, Julien Skrobek, helped me better understand the fine differences between styles of noise as he perceives them. He, like Vomir, argues that HNW is only to be used to describe a "static wall of harshness." If you add in "moving layers" of noise, it becomes a different subgenre, wall noise, which is sometimes associated with Texas, where a local scene thrives around a famous noisester who goes by Richard Ramirez. Meanwhile, any composition that includes elements of static noise but doesn't fulfill the pure definitions of HNW or wall noise would be given the tag "static noise." Conceptual dogmatism is important. For Skrobek, "if it's not pure, it ceases to be HNW and falls into a different subgenre according to me."

The idea of HNW is often traced back to Canadian noise musician The Rita, born Sam McKinlay, who is considered a pioneer of the concept of noise "walls." His moniker

---

16 *Vomir* is the French word meaning "to vomit," cycling back to the fact that the word *noise* has its origins in *nausea*.

comes from the name of the boat in *The Creature from the Black Lagoon*, one in a long line of references to horror and sci-fi films found in the noise scene. According to a 2007 interview with *Musique Machine* magazine, the inspiration for McKinlay's walls of noise dates to his university days, when he would create minimal visual art, culminating in a "large black-on-black painting." This work was inspired by the work of the abstract expressionist Ad Reinhardt, known for his extensive series of black paintings, which look like canvases painted black but, upon close scrutiny, reveal subtle combinations of black and nearly-black shades. The Rita's noise walls are the sonic equivalent to those black-on-almost-black squares—repellent blocks of harsh feedback that reveal their nuances under close examination.

Today, Romain Perrot is the scene's leading artist and philosopher. He is generally credited with establishing the concept of the *pure* harsh noise wall, working prolifically out of his home base in Paris. Since his debut, *Living Dead Noise*, Perrot has, as Vomir, had his stamp on over 350 individual releases on nearly as many different record, tape, and CD-R labels, many of them fitting the description of pure HNW.

Besides his massive body of work, Perrot has also emerged as a conceptual leader on the scene. He has even issued a manifesto, the "Manifeste du Mur Bruitiste," that describes HNW as more than a musical genre, and instead a way of life:

> *"The individual no longer has an alternative but to completely refuse the promoted and preached contemporary life. The only still free behavior is the noise and withdrawal, to never surrender to handling, socialization, and entertainment. The [Harsh Noise] Wall does not promise to repeatedly provide a direction and values with the lived existence. The opaque, dull, and continuous noise allows a total phenomenologic reduction, a means against the existential interpenetration: disengaged in the pure and unaltered bestial appeasing."*

It is hard not to see this sort of ideological grandstanding through the lens of art movements like Dada, Fluxus, and the Situationists, which helped define their ethos through weighty manifestos. Maybe it's a European thing.

If there is a foundational release in the HNW canon, a major contender would be *Total Slitting of Throats*, subtitled "An audible HNW manifesto." This was a 2005 CD-R that came out on The Rita's own label, Militant Walls. It compiles the efforts of five different noise acts: Mania, Sewer Election, The Cherry Point, Treriksröset, and The Rita himself. Each producer recorded their own wall, and then all five were overdubbed onto each other. The result is one single sixty-six-minute HNW—a constant, unchanging block of rough white noise. In a (one-star) review for *Tiny Mix Tapes*, critic S. Kobak makes reference to the "automatic" nature of the release: "It almost feels like the boys, most of who can be labeled as top-line experimental acts, left their oscillators buzzing while they went in the other room and took bong tokes."[17]

---

17 S. Kobak, 'Total Slitting of Throats - Total Slitting of Throats,' *Tiny Mix Tapes*, 2007 <www.tinymixtapes.com/music-review/total-slitting-throats-total-slitting-throats> [accessed 27 July 2020].

Certainly, there are many individuals, including those in the noise community, who are not sold on HNW's uncompromising conceptualism. If you want unfiltered opinions, go no further than online comments sections; sure enough, two separate commenters on Vomir's sprawling Discogs page poke fun at the interchangeability of his records, quipping that the "best song is untitled" and "untitled is best song."

Indeed, Romain Perrot is aware of how sonically similar his releases are. In the age-old tradition of HNW, he creates each noise wall by daisy-chaining several white noise generators and effects units together, setting their parameters, and then letting the resulting feedback play out unchangingly for a given length of time. This concept of interchangeability is also reflected in his attempts at anonymity. It is his trademark to wear a plastic bag over his head during performances.

The insert for the *Total Slitting of Throats* CD-R, featuring the first use of the acronym HNW. Image courtesy of Sam McKinlay, a.k.a. The Rita.

Perrot spoke to me from his mother's place in a small town in the Burgundy region of France. Perrot was born and lives in Paris, where he works an office job and raises two children with his wife. Yet this self-described "salary man and family man" has lived a parallel life for years, producing and performing HNW as well as other forms of experimental sound. Perrot tells me he loves pontificating on the theory of noise, but the real draw for him boils down to catharsis. "I've been to analysis, I've talked a lot about the different problems you can have as a human being," he explains. "But noise was so direct and so free in its blankness. It is like the avant-garde of Fluxus or the Lettrists, something like concrete poetry or sound poetry. You express feelings that are inside of you, but not in an intelligible way. You don't have to say complete sentences."

Nearing fifty now, he explains that he now knows a lot more about himself than he did when he started, and that his ability to put words to how he feels has advanced. "Noise is so blank, so free of any definite expression. That was absolutely perfect for me. I didn't have to put words to specific matters. It was just a letting go, an excess. It is a protest against everything, but of course it is against everything, so it is against nothing."

Echoing his moniker, he frames the HNW experience in visceral terms, describing it as "a way of saying I need to eject, to puke something out of me, to resist the world in which I am living." And yet he is clear to emphasize that, despite the impression abrasive noise walls may give as being violent in nature, they are not about aggression. "Noise is not to make people feel pain," he asserts. "Noise is not about pain. Noise is not about violence. Harsh noise is about being overwhelmed by this flow of sound, overwhelming sound, being processed in this big wave of sound that is just so cohesive. And that you can feel physically. It's a love of free expression."

Reflecting on the type of imagery that often shows up on the covers of noise and HNW releases—with extreme pornography and *Faces of Death*-style imagery abundant—he is careful to describe this transgressiveness as something like a rite of passage, emphasizing HNW's role as piercing the veil of normiedom. "At first glance, we confront you," he says. "We present you something that's a bit of a contrast to society, and then if you go through this first provocation and confrontational aspect of things, you get into exactly what noise is, what it is representing. And then you understand that this is just another way to look at society. And most of the time the pornography or the violence of the artwork are just a *deuxième degré*. It is not 'Oh, you should be really mean to women, or you should be a serial killer.' But it is more about: Just look exactly at your so-called normal society. And if I am different from my society, it's because I do not want to be part of this, I don't want to be a part of this very clean and proper, beautiful society that you are selling to me. This society is made of violence and crime and pornography and use of women. Degradation and everything."

While Perrot used to produce, record, and listen to noise every day, because his familial and career responsibilities have expanded, he now reserves a dedicated block of time on Friday evenings for it. He will set up chains of pedals and noise generators, hit *record*, and listen to his headphones. Sometimes he will have to halt the recording because the HNW isn't quite right: one frequency band overpowering the rest, taking away from his intended sound spectrum.

He tells me doesn't return to his old work at all. "Everything must be new," he declares. "I don't really revisit music I made in the past. My goal is getting the music recorded, and then I release it, and then I go to another project." This aesthetic choice helps contextualize his voluminous discography.

One thousand, eight-hundred and thirty-nine albums are classified as 'Harsh Noise Wall' on Discogs as I check right now—by the time you read this, the tally will certainly have cracked two thousand.[18] There is an LP by The Rita that's selling for over one hundred dollars.

Meanwhile, a six-CD-R Vomir boxed set called *Claustration*, put out by a Scottish noise label called At War With False Noise, features one noise wall each on the first five CD-Rs.[19] That is five hour-long discs of unadulterated noise wall! Skip to anywhere in a track, and the sound will be exactly the same. For an hour! Times five! Who listens to this?

---

18 As I review this paragraph, the tally has indeed bumped past two thousand—to 19,052! Clearly, I was underestimating HNW's exponential growth curve.
19 The sixth CD-R also contains noise but hews less strictly to the pure parameters of HNW.

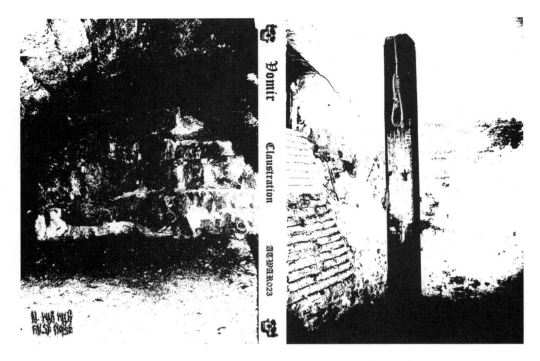

**The cover art for Vomir's *Claustration* 6xCD-R boxed set.
Image courtesy of Alastair Mabon of At War With False Noise.**

Well, I reached out to Al, the guy who runs At War With False Noise, to get his read on the harsh noise wall phenomenon. A friendly teacher from Kilmarnock, Scotland, who also harbors an interest in sixties and seventies European cinema, Al has run his label since 2005. AWWFN is not devoted to noise; its discography spans several stripes of experimental music.

Al speaks uniformly positively about Romain Perrot, praising his commitment to ideology as well as his personality. ("I love that he's not like most noise guys who you get over to play, who are usually pretty weird and lacking in basic social skills.") But curiously, Al's opinion on HNW has evolved over time—and his current opinions of the scene are less charitable.

"My thoughts on the genre are pretty straightforward; it's fucking stupid," Al states. "*Total Slitting of Throats*... that was a revelation! Vomir conceptualized it, and his total factory floor approach was a statement in itself. This harsh noise wall 'scene' I think is just lazy crap with no artistic merit at all. There was a point I was getting an email a day asking to release a tape from some HNW guy or another; I hate not responding to people who send me music 'cause I think it's disrespectful, but dear me. Too much."

"Less people listen to [HNW] than make it," Al suspects. "It's prolific entirely because it's easy to do. I'm pretty sure some people have just made a copy of a Vomir CD-R, taken the name of an obscure Giallo they've Googled, and released in an edition of 10."

Al is not alone in his opinion. Online noise discussion boards serve as archives of arguments between wall supporters and antagonists. These debates tend to follow a specific script. Someone will argue that HNW as a concept was cool for the microsecond it took to come up with the idea. Since then, it has become a lazy exercise in which wall creators produce walls for the sake of producing walls. As a result, the scene is home to more musicians than listeners, and the only reason anyone buys these releases is because, owing to their scant editions, there's the vague hope that one day they'll be worth as much as an early Merzbow release. Then an HNW defender will retort that fuck you, I like listening to HNW. And so on.

Given these differences of opinion, it seemed important to speak to some people willing to defend the almighty wall. I started cold-emailing people who ran particularly prolific HNW labels, as well as artists who had composed many of their own walls. And, contrary to some stereotypes that paint the scene as unfriendly and anti-intellectual, almost everyone I reached out to responded—eager to help me better understand the body of work that they care deeply about.

Julien Skrobek, mentioned earlier, is a thirtysomething English teacher who has lived in Paris his whole life. Over the course of his noise and HNW career, he has launched forty-four different projects. Nowadays, he runs an HNW cassette label called Hallucination Tapes as well as a net-label named Process that has an open-door policy to artists creating ANW—or ambient noise wall, a mellower cousin of HNW's. He also records as Sumbru. To create his walls, Skrobek uses an application on his phone that generates white noise, then sends this sound through several effects pedals.

For Skrobek, HNW is serious business from a theoretical standpoint. "I'm not sure HNW is even music anymore," he points out. "The composer just sets some parameters, and then it's up to the listener's brain to do the rest. There are changes, rhythms, and so on, but they are all in the listener's mind. With 'normal' music, it is the composer who purposefully introduces these elements. To me, HNW was another step in experimental music, abandoning some of music's tasks to the listener."

And while he claims he doesn't get too caught up in the philosophy of HNW, Skrobek, who has a personal interest in Dada and the French avant-garde Lettriste movement, sees HNW in the context of conceptual art that's come before it. "There is no composition work in the traditional sense of the word," he notes. "Once you've set your gear on a sound you like, that is the duration of a HNW track. You could make 20, 60, 90 minutes, whatever you need to fit a tape."

For Skrobek, this aligns with the artistic tradition established by the Situationists. He points specifically to Pino Gallizio's 1958 work *Industrial Painting*, a seventy-five-meter-long roll of canvas that was automatically painted using a machine he created. Similarly, the idea of setting up a string of noise generators to automatically produce a composition, then simply pushing the record button and waiting, alludes to both the convenience and hollowness of industrialization.

Skrobek also sees parallels with reductionism, a modern concept in improvised music. He brings up the Japanese guitarist Taku Sugimoto and the Austrian trombonist/

bass harmonica player Radu Malfatti. "These musicians open temporal windows by playing a sound, followed by silence," Skrobek says. "The silence can last, let's say, between 10 seconds and 2 minutes. Then there is another sound."

As Skrobek points out, both HNW and reductionist music work "on the brain," in a manner distinct from other music. "Quasi-silence and continuous noise are the same because it is the memory of the listener that tricks him into coloring the sound one way or another." For Skrobek, a big part of the appeal of unchanging, static noise is the idea of "trick[ing] your brain into hearing things that aren't really there."

Treven Hall is one half of Big Pharma Records and performs HNW as Ragk. He is a high school student who lives in Leavenworth, Kansas, with his parents and little sister, describing his day-to-day life as "I mostly drink orange soda—Sunkist is a favorite— and watch cartoons." His entry port into the world of HNW was *Claustration* by Vomir (that 5-CD-R HNW box we discussed earlier), which he found "pretty neat at first glance but also really gimmicky."

For him, HNW's draw is its ability to induce an altered state of consciousness. "At first, I was using *False Security* and *Never Safe* by [HNW artist] Female Pedophile as things to listen to while I did homework. It wasn't working, though, because as I was working, I would get very distracted, losing myself to the wall. It's mesmerizing, really, and you have to listen to a wall for a long time, but if you listen to it long enough, you start to fall into a trance-like state. For me, it's very comfy and warm and fuzzy and cozy."

Hall is not alone in remarking on the trance effect. James Shearman, who is twenty-two years old and lives in Northeast London, curates an HNW net-label named HNW Netlabel and produces walls under the name A Raja's Mesh Men. When he heard his first HNW release three years ago, he was struggling with insomnia. That track was Clive Henry's "Supreme Isolation in a Map of Hell," which was released on a 2011 split with Vomir. "Zoning out to a wall of enough length can induce/inspire auditory hallucinations," Shearman tells me. "With this particular wall, and the particular headspace with which I approached it at the time, I began to experience some really evocative hallucinations that opened up to me this idea that a subgenre form founded on static minimalism could be much more than I had initially conceived. There could be worlds within the walls—sonic worlds…"

Liam McGeorge, meanwhile, is a twentysomething from the UK who's known for recording HNW under the prolific Distorted Souls Within A Corrupt Vision moniker. He recently stopped recording under this name and now produces HNW as Shurayuki-hime, a project themed around "feminism and femininity in Japan, using artwork which is cute and fun." For him, a major part of the appeal of HNW is in the genre's interchangeability. But it's the interchangeability of the listener's experience that captures McGeorge's interest. "One thing I love about HNW is that the sound is purely neutral," he points out. "Although due to our constant subjection of music, tonality, melody, and rhythm, some may say otherwise. But I see HNW as an empty book. You can create whatever feeling, emotion, or agenda you see fit."

There is still the question of why there needs to be so many HNW releases, when they all seem a bit similar. Skrobek relates this to the methods of automatic art production pioneered by the Situationist movement. When asked, McGeorge points out that there is something innately obsessive about HNW and its enthusiasts, which fuels the genre's productivity. Al, if you recall, believes the genre is prolific simply because it's easy. Treven Hall essentially feels the same way—but sees that easiness as a positive, an opportunity for exploration.

"With no other genre can you have the potential to release 50 albums in a week, and they might all be really good by genre standards," Hall revels. "Because HNW doesn't take a lot of time or preparation or work honestly. You just bump a pedal on a white noise generator, leave it running for 30 minutes, and call it good. So long as your low end is good and your distortion is crunchy, go for it, have 500 releases in a year. No other genre opens up that opportunity in my opinion."

For James Shearman, like Liam McGeorge, obsession is the key. "Viewing HNW outside of the lens of obsession, or worship, or an overly meticulous interest in something makes it seem quite alien," he tells me.

I still wasn't sure I was understanding the *point* of a genre where hour-long tracks of static noise are the norm, so I tried to reason it out.

For one, noise walls can be useful. People use white noise generators to drown out atmospheric noise—to better focus on work, or even to sleep. While there are apps and products that serve this role, HNW allows artists to customize and document their unique strain of white noise.

Second, HNWs are not fundamentally artless. There are different qualities to HNWs—they vary in terms of timbre and pitch, and they may have larger or smaller "grains" of noise. At least some thought must go into making them—or if not a thought, then at least some action, like, say, turning a knob or two.

Finally, HNWs are conceptually pure. Given that it's just noise, and it doesn't change appreciably from start to finish, there is absolutely no concession to accessibility. Walls boast a blend of nihilism and outsider deterrence that appeals to audiences in the same way that metal, and all its successively pigeonholed extreme subgenres, do. These extreme music scenes revel in the catharsis of harshness, the joy of cultdom, and the ugly appeal of meaninglessness.

Harsh Noise Wally is an online comic strip in which *Dilbert* cartoons are doctored, their original speech bubbles replaced with new text. The premise is that *Dilbert's* characters, and in particular Wally, work in an office that produces harsh noise walls for the public.

In one strip, a robot, speaking to Wally, says, "I listen to nothing but harsh noise walls all day, every day. I ceased caring about anyone and anything, all my flesh and muscles rotted off, leaving me a soulless husk carried by a robotic frame."

Wally, his face stoic, responds, "I'm still waiting to hear the downside."[20]

20 harshnoisewally.tumblr.com/

HNW ESSENTIALS

Establishing a canon for a genre composed of interchangeable walls of static noise may seem like a fool's errand, but here it is anyway.

V/A, *Total Slitting of Throats* (Militant Walls, 2005) The second release on The Rita's CD-R label, Militant Walls, this is billed on its cover as an "HNW audible manifesto." As far as dense blocks of noise go, it's a bruiser: It takes five walls by five artists, then dubs them all on top of each other to produce one ultra-wall. A widely regarded seminal release in the HNW genre, it has been reissued twice, once in 2007 by Troniks and again in 2017 by the Toronto label dod-ecaphony.

THE CHERRY POINT *Night of the Bloody Tapes* (Troniks, 2005) The Cherry Point is Phil Blankenship, and this release is not one wall but four separate tracks, culled from three years of tapes. Perhaps not as pure as the genre would become, the no-frills, void-oriented aesthetic is in full gear here, and it was billed at the time as an advancement in noise extremeness. As one 2006 review put it, "The constant stream of noise it provides eventually blanks my mind completely."[1]

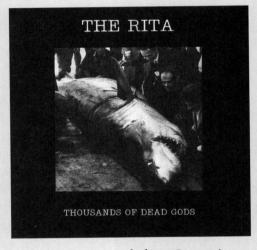

THE RITA *Thousands of Dead Gods* (Troniks, 2006) From the HNW scene's originator, this highly regarded album is built out of underwater recordings taken during shark cage diving, which were then reduced to noise walls. An unconventional methodology for recording HNW, and arguably more proto-HNW than true HNW, its backstory contributes to its mythology. One reviewer, trying to describe the experience of listening to this album, posed the question: "Have you ever smoked so much pot that you actually sobered up?"[2]

VOMIR *Claustration* (At War With False Noise, 2007) Six CD-Rs worth of uncompromising harsh noise walls from the Parisian thought leader of the genre. As the *Noise Not Music* blog put it after listening to all six discs straight, "I've never felt so isolated by music before, the rumbling, warm noise wrapping itself around me and not letting go until the end."[3]

1   Lucas Schleicher, 'The Cherry Point, "Night of the Bloody Tapes,"' *Brainwashed*, 2006 <brainwashed.com/index.php?option=com_content&task=view&id=4430> [accessed 27 July 2020].
2   Seth K, 'The Rita - Thousands of Dead Gods,' *Tiny Mix Tapes*, 2006 <www.tinymixtapes.com/music-review/rita-thousands-dead-gods> [accessed 27 July 2020].
3   Jack Davidson, 'Thoughts: Claustration by Vomir,' *Noise Not Music*, 2017 <noisenotmusic.com/2017/11/06/thoughts-claustration-by-vomir/> [accessed 27 July 2020].

VOMIR *Proanomie* **(At War With False Noise, 2008)** If *Claustration* is too much for you—and it really should be—then this is likely the second-best-known Vomir release, also on Al's At War With False Noise label. At seventy-three minutes of unchanging harsh noise wall, it is still far from a compromising experience. Godflesh's Justin Broadrick selected this as one of his current favorites in an article for *The Quietus*, describing Vomir's music, played at loud volume, as "the ultimate black hole, it is the fucking void of birth and death right before you, you know what I mean?"[4]

HNW books

At least two individuals have put out what they consider the literary equivalents of harsh noise walls. Joseph Szymkowiak released *HNW*, a 586-page paperback whose pages are just monochrome static.[5] Noise artist Cementimental, meanwhile, released an untitled "harsh noise graphic novel" comprising "300 pages of pixel-noisescapes," which he designed using an "antique" piece of shareware called *LightningPaint*.[6]

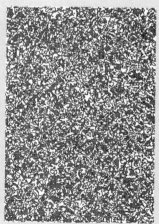

Cover and sample pages from Cementimental's harsh noise graphic novel. Image courtesy of Tim Drage, a.k.a. Cementimental

4 Kate Hennessy, 'Central To Process: Justin Broadrick's Favourite Albums,' *The Quietus*, 2014 <thequietus.com/articles/16496-justin-broadrick-godflesh-favourite-albums-interview?page=8> [accessed 27 July 2020].

5 'HNW BOOK (Seclusion Room) | Nahàsh Atrym Productions,' Bandcamp <nahshatrymproductions.bandcamp.com/merch/hnw-book-seclusion-room> [accessed 27 July 2020].

6 Winterᴊte, 'Introducing — Cementimental,' *Medium*, 2017 <medium.com/@wintermute2097/introducing-cementimental-b23713166a0b> [accessed 27 July 2020].

1.2 QUIET

If loud music has become an arms race toward sonic massiveness, reaching its apogee in the form of the harsh noise wall, at the other extreme is a somewhat quaint anti-battle toward quietness and simplicity.

Defining quiet music, much like loud music, is complicated. I made the mistake of conflating it with minimalism, which has been around for generations of art history in every creative medium. Visual artist John McCracken, for example, is famous for constructing monochromatic planks. His *Black Plank* sculpture, a black rectangle made of resin, plywood, and fiberglass, sold for over $350,000 at auction! Raymond Carver's stripped-down, matter-of-fact stories are considered examples of literary minimalism.

A group of composers from New York including La Monte Young, Philip Glass, and John Cage are often credited with establishing the role of minimalism in music, an idea first put down in words by Michael Nyman in a 1968 article for *The Spectator* titled "Minimal Music."[21] Cage's *4'33"*, composed and premiered in 1952, was a four-minute-and-thirty-three-second concert performance in which a pianist sat onstage at a piano but declined to play a single note. The resulting silence and the incidental noise of displeased audience members were the point of the composition.

But musical minimalism is not the same thing as quietness, although the two are commonly conflated by listeners and critics. More than quietness, a defining feature of minimal music is repetition. Eric Satie's *Vexations*, for example, is a brief few lines of sheet music intended to be repeated 840 times in a row—a composition so impractical, it wasn't publicly performed until nearly forty years after Satie's death. (That performance lasted over eighteen hours.) In the case of *Vexations*, minimalism refers to the use of limited musical materials—a single phrase is repeated over and over without any change or musical development. Harsh noise wall is a classic case of minimalism: many HNW artists twiddle some knobs, then let a machine automatically populate their recording with unchanging noise.

I learned that pinning down the concept was as complicated as defining what makes music loud. Perhaps quiet music refers to music that is mastered at a low volume—music that occupies a relatively low proportion of the potential sound spectrum encoded on a CD or other format. But a listener could achieve the same effect by turning the volume down on their stereo.

Drone music is quiet because relatively little happens in it—the sound itself can be loud, but it is defined by its slow-moving, sometimes gentle manner. Lowercase music embraces both silence and a low-key attitude, expecting the listener to consume it at a barely perceptible volume. And, on the extreme end of the spectrum, onkyô and no-input music are conceptually the sound of nothing at all—but not exactly silence.

---

21 Michael Nyman, 'Minimal Music,' *The Spectator*, 221.7320 (1968), 518–19.

EXTREME MUSIC

I.2.1 Drone

In their purest form, drones are continuous lengths of sound that change very little over, say, a twenty-minute composition—a bit like holding down several keys on a synthesizer. To call drone "quiet" is not entirely accurate, because some drone music can get pretty loud. Better descriptors might be slow, docile, or tranquil.

The use of drones in music predates most of the phenomena covered in this book. The tanbura, the instrument responsible for the familiar background drone that appears in some classical music from India, is a stringed instrument that's been around since the fifteenth century at least. Predecessors of the hurdy-gurdy, a cranked string instrument that contains "melody strings" and "drone strings," have been traced back to the eleventh century!

In the 1960s, La Monte Young established a project called the *Theatre of Eternal Music*, devoted to staging lengthy performances of slow-moving and little-changing music. Young thought of his music as having two separate components: "primary" and "secondary" drones. "Primary drones are defined to be those drones that sound continuously during an entire performance," he explains in an essay on the history and composition of his work. "The primary drone usually remained constant (the same pitch) throughout most or all rehearsals, performances, and recordings of a particular evolving section of the work."[22] Secondary drones, meanwhile, would come and go during a piece, although they would generally also be sustained for long periods of time.

Most of Young's essay deals with his bitter quibbles about who was the true composer of the music performed by the *Theatre*, a source of disagreement between *Theatre* performers that eventually led to the acrimonious breakdown of the collective.[23] Today, because of these disagreements, only one recording of the *Theatre*'s work has been publicly released, although an entire archive apparently exists.[24]

Following these early experiments, the Velvet Underground worked drones into their classic records. In the seventies, adventurous German bands like Cluster, Can, and Neu! established drones as an integral component of the krautrock scene. And as follows, an upstart genre associated with mystical themes began using drones for spiritual enlightenment and profit.

I.2.2 New Age Music

The term was coined in 1975, when guitarist William Ackerman used it to describe the output of his label, Windham Hill. Back then, most of Windham Hill's releases were drone-free acoustic instrumentals that were designed to help listeners relax. In some ways, the music released by the label was genre-agnostic, including a mish-mash of everything from krautrock to the "furniture music" of the minimalist Erik Satie, who aspired to make music that blended into the background, like furniture in a room.

---

22 La Monte Young, *Notes on The Theatre of Eternal Music and The Tortoise, His Dreams and Journeys* (New York, 2000) <www.melafoundation.org/theatre.pdf> [accessed 28 July 2020].

23 The longest section of the essay is titled "*The Tortoise, His Dreams and Journeys* is a composition by La Monte Young," *The Tortoise*... being one of the pieces performed by the Theatre. Its subtitles are "Public Opinion," "The Opinions of Informed Individuals," and "My Own Opinion."

24 La Monte Young, 'Statement on Table of The Elements CD Day of Niagara April 25, 1965,' MELA Foundation, 2000 <www.melafoundation.org/statemen.htm> [accessed 28 July 2020].

Robert Rich's *Somnium*. Image courtesy of Robert Rich.

To cynics, New Age music is a marketing term—a way to cross-market a broad range of music styles into the then-booming New Age movement. Jazz clarinetist Tony Scott emerged as a respected soloist in the fifties, once described by legendary jazz writer Leonard Feather as being "among the new true masters in contemporary jazz." By the end of the fifties, while in Japan, he met a koto player named Shinichi Yuize, as well as the musician Hōzan Yamamoto, who performed on a bamboo flute called a shakuhachi. *Music for Zen Meditation*, recorded in 1964 and often cited as a proto-New Age landmark, featured Scott improvising alongside his Japanese colleagues.[25]

Scott, Yuize, and Yamamoto's tranquil music does not drone. But the proliferation of inexpensive synthesizers in the eighties made it easier to compose peaceful soundscapes, and a good chunk of New Age music would come to be associated with sustained, enveloping keyboard tones. Vangelis, long associated with the genre,

25 Graham Reid, 'Tony Scott: Music for Zen Meditation (1964),' Elsewhere, 2018 <www.elsewhere.co.nz/essentialelsewhere/8331/tony-scott-music-for-zen-meditation-1964/> [accessed 28 July 2020].

famously opined that New Age music "gave the opportunity for untalented people to make very boring music."[26]

Despite its detractors, New Age music was big business. There were radio stations devoted to the genre, beginning with *Hearts of Space* in 1973, nationally syndicated in the early eighties. At the zenith of New Age mania, an L.A. rock music station was rebranded as a "mood service" called The Wave; it got rid of DJ chatter and required listeners to dial a toll-free number to learn the names of the songs they were hearing.[27] Over its course, the New Age scene has established and nurtured the careers of bona fide stars like Enya, Enigma, Yanni, and Kitarō.

Beyond the big names in New Age, there is a fascinating underworld of lesser-known works, including mysterious records released on one-off vanity labels. Titles like *Harmonic Brainwave Synergy* by R. Brian Caldwell (Neurosonics, 1990), *Crystal Illumination* by Aeoliah (Oreade Music, 1989), and *Valley of the Birds* by Emerald Web (Stargate, 1981) typify the scene's collision of pseudoscience, mysticism, and swindle-ism.

The reissue label Light in the Attic put out a triple-LP compilation called *I Am the Center*, which collects tracks from private-press records and tapes by these small-scale New Age artists. Douglas McGowan, an L.A. record collector, runs Yoga Records, a reissue label dedicated to these types of releases. In an interview conducted by Light in the Attic, McGowan says he sees New Age's appeal as escapism, calling it "a healthy, mindful way to distance ourselves from the clamor of the present moment."

One of the more noteworthy artists featured on *I Am the Center* is Iasos, whose "Formentera Sunset Clouds" is an appealing passage of shimmering synthesizer chords and crashing ocean waves. Iasos claims that his music, first released on LP by an obscure early New Age label called Unity Records,[28] is actually the work of a "higher dimensional being," who uses Iasos to channel his music to humankind.[29]

Iasos was born in Greece but moved to upstate New York as a child. He learned to play the piano and flute growing up, and eventually studied cultural anthropology at Cornell, graduating in 1968. It was in Ithaca, New York, that he reportedly began to hear "paradise music" in his head, leading to a move to California and a shift in his career aspirations. As he outlined in a 2014 interview:[30]

"I had an experience where I suddenly became aware of a higher dimensional being, and it ignited an aha moment. I realized he and I had made an agreement together before I was born, and the agreement was that he was going to transmit music to me, and his visual ideas also, and my job was to receive them, manifest them, and get them out there to the public."

Iasos identifies this higher being alternately as Vista and Cyclopea, purportedly "the Elohim of the 5th Ray." This spiritual terminology comes from Theosophy, an

---

26 Peter Culshaw, 'My Greek Odyssey with Alexander,' *The Telegraph*, 2005 <www.telegraph.co.uk/culture/music/3634447/My-Greek-odyssey-with-Alexander.html> [accessed 28 July 2020].

27 Judith H. Balfe, *Paying the Piper: Causes and Consequences of Art Patronage* (University of Illinois Press, 1993).

28 That LP, *Inter-Dimensional Music*, is worth a fortune on the secondary market, and has been reissued several times in a variety of formats.

29 Emma-Lee Moss, 'High Times with New Age Pioneer Iasos,' *Noisey*, 2014 <www.vice.com/en_ca/article/68z746/high-times-with-new-age-pioneer-iasos> [accessed 29 July 2020].

30 Moss.

esoteric religious movement established by occultist "Madame" Helena Blavatsky in the late nineteenth century. Theosophists believe in several Ascended Masters, each of which oversees a specific Ray, the fifth Ray being associated with nature. Iasos describes Vista as "always whispering ideas in my ear, you know, 'Iasos, try this.'"

Iasos put out his first releases in the seventies and has not stopped. Over the years, fame has eluded him, and he has self-released most of his tapes and CDs. According to Iasos' official biography, NASA used his recordings for a multimedia presentation, which was circulated across the United States to planetariums.[31] In 1989, a Plymouth State University scientist named Joel Funk used Iasos' track "The Angels of Comfort" in experiments on near-death experiences (NDEs). One study recruited people who claimed to have had an NDE; they ended up ranking Iasos' piece as the one that most resembled the music playing during their NDEs, apparently by a wide margin.

The 2010s were kind to Iasos, fueled by a renewal of interest in New Age music within hipster circles. Previously relegated to performing "virtually anywhere there's been a world peace festival, a harmonic convergence event, or a celebration of an equinox or a solstice," as one critic put it,[32] now he's in his sixties and performs to lofts full of young people, some of whom have set off on transcendent drone careers of their own.

I.2.3 Ambient

Although there were other earlier precedents, the arrival of ambient music as a scene is generally attributed to Brian Eno. In 1978, he put out *Ambient 1: Music for Airports*, a break from the pop music he'd previously recorded. Like Satie's concept of furniture music, the music on *Ambient 1* was designed as environmental music, specifically as a salve to the tense atmosphere of the modern airport. Its four expansive tracks are a tranquil history lesson in synthesizer technology, the Yamaha *ahhh*s of the synthetic chorus a charming blast from the past.

"Ambient" became synonymous with a subcategory of electronic music variably known as ambient house, ambient techno, or chill-out music. A hierarchy of star producers emerged, among them Orbital, Boards of Canada, and The Orb. Drones were present in some but not all ambient music—they're an integral component of The Orb's glorious twenty-minute single, "A Huge Evergrowing Pulsating Brain That Rules From The Centre Of The Ultraworld," which managed to earn a place on the UK Singles Chart. British act The KLF, also known for punchy dance music and weighty countercultural statements like incinerating one million British pounds,[33] put out an ambient record named *Chill Out*, a continuous abstract collage of synthesizer fog and pilfered samples.

31 'Iasos - Biography + Resume + Discography' <iasos.com/bioresum/> [accessed 29 July 2020].

32 Lara Pellegrinelli, 'The New Age of New Age: Genre-Founding "celestial Musician" Iasos Transfixes Bushwick,' *Politico*, 2012 <www.politico.com/states/new-york/albany/story/2012/05/the-new-age-of-new-age-genre-founding-celestial-musician-iasos-transfixes-bushwick-067223> [accessed 29 July 2020].

33 Andrew Smith, 'Burning Question | From the Observer | The Guardian,' *The Guardian*, 2000 <www.theguardian.com/theobserver/2000/feb/13/life1.lifemagazine4> [accessed 29 July 2020].

EXTREME MUSIC

Geir Jenssen, who records his ambient music under the name Biosphere, is one of the most enduring producers of drone-oriented ambient music. Though he has reservations about the term ambient because it suggests background music,[34] his body of work is widely acknowledged to include many classics of the genre. Working out of his home in Norway, his music seems to evoke the country's polar landscapes. His first album under the Biosphere name, *Microgravity*, is beat-oriented, while his 1997 album, *Substrata*, is built out of subtle drones and natural field recordings. It's the ultimate album for a cold winter night.

Ambient artists Steve Roach and Robert Rich have devoted much of their careers to long, droning epics, and both have produced sprawling, daunting discographies. An unheralded gem is Roach's *Immersion* series, which uses drones explicitly as a tool to explore the hypnagogic period between wakefulness and sleep. Roach proposes in his accompanying press release that these albums are for settings where "traditional music could be considered invasive."[35] The third volume in the series comprises over three and a half hours of shifting drones, perfect for bedtime deployment.

While he was studying computer music at Stanford University in the early eighties, Rich started staging overnight concerts where audience members would bring sleeping bags and rest on the floor while the music played. Skyping from his solar-powered house in Mountain View, California, he explains that the idea of a sleep concert revolved around the unique effect of music on sleep. He points out that sleep becomes shallower when there is sound in the background, which in turn leads to more moments of wakefulness through the night. His excellent *Somnium* album is a recorded version of a sleep concert, spanning seven hours of metamorphosing drones and nature recordings. It was apparently the longest commercially released recording at one point, issued on DVD instead of CDs so that all the audio could play without interruption.

The term *dark ambient* is often used to describe the eerie and cavernous work of Roach and Rich, along with even creepier producers like :zoviet*france: and Lustmord. Elsewhere, critics have lumped Roach and Rich in with the New Age movement, an association Rich scorns. Regardless, in the year 2018, Steve Roach was nominated for his first Grammy Award, when his *Spiral Revelation* made the shortlist for—you guessed it—Best New Age Album.

So what exactly differentiates New Age music from ambient music? Music critic Mark Richardson summarizes their distinctions and similarities best in a *Resonant Frequency* column:

"Ambient music by a baby-booming hippie geared toward soccer moms is filed in one place, while ambient music made by former club kids and aimed at indie record fans winds up in another. One man 'relaxes' while the other 'chills,' but we're all hoping to tune into the kosmische erschütterung."[36]

34 Andrew Ryce, 'Biosphere: Introverted Music,' *Resident Advisor*, 2016 <www.residentadvisor.net/features/2805> [accessed 29 July 2020].

35 'Steve Roach: Immersion Three' <www.steveroach.com/store/store.php?item=373> [accessed 29 July 2020].

36 Mark Richardson, 'Soothing Sounds for Hipsters,' *Pitchfork*, 2002 <pitchfork.com/features/resonant-frequency/5857-resonant-frequency-12/> [accessed 29 July 2020].

I.2.4 Homemade Drone

In the 2000s and 2010s, a vibrant folk scene of drone musicians putting out limited-edition releases on CD-R and cassette emerged, often building entire albums out of prolonged synthesizer chords or various permutations of guitars and effects pedals. The scene channels a hodge-podge of influences; sound projects like Pine Smoke Lodge, Flowery Dreamcatcher, and Tuluum Shimmering harken back to New Age's spiritualism. One label, Rotifer Cassettes, even reissued the grand mystic Iasos' debut album.

Tuluum Shimmering is an interesting case. His real name is Jake Webster, and he's based in England, but that's about all there is to know—there are no photographs available, and he doesn't play live, citing his shyness.[37] His music started appearing on tapes in 2008, seeming to embrace a very New Age aesthetic; his music was once described as "rootless World music."[38] Webster's drones were recorded at home using a looping machine, resulting in longform meditative works that merge flittering flutes, textural hand drums, and violin drones, all apparently recorded live without overdubs. In 2010, when he announced in a rare *Musique Machine* email interview[39] that he believed music should be free, he subsequently gave up on physical releases altogether and instead made every future recording available for download on his website.

Tuluum Shimmering's *In the Great Swamp You Were Conceived* tape, released on Rotifer Cassettes.

Webster claimed that, two or three years before he released his first album, he had no interest in music at all. He didn't own any records, nor did he listen to the radio.

"Then I had a strong feeling that I in fact loved music, just had never heard the right kind. So I raided my dad's LP boxes, playing everything indiscriminately, without the slightest clue who the artists were, what it might sound like and so on. I found that my impulse had been correct, with Coltrane's *Ascension*, Ornette Coleman's *Free Jazz*, Dylan's *Basement Tapes* and Beefheart's *Trout Mask Replica* all having a colossal and instant impact."[40]

Since then, his passion for music has taken on a devotional valence, not unlike the reverence conveyed by many New Age artists. But when asked by *Musique Machine* about the spirituality of his recordings, he drew a clear line:

"I don't believe in anything supernatural, and I'm not religious in any sense. I do, however, very much think that music and all human creativity should not just be a central 'part' of people's lives, but not be considered in any way separated from life at all."

---

37 Delirious Insomniac, 'Unbroken, Shifting Tradition,' *Musique Machine*, 2010 <www.musiquemachine.com/articles/articles_template.php?id=190> [accessed 29 July 2020].

38 Matthew Phillips, 'Tuluum Shimmering - Ulau Tau / Spirit of Sun,' *Tiny Mix Tapes*, 2013 <www.tinymixtapes.com/music-review/tuluum-shimmering-ulau-tau-spirit-of-sun> [accessed 29 July 2020].

39 Delirious Insomniac.

40 Delirious Insomniac.

Webster has even started up his own label, Tuluum Shimmering Records, and while he hasn't entirely maintained his promise not to release physical albums—all his label's releases have come out on CD-R—he has made them all available for download via Bandcamp at low cost.

It is not uncommon for contemporary drone artists to put out dozens upon dozens of releases. One such prolific artist was Josh Burke, about whom very little is known. Between 2008 and 2011, he put out hundreds of tapes under a complex web of pseudonyms like Sky Limousine, Futuresport, 56K, and Silk Fountain. He also operated at least three different tape and CD-R labels, each given its own whimsical name: Avocado Jungle Tapes, Midnight Star Media, and Clear Video & Audio Cassettes. Then he disappeared. There are no interviews available online, nor any photographs. All that exists is a convoluted body of work, only some of which is available for download.

The knock on the drone scene and its myriad limited-edition releases was that it embraced a paint-by-numbers ethic, with artists pumping out piles of indistinguishable work. Emeralds, one of the most seminal drone acts, were themselves guilty of mass production, releasing reams of CD-Rs, tapes, and the occasional record from 2006 to 2010. But they also were willing to poke fun at that phenomenon, naming one of their CD-Rs *Bullshit Boring Drone Band* (American Tapes, 2006).

The vast majority of these drone releases are distributed in quantities of fifty to one hundred copies and usually traded or sold at close to cost. Most releases are promoted through the label's social media outlets, free-hosted website, and Bandcamp page, and are sometimes circulated to a few small-scale distros. The scene, much like the noise scene with which it overlaps, emphasizes collaboration and socialization over the veneration of auteur producers.

At drone's peak in the late 2000s, a few bands and artists crossed over to the indie mainstream. Emeralds was the first to land, signing to avant-garde label Editions Mego, opening for underground stalwarts like Caribou and Throbbing Gristle, and playing at two All Tomorrow's Parties festivals. Even bigger was Oneohtrix Point Never, the much-lauded sound project of Daniel Lopatin, who placed a track on the soundtrack for Sofia Coppola's *The Bling Ring* and established a career scoring indie films. His work has subsequently extended into other, drone-tinged genres—among them vaporwave, another nostalgic genre that venerates the synth-slathered neon pop of the 1980s, especially the mood music one might have heard in shopping malls and elevators.

1.2.5 Lowercase

Quiet music would get even quieter in the late nineties thanks to a sound art movement known as lowercase. The genre's name was first documented in a 1997 interview in *The Wire*, when experimental producer Steve Roden said he had been using the term for years to highlight the understated quality of his sonic portfolio. As he described in an essay accompanying the ten-year anniversary reissue of his best-known album, *Forms of Paper*:

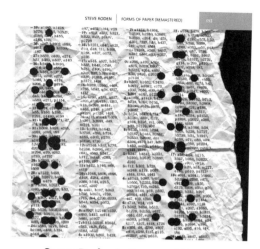

Steve Roden's _Forms of Paper_

"I had been using this phrase since the mid-1980s to set my work apart from the bombastic nature of painting at the time via artists like Julian Schnabel. While the artworld and popular culture seemed to favor spectacle, I was interested in silence, humility, intimacy, and thus began to describe my work as having a lowercase aesthetic—and I viewed the term as a quiet form of protest."

Something about Roden's interview inspired several other artists who identified with his lowercase methodology. A couple of years later, he was approached by James Coleman, an improvisatory musician, who wanted to start a listserv called *lowercase-sound*. This mailing list's mission statement was to discuss and publicize music that explored "some or all of the characteristics of low volume, silence, soundscape/ environmental/field recordings, indeterminacy, psycho/acoustic treatments of space, environment & context." It rapidly became a bustling online community for people who embraced the lowercase ethic.

Once the *lowercase-sound* list was in full force, a San Diegan named Josh Russell started a record label, Bremsstrahlung, to showcase the lowercase scene, naming it after the tiny amount of electromagnetic radiation that results from the slowing of a subatomic particle as it collides with another particle. Bremsstrahlung kicked off in 2000 with a two-CD compilation, *Lowercase*, thoughtfully curated and accompanied with detailed liner notes to help contextualize the growing lowercase movement. In an unusual move, each copy came with two copies of the release—four CDs in total—so that the owner could donate the extra copy to "another curious listener."

Steve Roden's landmark 2001 album *Forms of Paper* is now a key work in the lowercase canon. Conceptually, it is a study in understatement, *reductio ad absurdum*— it came from Roden being commissioned to create music to be played at a local library! Roden prepared for the recording by removing the pages of an old textbook, folding each sheet, and using a hole-puncher to make holes in each page. He then spread the sheets of paper in front of him and placed a combination of standard and contact microphones on top of the pages. Speakers amplified the soft sounds of his hands interacting with the paper.

Roden intended for *Forms of Paper* to be listened to at very soft volumes. Misunderstanding his intentions, however, his record label, Line, boosted the volume of the whole album during the mastering process to match contemporary standards for recorded work. When Roden finally got around to listening to the release—after it had already been distributed—he was dismayed to discover a bunch of extra sounds that were not obvious at the intended volume level. Although it became his most widely circulated release, for years Roden grimaced at the thought of it and avoided playing it.

It was only in 2011, for its ten-year anniversary, that he finally got around to listening to a remastered version, restored to the original, near-silent volumes that he had initially intended. Over fifty-four minutes, the listener is treated to occasional thin blips of sound—light smudges of static or the occasional, unassertive digital chirp. There is nothing here that sounds like sheets of paper being manipulated. Despite its understated aesthetic, it became one of the lowercase movement's highest-profile releases, featuring in a prominent article in *Wired* Magazine.[41]

For Roden, the conceptual basis for his lowercase music has nothing to do with staking out a musical extreme. Instead, he says that his ideology is rooted in the letters of poet Rainer Maria Rilke. Rilke articulated an idea of "inconsiderable things," meaning things so understated that only a sensitive soul is likely to detect them.[42] In the constant din of today's soundscape, these inconsiderable things are the soft and subtle sounds barely perceptible in the margins.

Interestingly, even Josh Russell seems to get Roden's aesthetic only half right. In the liner notes to Bremsstrahlung's inaugural compilation, he writes of the "moment of pure attention that one's sense of self simultaneously disappears and swells to encompass the surroundings," and of "forc[ing] the listener to pay focused attention to sound." And while he also acknowledges the subtle interplay between lowercase music and the incidental sounds of the surrounding world ("the hum of the refrigerator, the refuse truck backing up in the alley, a plastic bag trapped in the fence rustling"), he also recommends using "good headphones at high volume," an idea that would certainly be opposed by Roden.

As the scene developed, lowercase would continue to deviate from Roden's original vision, eventually becoming a term used to refer generally to music that drifts between silence and almost imperceptible sounds. One specific breed of lowercase music saw recordings focused on particular source material, typically on a small or even microscopic scale. Ronnie Sundin's *Seismo* mini-CD-R, for example, included among its sound sources the amplified sounds of an anthill. Steve Roden's *Light Forms* uses light bulbs as its basis. Bernhard Gál's "Zhu Shui" is crafted from the sounds of water boiling in four kettles, its press release tracing its range of sounds "from the pianissimo of the steam to the fortissimo of the kettles' whistling, from the crackling of the cooling metal kettle to the sizzling evaporation of condensed water droplets."[43]

In 1993, the avant-garde German composer Bernhard Günter put out a record entitled *Un Peu de Neige Salie*, which many consider the first lowercase release, even though it predates the term—and despite the fact that Günter himself resists the label.[44] When it came out, it was a sharp break from the prevailing aesthetic of noisy bluster on the scene. Both the record label's owner and the CD manufacturing plant supposedly

41 Leander Kahney, 'Whisper the Songs of Silence,' *Wired Magazine*, 2002 <www.wired.com/2002/05/whisper-the-songs-of-silence/> [accessed 29 July 2020].
42 Rainer Maria Rilke, *Letters to a Young Poet* (San Rafael, California: New World Library, 1992).
43 Bernhard Gal, 'Zhu Shui. Sound Installation at the Phonomanie-Festival, December 2000.' <www.bernhardgal.com/zhushui.html> [accessed 30 July 2020].
44 Dan Warburton, 'Bernhard Günter Interview,' *Paris Transatlantic*, 2003 <www.paristransatlantic.com/magazine/interviews/gunter.html> [accessed 30 July 2020].

called Günter to let him know that his master tape was defective, reduced only to pops and clicks.[45] Yet that seemingly malfunctioning master recording has accumulated accolades and has been reissued several times. The influential music magazine *The Wire*, the authority on experimental music, listed it as one of their *100 Records That Set The World On Fire (While No One Was Listening)*.[46]

Günter, who runs the experimental label trente oiseaux (yes, that is in lowercase) and studied at IRCAM, has claimed that he could build a whole piece around "a single violin note."[47] He has also remarked that he doesn't much like the associations that people have drawn from Roden's term, *lowercase*, although he does make a point of putting artists' names in lowercase on his label's releases. Günter figures lowercase really refers to "an art form of enhanced attention," which is something critics have picked up on when engaging with his work. Reviews of *Neige Salie* comment on how the sonic subtlety and the way Günter's quiet music constantly interacts and competes with the surroundings lead to an increased demand on the listener's concentration.

Much of Günter's discography is quiet. *Univers Temporel Espoir*, which came out six years after *Neige Salie*, is even quieter than its predecessor. One online commenter even goes so far as to call it "the infrared region of sound."[48] On the other hand, Steve Roden's releases are often focused around specific concepts or use restricted sound sources. The audio on 2002's *Winter Couplet* was made using only two teacups. 2003's *Resonant Cities* solely comprises field recordings collected in different cities. In line with his original vision of his music as akin to Rilke's "inconsiderable things," many of his releases include a simple request in the liner notes: "Intended to be listened to at low volume."

Another player in the quiet music scene is Richard Chartier, who has referred to his own work as "ultra minimal." In 2000, he put out his impressively quiet album, *Series*, on his own label, LINE.[49] In a review for AllMusic, critic Jason Birchmeier wonders if there might be more silence than non-silence on the disc, which he is a little ambivalent about: "It's just as easy to dismiss *Series* as highbrow digital-age rhetoric that is ultimately void of substance as it is to champion the album as visionary."

In a 2001 interview with *AmbiEntrance* magazine,[50] Chartier explains that his music *technically* isn't quiet at all. It's just that he uses very high and low frequencies which, even when played loud, sound quiet due to the physiology of our ears, which are less sensitive to sounds at either extreme of the frequency spectrum. Chartier's music embraces these spectral fringes. "Many of the sounds on *Series* seem silent," he explains. "But if you watch *Series* on a level monitor on your amplifier, you can see that it is actually quite active or 'loud' ... [there's] a lot of energy in the sounds, but they seem quiet."

---

45 Caleb Deupree, 'Un Peu de Neige Salie - Bernhard Günter,' AllMusic <www.allmusic.com/album/un-peu-de-neige-salie-mw0000049595> [accessed 30 July 2020].

46 Ed Baxter, '100 Records That Set the World on Fire While No One Was Listening,' *The Wire*, 1998, 22–41.

47 Warburton.

48 SouthPacific, 'Univers Temporel Espoir by Bernhard Günter (Album, Lowercase),' Rate Your Music, 2008 <rateyourmusic.com/release/album/bernhard_gunter/univers_temporel_espoir_f1/> [accessed 30 July 2020].

49 Kurt Liedwart, 'Interview with Richard Chartier,' Tonschrift, 2009 <web.archive.org/web/20160530192357/http://mikroton.net/tonschrift/en/interviews/richard_chartier.html> [accessed 30 July 2020].

50 David J. Opdyke, 'Richard Chartier Interview,' *AmbiEntrance*, 2001 <web.archive.org/web/20130524032527/http://www.spiderbytes.com/ambientrance/intchartier.htm> [accessed 30 July 2020].

EXTREME MUSIC

Chartier's work is lumped in with lowercase, but his name is also invoked in discussions about a related concept, *microsound*, which shares many common ideas and artists. Microsound refers more to a method of producing music than it does to a genre or movement. It describes the process of using audio software to construct music on a micro level, sculpting individual bits of sound by the microsecond. Each little pixel of sound—an infinitesimal moment in time, a morsel of given wavelength—can be meticulously crafted and positioned. This method of sound production is also referred to as *granular synthesis*, which reflects the micro-partitioning of sound into individual grains.

In an excellent review article covering the genre, music theory professor Sonya Hofer points out that the microsound concept considers audio in terms of a physical metaphor—it imagines individual atoms of sound being custom-assembled to create novel sonic permutations. The idea of thinking about sound graphically has since become commonplace with the popularization of audio production software.

Chartier's *Series* is cited by Hofer as a key example of the microsound approach, its thin wisps of sound built over a white canvas of silence, intended to be played softly and subjected to deep focus by the listener. Much of the record was made using a now-primitive computer program called SoundEffect.[51] In the microsound tradition, it represented sound files visually, allowing the user to portion tiny bits of audio into a composition.

Although microsound and lowercase refer to different things—one a method of sound production, the other an intended style of listening—they both embrace minuscule extremes. They emphasize sounds on the periphery of perception, noises that might evade the most attentive listener's attention—ones that are too brief, too high-pitched, too low-pitched, or too quiet.

1.2.6 Onkyô

"I think these musicians' focuses are on hearing the sound, not physically playing musical instruments. Sometimes the instrument is an obstruction. They just want to listen more to the sound."

— Sachiko M, 2014[52]

In Japan in the very early 2000s, an unusual music scene called *onkyô*, which translates roughly as "sound," emerged out of a performance space known as *Off Site*. This was a tiny venue located in one of several old wooden houses amid the skyscrapers in Tokyo's commercial center, Shinjuku. *Off Site* had a floor space of six meters by two meters, fitting roughly fifteen people at a time. It was tucked next to several other houses, so that loud performances would irritate the neighbors; as a result, musicians were forced to explore a very quiet method of performance. As one member of the *onkyô* scene, musician Toshimaru Nakamura, put it: "We were only playing quietly because the

---

51 Liedwart.

52 Clive Bell, 'Off Site: Improvised Music From Japan,' *Red Bull Music Academy Daily*, 2014 <daily.redbullmusicacademy.com/2014/10/off-site-improvised-music-from-japan> [accessed 30 July 2020].

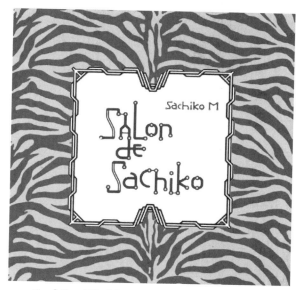

**Sachiko M's 2007 CD, *Salon De Sachiko*.
Image courtesy of Christopher Heron.**

neighbors would have complained if we played any louder."[53]

The limits of onkyô are contested, but the music produced by its artists tends to have certain things in common. One is an emphasis on silence. Onkyô recordings tend to feature a lot of negative space, including a high proportion of dead silence. A second common theme is the idea of *no-input music,* which is music played using electronic devices without any actual input running through them.

One no-input practitioner, Toshimaru Nakamura, uses a mixer without input. Since a mixer with nothing going in has nothing to mix, the sounds that occur are simply the incidental noises of the machine's mechanics. A listen to his 2013 album, *No Input Mixing Board #8* (Oral/The Dim Coast), reveals a shifting bed of electronic fuzz, ultra-high-pitched tones, and the occasional electronic pop.

For Nakamura, the appeal of no-input music is that the mixing board's unpredictability yields a different hierarchy between performer and instrument. In a 2003 interview, he put it this way:

> *"I think I find an equal relationship with no-input mixing board, which I didn't see with the guitar. When I played the guitar, I had to play the guitar. But with the mixing board, the machine would play me and the music would play the other two, and I would do something or maybe nothing."*[54]

Musicians often speak in reverent tones about their favorite instruments, but it is rare indeed for the player to become the played.

Another onkyô exponent is Sachiko M, who started off as a sound engineer for a theater company before transitioning into composing experimental music in the late 1990s. Her trademark approach is to improvise using pure sine wave tones. She also performs no-input music using a sampler with no actual samples, again relying on the machine's own unpredictable output. Her 2000 mini-CD release, *Detect* (Antifrost), is exemplary of her radical minimalism. The pervading sound is that of silence, but above the void are the occasional, seemingly random bits of digital detritus. Electronic pops,

---

53 David Novak, 'Playing Off Site: The Untranslation of Onkyô,' *Asian Music,* 41.1 (2010), 36–59 <www.academia.edu/2028497/_Playing_Off_Site_The_Untranslation_of_Onkyô._> [accessed 30 July 2020].
54 William Meyer, 'Toshimaru Nakamura Interview,' *Perfect Sound Forever,* 2003 <www.furious.com/perfect/toshimarunakamura.html> [accessed 30 July 2020].

like the sound of a cable being connected to an amplifier, occur intermittently, often in rapid-fire succession. Tidy bleeps and piercing sines enter the fray as well, the latter's high-pitched tones increasing in intensity as the record progresses. Many critics use the language of purity to describe Sachiko M's tones and pops, drawing out adjectives like "austere" and "clean," although no-input music, ironically, relies on the impure, incidental signals that flow through hardware that is intended to run silently.

Ethnomusicologist David Novak points out that onkyô composers' no-input instruments "create no sonic material, and so (unlike a saxophone, for example) will not make sounds that refer back to any recognized musical vocabulary."[55] Relieved of its recognizable referents, onkyô is a truly abstract genre, a break from other music scenes. Whereas even the freest jazz performances involve interactivity between instrumentalists, in onkyô, although their sounds co-occur, each performer's process is occurring independently.

It may be an oversimplification, by onkyô's no-input music seems like the logical extreme of quiet music. It's hard not to think of John Cage's 4'33" when listening to a record made by a mixer that isn't hooked up to an audio source. Is a no-input release the twenty-first century's equivalent of sitting in front of a piano in a packed auditorium and playing nothing for four and a half minutes? Are Sachiko M's digital crackles and pops the electronic analogs to the shuffling feet and rumpling programs of Cage's audience?

For Cage, the idea was to perform a concert devoid of organized sound. For onkyô's no-input clan, part of the appeal no doubt lies in a parallel paradox, a little like a perpetual-motion machine—the strange idea of input-free machines somehow producing output.

---

55 Novak.

I.3 VULGAR

Some genres are defined as much by their subject matter as their sound. Horror punk is punk music about haunted houses and ghosts, and witch house is a late-aughts electronic music genre that explores Wiccan and mystical themes.

Sometimes, these themes can push the limits of taste. Grindcore is an extreme genre on the periphery of hardcore punk and metal. If you can make it through the fast-and-loud climes of thrash and death metal, you'll reach grindcore, which in its most prevalent form consists of under-one-minute blasts of distorted guitar, mile-a-minute rhythms called blast beats, and vocals that sound like someone gargling their own vomit.

Few agree on what counts as the first grindcore album, although Napalm Death's *Scum*, released in 1987, is a usual starting point. Listening to *Scum's* sonic carnage now, it is hard to fathom that this stuff once made a significant dent in pop culture. But even though the band recorded an entire side of this LP for a mere fifty pounds, the British music press were all over Napalm Death in their heyday, and *Scum* reached number seven on the UK Indie Chart.

Although grindcore is an extremely niche scene, it has its own subgenres, each of which has accumulated a sprawling body of work. It isn't uncommon for a band to have over fifty releases to its name, with each one being put out in an edition of fewer than a hundred copies.

I.3.1 Blood and Guts

Goregrind is a subcategory of grindcore whose subject matter is restricted to gore. The titles and lyrics of songs produced by goregrind artists are committed to a fascination with viscera. Goregrind songs feature a focus on bodily organs and human pathophysiology, with song titles and lyrics designed to be as revolting as possible. For example:

Oozing chyme reeks as your duodenum is hacked
Secreting gastric juices, enzymes melt your faecal tract
Torn major arteries, your corpse with blood is drenched
Your mouth is ripped inside-out as your oesophagus is wrenched
> —Carcass, "Maggot Factory," from *Reek of Putrefaction*, 1988

Connoisseurs of goregrind generally recognize British band Carcass' debut album *Reek of Putrefaction* as the genre's very first record, one which spawned a movement. Even legendary BBC radio announcer and indie tastemaker John Peel was entranced, regarding it as his favorite album of 1988![56] And while you can rarely actually make out the words of goregrind songs, you can certainly recognize Carcass' song titles as articles of poor taste. Highlights on *Reek* include "Genital Grinder," "Vomited Anal Tract," and

---

56 Mudrian, Albert (2004). *Choosing Death: The Improbable History of Death Metal & Grindcore*. Los Angeles: Feral House. p. 132. ISBN 978-1-93259-504-8.

Carcass' *Reek of Putrefaction*

"Microwaved Utero Gestation." The album's cover, meanwhile, is a collage of photos snipped from medical journals.

As detailed in Albert Mudrian's detailed history of death metal and grindcore, *Choosing Death*, Carcass was composed of two vegans and a vegetarian, and the central idea behind their grotesque music was to suggest that animal and human meat are essentially the same. By depicting the dismemberment of the human body so vividly, Carcass were hoping to evoke a reaction that would lead the listener to ask themselves what made eating animal flesh any different.

Today, Carcass' opuses seem tame in comparison to the downright anatomical detail of contemporary goregrind music. There has also been an expansion into a sister genre, *gorenoise*, which eschews rock-based sounds in favor of harsh noise. Contemporary gore-meisters have upped the ante by digging deeper into their medical pathophysiology tomes, occasionally garnering the genre name *medicore* for their jargon-rich productions.[57] For

57 "Medicore" serves as a reference to the genre's esoteric medical terminology—and is only a mere letter away from "mediocre."

example, in 2013, the Regurgitated Stoma Stew Productions record label put out a collaborative album between two bands, one named Carcinomatous Hepatocancrogastrojejunostomy Following Ureterarterialnecroticfaciotomy and Urethropancrejejuniumuterostomy, and the other called Urinary Tract Infection From Severe Pus Clots.

The Regurgitated Stoma Stew Productions label is no stranger to gory mouthfuls. Let's examine the track listing from a CD-R EP named *An Abnormal Condition Characterized By Hypertrophy Of The Interventricular Septum and Left Ventricular Free Wall Of The Heart*, by a band named Enterococcal Infection of the Urinary Tract Causes Severe Urinary Incontinence:

Escharotomy For Necrotic Tissue Left From A Third-Degree Burn Of The Torso
Inflammation Of The Mucosal Lining Of The Esophagus
The Surgical Creation Of A Direct Passage From The Esophagus To The Jejunum
A Rare Condition Characterized By Deposition Of Type II Cryoglobulins
   Without A Detectable Cause
An Abnormal Condition Characterized By Gross Hypertrophy Of The
   Interventricular Septum And Left Ventricular Free Wall Of The Heart
Surgical Repair Of Perforations Of The Eardrum With A Tissue Graft
A Disease Of Unknown Cause Resulting In Fibrous Induration Of The Corpora
   Cavernosa Of The Phallus
A Crisis of Uncontrolled Thyrotoxicosis Caused by the Release into the
   Bloodstream of Increased Amounts of Thyroid Hormone

According to the music cataloging website Discogs, this is one of 353 releases to exude from the Regurgitated Stoma Stew label since its formation in 2009. That is an impressive but not unprecedented tally when it comes to goregrind labels, where the norm is to have discographies above the one-hundred mark. So you can only imagine just how much medical terminology has been dredged up over thirty years of goregrind.

In some ways, the *grossness* of the gore is neutralized by the technical nature of the medical nomenclature and its inaccessibility to a lay audience. With that said, frequent references to pus, vomit, and blood do manage to turn one's stomach a tad. I began to wonder if they were pulling their lyrics and song titles from the medical literature, and indeed, I noticed that many of the tracks on that Regurgitated Stoma Stew EP were just definitions of medical terms. For example, "Inflammation Of The Mucosal Lining Of The Esophagus" refers to esophagitis, and the other track titles also revealed themselves as definitions, including technical descriptions of the terms esophagojejunostomy, essential mixed cryoglobulinemia, hypertrophic cardiomyopathy, myringoplasty, Peyronie's disease, and thyroid storm. A web search of each track revealed that they were pulled directly from *Mosby's Medical Dictionary*.

Arnaud lives in Montreal and has run Sulfuric Diarrhea Records since May 2015. He trades and sells his CD-R and tape releases through Facebook primarily, and in true gorenoise tradition, his Facebook account's cover photo features crossed-out musical notes superimposed over a photo of a bent-over man with greenish-yellow diarrhea streaming out of his bare bum. Despite the seeming misanthropy of a scene that celebrates organs spilling out of abdominal cavities and the stench of rotting flesh, he appreciates the relationships he has established through the scene.

"I've always been fascinated by biology in general, but mostly about death," Arnaud reflects. "The stages of decomposition which the human body goes through just seem beautiful to me. What normal people consider disgusting, I consider beautiful."

But it was also the extremeness of the sound itself that gripped him. "The first time I heard a gore-noise project, my quest for the ultimately horrible music ended. I listened to a lot of different styles of music in my youth, always going into more brutal and violent stuff. When I discovered the Mexican band Disgore, I thought I was at the end, but then I heard about Last Days Of Humanity. After that I wondered what could possibly beat that. At that point, I stumbled across Hemorrhoidal Anal Suffering, Agonizing Excess Bowel Acid Dissolving The Intestines Causing Massive Organ Trauma, Pseudocyst, Urinary Tract Infection With Severe Pus Clots, and many more. After listening to those, I knew that was the style of music I wanted to make."

Arnaud produces music and releases tapes with the free time he has from his work as a welder, and everything he does is homemade and on the cheap. He uses free software to compose music, sourcing his drums from a program called Hydrogen and recording the rest with Audacity. He assembles his covers with Photoshop, prints them, cuts them, and then dubs his cassettes manually. For Arnaud, it's clearly a labor of love.

His interest in gore arose at an early age. "My fascination started young, around thirteen to fourteen years old. Like most teenagers my age, I played *Doom*, *Call of Duty*, and other violent games, watched horror movies, stuff like that. The more I watched, the more I wanted to see gore."

I wanted to know what things inspire his ongoing immersion in this gory world. "Putrefaction, surgery, murder, abortion, autopsies, the mind of a psychopath," he listed. "The music itself feels like a soundtrack to all those. When I hear harsh-gore-noise like Wormclogged Blisters or Carnal Excrement, I like to think that this is what a psychopath is hearing when he's taking his victims' lives. All the pictures are real; this is what morality doesn't want you to see. But these things are just the day-to-day for some of us. Rape, murder, torture, and exploitation of all sorts. People live these things every day, we all know it's wrong, but a lot of people close their eyes on it. Popular music shows all the sweet sides of life—we like to show the ugly part, the truth."

He considers himself a lifer. "I just love it, man. It's a passion, a hobby, a way of living," he says. "Almost all my free time is dedicated to this. I see myself doing this all my life, if possible with a greater budget but anyhow I will make gorenoise tapes until I'm in the grave. If I find death in a brutal way, the best epiphany for me would be to have the photos of my carcass used for the last Sulfuric Diarrhea Records ever."

For Erik Raddatz, who runs a goregrind and goregrind noise label called Running Through the Blood Productions, the appeal of this music is existential. "This genre taps into the most depraved, real, honest aspects of death, dying, and perversion," he explained to me via email. "It doesn't hold back and allows a creative and safe healthy release of these thoughts, feelings, and actions. It takes the roots of death metal to a more personal level with graphic death and its aftermath. Autopsy means to see with one's own eyes, so this is not only a peek inside bodies, organs, viscera, disease, etcetera, but also a peek into most people's greatest fear, which is dying."

He emphasizes that Anal Birth, a project by Adam Rotella, represents the beginning of gorenoise music. "Anal Birth was the birth of gorenoise to me. The grotesque imagery and inhuman/subhuman sound of gorenoise combined with its pure death, dying, forensic, pathological approach appeals to my misanthropic mind." His cover art, which he assembles together with his "graphics genius" girlfriend, is inspired by the gore-collage on Carcass' debut album. "*Reek of Putrefaction* set the standard for forensic cover art, and in today's age, it is quite simple to Google something foul and grotesque and have hundreds of pics to choose from. Is this overdone? Absolutely! But what else really expresses pathological goregrind and gorenoise? Something artsy? I think not."

Ivan Loi, who lives in Bologna, Italy, is thirty-four years old and works as a carpenter but is currently transitioning careers. He runs the Viscera Records label and performs goregrind under the name Cannibe—though he's also put out music under about forty other pseudonyms. He isn't sure what it is about goregrind that captured his mind sixteen years ago, but it's been a persistent passion. "There is no specific reason for how I got into this insane and sick musical world," he tells me. "Nothing of my personal problems. Many years ago a friend of mine made me listen to some gore bands, and from that day, I decided to be part of it too, playing and releasing rotten bands."

Like Arnaud, he likes that goregrind has connected him with other fans, near and far. "In all these years, the 'musick' has allowed me to meet a lot of really interesting, cool people. With those who live closest I have established a very good friendship, but with others who live in other parts of the world, unfortunately, for now, it is an internet friendship."

Despite goregrind's graphic subject matter, Loi doesn't accept all forms of boundary-transgressing. In fact, acceptance of difference is important for him. "This community is true! There are no psychopaths, of course; there are simple people who have many passions in common with me. Nazis, sexists, homophobes: they are the true psychopaths!!!"

Reading through interviews in fanzines, I often felt as though interviewers and interviewees were vying to be as nihilistic, grotesque, and politically incorrect as possible. And while the scene is not immune from homophobes and supremacists, it can sometimes seem that much of the gruesome posturing is an act. For instance, in an interview for Indonesian fanzine *Anorexia Orgasm*, zine owner Putra attempts to out-repulse Last Days of Humanity drummer Marc Palmen, and Palmen briefly breaks the fourth wall, reflecting upon the gamesmanship of continuously upping the ante. (Warning: themes of sexual assault are involved.)

Putra: What do you think about Sex, Drug, and Satanism. How many times do you fuck your girl friends? And have you ever heard a story about a little girl who was raped by her father and tortured to death? If you were her father, what would you feel about it?

Marc: What I think of Sex? I prefer to call it PORNO, I love it!!!! Drugs are stupid and Satanism is the most pathetic bullshit I have ever heard!!! I'm sorry to say but I haven't got a girlfriend at the moment, I'm working on it!!! About your story, I can't come up with something shocking at the moment. You own me this one!!

Anthony Julius, a British lawyer and academic, provides a framework for thinking about "transgressive" art in his book, *Transgressions: The Offences of Art*. In this dense tome, he divides transgressive art into three categories: art that transgresses the rules of art (i.e., by going against the art canon), art that is politically transgressive, and art that transgresses taboos. Goregrind primarily falls under taboo-transgressing art, since it operates at a comfortable remove from the fine arts world and seldom gets political, apart from testing the boundaries of political correctness and good taste.[58]

There are many historical examples of taboo-breaking art, although Julius observes that the form has become less subtle and a lot more confrontational. For Julius, taboos are distinct from morality, taboos being "certain values by which we live but which cannot (or not without a stretch) be described as moral principles."

Julius charts the history of taboo in terms of two stages. In the first, there is "the story of our emancipation from a magical, non-ethical superstition, from taboo … and our development towards the enlightened, self-aware rationality of a universal morality." As an example, he cites J.G. Frazer, an anthropologist who studied diverse cultures' myths and identified several common themes despite each society's disparate origins. Frazer argued that early, primitive taboos eventually give way to the more refined, contemporary systems of law and morality, although as he intolerantly notes, "the swine of modern society are still content to feed" on these ancient superstitions.

For Julius, the second part of the history of taboo is a coda. Friedrich Nietzsche, in his self-proclaimed "campaign against morality," revealed even the so-called enlightened morality is "mere superstition, custom, etc … a sham." He saw our society's unquestioningly accepted codes of conduct as nothing more than a series of irrational taboos and rituals. In the end, Julius argues, this leads to a return to the custom, convention, and taboos.

As Julius sees it, taboo-breaking art "exploits the tension between these two stories." On one hand, there is the idea that we've overcome taboos and instead live moralistically, and on the other hand that our accepted codes of morality are nothing more than taboos and rituals. This type of art "exposes our attachment to sentiments that, though they share certain characteristics with morality, are not moral." It also "intimidate[s] us with its nihilism when it values at zero what we justifiably esteem," and as a result can also be seen as a form of cruelty.

---

58 Although one could argue that the goregrind ur-text, Carcass' *Reek of Putrefaction*, is politically transgressive given that its objective was to confront meat-eaters by comparing human flesh with meat.

Where does the vividly graphic content of goregrind fit into this system? As it turns out, there are direct parallels in the world of fine art. For her 1997 book *Post Mortem*, photographer Sue Fox took over a thousand photographs of dead bodies in a Manchester morgue[59] and received considerable flak when these images were exhibited. By removing the bodies from their medical context, her work parallels the time-honored goregrind practice of putting autopsy photos on album covers. In 1992, photographer Andres Serrano, no stranger to controversy, also exhibited a series of photographs of dead bodies in a morgue. Julius argues that these works appear to offend audience members on the basis of moral principles. For one, they depict people who may have been unlawfully killed—and images of their cadavers are violations of privacy. But he argues that these reasons don't adequately explain the feelings they evoke—feelings of "disgust, aversion, ugliness, distaste." These emotions are rooted in the fact that this art violates expectations that art will stay within a familiar realm of "safe" and "customary" content. "Violating bodies or picturing their violation puts our sense of our own bodily integrity into momentary jeopardy," he points out. These perspectives echo Erik Raddatz's perspective on goregrind as confronting people with their fear of death.

Julius argues that, in some cases, the taboos can themselves be harmful. "When they are aggregated into collective terms such as 'public decency' or 'community standards,' they can be used as a cudgel to bludgeon heterodoxy, dissent and even simple eccentricity," he writes. As an example, he points to New York mayor Rudy Giuliani's call for a "decency panel" that would censor programming decisions made by publicly funded museums.

Extreme metal scenes like goregrind consider their marginality as integral to their identity. Grisly cover art alienates the masses and ensures an in-group of dedicated and steel-stomached scene members. The content frequently violates taboos held by the general public, but then again, this music is hardly intended for the masses. Most goregrind releases are put out in editions of under a thousand, and many are issued in sub-fifty pressings. They are intended to appeal to the few who are already indoctrinated.

While Carcass' *Reek of Putrefaction* was taboo-breaking, can we really consider the ten-thousandth goregrind CD-R to arrive in its wake, thirty or so years later, taboo-breaking? Perhaps the most taboo-breaking thing to do within the goregrind world would be to put out an album about teddy bears and rainbows. In fact, that's something that the notorious shit-disturbing grindcore band Anal Cunt did in 1998, putting out *Picnic of Love*, a cheerful acoustic album adorned with falsetto vocals and pithy lyrical treasures like "Greed is something that we don't need."

Perhaps goregrind is a form of rebellion rooted in one's own, personal social context—its very repugnancy a way of embracing one's status as an outsider. Perhaps goregrind's misanthropy serves, for some, as an expression of anger about aspects of their life. After all, many goregrind bands and labels gripe about their small towns and lack of money in interviews. At the extreme end, I also wonder if a minority of goregrinders experience a sexual thrill premised on a fetish for sadism.

The extremeness of goregrind's musical content pushes these artists to the margins of popular culture, but in those fringes, they find one another. And thus, even if the

59 www.independent.co.uk/life-style/visual-arts-vile-bodies-1152137.html

music's basis is in anger and misanthropy, a camaraderie emerges. That they can tolerate and even celebrate their gory fantasies establishes a tight-knit in-group. But, as the next section will explore, there's an awkward gender line that emerges among the extreme metal community.

1.3.2 Pornogrind

Goregrind is not alone as an extreme subgenre of grindcore, and it's not the most disturbing subcategory either. Scrolling through appropriated medical terminology, I started to feel that a band name like Perforated Bowel Syndrome With Oozing Faeces was more folksy than truly offensive, a notion matched by the good natures of the scene members I connected with. Guyome, a member of long-running French goregrind band Pulmonary Fibrosis, once signed off a 2013 interview with *BrainDead Zine* by saying that "there is no fans but friends."[60]

The more malevolent grindcore subgenre is something called *pornogrind*, along with its noise cousin, *pornoise*. This is a much more controversial breed of chaos that combines grindcore with graphic sexual imagery and descriptions of gratuitous violence, reeking of sexually sadistic overtones. (As an illustrative point, there is a sub-sub-sub-genre called pornogore that merges gore and pornography to synergistically appalling effect.)

An article by Amanda Hess, published in *Washington City Paper*, comments that the content of pornogrind albums "would keep them out of most stores,"[61] which is quite the understatement when you consider a genre whose albums and song titles bear names like *Drink Vaginal Soup or Die!*, "Fistful of Sperm," and "Twat Enema"—all by prolific band GUT. The fact that the cover art often provides depictions of the titles' acts does not help their retail sales. And yet this doesn't deter audiences. GUT's *Drowning in Female Excrements* single, one of countless pornogrind releases, has sold out three separate pressings—over 1,500 copies in total—and copies have sold for nearly forty dollars as collectors' items!

Sonically, pornogrind diverges from regular grindcore by its slower pacing and a greater reliance on groove. There is a big scene in Germany, where core bands like GUT and Cock and Ball Torture both originate, although a group of homophobic Californians called the Meat Shits are also often cited as early exponents of pornogrind filth. Inspired by these bands, a panoply of different acts has sprung up across the globe.

Perhaps the only pornogrind band I can stomach is the humbly named Cock and Ball Torture, who at least seem to revel in the humorousness of their exploits. A fan-made video for their "Aphrodisianus" features a bunch of middle-aged celebrants at a wedding reception dancing along to dense riffs, a breakneck rhythm section, and vocals that are more burp than voice.

GUT is another canonical pornogrind act, a collective that kicked off in 1991, initially playing standard grindcore. The aforementioned demo, *Drowning in Female Excrements*, is a shoddily recorded assembly of horror movie samples, cavernous bass guitar rumble,

60 'Interview with PULMONARY FIBROSIS - French Gore/Grind,' *Braindead Zine*, 2013 <www.braindeadzine.net/interviews/pulmonary/> [accessed 2 January 2021].

61 Amanda Hess, 'Brick and Mordor,' *Washington City Paper* (Washington, D.C., 18 January 2008) <washingtoncitypaper.com/article/236334/brick-and-mordor/> [accessed 2 January 2021].

and pig-gargle vocals. Their focus appears to be on gore, although "Confessions of a Necrophile," as well as the cassette's title, nudge toward sexual themes. Throughout the early and middle nineties, the band would refine its style, pulling toward increasingly perverse concepts. Seven-inch EPs *Pussified/Assified* and *Hyperintestinal Vulva Desecration* would see the band embracing the collision of sex and violence that would come to define them. The former begins with an audio clip of a woman screaming in terror, right before the music hits. Thereafter, the band's customary burpy vocals and guitar sludge are augmented with a more groove-oriented sound backbone. That groove became part of the definitive GUT sound and a standard feature within the pornogrind subgenre, which is generally considered more groove-oriented than other forms of grindcore. Like many pornogrind releases, the cover of *Pussified/Assified* is explicitly sexual, depicting a dirty hand stroking a woman's pubic hair with a grimy brush.

Interestingly, as GUT progressed into the 2000s, their sound would evolve in interesting directions. *The Cumback 2006*, which followed a brief absence from the scene, crossbred their pornogrind with a goofy strain of hip-hop, a sort of pornogrind nu-metal. Unsurprisingly, this overhaul divided the band's fans; some embraced the new direction, but there were also many disgruntled tirades online, e.g.: "it sucks cock so fucking bad that it almost seemed to me that it was on purpose," per one YouTube commenter. Despite the new sound, GUT's content remained the same. The track list is a medley of porn star names and casual misogyny ("Jenna Haze (You're a Pro)," "I Hate Chicks (But I Love Pussy)"). They've even gone to the trouble of interspersing snippets of porn audio among the songs.

GUT's albums were almost deliriously offensive, and what little interview content exists online is also characteristically vile. In a 1992 interview conducted by Billy Nocera of death metal/grindcore zine *The Coven*,[62] a fourteen-year-old Nocera is treated to GUT vocalist Oli Roder gleefully recounting a dubious story of desecrating his aunt's corpse. "All members of GUT are sick and disgusting, and I really like that," Roder boasts.

It's tough to stomach the antics of a band like GUT, but the Meat Shits are a true exercise in awful. They were one of the key early bands in pornogrind and also one of the most controversial acts in extreme metal. The Meat Shits were formed in the late eighties in the small town of Modesto, California, which is ironically the Spanish word for "modest." Helmed by Robert Deathrage from the start, they quickly gained a reputation for their brash and inflammatory antics, with Deathrage's songs stoking up deliberately crass subject matter: homophobia, misogyny, racism, anti-feminism. Their song titles and album art celebrated pornography, often appropriating full images from the pages of extreme porn magazines—one area where the Meat Shits' influence would leave an indelible mark on the pornogrind genre.

By all accounts, Deathrage truly was a homophobic, sexist racist. A 2001 interview[63] in long-running metal fanzine *Canadian Assault* offers a glimpse into his psyche, as well as plenty of historical context. By then, he was on the third of many reunions of

62 'GUT INTERVIEW TAKEN FROM RAZORBACK RECORDS WEBSITE A Tribute To The Gore Legends,' *PORNO DEATH-GRIND-WEB-ZINE* <goregrind.20megsfree.com/gut_interview.htm> [accessed 2 January 2021].

63 www.canadianassault.com/meatshitsinterview.htm

the band, its roster all new, and in the interview, he blames the band's first breakup on newfangled politically correct values that had permeated the underground music scene, which "succeeded in poisoning impressionable minds with their pro-gay/anti-sexist propaganda." According to Deathrage, the Meat Shits initially attempted to counteract this tendency by bringing increasingly offensive material to the table, but several record labels backed out of putting out their vile new records. So Deathrage decided to call it a day.

He then lost his job after Modesto was flooded and moved to Ogden, Utah, to become a carpet installer. It should surprise nobody that Deathrage was unhappy in a state where pornography is illegal. "I used to have to travel to Evanston, Wyoming, if I wanted to buy real beer," he recounts. "And towards the end of my stay in that toilet, the UHP (Utah Highway Patrol) would wait outside of the liquor store in Wyoming waiting for anybody with Utah plates to attempt to bring illegal liquor back into the state." As a result, Deathrage moved to Stockton in central California.

Online message boards also relate how Deathrage has completely fallen off the map for years at a time, leading to rumors that he had died of a heroin overdose. Lo and behold, he would turn up again, hawking Meat Shits merchandise and playing "reunion" shows, only to again disappear, often leaving band members and record labels in the dark.[64]

There's a rumor about the Meat Shits that, at their second-ever show, opening for Primus at a local restaurant, one of the older waitresses was so offended and overwhelmed by the band's noise that she went into convulsions and later died. Deathrage confirms this story with pride in his interview, although it's hard to know whether this truly happened or whether it's merely a figment of Deathrage's insatiable bravado.

Many members of the extreme metal scene disown the band. Critic Stefan Franke, in his review of a Meat Shits album for *Voices from the Darkside* magazine, describes them as "nothing but a bunch of redneck imbeciles, who try their best to be provocative but turn up being totally stupid."[65] In a review for the *Deadtide* website, reviewer K. Huckins pans the same album as "noise meets stupidity," again skewering the band's backward politics: "Anytime I see anyone spewing this much homophobia, I have a tendency to assume that they live in a very small place—something, say, closet-sized."[66]

The latter review also references Varg Vikernes, a Norwegian black metal performer who was convicted of burning down churches and murdering one of his bandmates. While in prison, he became involved in the blood-and-soil nationalist Heathen Front movement, considered by many to promote neo-Nazi, white-supremacist values. Many of Vikernes' writings through the nineties and aughts are unabashedly racist and anti-Semitic. He also apparently tried to mail a letter bomb to Israeli metal band Salem.

---

64 www.nwnprod.com/forum/viewtopic.php?p=870425&sid=26f37d92919faefaa5ebfbf437eb3776
65 Stefan Franke, 'MEAT SHITS Review,' *Voices From The Darkside* <web.archive.org/web/20180608035444/http://www.voicesfromthedarkside.de/Albums-EPs-Demos/M/MEAT-SHITS--2090.html> [accessed 2 January 2021].
66 www.deadtide.com/reviews/albums/page.php?id=372

The trouble with Vikernes is that he was also the guy behind the one-man band Burzum, a canonical black metal act whose albums are considered classics of the genre. As a result, metal fans have struggled to reconcile their love of Vikernes' music with his detestable values.

In his article for the online magazine *PopMatters*, "A Very Dirty Lens: How Can We Listen to Offensive Metal?," writer Craig Hayes uses nationalist-socialist metal, including Vikernes' work, to argue that listeners are always making ethical and political judgments when choosing whether to listen to offensive metal, even if they considers themselves to be apolitical in their music appreciation.[67] He challenges the argument that metal lyrics are mere fantasy, that they have nothing to do with ethics. Most people draw the line somewhere, he argues, and it's where the individual fan draws the line that comprises an ethical choice. He reflects that "metal's history of in-built transgression and controversy has caused fans to make deeply personal decisions on how to conceptualize offensiveness, even if that's simply to say 'More entrails, please.'" For him, "rejecting the place of ethics in metal is an ethical decision" in itself.

Jill Mikkelson, in a 2016 opinion piece for *Noisey*,[68] describes her history as a fan in the male-dominant extreme metal scene. As she grew older and wiser, she started to challenge the lyrical themes of sexual violence that pervade much brutal metal, including pornogrind. She concluded that the sexism of these lyrics serves to "preserve a patriarchal power structure, maintain the status quo of women as disposable sex objects, and it's very likely that they're insidiously affecting men's attitudes towards women, both in the context of metal and outside of it."

She rejects the counterargument that these forms of extreme metal are just fantasy. Pointing to the staggering rates of violence against women in the general population, she sees this argument as a naïve attempt to excuse metal from society at large. She points to the many stories of sexism shared by women on the metal scene and the stream of death threats received by one-woman death metal act Murkur.

Mikkelson, notably, does not make the argument that bands and artists need to stop performing this music. Instead, she criticizes the attacks that people invariably face when these objections are raised. She wants this sort of discussion to be accepted, to foster a dialogue that might help change sexist attitudes.

With all this in mind, I began to wonder if there really was a defense for music as extreme as pornogrind. I have yet to hear a foolproof one, but while lurking on online message boards, I encountered one defender on *ilxor*, a forum for music nerds frequented by many music critics. That user sees goregrind as an opportunity for trauma survivors to explore their experiences. "Goregrind is specifically about vicariously relating to positions of extreme exaggerated power over the helpless," they suggest.[69] "I personally think there's value in an aesthetic space where that sort of identification can take place."

---

67 Craig Hayes, 'A Very Dirty Lens: How Can We Listen to Offensive Metal? — PopMatters,' *PopMatters*, 2013 <www.popmatters.com/a-very-dirty-lens-2495726632.html> [accessed 2 January 2021].
68 noisey.vice.com/en_ca/article/death-metal-misogyny
69 'Rolling Metal Thread 2014,' *Ilxor*, 2014 <ilxor.com/ILX/ThreadSelectedControllerServlet?action=showall&boardid=41&threadid=98699> [accessed 2 January 2021].

EXTREME MUSIC

This opinion is the product of this one's person's experiences, who sees this from the perspective of their own trauma. I suspect this is not the guiding influence behind most individuals' fandom, although I can imagine that there are many members on the scene who have suffered their own personal adversity. To my mind, this doesn't excuse the genre's many transgressions, but it does suggest a unique way to appreciate this work.

Returning to Anthony Julius' theories about transgressive art, I would argue that pornogrind, unlike goregrind, transgresses not just taboos but also ethical positions. While some might argue that the genre can serve as a fantasy, or a sort of catharsis or vehicle for exploring one's own psychology, the point stands that sexual violence is a socially destructive phenomenon that occurs with great frequency. Pornogrind is transgressive because it inhabits and often glorifies this space—for example, in a GUT song like "Pissmop (Maybe You Can Be One Too)." Given the deleterious effects of gender-related violence on society and individuals, it's not a mere "taboo" that's being violated, but a fundamental ethical wrong. Whether you think this means the genre is a problem, or that it is worthy of being censored, is for you to decide.

SEVERAL ELABORATELY ANATOMICAL GOREGRIND BANDS

Perforated Bowel Syndrome With Oozing Faeces

You, & me...and a meathook makes three

This is one of the many one-man-bands of Bobby Maggard, a goregrind/gorenoise linchpin who runs one of the most prolific DIY gore labels around, Regurgitated Stoma Stew Records. He estimates in an August 2019 interview that he has put out 1,018 releases total[1]. Although one of his other "bands," Urinary Tract Infection From Severe Pus Clots, is even more popular than this one, I'm partial to anything with Oozing Faeces in its name. <u>Recommended release:</u> *You, & Me... And A Meathook Makes Three* mini-CD-R (Regurgitated Stoma Stew Productions, 2016). I'm a sucker for a rhyming title.

Melanocytic Tumors Of Uncertain Malignant Potential

The gorenoise project of Ivan Loi, member of Cannibe and owner of Viscera Records, whom I interviewed for this book. Melanocytic Tumors, one of many projects Loi has helmed, has put out a couple dozen releases since its formation in 2011. <u>Recommended release:</u> *The Breakdown Of Proteins In A Decomposing Carcass Is A Spontaneous Process But One That Is Accelerated As The Anerobic Microorganisms* CD-R EP (Land of Fog Records, 2013). Bonus points for the extremely long title, complete with spelling errors. This one seems to be part of a medical dictionary's definition of "putrefaction."

---

1   Rudolf Schütz, 'Practicing Surgery with Bobby Maggard (Regurgitated Stoma Stew),' *Rubber Axe Zine*, 2019 <www.rubberaxezine.com/practicing-surgery-with-bobby-maggard-regurgitated-stoma-stew/> [accessed 2 January 2021].

Agonizing Excess Bowel Acid Dissolving The Intestines Causing Massive Organ Trauma

Called Agonizing Excess for short, this is one of many one-man-bands helmed by Bob Macabre, a.k.a. Bob Egler, a burly, beardy man from the small town of New Alexandria, Pennsylvania. Also the owner of Macabre Mastermind Records, Bob has been known to dabble in various subgenres, putting out dozens of releases per year.[2] Recommended release: *Obstructed Colon Causing Intestinal Eruption* CD-R (Noize Black Music Manifestation, 2013). So good, it was reissued by Running Through the Blood Productions!

Carcinomatous Hepatocancrogastrojejunostomy Following Ureterarterialnecroticfaciotomy and Urethropancrejejuniumuterostomy

There are other long goregrind names, but this one is a real mouthful. The story behind it is even stranger. This is one of many projects by an anonymous producer who went by The Love Doctor, who used to run a Bandcamp account that was filled with music noted by critics to be especially skillfully arranged and performed. A blog named *Burning Ambulance* tracked the mysterious Love Doctor down in 2013, only to learn that he was a fourteen-year-old who aspired to become a forensic pathologist.[3] At the time, he claimed to have started recording music two years earlier—when he was just twelve! When asked what his parents thought of his gory music, he responded, "My dad likes my more musical death/grind projects and my mom hates my vocals. Hahahahahaha." His Bandcamp has since been taken down and he has been silent for a couple years, so the mystery lives on—but he would presumably be in his twenties now, possibly on his way to a pathology career.

Recommended release: *Rancid Jejunostomy and Pancreatomy Resulting in Gastrointestinal Carcinoma* CD-R (Necrotic Jejunostomy Productions, 2012). Featuring the hit single, "The Chunks of Juice Spill out of the Tracheostomy Stoma are Filled With Multiple Infectious Bacteria and Biochemical Substances," this album makes eight separate references to the most underrated part of the digestive tract, the jejunum.

Disgorgement Of Intestinal Lymphatic Suppuration

This goregrind band from Angers, France, is made up of three members: Pierre, Vincent, and Tony LeGrinder. They've released droves of splits but only a couple albums. Recommended release: *Hospital Holocaust* CD-R (Septic Aroma Of Reeking Stench, 2007). A fifty-three-track album on a Greek label with *that* name? What's not to like?

2 Wulf, 'Interview with Bob Macabre of Chainsaw Dissection / Psychotic Homicidal Dismemberment / Satanic Impalement!!', *Malicious Intent*, 2011 <maliciousintent666.blogspot.com/2011/04/interview-with-bob-macabre-of-chainsaw.html> [accessed 2 January 2021].

3 Phil Freeman, 'The Strange Case Of The Love Doctor,' *Burning Ambulance*, 2013 <burningambulance.com/2013/09/03/interview-with-the-love-doctor/> [accessed 2 January 2021].

I.4 FAST

"My father once commented, 'You don't listen to music at the right speed, do you?'"[70]
—Zoe Mindgrrind, Splatterkore collective founder

As the loudness and softness wars played out, another battle emerged in the world of electronic dance music. This was the speed war.

To understand the context behind this often esoteric rivalry, it is important to first review some basic electronic music history.

In the early 1980s, two major electronic dance music genres developed: house in Chicago and techno in Detroit. Both genres were centered around a prominent 4/4 kick drum, that familiar *thump-thump-thump-thump* bass beat that forms the backbone of most eighties and nineties dance music. This beat came to be known as 'four on the floor,' and in most songs, it would beat between 120 and 150 times per minute. This metric came to be known as a track's beats per minute or BPM, an important statistic for DJs who carefully match songs' rhythms so they can seamlessly mix them during sets.

Not long after they emerged in America, house and techno took hold in Europe. For most of the past few decades, these genres have managed more mainstream success with European audiences than North American ones.

In the nineties, a faster and harsher strain of electronic music called hardcore took root in raves in Europe. The term hardcore doesn't quite refer to one sound; instead, it comprises many subgenres. These subgenres would often test the limits of speed, wading into the territory between 150 and 200 BPM—edging past three beats per second!

Gabber, a Dutch breed of hard, angry hardcore, was one subscene that tested the limits of danceability. The much-maligned subgenre known as happy hardcore, meanwhile, offered a counterpoint to gabber's world-weary grit—it was cheerful, typically matching bouncy synths to sped-up vocals. Electronic music purists often compared happy hardcore's sound to Alvin and the Chipmunks.

Not every subgenre of hardcore stuck to the four-on-the-floor beat. One of the cardinal electronic music genres, known as drum and bass, uses something called a *breakbeat* as its rhythmic backbone. This is a complex drum rhythm that was originally sampled from the drum solo of a vintage soul single titled "Amen, Brother" by The Winstons—that widely used sample is now known as "the Amen break." Drum and bass producers would later pull breakbeats from several different soul records and eventually started creating their own beats, using audio software to surgically extract each drum hit from old drum solos, which they would then meticulously rearrange into custom patterns.

In the 2000s, an extreme version of breakbeat-driven music emerged under the name breakcore. This was music that took breakbeats and amplified their speed and complexity to previously inconceivable highs. Breakbeats themselves are fast and complicated beats to

---

70 'Interview: Mindgrrind Settles the "Core,"' *Unscene Berlin*, 2013 <unsceneberlin.blogspot.com/2013/04/interview-zoe-mindgrrind-settles-core.html> [accessed 1 January 2021].

begin with—so when they're turned up to 200 BPM, it's a truly blistering sound. Breakcore peaked in the mid-aughts with the critically acclaimed work of solo acts like Kid606, DJ/Rupture, and Venetian Snares, who emerged as a clan of beat scientists. In one notable example, Venetian Snares and his then-girlfriend Hecate, also a prominent breakcore producer, used high-fidelity microphones to record themselves having sex. They then chopped up the resulting audio to make a full album, *Nymphomatriarch*, built exclusively out of those dissected sex noises. With one notable track featuring a memorable spank as its snare drum, the record inevitably raised eyebrows; it was even written up in *Playboy* magazine, a rare brush with popular culture for extreme music.

1.4.1 Speedcore

The speeds achieved by gabber, happy hardcore, and breakcore were snail-like compared to an obscure underground movement that emerged out of hardcore's ultra-rapid fringe. As those genres maxed out around 200 BPM, a genre called speedcore aimed to push the envelope, using 250 BPM as the lower limit of tempo. Speedcore tracks indeed can hurtle up to 500 BPM, which amounts to over eight beats per second—an absolutely boggling figure. To get a sense of just how absurd that is, try tapping your finger eight times in a second, and you'll see that these are distinctly supraphysiological speeds.

Members of the speedcore scene are a dedicated bunch, churning out content at an impressive clip. Much of their output is released digitally, often made available online for free, resulting in a complex network of netlabels and YouTube accounts. Despite this sizable online footprint, the history of speedcore is poorly documented, and even the definition of speedcore remains contested. Simon Reynolds, in his seminal history of electronic music, *Energy Flash*, makes only passing mention of some proto-speedcore acts, also filing them under the gabber tag. And DJ Distortion, member of the gabber collective Rotterdam Death Corps, believes that trying to precisely define speedcore misses the mark entirely: "Naturally, some people start giving it different names the faster it gets, like terrorcore, splittercore, or speedcore...but really it's all derived from the same thing, and that's house."[71]

Yet there is most definitely a group of people who consider speedcore a distinct scene, not just an appendage of gabber. Despite this, there is no definitive history available online, perhaps reflecting a scene that has largely taken place live. The digital evidence of speedcore's origins amounts largely to a smattering of disorganized and often contradictory message board posts, many in Dutch. To try to gain some clarity, I enlisted help from Tuomas Kinnunen, a speedcore producer from Finland who has spent untold hours trying to make sense of the genre. He generously shared his vision of the frenetic scene, emailing me a detailed breakdown painstakingly cross-referenced with forum posts and YouTube links.

In the beginning there was hardcore, and then there was gabber—that breed of fast, aggressive music primarily out of Europe. As the BPMs got faster, some producers experimented with extreme speeds as one-off endeavors. These can be considered

71 'Rotterdam Terror Corps' DJ Distortion Talks Gabber History | Telekom Electronic Beats,' *Electronic Beats*, 2015 <www.electronicbeats.net/rotterdam-terror-corps-dj-distortion-talks-gabber-history/> [accessed 1 January 2021].

proto-speedcore, if you will: "songs" that were designed to see what music sounded like when rhythmic parameters were brought to their logical extreme.

Interestingly, some familiar names got into the mix. Moby was one. In the early nineties, he was an established electronic producer, though still years away from the international ubiquity of his *Play* album. In June of 1993, he put out a single whose A-side, "I Feel It," was a riveting rave track that would go on to be included on the soundtrack to the movie *Cool World*.[72] But the significance of "I Feel It" may have been eclipsed by its B-side, "Thousand," which ended up in the *Guinness Book of World Records* for boasting the fastest tempo ever heard on a commercial single. Utilizing an iconic sample from the 1983 disco classic "Let No Man Put Asunder" by First Choice, it starts off with a plodding four-on-the-floor beat that runs at a normal tempo. But the speed quickly starts to accelerate, whizzing toward a peak of approximately 1014 BPM before cutting out, then starting the climb again. While the original sample from "Let No Man Put Asunder" is a joyful cry of "Oh, yeah," here the singer's ecstasy is distorted into a menacing blur, bludgeoned by the turbine rhythm. Moby used to play "Thousand" during sets in the mid-nineties, sometimes while smashing his equipment, rock-star-style.[73] Interestingly, despite its absurd pace, "Thousand" retains an excitement that could work on the dance floor—albeit one located in the deepest recesses of Hell.[74]

In January of 1993, Cybersonik, the duo of techno stalwarts Dan Bell and Richie Hawtin, put out a single featuring the tracks "Jackhammer" and "Machine Gun (Circuit Breaker Remix)" on Probe Records. Like some of Hawtin's work as Plastikman, the titles are designed to be descriptive, and the tracks use little more than percussion to achieve their effect. "Jackhammer" pits an abrasive drill noise above a hyper-kinetic kick, while "Machine Gun" starts off as a mid-range 140 BPM techno track before abruptly doubling the bass drum to a rowdy 280 BPM, simulating the battering of an automatic gun. Years later, Hawtin would reveal in Simon Reynolds' *Energy Flash* that the entire single was intended to lampoon what they saw as a rave scene that had lost its way. "We don't even like that record," he said. "It was a statement [to the rest of the rave scene]—kind of 'We don't know what you guys are doing, but it's not what we're about.'"

That same year, the German group Atari Teenage Riot unveiled a new live track called "319." ATR specialized in a confrontational brand of punk-infused gabber that came to be known as digital hardcore, and "319" is a fitting example of their boundary-walloping attitude, its title a direct reference to its peak BPM. ATR's regular tracks are pulverizing in their intensity, so this piece was a fitting way to cap off their performances on a note of ecstatic frenzy. There has been no official studio release, so the only official documentation of this beast is a rare live recording that was included on a limited-edition bonus disc.[75] On that recording, "319" is little more than a kick drum and synth pulse blaring above a shifting tide of feedback noise, dissonant even by the usual standards of ATR.

---

72 "I Feel It" was known as "Next Is the E" in the States, where it peaked at number eight on the *Billboard* dance chart.

73 Kevin Holmes, 'An Interview With Moby: The Man With Two Facebook Accounts,' *Noisey*, 2011 <www.vice.com/en/article/535qyq/an-interview-with-moby-the-man-with-two-facebook-accounts> [accessed 1 January 2021].

74 Twenty-one years later, Moby was sued for unlicensed use of the First Choice sample in both "Thousand" and "I Feel It."

75 "319 (Live At Eurobeat 2000, London 1993)," from Alec Empire & Atari Teenage Riot, *Sixteen Years Of Video Material* (Eat Your Heart Out / Monitorpop Entertainment, 2008)

Other proto-speedcore exploits from the year of 1993 include two obscure German entries: "Double Speed Mayhem"[76] by 303 Nation, which appears only on a compilation titled *Frankfurt Trax: Volume 4,* and "Summer" by Sorcerer, which precedes its cavalcade of 250+ BPM chaos with a clip of Darth Vader urging you to "release your anger." The birthplace of gabber, the Netherlands, also holds its own with The Dreamteam's "Killer Machinery," an obscure forty-second track, kicking off with a rhythmic loop that increases its tempo with each iteration up to a momentary peak of, apparently, 1920 BPM.

While the likes of Moby and Richie Hawtin were fooling around with the settings on their drum machines, a subset of lesser-known gabber producers started to up the ante, recording tracks that matched increasingly breakneck speeds with dark and aggressive sounds. Called speedcore, the word seems to have been first used to refer to a variant of electronic music that fused hardcore techno with metal samples. This sound emerged in 1994 on several releases put out by the French label Gangstar Toons Industry label and by New Yorkers like the Disciples of Annihilation, a trio of Italian Americans often referred to as D.O.A.

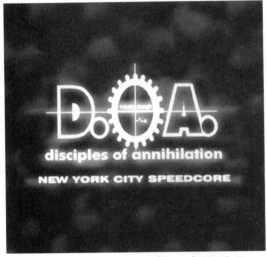

Cover art of *NYC Speedcore,* by D.O.A. Image courtesy of Industrial Strength Records.

D.O.A.'s 1994 EP, *Industrial Strength 9d4,* was released on the fledgling Industrial Strength label and is a typical example of the style. Dark synths and samples of distorted guitar riffs bound off relentless kick drums, which momentarily reach 280 BPM on the blaring "Ya Mutha Part II." D.O.A.'s vicious energy led them to be signed to the British grindcore label Earache, which made a brief foray into extreme American electronic music in the mid-nineties.

Dutch scenesters, meanwhile, will point to incipient speedcore from their homeland, such as a 1992 remix of Euromasters' "Alles Naar De Fl—te" that clocks in at 250 BPM. Despite its whopping speeds, "Alles Naar De Fl—te," which means "All F–ked Up," made the Dutch Top 40 for three weeks, reflecting the unprecedented success of the extreme genre in the Netherlands. Euromasters were noted for representing their hometown, Rotterdam, in its notorious feud with the Amsterdam music scene. (Their first, most famous single translates as "Amsterdam, Where's That?")

The first time speedcore was referenced by name on an actual release came in 1996, on D.O.A.'s album, *Mothafuckin' New York Hardcore.* It featured a track titled "N.Y.C. Speedcore," its name emphasizing that it was not a Dutch production. Many of the tracks on the album were created by layering heavy metal samples over a maxed-out drum machine; "N.Y.C." itself pulls riffs from Type O Negative's goth-metal cover of

---

76 This track was used in a nightclub scene in the 2002 film *Morvern Callar.*

the seventies soft-rock tune "Summer Breeze." These days, *Mothafuckin' New York Hardcore's* sound has more in common with a genre called terrorcore, a kind of gabber that distinguished itself from cheerier commercial gabber through its heavy intensity.

But in addition to being heavy, "N.Y.C. Speedcore" also turned attention toward the central aesthetic of speedcore: *speed*. Around this time, producers started to compete in earnest to up the BPM ante while still making coherent music. Beats per minute figures, often listed on a record's center sticker to help DJs mix tracks live, edged higher and higher.

Throughout the nineties, *speedcore* was invoked to refer to fast music above 200 BPM, but at some point in the late nineties or early 2000s, the term came to specifically refer to music above 250 or even 300 BPM, relegating everything beneath that to mere hardcore or terrorcore. The advent of a short-lived record label called United Speedcore Nation was an important landmark. Run by Karle, a.k.a. Karl-Christian Baginski of Germany, the label made many tracks available online for free as MP3s, and also released a bunch of vinyl, including their first record, a 1999 compilation named *Tag Der Zerstorung*. Despite only existing from 1997 to 2001, after which Karle seemed to vanish, it achieved a disproportionate influence, perhaps because its overarching goal was to build a speedcore community instead of just a label. I was able to find a blurb from an archived version of USR's website circa 2001, which gives an idea of USR's mission:

Under the name of United Speedcore Nation, some Artists have united, who only want to have fun in producing and don't want to know anything about commercial shit. The Reason is simple: From the money we get, we pay for our upcoming projects, for example another Label (or labels), Shirts, Party's etc. This is the interest we have, and we get no money from the Label for ourselves, but instead we save it for the upcoming Releases etc. We are happy if other producers and/or newcomers share our non-commercial interest because we want to grow to become a big community. If you are interested in joining us, please contact us.[77]

Another key moment in speedcore was the 2001 release of the envelope-pushing "Holland Is G.V.D. Het Hardste!!" single on a Dutch label named Cunt Records. The mix on the A-side reached a preposterous 666 beats per minute! "Holland" is the work of the producer Noisekick, a Leeuwarden, Netherlands, native named Rudmer Reitsma who is known for wearing a monster mask during his DJ sets. Now in his thirties, Reitsma was only twenty when that single came out.

In a 2016 interview for *DJ Mag NL*, Reitsma explains that he created "Holland" on an old computer using an early music sequencing program called *FastTracker*.[78] He got some help from an established terrorcore producer named Drokz to assemble the demo CD, which Drokz then released on his Cunt label. The infamous "666 BPM Mix" begins with a cheerful house sample announcing that "it's party time," which is then interrupted by a man shouting angrily in Dutch, after which a wall of jagged beats rains down.

---

77 web.archive.org/web/20010401090816/http://u-s-n.de:80/

78 translate.google.ca/translate?hl=en&sl=nl&u=https://djmag.nl/thunderdome/02272016-1331/noisekick-vertelt&prev=search

My speedcore guide, Kinnunen, explains how the genre's sound has shifted through the nineties and aughts. Over time, as the speed limits increased, the technical aspects of audio production also shifted. In the nineties, the rhythmic bedrock of speedcore tracks was a distorted kick drum played by a drum machine called the Roland TR-909. But in the aughts, producers shifted to digital production, crafting their tracks' machine-gun bass pulse using digital tones as a stand-in for the beats. This production method was embraced by Dutch artists like Noisekick and Noizefucker. As Noizefucker put it to me in a brief email exchange, the shift to computerized beat generation was a matter of convenience: "i like it easy haha so why all the trouble if you can do the same with wav files?"

Listening to Noizefucker's 2007 track, "Dedicated to Peter a.k.a. Pappa Speedcore," it's impossible to imagine how his breakneck sound could have been created prior to the digital age. Beginning with a mournful sample from an aria, he proceeds to subject the opera to a barrage of impossible rhythms, unpredictably switching the BPM from gear one to gear one million.

The center label of *The New Head EP*, by Noizefucker vs. The Destroyer. Features the track, "Dedicated to Peter a.k.a. Pappa Speedcore." Image courtesy of Erwin van den Bosch, a.k.a. Noizefucker

As I soaked my ears in this extreme sound, I decided on a whim to email Simon Reynolds, the author of *Energy Flash*, asking the electronic dance music scene's most reputable historian if he would share his reflections on the scene.

Speedcore became a thing after Reynolds stopped avidly following gabber, so he is aware of the proto-speedcore acts but not subsequent developments. But he tells me about a syndrome he calls the *zone of fruitless intensification*, which first arose on the drum and bass scene. Between 1991 and 1993, drum and bass producers accelerated the tempo of their music from 120 BPM to 150 BPM. At the time, Reynolds explains, this felt "like this huge threshold being crossed, the increase in speed had a drastic effect on the intensity/radicalism of the music," which also alienated those who couldn't handle the rhythmic potency. Yet in the years thereafter, as drum and bass insidiously increased its tempo by an additional 30 BPM, it was a case of diminishing returns—for whatever reason, past a certain point, the tempo rise no longer led to a major boost in intensity.

It seems to Reynolds that the denizens of speedcore were immune to the zone of fruitless intensification. Reynolds cited the outer fringes of noise and extreme metal as examples of genres that turn into arms races toward increasing intensity. He also mentions another hypothesis, wherein certain increasingly extreme genres "advance through self-parody." Essentially, someone decides to push the envelope as a joke, and then others pick up the idea and run with it; what was once a joke gets taken seriously. This brings to mind Richie Hawtin and Dan Bell's satirical "Machine Gun" single, discussed earlier, which was described by Hawtin as a communiqué to the rest of the hardcore scene that "we don't know what you guys are doing, but it's not what we're about."[79]

As it advanced deeper into the 2000s, speedcore went international. There was a Canadian Speedcore Nation. Two defining speedcore artists, Frazzbass and Komprex, headed up an increasingly robust Italian contingent. And the unlikely locale of Australia, hardly a hotbed for electronic music, fostered a zesty producer by the name of Passenger of Shit and a controversial gabber act named Nasenbluten.

Passenger of Shit, born Swift Treweeke, is the son of Vernon Treweeke, a painter who rose to prominence in the sixties as the "father of psychedelic art in Australia." Swift also runs the Shit Wank label and traffics in a combination of speedcore, shitcore, and breakcore. His album covers employ a Dali-meets-Botero-meets-R.-Crumb aesthetic, except the content is rich in genitals, feces, brains, and worms—a fitting tribute to the über-fringe music and an homage to his father's reputation as "Australia's leading practitioner of abstract eroticism." Several of his albums feature cartoon images of veiny, scabrous penises in various stages of ejaculation and lumpy turds of multitudinous colors, often in tandem.

Swift is now in his fifth decade, but still names his songs things like "Exposed Entrails Marinated With Cock Snot." He started writing music at age twelve, and in his teenage years, he began experimenting with music software on an old Amiga 500 computer and recording "harsh screaming shit noise" with his buddy Krishna Thorburn (who continues to collaborate with Treweeke as Virya Dadura Vamana). They first formed the band Vomit Junction before changing their name to Rancid Shit Wank, then forming the Shit Wank record label in 1997.

His first released work under the name Passenger of Shit was a 1999 track on a Sydney CD compilation titled *Terra D.A.T Kill Pope Free*, which set the stage for his first full-length release in 2000, which he put out in an edition of thirty. The second album, *2*, was released the same year and can be heard in full on PoS' Bandcamp page, offering a glimpse into the early sound—recorded when Treweeke was approximately twenty. It's a sometimes exhausting tract of variably paced 4/4 kick drums laced with juvenile samples, simple toy melodies, and microphone-bleeding screams, with song titles like "Stick Dick in Concrete," "Rip Ya Tits Off," and "Vomit Up Your Ass." The standout track "Artificial Vagina" may feature vocal thrills not far from the intimidating excesses of the power electronics genre, as well as scattered clips from an instructional recording of gynecological surgery, but its main focus is its pounding beats. Though he's mired in an obsession with vulgar subject matter, a track like "Brutalise My Penis" demonstrates Treweeke's undeniable production talent, matching beats with expertly selected melodic fragments. His skill is beyond that of many similar DIY recording acts, but his enthusiasm for feces and genitalia relegate him to a life on the fringe.

79 Simon Reynolds 1963-, *Energy Flash : A Journey through Rave Music and Dance Culture* (London: Picador, 1998, 1998) <search.library.wisc.edu/catalog/999843312202121>.

EXTREME MUSIC

Treweeke gives me a sense of the concept behind his aesthetic, including his crass taxonomy, by telling me that Passenger of Shit came about after a few years spent engrossed in noisier climes. "I was making music that was purely screaming (harsh noise and shitnoise) for a few years. Then, after working out how to make my own analog kick drums using my 4-track, I wanted to make tracks inspired by the pioneering Bloody Fist artists like Nasenbluten and Syndicate (for their angry speedcore, swearing, and dark sinister breaks), Fraughman, and Memetic (for their harsh noise and breakcore / speedcore), and also to create a breakcore/noise fusion, trying to go harder and more extreme! I think many artists at this time were seeking and finding ways to combine noise and dance music—that was the main inspiration."

He explains that the colorful content of the lyrics has been misconstrued at times. "My inspiration for the shitcore lyrics, or anti-lyrics, was maybe seen as a kind of piss-take of serious hardcore, but really was just my own self-expression and love of absurd surrealist imagery. Much inspiration comes from the dream world and, of course, this poetry is metaphorical and metaphysical. Typical surrealism. I guess I've been a surrealist since as far as I can remember. The inspiration in my more recent works is around making pieces that are both disgusting and beautiful, horrifying and cute, et cetera." Indeed, much of Treweeke's recent cover art showcases this juxtaposition of beauty and the macabre. His 2016 album, *Erotic Speedcore Coprophilia*, takes a pretty face as its centerpiece, surrounded with goopy viscera and augmented with pins in its eyes and ears.

In an intriguing twist of fate, PoS was selected by Nick Cave to perform at the Australian edition of All Tomorrow's Parties, a renowned series of music festivals curated by leading artists. Cave had apparently stumbled across PoS' MySpace and felt the chaos was a perfect fit. Nasenbluten, meanwhile, was a group of three Aussie producers named for the German word for "nosebleed." Their sample-heavy brand of hardcore is perhaps more suitably called gabber, with tempos rarely pushing into speedcore territory. Though many of their releases were put out on their own Bloody Fist label, their classic *100% No Soul Guaranteed* EP came out in 1995 on Industrial Strength, who put out the early Disciples of Annihilation records. Dark samples, noisy dissonance, and front-and-center kick drums are the name of the game, rendering even a blown-out clip of James Brown's "Sex Machine" into empty-warehouse gray.

Nasenbluten gained notoriety for a limited-to-fifty, lathe-cut seven-inch record they gave to friends in 1996, featuring the songs "Rainbow Up My Arse" and "Show Us Yor Tits." The latter was a gabber track interspersed with sampled news reports about Anna Wood, an Australian teenager who died after taking ecstasy at a rave, leading to panicked media coverage and a series of anti-rave reforms in the country. The record's center label features an image of Wood, with eyes censored, surrounded by the text "I'm having the greatest night of my life!" Considered by some to be in poor taste, and by others to be a piece of biting social commentary, it was never given an official release, and today, rogue copies sell for thousands of dollars online.

If scenes in Australia and Italy weren't enough to convince you that speedcore has gone international, consider that a Japanese scene also emerged at the start of this millennium. At first disseminated via peer-to-peer networks,[80] several Japanese producers explored the rhythmic intensity of hardcore techno, often trading gabber's hard elements for a happy, synth-laden sound. J-core, as the genre has been dubbed, isn't necessarily limited to the blistering tempos of speedcore.

One major J-core exponent is the charismatic Yosei Watanabe, who goes by m1dy and routinely traverses the 400 BPM limit. He also runs a couple of labels that issue J-core music on CD: the PORK label primarily releases his own albums, while Maddest Chick'ndom has issued releases by several artists. Considered by some to be "The King of Japanese Speedcore," he is a stocky, middle-aged Japanese guy with bleached blond hair who's frequently pictured wearing sunglasses. There is little definitive information about him, but a Japanese interview suggests that he was a high-school punk rocker in Osaka who discovered samplers and drum machines, after which he ditched his band members and committed himself to electronic music. When he discovered ultra-BPM music online, he figured he could do it too, favoring an upbeat sound over the dark and abrasive climes of gabber.[81] This led to him releasing some tracks on the early music sharing website mp3.com, including his now-iconic song, "Tokyo Style Speedcore,"[82] a blistering two minutes of variegated beats and looped samples.

1.4.2 Splittercore

As brave producers pushed past the 500 BPM mark, a new term began to crop up: splittercore. At these speeds, beats start to lose their rhythmic quality and instead become more like textures. Accordingly, there is considerable crossover between splittercore and the noise music scene.

My speedcore guide, Tuomas Kinnunen, pointed out that the word "splittercore" comes from a DJ set by speedcore producer Pengo from around 2005, which she posted online with the title "Splitterkrötenterror." And while fans will debate whether this fast brand of speedcore needs its own name, several net labels have used the label, including Splitterblast Records and the prolific Splitterkor Rekords Dziwko!!!

Czech native Martin Ritter used to run Splitterblast Records and now runs a label, KyokudoCore Records, which specializes in J-core. According to him, splittercore came about as producers were experimenting with speeding up speedcore vinyl, playing 33 RPM records at 45 RPM. Once this caught on, they started producing tracks at these high speeds.

Some perspectives on splittercore are more cynical. Speedcore Dave, né Sean McMillan, a speedcore producer and university student in music technology, tells me that the emergence of splittercore in the mid-2000s was the result of a "pissing contest between producers to make the fastest and most extreme sounds they possibly could." As that happened, the body-moving attributes of speedcore evaporated.

---

80 Dave Jenkins, 'Beyond J-Core: An Introduction to the Real Sound of Japanese Hardcore | Bandcamp Daily,' *Bandcamp Daily*, 2018 <daily.bandcamp.com/scene-report/j-core-japanese-electronic> [accessed 2 January 2021].

81 'The First Interview Project!,' *Hardcore Life*, 2005 <web.archive.org/web/20071214135923/http://www.guhroovy.com/blog/archives/cat17/index.html> [accessed 2 January 2021].

82 Chipicato, 'M1dy,' 2016 <core-assault.blogspot.com/2016/09/m1dy.html> [accessed 2 January 2021].

EXTREME MUSIC

"It went from speedcore which was (vaguely) danceable to something that was just really heavy and distorted and was filled with kickdrums, just because it could be done," he explains. "It really took off in the mid aughts because by then, people had access to pretty decent internet speeds and connections, so web labels could flourish. With these web labels, there was no upfront cost of producing records, and it was being offered to people for free. Splittercore itself relied on this because it was very, very out there, and most die-hard speedcore/terror fans thought splittercore was just far too much to handle—DJs as well. Think about it. It's quite easy to mix tracks that are in the two-hundreds of BPM, as you can pitch things up and down, but with splittercore, it gets nuts and downright impossible in some cases. Very few splittercore tracks had dance-floor appeal."

One of the many artifacts of the splittercore scene is *Splitter Destruction*, a compilation put out as the inaugural release on the Splitterblast label.[83] These tracks are short; over a quarter are under two minutes. Many techno and house songs exceed seven minutes, but *Splitter Destruction* squeezes in twenty-nine frenetic tracks. Egnal Ramd, a Dutch producer who credits the Euromasters as the reason he got into speedcore,[84] collaborates with the mysterious MC Shithead on three tracks. Their typical approach is to drench their manic beats in feedback, emphasizing the continuum with harsh noise. Russia's Okcid, who co-runs a speedcore label called MindNepping Records, accomplishes the same with piercing industrial textures and distorted yells. A highlight is DJ Antitiesto, a Czech producer named Martin known for merging extreme speedcore with 8-bit chiptune sounds. But for *Splitter Destruction*, he submits a splittercore evisceration of the Police's "Walking on the Moon," mincing pitched-up samples and tossing them into a vortex of digital noise and propeller beats, naming the result "Wanked On The Moon (Splittertone Break Mix)."

Ritter, the man who used to run Splitterblast Records, tells me he sees splittercore as a countercultural statement—"music without any limits, music against any standards or rules," as he puts it—as well as an aesthetic preference. "It's extreme music for the people who like it hard and fast," he expounds. And while his pronouncement that splittercore beats sound "like a machine gun raping your soul and body like bullets" sounds a little hyperbolic, he argues that its aggressiveness, paradoxically, does not engender violence in its listenership. "I must admit people listening to this stuff are rarely aggressive," he reflects. "In fact, listening to extreme music makes you calmer and more positive."

Much like Ritter, Speedcore Dave got into this frenetic music because "it was the ultimate, like, 'fuck you' type of music." He sees it as a "weird counter-counter-counter movement of mainstream music," a form of exponential rebellion toward music's tendency to lose its edge as new ideas are assimilated. "Pop was too mainstream to people, so they made gabber," he reflects. "Gabber became too mainstream and people wanted harder and faster sounds, so speedcore became a thing. Then the exact same thing happened with splittercore. It's kind of funny, really."

Funny, perhaps, but this is serious stuff for those who spend their days producing tracks and unleashing albums worth of music onto the internet. Noizefucker, a.k.a.

---

83 Splitterblast made this compilation available free online: archive.org/details/splitterblast001v.a.-SplitterDestruction
84 Egnal Ramd, 'Welcome 2 Hell! - About' <web.archive.org/web/20101017180105/http://www.egnal-ramd.tk/about.php> [accessed 2 January 2021].

Erwin van den Bosch, works in "factory production line kinda work" by day so that he can fund his music production hobby. He doesn't get hung up on distinctions between speedcore and splittercore, but when I ask him what his life is like outside of music, he seems confused by the question. "uh must say that it is much music in my life," he reflects. "when i am off from work i listen to music or dj or make music haha."

1.4.3 Extratone

Splittercore, by our definition, is speedcore pushed past the 500 BPM mark. But there is a genre that exceeds the standard BPM range of splittercore. Interestingly, this hyperspeed breed came about long before the advent of splittercore, when two French producers started experimenting with audio production software. One of those music-makers was the enigmatic Einrich 3600 BPM, who's described in one of very few online mentions as "a french-belgium guy [who] won his nickname from his friends who salute his passion for germany." The other producer, Lawrencium, developed a passion for extreme sounds while recording electronic music as i2. Einrich and Lawrencium's music is mainly known to us because of their posts on United Speedcore Nation's message board, where they shared tracks and published barely comprehensible screeds about the mechanics of music that goes beyond 1000 BPM. They gave their creations the genre name *extratone*, which references the fact that, at ultra-rapid-BPMs, beats stop being perceived as individual units, but instead just smooth out and sound like tones—the "extra" tone, perhaps.

How does this work acoustically? A tone is, essentially, the effect of sound waves cycling at a given frequency. A particular tone's frequency is defined by the number of cycles of the soundwave that occur each second. That measure of *cycles per second* is typically referred to as hertz (Hz). The lowest note on a standard piano is 27.5 hertz, or 27.5 cycles per second. Multiply 27.5 cycles per second by sixty seconds per minute, and that equals 1650 cycles per minute. This means that a beat running at 1650 BPM would sound like a tone whose pitch is that of a piano's lowest note. At 1000 BPM, the lowest limit of what qualifies as extratone music, the beats produce a 17 Hz tone.

Most of the appeal of extratone seems to lie in the transitions between beats and tones, which serve to accentuate just how blisteringly fast things are moving. Thus, a track's BPM will frequently waver between normal speedcore rhythms and the rhythmic extremes of extratone's upper reaches. It is viciously experimental by design and, as a result, more closely connected to the world of noise music than electronic dance music.

The story of extratone is obscure and very poorly documented. The most definitive account we've got is a series of bizarre YouTube videos featuring dense black-on-white text and a soundtrack of montaged extratone tracks, published by the aforementioned Einrich 3600 BPM.' In the videos, Einrich explains, in text, that his explorations supposedly began in 1994, when he was studying the BPM of various speedcore tracks, modifying them by twiddling his turntable settings up to 78 rpm. Increasingly obsessed by their tempos, in the summer of 1998, he started hosting a show called *600bpm* on a local radio station, which focused on music with blistering tempos. At the time, he

**Definitive compilation *Develop Your Extratone*.
Image courtesy of 1000+.**

suspected that 600 BPM was the point in which beats stopped being perceived as individual units, but his big discovery came shortly afterward, when he ran his high-speed music through an oscillograph. This hammered in his essential principle—ultra-high beats were visible as discrete units on an oscillograph but sounded like tones to the ear. Hence "extratone," a German portmanteau of "extra" (as in "to extract") and "tone" (as in "tone").

Somehow, he settled upon the "fantastic number" of 3600 BPM, which translates to a tone of 60 Hz, and this number was apparently so compelling that he named himself after it. Einrich's first composition was called "Oszillograph Ekel," which hits a maximum tempo of 3859 BPM. He would continue to release a spurt of tracks on his own "Immer Schneller" (Always Faster) label, which seems to have released Einrich 3600 BPM CDs or CD-Rs, although there is no record of these collectibles existing outside of a few pictures on one of Einrich's YouTube videos.[85]

Einrich's speed peak was an outlandish 639,532 BPM, on "Fréquences Outrancières," a 2001 collaboration with Lawrencium. After this, he disappeared from the scene, only to briefly reemerge with an extratone remix of the Belgian national anthem in 2010.

Einrich has become a cult figure on the extratone scene, a pioneering experimenter whose work appeals to a small cadre of experimental music enthusiasts. There is little to differentiate it from noise music, but its obsession with technical detail leads to it lacking the visceral appeal of much harsh noise. It's largely structureless, procedurally meticulous, and not remotely danceable—the musical equivalent of a highly technical journal article.

But 1000-BPM music is not ALL grooveless. A hardcore producer named Annoying

---

85 Since I wrote this, three Immer Schneller CDs, all by Einrich 3600 BPM, appeared on Discogs, albeit apart from their title, cover, and year (all of them supposedly came out in 2000), there is no existing information about their track listing or any other data. The highest catalogue number is 11, which suggests that several more exist. (www.discogs.com/artist/2341472-Einrich-3600-BPM)

Ringtone put out "Extratone Pirates" in 2010. It's a mashup of "Keelhauled" by Alestorm and "Disturbia" by Rihanna, matched with frenetic beats that intermittently ratchet up to 1000 BPM. Dave figures it's the only extratone track that really gets played on dance floors.

Annoying Ringtone is a man from Aberdeen, Scotland, who sets mashups to rapid beats and also manages a netlabel called Dance Corps. He is like the pop-lite of extreme speedcore, equal parts populist and troll. Annoying Ringtone essentially sets pop songs to extreme speedcore beats, only breaking the 1000-BPM barrier for moments at a time, perhaps so that he can claim that his tracks are extratone. Check out his chipmunked rendition of LMFAO's "Party Rock Anthem," titled "Party Speedcore Anthem," for a rough mission statement. LMFAO and Annoying Ringtone seem to be a match made in heaven, even if one has landed songs on the *Billboard* chart while the other subsists in relative obscurity—both are unapologetic, obnoxious, and essentially committed to fun.

Extratone-associated record labels include 1000 + and Extermination Recordings. The man behind the 1000 + label, DJ Ninja Love Mistake, recently died, but his label serves as a valuable document, having released definitive extratone compilations like *Absolute Extratone Anthems Vol. 1* and *Develop Your Extratone*. These are all available free online and are worth your attention.

1.4.4 Flashcore

There is more to the speedcore fringe than just BPMs. An experimental subgenre called flashcore represents the experimental end of the hyperspeed scene. Led by French artist La Peste, flashcore takes speedcore's hyper-paced kick drums and uses them to design abstract soundscapes, shifting the tempo and pitch fluidly to reduce beats to floating strata of ambient sound. According to a thorough history of the genre written by Jon Weinel for *Spannered* magazine,[86] one innovation of flashcore was to vary the pitch of the kick drum throughout a song, these unpredictable deviations untethering them from their traditional rhythmic function.

In the world of flashcore, La Peste functions as a sort of guru. He is prone to issuing the odd manifesto, including one claiming that the music's turbulent beats are designed to modify consciousness by their effects on individual "air molecules."

Flashcore is the spatial and temporal conception of air landscapes of which 'sonic atoms' (=the smallest particle of sound which is thought as an entity in itself) are being controlled with the exclusive aim of making us explore our minds and perceive any kind of transcendence. As for atomic energy or drug action, we are reaching a point where it's possible to provoke nano-audio-explosions with quite some big results for the minds.

Born Laurent Mialon, he coined the term *flashcore*, and purists have argued that the only true flashcore is music released by him. Born in Bordeaux and raised in the southwestern part of France, he has cited the crashing waves of the Atlantic Ocean and the region's terrific thunderstorms as early audio inspiration. When he attended his

---

86 Jon Weinel, 'Flashcore | Earth, Atomizer, Let's Go!', *Spannered*, 2007 <www.spannered.org/music/1181/> [accessed 2 January 2021].

first rave in 1991, it was a revelation.[87] He subsequently honed his audio production chops in the mid-'90s speedcore scene, then started a record label, Hangars Liquides, in 1998. The first release on his label was the *Haikumputer* 12" by his friend Ronan Le Roux, who was then recording as EPC. The music on that record has been called "deconstructed rave,"[88] which is a fitting tag for its disjointed rhythmic loops, which seem to mimic the creaking and clanking of industrial machinery.

It isn't until the label's twenty-first release, the 2001 La Peste single, "Le Syndrome Des Draps Cassants" b/w "F-117 Crash," that the flashcore sound starts to emerge. Weinel notes that, in flashcore, the kick drums are no longer tasked with producing a danceable rhythm, and instead are intricately decomposed, the focus being "instead on twisting and contorting the rhythmic forms into complex structures, as this provides interest to the music." The main component of "Le Syndrome Des Draps Cassants" is an unpredictably skittering beat, like an isolated rhythm track from an Autechre record. Indeed, writer Andrea Migliorati has described flashcore as a hybrid of intelligent dance music and speedcore.[89]

In 2006, La Peste released an untitled 12" as Hangars Liquides' twenty-fourth release, which he reportedly considers his "most flashcore record" to date.[90] Here, the beats are reduced to flailing strata of noise, all texture and no rhythm. Fittingly, Mialon acknowledges the influence of experimental composers like Iannis Xenakis, claiming in his manifesto that his hope for flashcore is to "rethink music as something that clearly goes beyond harmony and rhythm."

The paradigm of speedcore, which aims to compress scads of rhythmic stimuli into short timeframes, is an ideal one for Mialon's flashcore experiments, which emphasize the atomic properties of sound. La Peste has used the term "nano-audio explosions" to describe what Weinel describes as the "very detailed, complex structures of short, fragmented sounds" that make up his work, designed to "[achieve] as many micro-emotional responses from the listener in as short a space of time as possible."

Over a decade after he wrote his genre-defining article, I reached out to Weinel to get his updated thoughts on the flashcore canon. He recognizes that it can be hard to separate his own psychedelia-informed ideas about La Peste's work from the intentions of Mialon himself. But he is convinced that the supraphysiological possibilities of audio production software can influence both physiology and psychology in profound ways. "I see these projects in a broad sense as interrogating the potential for technology to represent and induce powerful experiences, which may include various cognitive and emotional dimensions, perhaps even seeking the 'transcendence' Laurent Mialon mentioned in the HL manifesto," he tells me.

Our Finnish speedcore guide, Tuomas Kinnunen, figures that speedcore proper has stagnated in the past decade or so, leaving the real innovation to subgenres like flashcore. Perusing the web, you might notice that most acts cross-identify with multiple genres: splittercore, hardcore, speedcore, gabber, extratone, noise. Genre boundaries

---

87 Andrea Migliorati, 'PORTRAIT#7: La Peste - "Para La Santísima Muerte Flashcore Live Set,"' *PAYNOMINDTOUS*, 2016 <www.paynomindtous.it/portrait7-la-peste/> [accessed 2 January 2021].
88 'Haikumputer by EPC (EP, Industrial Hardcore)', Rate Your Music <rateyourmusic.com/release/ep/epc/haikumputer/> [accessed 2 January 2021].
89 Migliorati.
90 Weinel.

THE SPEEDCORE CANON

There is no easy way to develop a list like this, and I suspect any speedcore fan would criticize certain releases I have chosen to include and those I have omitted. Regardless, this is a list of speedcore essentials, synthesizing my many emails to contemporary speedcore producers and label owners.

Proto-speedcore

Moby, "Thousand"

Cybersonik, "Machine Gun" and "Jackhammer"

Atari Teenage Riot, "319"

303 Nation, "Double Speed Mayhem"

Sorcerer, "Summer"

Early speedcore

DJ Skinhead, "Extreme Terror" (1994, Industrial Strength Records)

D.O.A., *Industrial Power 9d4* (1994, Industrial Strength Records)

Embolism, "This Means War" (1995, Bloody Fist Records)

D.O.A., *Mothafuckin' New York Hardcore* (1996, Industrial Strength Records)

Various artists, *Tag Der Zerstorung (Day of Destruction)* (1999, United Speedcore Nation)

Speedcore

Lord Lloigor, "Beyond The Green Light" (1999, Brain Destruction)

Noisekick, "Holland Is G.V.D. Het Hardste!!" 7" (2001, Cunt Records)

Splittercore

Pengo, "Splitterkrötenterror" DJ mix (circa 2005)

Various artists, *Splitter Destruction* (Splitterblast Records)

Extratone

Einrich 3600 BPM, "Oszillograph Ekel" (1998, Immer Schneller)

Einrich 3600 BPM, "Fréquences Outrancières" (2001, Immer Schneller)

Annoying Ringtone, "Extratone Pirates" (from Annoying Ringtone & Distonn, *Nightclub Annihilator*, 2011, Dance Corps)

Flashcore

La Peste, "Le Syndrome Des Draps Cassants" b/w "F-117 Crash" (2001, Hangars Liquides)

La Peste, *Untitled (HL 024)* (2006, Hangars Liquides)

GUIDE TO BPMS:

250–500: Speedcore

500–1000: Splittercore

1000+: Extratone

are imprecise, and pigeonholing into one scene limits your ability to appeal to diverse audiences. Simon Reynolds would describe these divisions as emblematic of dance music's "semantic excess"—"a taxonomic frenzy of differentiations that seem ever more minute and barely perceptible to outsiders but remain absolutely urgent distinctions for people fanatically involved in the scene."

Many see the combinatorial explosion of nomenclature as an opportunity to make their mark on electronic music history. Over the years, a litany of 'cores have sprung up, including Frenchcore, Polcore, suizidcore, and so on. He isn't sure, but Reynolds himself suspects he may or may not have coined gloomcore. And Kinnunen is working on shamancore, a merging of "ritualistic/shamanic music with hardcore/speedcore." He conveys a remote optimism about his aspirational nano-genre:

Maybe it will become a thing someday, who knows :)

Perhaps this all fails to answer the singular question: what is the fastest track in history? We must go way back to 1996, when a producer named Johnny Violent, who was once dubbed "the Quentin Tarantino of techno,"[91] capped off his *Shocker* album with a 1:45 track called "Burn Out." It takes the form of a call-and-response composition; Johnny shouts out a BPM value, then has a drum machine play a short bit of rhythm at that speed. He starts at 250 BPM, escalating in increments toward a finale of *twenty million BPM*. As the BPMs escalate, what starts off as a recognizable pattern of kick drum beats becomes a single tone, then a short stab of noise, and finally, at 20,000,000 BPM, just a single click— all the beats compressed so closely together that they are barely perceptible.

91 Paul Kilbride, 'Ultraviolence - Blown Away 94-04,' *Sandman Magazine*, 2005 <web.archive.org/web/20110716032319/http://www.sandmanmagazine.co.uk/oldsite/york/newreleases/nr008/nr008.html> [accessed 2 January 2021].

1.5 FOUND

What if you discovered your own voice on a publicly released recording? It could happen.

Mangdisc is a tape and CD-R label run by Maine noise musician Skot Spear, whose every release comes in unique packaging. His label's catalog includes dozens of concept releases and exercises in Dadaist cacophony, but an obvious highlight is his twelve-disc *Found Series*. This project compiles the highlights of Skot's staggering collection of found audio, most of which he collected from thrift stores.

Skot, who also records under the moniker id m theft able, explains to me the basis for these releases. "I have an archive of over a thousand found cassettes that I've found over the last 20 years. A lot of them aren't terribly interesting, but I don't have the heart to get rid of or record over them. I used to find them at thrift stores, but that's getting harder and harder these days. I have one particularly fond memory of an ex-girlfriend volunteering to have me put her in a dumpster so she could fish a cassette out of there. The tape turned out to have some amazing recordings of children singing somewhat obscene songs on it."

A tour through the *Found Series* reveals recordings that are simultaneously fascinating and banal. The series kicks off with one of Skot's personal favorites, *eeee eeeee*, described online as "a frustrated 6th Graders [sic] solo album of primitive rock and absolutely gorgeous drum machine/keyboard solos." According to Skot, this was a recording made by a friend's younger brother, found in that person's basement. As Skot said at the time of its release, "My best guess is that he would not approve of my giving copies of this to people, but I and everyone I've played them for have enjoyed them so much that I feel they warrant sharing regardless."

One tape reproduces a recording of "several doctors describing the removal of a cyst from the vulva of a 'well-nourished' and 'obese' woman with 'pendulous' breasts." *Low Noise Quality Tape Thirty Minutes Per Side* is described as follows on the Mangdisc website:

A compilation of sounds from two cassettes that were found together, assorted recordings from a group of young girls. An adolescent girl renders gorgeous versions of songs such as Mötley Crüe's "Home Sweet Home" and "From A Distance," while a group of other, younger girls tries to form a band. Punctuating all of this are occasional 1980's radio commercials, and long lulls where someone forgot to turn the tape recorder off.

Skot rebuffs my attempts to intellectualize the appeal of these found recordings. "I don't have any particular ideological or philosophical angle to it all, I'm literally just issuing recordings that I find engaging in some way. Some are funny, some are deeply depressing, some are enthralling, some are fascinatingly boring."

The process of exhuming old recordings ends up converting otherwise banal audio into real drama. Without context, the listener can't help but try to fill in the gaps in the stories. Who are these people captured on tape? What are their stories? What do they mean when they say what they say? As the mind builds a narrative out of scraps, the sound is imbued with a heightened emotional valence—what is mundane becomes funny, or anxiety-provoking, or melancholy.

This is a notion that resonates with Jacob Smigel, an emergency room physician who works in a rural hospital an hour out of Austin, Texas. He is responsible for assembling one of the most absorbing relics of the found sound scene, a CD-R compilation named *Eavesdrop* that came out in 2007. Smigel generously regales

The cover of Jacob Smigel's found sound compilation *Eavesdrop*. Image courtesy of Jacob Smigel.

me with background details and shares some of the "director's cut" versions of the recordings that made it onto *Eavesdrop*.

Smigel's interest in old tapes dates to his teenage years growing up in Las Vegas, where he worked in a Friends of the Library warehouse, combing through thousands of donated books. He found himself sifting through a mom-and-pop thrift store that "doesn't filter the contents of their shelves," and discovered a tape for ten cents with a handwritten label reading *The Powers of Magnetism*. Listening to it in his station wagon, it was a radio show about the powers of magnetism, but it abruptly switched to a woman speaking into a microphone, dictating a taped letter. "I thought, this is amazing. This is really special. And I felt a little guilty—I'm not supposed to be hearing this!"

Soon he was visiting several thrift stores with a Walkman, picking out tapes that looked home-recorded to see if they were just people's mixtapes or transferred LPs. A slim minority of the tapes would have people's voices on them, be they audio diaries, tape letters, or other miscellaneous treats. He'd buy these "ten at a time," then pop them in the car stereo for his daily commute. After a while, he started to imagine them forming an album. Smigel is also a musician who has released several albums, including a few for the Not Not Fun label. But *Eavesdrop*, a personal project that developed out of a lifelong hobby, became his own self-released project.

One thing that makes Smigel's compilation stand out is its liner notes. For each clip, Smigel tries to piece together the story behind the recording. "I think the tracks stand alone. They don't need me to do all that, but it was such a pleasure. That's why the liner notes are longer than my college thesis."

But even among the greatest hits, there are several weird highlights. One is the recording of two older socialites scoffing at the supposedly bisexual owner of a local hamburger store. Another captures a humiliating round of karaoke. But the apogee is the audio diary of Carol, a sardonic twentysomething woman living in the Bay Area in the early seventies. According to Smigel, this six-minute excerpt is a mere piece of the puzzle. He found several tapes marked with her name in a thrift store in Las Vegas, which essentially served as a chronological document of her highs and lows over two years. The recorded tidbits include her bemoaning her job at a coffee shop, ruminating on her binge-purge relationship with food, harping on her crush on a gay video store clerk, and, in an especially vivid moment, using a vibrator while fantasizing about Mick Jagger.

"Carol" is found sound at its most sublime. In a mere six-minute excerpt, the listener is pulled into its thrall. Carol's words are, in turns, scintillating, depressing, and relatable. Because of its captivating content, Smigel makes available a full version by special request, which apparently so intrigued Andrew W.K. that they discussed putting together a theatrical production of it! To this day, Smigel will sometimes act out bits and pieces during music shows.

As a curious aside, Jacob's brother believes he encountered Carol working at a dive bar. She seemed the right age, her name was Carol, and the voice was familiar. He tried to figure it out by asking her questions but couldn't confirm his suspicion definitively.

Smigel also found another tape, "Band Nerd Love," which was a lovelorn high school senior's audio diary and which he did put out as a limited-run CD-R release. Both tapes raise the question of ethics, an obvious concern when it comes to found sound. Jacob Smigel is not blind to that; after all, he titled his collection *Eavesdrop*, hinting at the illicit nature of the experience.

Smigel tells me he recognizes that each recording represents the intellectual property of those who recorded them and that the album itself is a copyright violation. After its release, *Eavesdrop* elicited a minor media blitz, and Smigel even recorded an interview about the disc with NPR's *Good Morning America*. He tells me he had mixed feelings at the time, worrying that the recordings would become overexposed and that he'd end up sued. The NPR interview was never aired, which Smigel considers a blessing in disguise. He is clear to emphasize that his project is not at all about ridiculing the people on record and he goes to lengths to humanize his subjects in his thoughtful liner notes. He hopes that, if someone ever hears their own voice on *Eavesdrop*—which, as far as he knows, hasn't happened—they would be pleasantly surprised.

Skot Spear of Mangdisc also reflects on the ethics of the situation, noting that the internet has changed things. "When I was younger I didn't really think too much about the ethics of it, but lately, there are certain recordings that I find that I don't feel like I can or should share via the internet," Spear tells me. "The whole culture of 'things going viral' didn't really exist when I started releasing these recordings in 2001 or so. Now, even the off chance that a release could get a lot of attention, including, perhaps, the attention of the person who made the recording, gives me pause before releasing certain recordings."

Hilarity and Despair is a collection of cassettes pulled from answering machines in thrift stores, put out in 2006 on vinyl as the inaugural release on the Sebastian Speaks label. The compilation was assembled by William Tyler, an alt-country singer/songwriter and member of Lambchop. Since 2006, his musical career has taken off, and he now puts out albums on stalwart independent label Merge Records.

EXTREME MUSIC

Tyler explains to me that *Hilarity and Despair* was assembled from the pooled collections of two friends who had been amassing answering machine tapes from garage sales and thrift stores. Tyler says he was most attracted to the subtle characteristics of the sound itself, "the analog static of tapes, the music playing in the background on some of the calls, the timbre of voices."

Of course, answering machine tapes are private communications, and while you can blame the original owners of the machines for neglecting to either remove or erase the tapes before they dropped them off at the thrift store, you can also argue that the voices on the tape are almost never the voices of the tape owners themselves.

As the title *Hilarity and Despair* presages, one issue that arises with this type of release is that the audience is invited to laugh at someone else's misfortune. Notorious phone hound Longmont Potion Castle built his cult career on the profane escalations of his molestees, whose patience invariably thinned after multiple prank calls. Similarly, painful emotions underpin several of *Hilarity and Despair*'s contents. For example, "Terry" is a sequence of increasingly exasperated calls from the title character's parents, desperately pleading for him to pick up his phone. "Terry, pick up the phone, if you're there, come on!"

This is not lost on William Tyler, and interestingly, he now concludes that he would not do it again. "My perspective on it has changed," he explains. "I was 25 when I put out *Hilarity and Despair* and I don't think I would do it now at 36. I think there is a sort of preservationist value in found sound and visuals, but it also is, by its nature, voyeuristic, and at worst exploitative. It's not like trudging out there and pretending to be Alan Lomax. It's someone else's detritus that you are using for artistic license."

Hilarity and Despair is far from the most dubious recording out there. Certain other found sound recordings supposedly comprise audio that is surreptitiously recorded. I'm aware of two such releases, and perhaps unsurprisingly these records are difficult to track down—they are old CD-R releases, produced in micro-editions and distributed in scant quantities. One such release is a disc entitled *Today's Voices*, released on the Hyperscan Records label, which I believe was formed just to put this record out. This record is only mentioned in a select few places; it is described in the Aquarius Records catalogue, and a couple of tracks were played on New Jersey freeform radio station WFMU and campus radio station KSZU. Only very recently did a Discogs entry surface.

It's a collection of recordings produced by technology that can tap into cell phone signals. The very limited information available online about *Today's Voices* includes the fact that someone named Sarah Lawson is its editor, as credited on the album cover.

For the longest time, the only way I could hear bits of audio from this album were by scouring the WFMU archives, and a couple of the tracks from *Today's Voices* can still be listened to online by this method. Those few tidbits are, at times, salacious. The cell signal device only captured the audio from one end of each conversation, and as a result, we are usually privy to only one half of any given call. The voices themselves are cast against the unsettling din of cellular feedback.

Many of the calls are sex-related. I suspect this may reflect Lawson's editorial discretion. One recording captures someone scrolling through their private messages on a pre-internet stag line used for organizing sexual liaisons. Another features a thickly accented woman awkwardly engaging in erotic talk, likely as part of a 1-900 call: "I remember how good it was when you fucked me, in this special way, the way we do when we're together."

Elsewhere, a young woman gossips about the strange customs of her brother's Panamanian "ultra-shy" girlfriend, whose family is unfamiliar with his American chivalry: "In Panama, the women just serve, serve, serve; the men just take, take, take; the men don't open doors [for the women]." On another call, a woman discusses the Bible, wide-eyed at the mysticism inherent in ordinary life. ("All this stuff in the Bible, a lot of it happens in your daily life if you look at it.") In one of the few recordings where both audio from both sides of the conversation is captured, two men argue brutally, one calling the other's daughter a "nasty slut."

Today's Voices is subtitled "Their Vices, Their Phones," and it certainly captures the bleak end of humanity. The probability that someone would recognize these voices is certainly low, given the limited pressing and the fact that Hyperscan Records is now defunct, with no remaining online source to buy copies. But at the same time, the listener here is invited to chuckle at the sordid personal details of real people—their unattenuated moments of desperation, anger, and arousal. Is that exploitative? Is it any different from filming someone through a window and posting that online?

Today's Voices is not alone in this esoteric subgenre of secretly recorded audio. An old catalog from San Francisco's seminal record store Aquarius Records lists an album by Petros Drecojecai called *Mistaken Receptions*; according to the blurb, Petros was an anthropologist from Hungary who visited the States in the nineties to attend conferences and pursue his academic career. He used a radio to tune in to what he believed were American talk radio shows, but apparently the lines were crossed, and he was in fact picking up signals from people's wireless phones. He recorded these transmissions, thinking they were American artifacts, and sent them back to Hungary as a tape, which much later made its way back to the U.S. in the form of a limited CD-R release. According to the copy, it included "Diet tips, sex tips, court tips, junkie poets, stripping, reading the riot act to would be boyfriends, and much more."

I reach out to Peter Conheim, a member of plunderphonics act Negativland, who was involved with the release. "The guy who made these recordings and shared them with us was a neighbor many years ago in a nearby building in downtown Oakland, California," he explains. "I can't even remember his actual name! He was a pretty weird and funny fellow who spent most of his time inside his apartment. He became clearly paranoid and used to talk about how an old lady in the same apartment building died on the floor below him, directly under his room, and he says he could actually smell her flesh rotting for days before someone eventually found her body. This much is definitely true, as I remember going to the building after the coroner had just left and disinfected the whole place, which still had a terrifying rotting meat odor lingering.

"We have long ascribed his slow descent into ultra-weirdness as seemingly 'triggered' by that event. Because before this woman died, he seemed a pretty straightforward chap. We started chatting over mutual love of avant-garde classical music and such. He was on some sort of confusing work-exchange program from, I think, Bosnia-Herzegovina. This was *right* after the war, if I recall right. And we'd swap cassettes and such. And at some point after the woman died, he started to talk about his 'interceptions,' which seemed to be, uh, illusory, but then he shocked us by playing some recordings, and we were amused/blown away and agreed to sneakily press them up onto a CD-R in cahoots with him. I lost contact with the guy shortly thereafter, before we'd even sold one. Indeed, I remember he never even got a copy of the disc! He wasn't answering the door, and I never had his phone number (and this is before cell phones), and I wound up moving out of the country myself for a few years, and out of that neighborhood. So, it's all a great and baffling mystery!"

<center>~~~~~~~~~~~~~~~~~~~~~~~~~~~~~</center>

Another genus of found sound recordings raises yet another ethical issue, namely content that's produced by people with severe mental health issues. We see this same problem in outsider art, which often walks a fine line between open-mindedness toward personal expression and fetishization of the unusual thoughts and behaviors of those with severe psychiatric disorders. Wesley Willis, a street performer with schizophrenia, developed a cult following for his whimsical keyboard compositions, leading to several professionally released albums and even a tribute song by Rob Crow. His commercial appeal is neither solely a response to his unfiltered artistic expression nor exclusively a reflection of our fascination with the mentally ill; it falls somewhere in between.

The appeal of this sort of audio lies in the fact that people find unpredictable, emotional, or irrational behavior funny. Perhaps one of the earliest examples was *Daddy's Curses*, a recording of a man named Bruce yelling and cussing in frustration while attempting to fix a piano. Supposedly taped by Bruce's fourteen-year-old son in 1987,[92] it captures a mélange of quotable vulgarities like "phooey and nuts" and "you dog licker!"

After seeing a WFMU blog post about *Daddy's Curses*,[93] in which one commenter named Matt remarked that he knew the family responsible for the recording, I follow an internet rabbit hole to track this person down—which involves me cold-emailing his weightlifting gym, then being referred to his former gym, and finally getting to speak with the man himself.

Daddy's Curses was recorded in the Flemingdon, New Jersey, area. Matt tells me that his friend's sister made the recording of her father fixing a piano, along with a friend

---

92 Nick H., 'Planned Obsolescene,' *Flushed Down the Blog*, 2009 <fdtb.blogspot.com/2009/11/planned-obsolescene.html> [accessed 7 July 2020].

93 Listener Therese, 'The Ravings of Bruce The Piano Man (MP3),' *WFMU's Beware of the Blog*, 2006 <blog.wfmu.org/freeform/2006/11/phooey_and_nuts.html> [accessed 7 July 2020].

of hers. This was back in 1991; Matt was ten and these kids were in freshman year at high school. At that time, students made copies on tape and shared them. Somewhere around 1998 or 1999, Matt made a digital copy and, because it wouldn't fit on email servers, put it up on a peer-to-peer file sharing medium, possibly Kazaa. "Nobody knows how it got spread online," he tells me.

Matt still has a copy of the tape; it contains Bruce's full name and the year of recording. Matt tells me that Bruce, whom he believes is still around, was an aerospace engineer.

He recognizes that there's thorny ethics involved with a recording like this. This was meant to be circulated by friends, not distributed widely. Recently, Matt was watching a Netflix documentary about another covert home recording, titled *Shut Up Little Man!*, when a clip of *Daddy's Curses* was played during a section about the history of audio verité recordings. Shocked to learn about how widely the recording had been disseminated, he contacted the friend whose sister made the recording, but neither she nor her sister were aware that it had spread. When word did finally reach Bruce himself, he was apparently displeased—according to Matt, it represented a rougher time in his life.

Shut Up Little Man!, a string of recordings that capture the incessant arguments between two alcoholic roommates in a low-rent apartment building in San Francisco, is even more notorious than *Daddy's Curses*. Recorded by the roommates' next-door neighbors, it's an extensive catalogue of slurred obscenities and pointed death threats from two people whose hatred of one another is clearly the by-product of a long period of cohabitation and a complete lack of sobriety.

Moving beyond alcoholism, in the realm of psychotic illness, there is a CD-R titled *The Meaning of Life*, released on the Chalfont, Pennsylvania, label Narbin Deeber Productions, run by Eric Prykowski and Brad Wind. The recording itself features an intense male voice talking to someone else, perhaps over the phone or perhaps to voices only he can hear. The man is clearly psychotic, as he expounds upon incoherent and fantastical themes, often involving outer space.

In today's digital age, it didn't take long for people to identify the voice on the recording—online experts connected it to a man from New Jersey who blogs prolifically in a distinctive manner, using familiar terminology both online and on tape. It even turns out there are other tapes featuring his voice. Prykowski tells me that one obsessive fan mailed the Narbin Deeber folks a selection of annotated quotes from this man. Prykowski doesn't know if the man is aware of the release itself. However, the man has blogged about another website that discussed the recording, angrily referring to it as his "personal hatepage."

I ask Prykowski if there was a philosophical orientation behind this release, to which he clarifies that the goal for putting it out was strictly because "it's entertaining." On the ethical question, however, he recognizes there is an inherent sketchiness. "I guess there is somewhat of an ethical dilemma in releasing something like *The Meaning of Life* and not knowing him personally, and I'm sure some listeners are laughing at his ranting and delusional ideas."

EXTREME MUSIC

It is hard to know how much true harm has been done to the man in question. He is at least vaguely aware of public fascination around him. When people are laughing at the content of *The Meaning of Life*, are they laughing at the absurd and whimsical things this man is saying, or are they laughing at him?

Other found sound releases augment found sounds with musical touches. One example is TAS 1000, a group from Vancouver that named themselves after the model of an answering machine that they found in a thrift store. That machine, previously owned by a woman named Marta, contained a cassette filled with mundane messages, which became the source material for the band's *A Message For Marta* album. TAS 1000 chopped the tape up into samples, then laid them over a bedrock of catchy instrumental rock. Once the record was disseminated online, a cult emerged around the band—a song from the album was used in a children's video game, a tribute band named TAS 2000 sprang up, and all the hoopla inspired several fan sites. One blog in particular set out to document the full phenomenon and hunt down the people on the tape, and the writer eventually found Marta and spoke with her via instant messenger. Though gracious, her responses are remarkably nonplussed. When asked what question she'd most like to ask the members of TAS 1000, she replies, "So.....do you have day jobs yet?"

Lucas and Friends is the project of Pea Hicks, whose instrument of choice is the Optigan, a desktop electric organ from the seventies. When a key is pressed, the organ shines light through a spinning celluloid disc, and the machine processes the resulting visual image as sound. You can put different discs into the instrument to achieve different sets of sounds; some of the discs were sold under exotic names like *Polynesian Village* and *Champagne Music*.

For Lucas and Friends' sole album, *Discover a World of Sounds*, Hicks sets a number of thrift store tapes to the Optigan. The name comes from one particular tape, labeled "Lucas," but draws upon a variety of sources.

In an interview for the February 1998 issue of *Exotica/EtCetera* magazine, Hicks says that the idea for releasing found thrift store tapes originated from a project of *creating* tapes for secondhand shops. "It was called the 'Poor Music Series,'" he explains. "I'd put together tapes of odd material, record copies on cruddy old tapes that I found in the thrifts, write things on them like 'Grandma playing organ 1972' and disperse them back out into the tape bins. The idea was that, if someone bought one of these tapes and thought it was legitimately someone's grandma from 1972 (even though it sounded much more obscure than that), then if they were anything at all like me, then they might just think it was the single most weird thing they'd ever come across."

Discover a World of Sounds arose out of a convoluted series of events. "I thought it would be funny to put out a CD of a bunch of bands doing covers of Merzbow pieces. It was originally a joke, but enough people took it seriously that it actually happened and became one of [the Vinyl Communication label's] big sellers.

Front cover of Lucas and Friends *Discover a World of Sounds*. Image courtesy of Pea Hicks.

Anyway, one of the tracks on that CD was actually a bit of noise that I found on a thrift store tape. The kid who made this tape was named 'Lucas,' and there was a spot on it where the batteries were going dead on his Fisher-Price tape recorder and the distorted sound that resulted sounded remarkably like a Merzbow track, so we stuck it on the CD. The CD had contact info for all the bands, so for the contact info for Lucas we just put 'Write to Lucas c/o Pea Hicks...' I got a postcard from some record label in England, addressed to Lucas—they wanted to hear more of his stuff and possibly put out a CD!

"Well, this got me thinking: If I actually did try to put out a 'Lucas' CD, what would be on it?? I figured I could just make a big collage of all my favorite found bits from the thrifts. It took me a while to get around to it (and about three months to put together), but that's how 'Lucas' came about. Somewhere along the way I decided to do all the song accompaniments too, just to break up the spoken word stuff and make it more musical. I sent a copy to that label in England and never heard back from them, so we just put it out on [Vinyl Communications]."

The Optigan

Hicks provides me with a digital copy of the album. It starts with a boy saying "asshole," then proceeding to spell it, and spins off from there. The ensuing collage is robust with kids' peculiar witticisms ("Oh, Kleenex, my baby Kleenex, we'll be together forever . . . Kleenex, I love you fore-eh-ver"), fart sounds, goofy fights between siblings, and various other foibles, sometimes replete with parental intervention:

Child: *I love you and you love me, we'll love together.*

Mother: *TREVOR, GET DRESSED!*

The record's greatest moments are those where Hicks finds recordings of people singing into their recorders with varying degrees of competence, then adds in an Optigan backing via overdubbing.

As Pea Hicks puts it, the mystery of found audio is inherent in the process of finding a tape. "The more serendipitous or unlikely the circumstances, the better. I actually *don't want* to know the identity of the people that made this stuff. I get people all the time telling me things like 'Oh, I have this crazy tape we made when we were kids that would be perfect for one of your art projects!' and honestly, I couldn't care less."

Hicks is not blind to the potential ethical pitfalls of found sound. "It's a bit tricky if you start to think about it," he reflects. "But I guess for me the bottom line is that, even if I happened to know the identity of the people on the recording, I wouldn't make that information public, so combined with the fact that almost all the materials I use are fairly old (often many decades old), it's highly unlikely that anyone featured would end up finding out about it, or would be found out by others. And even so, most of the material I use tends to be relatively innocuous. I mean, it's not like I have people seriously incriminating themselves in some way."

From Hicks' perspective, the positives outweigh the remote risks. "For me, if a bit of found material is compelling in some way, putting it out there for others to enjoy is a greater priority than worrying about whether the unknown person on the tape might ever become aware of their privacy having been violated, especially considering the odds of that happening."

Hicks tells me he continues to amass a vast library of found audio, and he has more than enough for another Lucas and Friends compilation, but he's been busy with other things. He points me to a page on his website called The YakBak Experiment.[94] The YakBak was a children's toy from the nineties that allowed kids to record short bits of audio and replay them. But "kids would walk down the toy aisle and record little secret messages on the YakBaks, with no intention of actually buying the toys." Hicks and his friend Llyswen went around documenting "this odd little underground audio bulletin board system" and made the mysterious blips available on his website.

One early precedent for found tape comes from the world of fine arts, in the form of Edinburgh-based artist Zoë Irvine's *Magnetic Migration Music* project, an early foray into mystery of found audio. Irvine tells me that she has loved audio cassettes since she

94 Pea Hicks, 'The YakBak Experiment,' *Optigan* <optigan.com/about-pea-hicks/the-yakbak-experiment/> [accessed 7 July 2020].

was a child and was once a tape editor for *Audio Arts* magazine, a legendary arts journal published on cassette.

In the late nineties, she started paying attention to the lone ribbons of magnetic tape tangled in gutters, enmeshed in fences, and twisted in tree branches around London. "I got obsessed, really, collecting it and narrativizing how it ended up there, what led to the tape being smashed," she tells me. "This idea of sound being already on the move and really just freed from its container."

In 1998, she picked up a ribbon that had caught in the tree outside her window, then re-spooled it into an empty cassette. Intrigued, she started collecting these mysterious strips and mounting them to cassette cartridges in order to restore them to playable order. Most of them were commercial recordings of popular music, though in many cases, the effects of the natural environment had caused the audio to be altered in unpredictable ways. There were some home recordings, as well as audiobooks, recordings of conference presentations, and language learning tapes. As her collection grew, she established a Soulseek server with digital versions of all her finds.

Around 2001, she saw a bit of footage of Taliban soldiers reaching into cars and pulling out audiotapes, then tearing the tape from the cassettes because they considered music illegal. Around then, there were also reports of thousands of asylum seekers attempting to come to the UK, living in the Sangatte refugee camp set up by the Red Cross in France, just across the English Channel. This was when the idea for *Magnetic Migration Music* crystallized.

"It was the nearest massive physical border to me, and I thought, well, maybe I'll go to this border and collect tape and speak to people about their journeys," she explains. She applied to a funding body with the idea and was approved.

"Off I went. And I spent a few days going, 'What was I thinking?'" She was struck by the experience of walking around, "taking in the magnitude of the situation." She wasn't sure if she was even going to find any tape. Yet, she began talking to people and recording the conversations, encountering Spanish truck drivers, British tourists, and many asylum seekers. On day two or three, while cycling around the area, she found her first bit of tape caught in a fence, eventually gathering a total of twenty fragments.

"I was amazed to hear what I found," she recalls to me. "There were Kurdish drums, there was North African music, nothing from France. It was all music that had come from somewhere else. It was so poignant to me to think of someone taking, as one of the very few possessions they could, a Walkman or something, and then the damn tape breaks."

One particularly memorable ribbon of audiotape contained a recording of a father and son talking, the father teaching the son to play drums. What made it especially real was hearing them repeatedly asking one another, in Kurdish, if the tape recorder was running.

In those videos from Afghanistan, Irvine remembers seeing cities' "great big arches" covered in ribbons of tape. "This image really stuck with me," she tells me "And I began to think, *This tape is now free, this music is now free to cross borders that the people cannot.* And this idea of migration and music in this literal sense had a resonance with something much more potent."

Irvine extended her concept in many different directions. She would use her found tapes in live performances, collaging multiple different stretches of tape at different speeds. At galleries, she would invite attendees to donate their own found tape ribbons, circulating a submissions envelope. She would then invite participants to help respool these tapes—a process involving untangling them, wiping off the dirt and bird poo, getting them into the cassette shell, and then playing them. A CD release called *Interference* came out, composed of tape ribbons that she found in East London. One memorable find was a strip of tape that had an imam giving a service on one side and a recording of "Do They Know It's Christmas?" on the other.

By 2008, Irvine shuttered the project, mainly because ribbons of tape became less abundant in the urban setting. She continues to produce art, and her found sound project is well documented on her website.

Irvine's idea was borrowed and made more systematic by Harold Schellinx in his project, Found Tapes. He extended the concept by including both recovered ribbons of tape and full cassettes he encountered in the city. All audio had to be found in public places like garbage bins and road shoulders, not purchased at thrift stores or garage sales.

As Schellinx collected these tidbits, he itemized them by the date of their recovery, the location they were found, and their contents. He then compiled select excerpts from the tapes and published them on his website in brief collages, forming a database that has gradually grown to 710 tapes. And he's also performed specially curated bits of his collection at installations around Europe.

Schellinx tells me that the inspiration for Found Tapes was Zoë Irvine's call for tape ribbons.[95] He tells me that he developed a "sixth sense" for detecting magnetic tape in the urban environment, "how it moves and blinks." He would also pick up intact cassettes when he found them. At the start, he would just store the tape in envelopes, along with pictures of where they were retrieved. Later, he started to digitize them.

Like Irvine, Schellinx says he was drawn to the sonic qualities of these found tapes, the unpredictable changes in the sound due to weathering. "Almost all of the magnetic emulsion might be gone, and yet you can still hear (the audio) and make sense of it," he explains. "That's not available in digital media, where if something is amiss with the file, it's gone totally."

Schellinx is also drawn to the indeterminacy of finding tape. "Picking up bits and pieces of cassette tapes, taking random samples from all the possible sounds in the world." Patterns emerge in the randomness; he reflects that it is "statistics but not science." By logging them online and, in 2010, mapping them using Google Maps, they also serve as a sort of travelogue, documenting Schellinx's movements. He has also

95 In fact, before he moved to tape, he was collecting an entirely different found object—baby soothers.

taken certain parts of the tapes and assembled them into a fourteen-part collage, which is now available online.

Even today, he finds two or three tape ribbons per year. Though much of the tape captures popular music, he's also found answering machine tapes and personal dictations. On one occasion, he found an audio love letter by a Greek woman to her Dutch lover; it was "trashed in the streets of Amsterdam."[96] Another tape, found in Paris, was recorded in someone's pocket, capturing his exploits around town for an hour.

Schellinx figures that the recordings' anonymity helps protect from adverse consequences. He considers it very unlikely anyone would recognize anything they heard on his tapes, though on one occasion, someone contacted Schellinx because one of his uploaded found tapes was that person's band's demo—however, he was tickled, not annoyed.

Schellinx is also careful to preserve anonymity as best as he can. He gives an example of one tape, which captured a French musician's telephone conversations with Warner Brothers, in which he proposes recording a demo and then is told by a secretary that they won't put out his record. It's a tape with multiple potential identifiers, including the person's phone number, so that's one the Schellinx kept offline—though he's considered calling the number. He also edits out any names, numbers, and addresses included on tapes on principle.

Much like Irvine and her tape collections envelope, some artists have crowdsourced the acquisition of found audio. Atlanta noise artist Justin Waters runs Sounds from the Pocket, an all-purpose experimental label. He's put out his own releases under the names Autio-Ethik and Dubb Normal, has curated a series of compilations whose submissions come on microcassette (more on that later), and has overseen a three-part CD-R project devoted to found sound. Waters compiled these releases by issuing an open call for thrift store finds. The sounds represent a patchwork quilt of tapes from thrift stores across the planet. It has also attracted the interest of several icons of the experimental music scene: Radboud Mens, a prolific sound artist from Amsterdam, as well as British sound artist Janek Schaefer and the longstanding Bay Area troupe the Big City Orchestra, to name a few.

Waters tells me a bit about his attraction to the found sound concept. "My fundamental core is rabidly seeking the truth of all things, knowing that there is a 'public and private' position held by all living creatures," he reflects. "While I do enjoy staged performances, it is what is underneath the camouflage we all wear every day that truly fascinates me. I understand that an answering machine message not intended for me cannot completely remove all the layers, but it does give me a glimpse into the truth.

96 A full transcript is available online at www.harsmedia.com/SoundBlog/Archief/00687.php. Sample quote: "I want nothing for my life, I just want you. You, a bed, the sea, some dope."

An insert from Sounds From The Pocket's *Found Sound Version 3* compilation, complete with a found photograph. Image courtesy of Justin Waters of Sounds From The Pocket.

"So naturally, as soon as I discovered my first microcassette recorder, I set out to interview people whenever and wherever I could, at parties especially in which intoxication is present (to sometimes remove another layer). And I would press questions such as 'What is patriotism to you?' and 'What do you think of homosexuality?' It was quite fun to do, made me feel more comfortable to be in such social settings, as I am not comfortable just 'being' somewhere like that, and I have been that way forever. And having the document after the fact is great, to be able to play and replay the questions and answers, to hear the pauses, to feel the thinking going on."

He later discovered thrift stores. "At the time answering machines were piling up, almost all the time with the cassettes still inside. So I would pocket those (ha, *Sounds From The Pocket* is my label name) and eagerly listen ASAP.

"Must've been around '98 or '99 that I got my first home stereo real-time CD-R burner. Immediately, I began archiving all my precious originals from the past decade plus. And having a new iMac with iTunes really helped me to see it all at once. Amazing. I could edit length, order, and file by so many different variables. So of course, I wanted to do something with all of this—'my life's work,' LOL."

He concocted the idea for his *Found Sound* compilation and issued the online call for submissions. "Record your own record records, digital recorders, found CD-Rs, reel to reel, anything. As long as the contributor did not create the original sound, thereby opening this up to some creativity."

Like others, Waters feels the risks are outweighed by the benefits. "I don't believe anyone has ever let me know they heard themselves on any of these recordings. I feel like once you let go of that data, it becomes public. And why not? Most of it is harmless chitchat."

Still, some finds are less banal than others. "A friend named Kenny found a microcassette recorder wrapped up and tucked away in the attic of his parents' new house. On it is a recording of a woman talking, sort of a suicide letter, going on and on about the wrongs enacted upon her, and the speech seems to become increasingly slurred. I think Kenny said that the neighbors said the previous tenant was a woman who had attempted suicide several times, with no luck, and eventually moved out." Waters didn't release that recording.

He has encountered found sounds in several locations. "In a 'new' microcassette answering machine purchased at Radio Shack, in a microcassette recorder purchased at a pawn shop, in thrift store cassette decks, on the ground, in the trash..."

On one occasion, he found a CD-R laying in the street in Brooklyn. "It had someone talking to a girl [named Laurie], trying to win her heart back, and then asking her to listen to a song that makes him think of her every time he hears it (hahaha, Chicago, 'You're the Inspiration'). I love the idea that I was able to find it because Laurie threw it out of her car window after hearing it!"

He's even been pulled into the digital age. "One fellow sent me a disc of 'Mic In' files. I believe that's what he called them. He said he scoured the internet for uploaded audio files made on Windows using the built-in mic, and these files, if unaltered by the creator, all had 'Mic In' in the title as the default name. His guess was that some of these were perhaps made without the operator even knowing that they were actually recording."

Today, the line between public and private content has changed somewhat, and we have seen many pieces of information that were intended as personal documents become public and even go viral. Early examples include the Star Wars Kid and the "Numa Numa" video. The majority of found sound releases showcase content that's too mundane to risk viral propagation, although a touring found-video showcase called the *Found Footage Festival* has seen several nuggets spread through YouTube.

Compared to the frenetic pace of viral content, many of these early found sound documents, often distributed as limited-run tapes and CD-Rs, seem quaint. Their distribution was so scant that many of the compilers are likely right when they suggest that the risk of identification is low. And, with our easy access to streaming video, the likelihood of these tapes going viral is dramatically lessened.

EXTREME MUSIC

Many of these found sound artifacts represent an era when mystery still existed. The backstories of the recordings on Jacob Smigel's *Eavesdrop*, Justin Waters' *Found Sound* series, and the *Hilarity and Despair* compilation are unlikely to emerge since the source audio is now decades old. Instead, we're left to connect the dots ourselves.

If done often enough, hunting for mystery tapes can return full circle. Skot Spear, the guy who runs Mangdisc, once recovered a tape labeled "Trivia Party" from a dumpster, only to discover his own, much younger voice echoing back at him through his car speakers. "The handwriting looked vaguely familiar," he recounts. "So we get in the car, pop the tape in the player, and the first voice I hear sounds uncannily like my Uncle Connie... But then, a moment later, I heard my own voice. I have many recordings of myself from age six on and I immediately recognized my roughly twelve-year-old voice. This was an audio recording of my family playing Trivial Pursuit, as they would get together to do once a month. I couldn't believe it. The handwriting was in my aunt's handwriting, an aunt who had recently died, and her daughter had apparently brought a bunch of her things to that thrift store.

"They apparently saw no need to keep the cassettes, so they chucked them out, and I found them."

SECTION II
EXTREME DURATIONS

II.1 LONG

On July 31, 2010, an American conceptual band named Bull of Heaven released their two-hundred-and-tenth album, *Like a Wall in Which an Insect Lives and Gnaws*. Like many of Bull of Heaven's nearly five hundred releases, this one was composed of slow-moving drone loops and was distributed freely through their website.

However, this release caused a minor storm of discussion on the internet, even though nobody had actually listened to the whole of it. That's because it is three million minutes long. To listen from start to finish would take you 5.7 years. The MP3 file itself clocks in at four terabytes!

Bull of Heaven was originally the work of Neil Keener and Clayton Counts, the latter of whom died in late 2016. (Keener has, since then, continued the band on his own.) Counts was legally blind due to congenital detached retinas but did not let this hold him back from a long career of sowing chaos. In the nineties, he was reportedly monitored by the FBI after a series of prank calls to a conservative radio host. In 2006, he was handed a cease-and-desist notice for posting a mashup of *Pet Sounds* and *Sgt. Pepper* on the internet, credited to The Beachles. He has even faked his own death, which made for a whole lot of confusion after his actual death was announced.[1]

Bull of Heaven's music ranges from longform drone to pop to improvised psychedelic rock. But *Like a Wall*, one of several impractically long compositions Keener and Counts produced, is part of a unique sonic category: music that takes longer to listen to than it does to create. These pieces are designed using lengthy sound loops, which may comprise 250 to 300 hours of audio. These loops are then digitally stitched together, but "granulized, randomized, effected, and resampled many scores of times" to ensure each piece contains variety and progression. As Counts explained, it is a time-consuming process to produce such long-duration audio, even if the delays are technological in nature: "Just exporting these files takes weeks. Adding in the time it takes to upload them, you're looking at months."[2]

According to a 2009 interview,[3] part of what makes these pieces appealing is that they break new ground, exploring new potentials for music. "These extreme lengths are one of the last remaining unexplored territories of audio experimentation," the two artists explain. In that feature article, they present themselves as trailblazing adventurers, pioneering a whole new paradigm of musical creation.

"Now, the differences between songwriting and writing longer pieces of music are obvious," they observe. "But they are similar in the sense that, as the creator, you feel however you feel about it, and you strive for it to be some kind of cathartic experience."

---

1 Tom Murphy, 'When Clayton Counts Died, His Friends Thought It Was a Prank,' *Westword* (Denver, 11 February 2017) <www.westword.com/music/when-clayton-counts-died-his-friends-thought-it-was-a-prank-8781104> [accessed 3 January 2021].

2 'Bull of Heaven - Ambient with a Twist,' *ScoreHero*, 2010 <www.scorehero.com/forum/viewtopic.php?t=104485&postdays=0&postorder=asc&start=0> [accessed 3 January 2021].

3 Delirious Insomniac, ...'...But Only A Handful of The Pieces Are Longer Than 100 Hours,' *Musique Machine*, 2009 <www.musiquemachine.com/articles/articles_template.php?id=155> [accessed 3 January 2021].

EXTREME MUSIC

Yet they concede that some of their experiments fall along the lines of an "endurance test," with it being impractical for a listener to listen to the entire thing. "Whether anyone listens to them without interruption is beside the point," they say. "As with any other piece of music, they're meant to be explored in whatever way the listener deems appropriate."

Keener is now forty-two and resides in Peoria, Illinois, where his main band, Planes Mistaken For Stars, was formed. He grew up in Wheeling, a suburb of Chicago, and was an adolescent devotee of punk music who went to school with members of Cap'n Jazz and Braid. When he met Counts, Keener was in his mid-twenties and working in a coffee shop in Chicago; Counts was a customer who would sit in the café producing his signature mashups. Counts was known for being abrasive, but Keener tells me it was immediately obvious he was a "genius." When Counts got in legal trouble due to his *Pet Sounds/Sgt. Pepper* mashup album, he asked Keener if he could hide out at a warehouse that Keener was living in. In 2007, Counts moved in. At the time, Keener was frequently out of town touring as a member of Planes Mistaken For Stars, but when he was home, he would record his own drone music on a four-track recorder. Counts, a "mastering genius" by Keener's estimation, offered to digitize some of this music, and consequently Bull of Heaven was born.

Around the time, Keener was experimenting with playing "loud drone music" on his stereo while he slept at night. He wondered aloud to Counts about the logistics of producing an eight-hour track to be used at night as a sleeping accompaniment. Digital music, unrestricted by the limits of a physical format, seemed like the ideal vehicle for this concept.

Keener says that Counts had an "obsessive" personality, and this idea of producing longer and longer tracks consumed him. "I remember when we did the series of superlong pieces, Clayton called me and was freaking the fuck out, and was like 'I figured it out, I figured it out.' He had figured out the technical aspect of how to make those pieces work.

"That's why I say he was a genius. I don't use the term lightly. He figured out how to achieve something that he had in his mind. And I feel blessed to have been a part of it. We obviously did all the shit together, but in terms of the lengthier pieces, he was definitely pushing in that direction, because he just wanted to push that boundary."

Pushing boundaries was central to the Clayton Counts ethic. He would become embroiled in online feuds with people who posted negative reviews of Bull of Heaven's long tracks on the website Rate Your Music. "He was an extreme person. When people didn't like [our music], he felt the need to defend it in some way or another. People were pissed off, people were like 'This isn't music.'... Somebody who says that your art isn't art is entitled to that opinion, and I think he understood that, and I don't think he gave a shit whether or not they thought it was. But making that person think about that point of view that your art isn't art, and maybe consider that there are different ways of looking at it—that's what art's about, making people think about things. It's about trying to elicit a response in some way. I was happier that people either hated or loved it. Because if nobody gives a shit, then nobody gives a shit.

"Like, who fucking cares if I make a five-year-long piece that's fucking completely unlistenable? That's not the point—you know what I mean? Especially if you're dealing with more of a conceptual art project. Bull of Heaven's a band, I guess, but it's also an art project."

When I ask Keener now about the idea that Bull of Heaven's ultralong music was about reaching catharsis through a test of endurance, he agrees. "Sometimes I think about this concept of staying in a situation that's uncomfortable for a little bit too long and, by doing that, breaking through something mentally. These pieces give people an opportunity to do that, and I guess that's where this concept of catharsis comes in. With meditation, the longer you do something past your comfort zone, the more opportunity there is for growth and catharsis."

In the case of *Like a Wall*, because the file itself was enormous, they ran into trouble with their website's web hosting company. "We paid for unlimited space, right, but all of a sudden, we're trying to upload a piece that's four terabytes. And they're just like 'No, we're not doing this.' And they kicked us off the server. That's when we started moving everything to archive.org. These were all huge stresses for Clayton."

Keener agrees that listening to *Like a Wall* in its entirety is an absurd endeavor. One online reviewer jokes: "don't bother, this album is so bad I could hardly get past the third year."[4] Someone uploaded a nearly twelve-hour YouTube video that collects seven excerpts from the album's totality. Extracts include a second-long bass rattle looped for an hour, an endless track of grumbling noise, and a strange passage that intermingles several layers of garbled speech for nearly two hours. Nobody would choose to listen to five years of this. And yet it exists.

As I dug through the annals of long-music history, I learned that *Like a Wall* was not even the longest musical composition to be conceived up to that point. In fact, the concept of the profoundly long piece has been tackled so many times in the past, I started to wonder why it was such an attractive concept.

Robert Rich, the aforementioned composer and musician in Mountain View, California, put out a recording in 2001 named *Somnium* that was inspired by his sleep concerts. At eight hours, it had to be put out on DVD, since a CD could not fit all the requisite data. Its detailed liner notes explain that *Somnium* works best as an accompaniment to sleep.[5] *Somnium* is specifically intended to capitalize on the hypnagogic phase of sleep, when you're in that liminal space between wakefulness and sleep. During that period, people experience transitional hallucinations that are susceptible to the influence of external stimuli.

As Rich explains, "Hypnagogic images are often less organized than true dreams, and often come blended with a semi-awareness of your environment. If you pass from this stage into a deeper sleep, you will not remember these images and thoughts. But

4 rateyourmusic.com/board_message?message_id=2841857&board_id=1&show=20&start=40
5 Robert Rich, *Somnium* [Liner Notes] (Portland, OR: Hypnos Recordings, 2001).

if you can linger at the edge, slipping in and out of stage 1 sleep, you can ride along the edge of your own awareness."

Lingering at the edge has been compared by Rich to how "a surfer uses gravity to stay on the leading edge of a wave," leading to "dreamlike hallucinations, evoking fragile new mental landscapes." This can then alter how we experience REM sleep, either by carrying the images evoked by the music into our dreams or by slightly reducing the depth of sleep to make dreams more vivid and memorable.

Perhaps the most high-profile longform piece is *Longplayer*, a composition that is unfolding in real time. It started just before midnight on December 31, 1999, and is set to conclude at the very same time one thousand years later, on December 31, 2999.

The concept of Jem Finer, a founding member of Celtic punk group The Pogues, *Longplayer* achieves its tremendous duration through its simple yet elegant design. First, Finer recorded a piece of music that lasted 20 minutes and 20 seconds, played on Tibetan singing bowls. This was then digitally transposed to create six separate compositions, each one sped up or slowed down by a specific increment to ensure that it was a certain number of semitones above or below the original. All six compositions were then set to start at the same time, each one looped. Because of the way their durations are staggered, they will not arrive at their initial pattern of synchronicity until a thousand years have passed.

The whole thing is, of course, being invigilated by computers, and depends on the continued functioning of the internet to continue uninterrupted. If you do not want to trek out to the official listening post, set in a lighthouse at Trinity Buoy Wharf, London, you can listen to a livestream of *Longplayer* on the official website. But the persistence of the project is a logistical challenge, given that its duration is the whole point. As a result, there is talk of establishing a dedicated *Longplayer* radio frequency in the future.

Finer conceived of his longform project as a response to the turn of the millennium. "I started to wonder about how to make sense of a millennium," he reflects on the *Longplayer* website.[6] "That is, how to render as sensible or tangible the great span of one thousand years, not so long in cosmic terms but sufficiently longer than a human lifetime."

As one of the organizers, Michael Morris, put it, focusing on producing a piece of music one thousand years in duration can make long tracts of time seem more comprehensible. "In making time tangible, the continuum of *Longplayer* helps to reduce the vertiginous fear of infinity and somehow sweetens the fearful thought of our own mortality, enabling us to live with hope."

With that said, before *Longplayer* was even dreamed of, someone else had conjured up a similar concept, albeit one that extends much longer. Dr. Ian D. Mellish, who records under the name Mel, is an experimental composer from the UK with a PhD in composition from York University. Trained in violin and electronic music and with a special interest in tape works, he has been composing since 1979.

6 Jem Finer, 'Conceptual Background,' *Longplayer* <longplayer.org/about/conceptual-background/> [accessed 3 January 2021].

In 1987, he unveiled *Olitsky*, which is named after Jules Olitski, a pioneering Color Field painter known for staining his canvases instead of using brushwork as many fellow Abstract Expressionists did. *Olitsky* uses a similar methodology as *Longplayer*, working with multiple tape loops playing simultaneously. In this case, there are only four loops, but they are staggered at very slightly different durations (44'43", 44'39", 44'46", 44'54"). Like *Longplayer*, the track is set up so that all the loops start at the same time, and the piece does not conclude until they are all aligned again. But unlike *Longplayer*, *Olitsky* will not be through until 1,648,171 years, 7 weeks, 6 days, 10 hours, 23 minutes, and 33 seconds have passed!

Another key distinction is that *Olitsky* is not the beneficiary of the kind of grant money that comes with being a public art project, so it remains unrealized. The tape loops exist, but there is no location where it runs continuously, nor is there a trust ensuring that it plays out its entire duration, protected against the elements. But it has been exhibited now and then, and there was even a CD put out containing excerpts of the music, on a now-defunct Welsh label named Red Wharf. Listening to those recordings reveals an eerie, droning trip that drifts between different atonal clouds of chords.

Mellish explains to me that long works like *Olitsky* are along the lines of "environmental" or "wallpaper" music, similar in spirit to Erik Satie's furniture music. Along these lines, Mellish has composed other lengthy works using loops, including an earlier one named after abstract expressionist painter Mark Rothko, which lasted three weeks.

Mellish explains that visual art does not only occupy physical space. "Paintings also occupy temporal space—sitting on a wall for years, being occasionally noticed in passing—whereas a music work is over after some minutes or maybe an hour or three." So why not create a piece of music that is lasting?

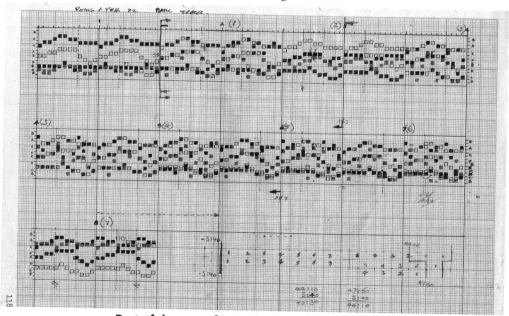

Part of the score for Dr. Ian D. Mellish's *Rothko*.
Image courtesy of Dr. Ian D. Mellish.

EXTREME MUSIC

"For *Rothko*, I visited the 'Rothko Room' at the original Tate Modern in London," Mellish tells me. "In those days, the room had skylights all around the ceiling and, as I was in a position to visit daily for a couple of weeks, I noticed that the paintings' colors changed and, because of the nature of the paintings, the various color-panels' edges shifted as the sun moved and the weather changed. From this observation, I was determined to reflect this changing in the composition of *Olitsky*."

The length of the piece was merely luck: The tape reels he was using were forty-five minutes each, and he opted to use four of them "to further vary the sound color and any resultant chords." The result was a piece of music that occupied seemingly infinite temporal space, and that was continuously shifting, just like Rothko's paintings fluctuating with the position of the sun above.

Unsurprisingly, John Cage fits into this long-music story somewhere, although he is not entirely to blame. In 1985, he wrote *ASLSP*, a relatively brief piece with indeterminate elements, for a competition. *ASLSP* stands for "As Slow as Possible," which is the instruction provided on the score itself. However, he did not include any specific guidance regarding tempo or dynamics, so it does not have a specified duration.

Since it was written for piano, any truly slow performance of it would include a whole lot of silence, because each piano note will only resonate for a short time. So in 1987, Cage produced an adaptation, *Organ2/ASLSP*, which is similar but intended to be played on an organ. An organ produces sound by blowing air through a pipe; if you hold an organ key down, it will blow air continuously, producing a sustained tone of indefinite length. Therefore, an organ-based adaptation can much more practically be performed as slowly as possible, without hours of silence between each note.[7]

The published score of *Organ2/ASLSP* is merely a title page, a short set of instructions, and four leaves of score, each containing two short pieces. Following Cage's death, a handful of musicians explored how to do justice to the piece, which up until then had only been extended to the neighborhood of several hours.[8] In 2001, their ambitions were realized, when a performance was started in a small church in a rural town in Halberstadt, Germany, population 44,000. With the help of a custom organ designed for the task, the organizers embarked on a performance of *Organ2/ASLSP* set to last for a whopping 639 years. This was achieved by modifying the organ pipes to produce different notes, with small bags of sand hanging on the appropriate keys to keep them pressed for years at a time. Thus, the organ will play its chords automatically; the "performer" need only show up every few years to change the pipes and shift the sandbags, which will then stay in place for several more years. These sporadic chord changes are such an event that people fly in from across the world to watch them happen.

A 2012 article in *Performance Research* documents a visit to the chapel. The authors are surprised to discover that the organ is inaudible from outside the doors of the relatively quaint, gutted chapel—despite reports of it being a "dial tone on steroids" that terrorized the locals. The organ itself is relatively small, its pipes stored in an attic and

---

7   Jeffery Byrd and John Fritch, 'Forever Ephemeral: John Cage's ASLSP,' *Performance Research*, 17.5 (2012), 5–8 <doi.org/10.1080/13528165.2012.728429>.

8   Terez Mertes, 'As Slow As Possible,' Violinist.com, 2008 <www.violinist.com/blog/Terez/20088/9005/> [accessed 3 January 2021].

only added or subtracted according to the needs of the score; at any moment, it only has the specific pipes needed to play the current chord.[9]

Like *Longplayer*, Byrd and Fritch relate this lengthy performance to Cage's affinity for time, which he saw as the "one quality" that silence and sound have in common. *ASLSP*, in its piano version, was designed to empower the performer to determine the extent to which time would be filled with sound and silence. The more slowly it was performed, the more silence there would be.

Recalling Finer's concept behind *Longplayer,* the 639-year performance of *Organ2/ASLSP* is seen as a reflection on "how fast time moves in contemporary society." By casting its scope beyond human lifespans, indeed across generations, they see it as encouraging people "to rethink their notions of time rather than viewing time as something to merely be filled." Indeed, listening to a years-long chord reverberate throughout the chapel's walls is said to evoke a sense of "timelessness." Byrd and Fritch expand, reflecting that "the one thing the sound does not do is move forward. This aural stasis has a way of holding the listener in its eternal now. The future seems beyond conception. The sound of the organ seems to erase all content beyond its serene audible presence."

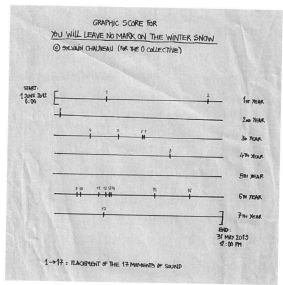

The graphic score for *You Will Leave No Mark On The Winter Snow.* Image courtesy of Sylvain Chauveau.

In a similar vein as *Longplayer* and the *Organ2/ASLSP* performance was a seven-year performance called *You Will Leave No Mark On The Winter Snow*, performed by an ensemble by the name 0. *You Will Leave No Mark* is almost entirely composed of silence; however, as represented by its inscrutable graphic score, the silence is punctuated, extremely sparsely, by "17 mysterious musical moments" produced using electronics and piano. As the ensemble's now-defunct website explained,[10] those moments "are either slowly fading in and out during several moments or very short, so that you'll have to listen as carefully as possible to check if you are hearing a silent or a sonorous part of the piece." Interested listeners were able to tune in to a 24/7 livestream on the website, where it played until its terminus on May 31, 2019. Of course, there was no way to know when one of those seventeen moments was going to occur, so curious listeners had to invest a lot of time and energy to hear one of them.

9 Byrd and Fritch.
10 web.archive.org/web/20130629223526/http://www.7yearsofsilence.com/

EXTREME MUSIC

But Sylvain Chauveau, the composer of the piece, says that Oliveros was not a direct inspiration for *You Will Leave No Mark*. For Chauveau, the goal was to use an extreme duration to produce something "outstanding." As he explained, "I know there are pieces that last hours. Days, that's much more uncommon. Weeks, months, even more. But I thought that years would be really, really rare, so that's what I chose."

Looking back, he notes that the extreme length allowed him to experiment with long stretches of silence, which is one of his favored compositional techniques. But the lengthiness is also an end in itself. He pointed out his Micro_concerts project, "a series of concerts that must not last more than two minutes" which he staged in Brussels, as well as a combined audio-visual installation which required him to perform live, seven hours a day, for three days.

Longplayer, Organ2/ASLSP, 7 Years of Silence, and *Olitsky*—these are either performances, or they exist in concept only. Bull of Heaven's longform experiments are freely available online but have no physical form. But James Whitehead, a contemporary experimental music iconoclast who is heavily involved in the noise scene, went one step further in 2013. Under his alias, Jliat, he put out a release that lasts 143.7 days and made it available in a physical format. *HNW510* is a set of 510 DVDs, each containing high-quality WAV files that are 6.7 hours apiece. The audio is a continuous length of unchanging harsh noise wall.

Whitehead tells me that *HNW510* sprung from the sense of wonder he experiences while contemplating the universe. "We have come to learn the vastness of the cosmos in space and time, also the incredible smallness in the quantum world," he says. "It is, if you like, now 'our world' or landscape, and it's this landscape I want to make art about. I've done many works around this idea. Limits and the limitless. You could say in a way I'm working in the tradition of landscape painters; my degree was fine art painting. Only our landscape is very big!"

For *HNW510*, the limit he is exploring is the limit of technology. In the nineties, he started creating computer programs to automatically generate WAV files. "It's fairly simple just to create WAV files by just writing numbers," he tells me, explaining that he created a whole series of discs called *Still Life* that were based on these auto-produced files. Setting every frequency in the sound spectrum to its highest possible volume, he ended up with a truly pure harsh noise wall.

HNW510 was actually preceded by a longer work called *1TB*, a set of 233 DVDs that each contained a seventy-three-hour harsh noise wall in MP3 format. Designed with the concept of "actualizing" the concept of a trillion—in this form, a trillion bytes—it was a colossal product, amounting to nearly two years of audio. "Art can actualize these abstract concepts, always has done," Whitehead says.

HNW510, though not as long, was a heftier production in terms of numbers of discs. Each disc contained a WAV file of four gigabytes, which was, at the time, the maximum file size. He chose the number 510 for no particular reason; he knew he wanted more than five hundred discs, for the purposes of getting "a very large wall of sound," and then chose to use 510 DVDs because they fit well into the aluminum box he had picked

A rare image of Jliat's *1TB*, comprising a whopping 233 DVDs inside a metal suitcase. Image courtesy of James Whitehead.

out. Importantly, each DVD contains a distinct WAV file: after creating each file, he wrote a program that changed each file by one byte apiece. "So it was not simply a copy of one CD, or a completely continuous repeated sound which has no difference," Whitehead emphasizes.

HNW510 was a time-consuming undertaking, and only one copy was ever produced. Whitehead tells me he sold it to "someone living in Scotland."

Many of the pieces discussed so far were composed using tape loops or by computers automatically generating sound, as opposed to being music produced in real time by human hands. Robert Rich's eight-hour *Somnium* was an exception, but it turns out there are even longer records produced by real people in real time. In 2011, the Flaming Lips put out a strange release called *7 Skies H3*, which was a single twenty-four-hour song contained on a flash drive that came housed within a real human skull. Limited to just thirteen copies, each one was made available for $5,000.

EXTREME MUSIC

The Flaming Lips are no strangers to this sort of novelty. Their 1997 album *Zaireeka* included four separate CDs, all of which were meant to be played simultaneously on four CD players for a surround-sound experience. They have also pressed their own blood into their records, collaborated with Miley Cyrus, and released an EP on a flash drive in the center of an (edible) gummy brain. If one gummy brain release was not enough, at one point, they were planning on releasing a live edition of their *Soft Bulletin* album inside a marijuana-flavored gummy brain.

But *7 Skies H3* is noteworthy because it is one of very few ultra-lengthy recordings that was actually performed by people. It is hard to know what the Lips' true motivations were, apart from novelty, but there are many reviews online that characterize it as remarkably listenable, if occasionally repetitive. Meanwhile, the band's frontman, Wayne Coyne, admits that he has never listened to the entire thing.[11]

Francisco López's untitled #305 SD card, featuring seven eight-hour compositions. Image courtesy of Francisco López.

In a less pop-friendly vein, there's Francisco López, who in January 2013 put out *Untitled #305*, a series of seven eight-hour compositions on an SD card, described as:

> *Seven ghostly nights of expanded time and occult sonic space. Venturing into deep realms of audio subtlety and ambiguity. Open to the hearing creativity, sleeping patterns, and dreams of the listener. A piece that blurs the limits between composition and sound environment.*[12]

López explains to me that these longform pieces are designed to straddle the line between composition and "sound environment." Whereas ambient music is designed to recede into the background, *Untitled #305* is intended to generate an "immersive and temporarily self-contained world" that garners the listener's full attention. López explains that the seven pieces, which were composed over the past thirty years of his career, use a host of musical techniques to captivate the listener's attention, including "wide dynamics," unpredictable changes in compositional structure, and "hidden complexity."

---

11 Tony Keefer, 'Wayne Coyne: SIX HUNDRED SECONDS WITH WAYNE'S BRAIN,' *The Music Room*, 2014 <themusicroom.me/wayne-coyne-six-hundred-seconds-with-waynes-brain/> [accessed 4 January 2021].

12 'Francisco Lopez – Untitled #305 (Seven Nights),' Soundohm <www.soundohm.com/product/untitled-305-seven-nights> [accessed 4 January 2021].

In other words, the extreme duration of *Untitled #305* seems to be about transfixing the person's attention, pulling them into a dense listening experience. As suggested by the press materials, this may include influencing the listener's sleep and dreams, in the same way Robert Rich's *Somnium* claims the audience's hypnagogic space.

As it turns out, Bull of Heaven's ultra-long compositions did not peak at 5.7 years. Although not all of Counts and Keener's compositions explore extreme durations, several do, and *Like a Wall* is far from the upper limit. Exploring the nooks and crannies of the band's sprawling discography, you will find something called *310: ΩΣPx0(2^18 × 5^18) p*k*k*k*. It is a 3.343 quindecillion-year[13] composition. Musically speaking, it is hardly a compelling audio experience—nothing more than a momentary bass pulse repeated incessantly for a span of time that is 2.4×10^{38} times the age of the universe.

Wesley D. Cray, an assistant professor in philosophy and East Asian studies at Texas Christian University, mentions *310: ΩΣPx0(2^18 × 5^18) p*k*k*k* in a journal article titled "Unperformable Works and the Ontology of Music."[14] In it, he describes several different types of music that are unperformable for different reasons. For example, compositions that require the performer to play faster than any human is capable of playing are "medically unperformable," while a hypothetical piece where each of three musicians is required to play louder than the others would be considered "logically unperformable." Bull of Heaven's *310* is "nomically unperformable," meaning that a performance would violate the laws of nature. This is because its duration is much longer than the projected lifespan of the universe.

As a thought experiment, imagine setting up a computer to play *310: ΩΣPx0(2^18 × 5^18) p*k*k*k*. How long would it take for the system to stop functioning? Equipment failure? The first power outage? The end of power production by humans? The universe collapsing into a pinpoint?

---

13 3,343,000,000,000,000,000,000,000,000,000,000,000,000,000,000,000 years.
14 Wesley D. Cray, 'Unperformable Works and the Ontology of Music,' *The British Journal of Aesthetics*, 56.1 (2016), 67–81 <doi.org/10.1093/aesthj/ayv047>.

LONG LPS

When the 33 RPM LP record was introduced, it was designed to play a maximum of twenty-three minutes per side, a huge gain on the 78 RPM records that were the standard at the time. Subsequent advances in technology allowed each side to play for a little bit longer than twenty-three minutes—initially up to twenty-six minutes and occasionally even past the half-hour mark. This was achieved by cutting smaller margins between each groove; however, each little bit was earned at the expense of sound quality.

That bargain between quantity and quality has not stopped several record companies from pushing the limits of LP length even further. Here are a few of the longest LPs to ever grace the market.

90 MINUTES: Arthur Fiedler, *90 Minutes with Arthur Fiedler and the Boston Pops* (1976, Realistic)

Often cited as the longest 33 RPM record, this easy-listening record was put out in 1976 by Realistic, the in-house record label for Radio Shack. It promised a "totally new Microsonic recording technique" but because the grooves had to be squeezed together, its dynamic range was squished. As a result, the recording jacket recommended the listener turn up the volume; however, this would also amplify the surface noise, submerging the already-thin sound in cracks and pops. As one record owner recalls, the lackluster pressing also had ripples in it, further worsening the signal-to-noise ratio.[1]

93–95 MINUTES: Beethoven/Tchaikovsky, *Eroica/Pathétique* Karajan 'Golden Coupling' Series (1970s, Toshiba)

The longest major label LP, this budget-line ("1,000-yen") Japanese pressing is somewhat shrouded in mystery, as very minimal information exists online about it (and much of what exists is in Japanese). There are a few scattered references to this pressing, which squeezes a symphony each by Beethoven and Tchaikovsky onto a single side of an LP, doubtlessly by sacrificing the dynamic range. (In comparison, each recording was previously released as a standalone LP on the record's American pressing.) This rare mega-LP bears the catalogue number EAC 30283.[2]

114 MINUTES AND 45 SECONDS: Johann Sebastian Bach, *Version Intégrale* (1970s, Trimicron)

In the early to mid-1970s, a purported "music lover" named Dr. Rabe developed a special type of LP with grooves that were spaced very closely together, presumably similar to Radio Shack's Microsonic technique. This method was sold by a firm called MDR (Magnetic Disc Recording) and was named Trimicron, which was also the name of the record label that released the records. However, because the grooves were shallower, the dynamics were lower, and the signal was apparently reduced by nearly 40 percent—meaning the listener had to turn up the volume by that percentage to hear it clearly. This meant that it was often necessary to use expensive turntables to get a good sound, although less discerning listeners may have considered the audio to be just fine.

---

1   'Longest LP Side Ever?' <groups.google.com/g/rec.music.classical.recordings/c/5uw3TA9Y2g4/m/Mgv6xoBTbkwJ> [accessed 4 January 2021].

2   '東芝音楽工業の廉価盤 (4) [1300円盤] (Low-Priced Board of Toshiba Music Industry (4) [1300 Yen Board])' <matsumo.gozaru.jp/music/page6h11.htm> [accessed 4 January 2021]; '世界最長収録のLPレコード？ － 「英雄」＆「悲愴」 － 私のレコード・ライブラリーから (The Longest Recorded LP Record in the World? -"Hero" & "Sorrow"),' 私のレコード・ライブラリーから (*From My Music Library*) <blog.goo.ne.jp/florian2896/e/8d8c096839dbe80a8497ba9295b78024> [accessed 4 January 2021]; 'Is This the Longest LP?' <rec.music.classical.recordings.narkive.com/GKfs9RyV/is-this-the-longest-lp#post5> [accessed 4 January 2021].

円盤

There were approximately thirty Trimicron discs produced in total, but the technology never caught on. Their Bach compilation, *Version Intégrale*, somehow fits recordings of his "Fantasia in G major" along with all six Brandenburg concertos onto one record. This one appears to take the cake for the longest 33 RPM LP in history, although a full Trimicron discography is not publicly available, so it is hard to know for sure.[3]

155 MINUTES: Beethoven "Symphony No. 5"; Dvořák "'New World' Symphony"; Schubert "'Unfinished' Symphony"; Prokofiev "'Classical' Symphony" (1957, VOX XL)

Perhaps a cop-out because it's not a 33 RPM record, this colossal classical disc is a 12" LP designed to be played at 16 2/3 RPM. That speed was below the standard at the time, but some record players could run at that speed. (Incidentally, in the radio industry, prerecorded programs were often recorded on 16-inch records that played at 16 RPM.)

This disc was part of a short-lived series of records put out by classical label VOX, which they released under the VOX XL sub-label, XL standing for "Extra Long." The masters were cut by audio engineer Rudy Van Gelder. This classical omnibus was the fifth release of the set (VXL-5), capturing performances of works by Beethoven, Dvořák, Prokofiev, and Klemperer, as conducted by masters Jascha Horenstein, Otto Klemperer, and Heinrich Hollreiser.

There are very few mentions of this particular LP available online, though there is an archived online auction that includes pictures of the cover and center label.[4] A *Billboard* article[5] from the time, "16 2/3 Speed Poses Program Challenges," notes that these listed for $6.95 apiece, as compared to normal VOX LPs, which ran for $4.95 each. Classical music fans are notorious about audio fidelity, so perhaps the lack of success was because the sound quality was inferior—or because only a fraction of the population had a record player that could play at that speed.

HONORABLE MENTION: Various artists, *The First Three Years of Blue Series Singles On One LP At 3 RPM* (2012, Third Man Records TMR143)

I have reservations about including this, because it is unplayable on nearly all turntables, and its length is merely a novelty. This is one LP that collects the first twenty-nine singles from Third Man's Blue Series, in which performers touring through Nashville are invited to record a song or two at the Third Man Studio, produced by Jack White of the White Stripes. Artists as varied as Insane Clown Posse, Tom Jones, Beck, and Dungen are included on this record, not to mention John C. Reilly and Stephen Colbert. In total, there are fifty-six songs on this one LP!

How did they fit it all onto one LP? They mastered it at 3 RPM, which means that the sound quality is severely compromised and almost no turntable can play it, apart from specialty models capable of moving at custom speeds. Copies of this ambitious experiment, pressed on translucent blue vinyl, were circulated at Third Man's three-year anniversary party and no doubt were restricted to a very limited edition. One online auction saw a copy go for $163 USD![6]

---

3 'Is This the Longest LP?' <rec.music.classical.recordings.narkive.com/GKfs9RyV/is-this-the-longest-lp#post1> [accessed 4 January 2021]; 'JS. Bach* - Version Intégrale (Gatefold, Vinyl),' Discogs <www.discogs.com/Johann-Sebastian-Bach-Version-Intégrale/release/5078155> [accessed 4 January 2021].

4 'Beethoven Dvorak Prokofiev Klemperer Horenstein Hollreiser Rare 16 RPM VOX VXL5 - Auction Details,' Popsike.com, 2013 <www.popsike.com/Beethoven-Dvorak-Prokofiev-Klemperer-Horenstein-Hollreiser-Rare-16-RPM-VOX-VXL5/360813202047.html> [accessed 4 January 2021].

5 Bill Simon, '16 2/3 Speed Poses Program Challenges,' The Billboard (New York, 25 November 1957) <books.google.ca/books?id=3ygEAAAAMBAJ&pg=PA77&lpg=PA77&dq=Horenstein+Klemperer,+Hollreiser,&source=bl&ots=scuW8ZlbrH&sig=Dhd8HwuNCb_4hdc-E2enbzMQZsc&hl=en&sa=X&ved=2ahUKEwjh2fbctMbfAhUC64MKHZAZD2MQ6AEwAXoECAkQAQ#v=onepage&q=Horenstein Klemperer%2C Hollreiser%2C&f=false> [accessed 4 January 2021].

6 'FIRST THREE YEARS OF BLUE SERIES SINGLES ON ONE LP AT 3 RPM Third Man Records - Auction Details,' Popsike.com, 2016 <www.popsike.com/FIRST-THREE-YEARS-OF-BLUE-SERIES-SINGLES-ON-ONE-LP-AT-3-RPM-Third-Man-Records/282184370374.html> [accessed 4 January 2021].

II.2 BRIEF

In 1987, the band Napalm Death put out their debut album, *Scum*. A work of extreme metal recorded on a shoestring budget, it is now considered a classic record that helped define the grindcore genre. And despite its inaccessible nature, it reached number seven on the UK Indie Chart and is included in Robert Dimery's popular tome *1001 Albums You Must Hear Before You Die*.

Scum is a direct record. Napalm Death's mission was to get their point across with expert efficiency—as a result, it fits twenty-eight tracks into just over thirty-three minutes. At the very end of the record's A-side, "You Suffer" clocks in at only 1.316 seconds. That precise figure earned a spot in the *Guinness Book of World Records*, which listed it as the world's shortest song for a while before dropping the category.[15] The song itself is little more than a couple of blast beats, a few power chords, and a meaty vocalization of the title by the band's then-singer, Nicholas Bullen.[16]

This short song, intended as a joke, was emblematic of the grindcore genre. Grindcore developed in the early to mid-eighties as a convergence between two extreme ends of already-extreme genres. On one hand, there was thrash, which was heavy metal's loud and fast fringe, combining metal heaviness with hardcore punk's speed. But grindcore takes thrash and adds an extra dose of hardcore, ratcheting up the chaotic tempos even further.

The first exponents of grindcore cropped up in the UK in the form of bands like Napalm Death and Carcass. The sound would later take seed in North America, where bands like Terrorizer and Brutal Truth became icons. At its apogee, grindcore artists flirted with marketability. Napalm Death's record label, Earache, was a major label subsidiary, and they even landed a track on the *Mortal Kombat* film soundtrack—a platinum-selling record. Today, grindcore may not have the same major-label profile as it did at its zenith, but its followers are true devotees, supporting an upper echelon of big names like Pig Destroyer as well as countless lower tiers of notoriety, some of which are trafficked via a labyrinthine network of underground vinyl, CD-R, and cassette labels.

There are a handful of musical devices that are characteristic of grindcore releases. For one, grindcore bands' drummers tend to communicate in *blast beats*—rapid-fire, unsyncopated drumbeats produced by hitting the bass drum, snare, or both on every sixteenth note. The lyrics, frequently growled or screamed, are often political or provocative, frequently both, and seldom intelligible. And, of course, many grindcore artists record short songs, a trend so notorious that some acts have been dubbed "blipcore" bands.

---

15 *Guinness World Records'* statement on the matter: "The nature of competing to make something the 'shortest' by its very nature trivialises the activity being carried out, and *Guinness World Records* has been forced to reject many claims of this kind. As such, we have been forced to cease listing records for the shortest song, shortest poem and indeed the shortest concert." Incidentally, "You Suffer" may also be the world's shortest music video. They filmed one in 2007 to coincide with a reissue of *Scum* on DualDisc—a double-sided DVD & CD.

16 Much like their songs, Napalm Death's members' stints could be short. Bullen left the band before *Scum* was finished, and Side B has a different vocalist as a result.

Napalm Death's *Scum*

There are several reasons grindcore acts tend to limit the duration of their songs. The principle of grindcore is to concentrate as much energy as possible into a given track by playing it as loud and fast as possible. That level of intensity is only sustainable for a brief amount of time, particularly for drummers, whose upper body muscles rapidly accumulate lactic acid, making it downright painful to continue for long stretches. Consult Pig Destroyer's classic album, *Terrifyer*—only two of its twenty-one songs pass the three-minute mark, and only two others surpass two minutes.

But beyond physiological limits, it could also be argued that the shorter a song is, the greater its density of intensity. In other words, brevity can imply extremeness itself, these short tracks seeming to encapsulate so much in such a short period of time. The same year that Napalm Death's *Scum* came out, another grindcore band called Sore Throat put out *Death to Capitalist Hardcore*, which fit twenty-eight songs onto one side of a seven-inch single. It quickly sold out its 1,000-copy run, and several iterations of bootlegs have been released to keep up with demand.

"You Suffer" is more than a little tongue-in-cheek. In *Precious Metal: Decibel Presents the Stories Behind 25 Extreme Metal Masterpieces*, drummer Mick Harris is quoted:

> There is a bit of novelty. Let's do the shortest, fastest thing you can do. And yeah, there are notes there. People think we just go "blllp" and that's it.[17]

In the same article, founding member Nicholas Bullen describes being amused by the world record they earned, joking that he wishes he had instead won for being the first human to breathe underwater. Interestingly, he also points out that Napalm Death weren't the first to the idea, describing "You Suffer" as their own take on an earlier song, "E!," by Wehrmacht. Wehrmacht, a thrashy "beercore" band from Portland, Oregon, included "E!" on their rare 1986 demo tape, *Beermacht*. Like "You Suffer," it is about one second long and sits at the end of the tape's A-side. But its lyrics are even shorter—just the letter E!

If "You Suffer"—itself a spiritual cover—is a goof, then the idea of *covering* it is even more absurd. But there are versions by Opeth, Soulfly, and harsh noise artist Kylie Minoise. And in 2011, a prolific French netlabel called Sirona Records put out an entire tribute album devoted to the song, featuring sixty different takes on the classic by sixty different bands—though many of them extend far past the original's run time.[18]

There were other related scenes that also featured microsongs. The Stormtroopers of Death (S.O.D.), a controversial crossover thrash band that spun off from Anthrax, recorded a 1985 demo named *Crab Society North*, which is sometimes cited as the first "blipcore" record. All its tracks are under one minute, with the longest clocking in at fifty-seven seconds. Over sixty-three songs fly by in fourteen minutes! According to an interview with band member Dan Lilken, the whole demo was an experiment in trying to make something extreme. Recorded on a "cheap tape deck with way too much input level so it sounded really distorted," it was never intended to be released, although it ended up being distributed by dedicated fans.[19] A few songs manage a riff for a few seconds before blasting off into chaos, and there is the odd intercessory joke, but the whole thing is tape-fuzzed beyond recognition. It is amazing that there is a collector's market for it.

Similarly, there is a style of music called noisecore that lurks at the extreme ends of hardcore, grindcore, and noise music. The central feature of this music is that it is played fast and loud and is condensed into seconds-long compositions. Napalm Death's "You Suffer" is a touchstone for this subculture, as is a 101-song EP by the band Sore Throat. Anal Cunt started off as a seminal noisecore band before branching out: their first release, out in 1989, was the *88 Song E.P.*, followed by the outlandish *5643 Song EP*, which was accomplished by the band like so:

"We went to a 16-track recording studio, and instead of using 1 track per instrument, we mixed all the drums, guitar, and vocals onto one track and recorded a whole side

17 Albert Mudrian, *Precious Metal: Decibel Presents the Stories Behind 25 Extreme Metal Masterpieces* (Da Capo Press, 2009).

18 The compilation is freely available online: archive.org/details/siro275VariousArtists-NapalmDeathYouSufferTributeCompilation

19 Sjouke Bakker, 'Dan Lilker Interview - February 2006,' *Official S.O.D. & M.O.D. Fansite*, 2006 <www.sod-mod.com/interviews/My_interview_with_DanLilker_Feb2006. htm> [accessed 7 July 2020].

of a 7" using only the first track. Then we recorded again using only the second track, then again on the third track, and so on and so on, so there is actually 16 different songs playing at once." (*5643 Song EP* liner notes)

The resulting EP ends up as one long tract of guitar feedback, growls, and scattered percussion that borders on free jazz.

One of Anal Cunt's earliest releases was a split with another cult noisecore band, Seven Minutes of Nausea. Their 1986 cassette demo, *Karen's Edge*, packed 102 songs into fourteen minutes, with a sedate narrator introducing each track by name just before the blast hits. The band would replicate their rapid-fire aesthetic on seven-inch singles like 1988's *Our Culture is Boring* (351 tracks) and 1992's *Disobediant Looser* [sic] (452 tracks). Seven Minutes contributed conceptually to the genre's obsession with brevity, inspiring international bastions in Europe, South America (Peru's Atrofia Cerebral and Brazil's Noise represent early manifestations), and Japan (where Final Exit is perhaps the most prolific noisecore act). One of the more distinctive exponents of noisecore is the Quebec band Deche-Charge, started in 1989 by Dan-Charge and Chain Saw. The band and its myriad side projects have put out hundreds of releases, many of them cassettes released with crude, hand-scrawled and Xeroxed cover art on the Gocharge Records label, run by Dan-Charge and his friend Frank Goshit. That label's aesthetic was described by Dan-Charge as "shit/noise stuff too horrible for most people to enjoy"[20] and was home to demos by bands with colorful names like Gargling Garbage, Clitoris Trafficker, Ultra Shit Crap, Doritos, and Burger Shit, the last of which is just recordings of Dan-Charge mumbling incoherently while riding his bike around town.

Eric Stemshorn and Wolfe Padaver run the Crn Vnv label out of Salt Lake City. Their fifth release is a compilation of one-second songs, pressed on a clear, lathe-cut record in a limited edition of twenty-five copies. While many artists submitted multiple tracks, the majority of the 419 tracks are credited to completely different names. According to Crn Vnv's website, a significant proportion of the tracks were anonymously submitted, so there is no way to track down their creators. Instead, we get an inscrutable list of colorful band names, ranging from concise obscenities (Anal Bagel, Johnny Applesemen) to long-winded curios (Shakespeare's Unpublished Powerpuff Girls Femslash Fanfiction, The All-New Nissan Pathfinder With 0.9% APR Financing).

This compilation was no cinch to put together, so I was surprised to learn that Stemshorn and Padaver are high school students. Padaver explains that the internet was a major influence for them, citing the abbreviated nature of social media posts as inspiration. He notes the influence of the video streaming platform Vine, which limits submissions to six seconds. "Six seconds is barely any time at all," he tells me. "It's not enough time for a knock-knock joke, or any conventional joke, really. However, these Vines are still hilarious. They display funny situations, make good jokes, and even have slight characteristics of larger works such as character development and a climax. For

---

20 sorenauseaheadache.wordpress.com/2010/01/11/deche-charge-interview/

CRN VRV RECORDS
VRV05

THE SECOND ALBUM
THE FIRST OF ITS KIND

Crn Vnv Records' *The Second Album* **compilation, a record containing second-long tracks. From author's collection.**

us, we decided to take a sixth of that time and use it in the same sense. There are certainly a lot of joke tracks on the *Second Album*, and they establish comedy in one tick of the clock. It's amazing to think that's all it takes."

Vine caught flak for catering to short attention spans, and the same criticism could be directed toward this record. The subtext to Stemshorn and Padaver's challenge to their artists—to convey something in one second—is one of efficiency. Just as grindcore compresses maximum intensity into minimum time, *The Second Album* promises to compress a full song's worth of feeling into 1,000 milliseconds.

I bought a copy of the highly limited-edition vinyl version of *The Second Album*.[21] Padaver argued that, like the short clips posted to Vine, the artist's task here was to convey something coherent in a mere second. In practice, however, the effect is limited by the brain's processing speed. Trying to discern the discrete identity of each composition, or to pinpoint a specific narrative or feeling, is impossible when the tracks are whizzing by so quickly. Inevitably, it's the more in-your-face jokes that tend to stand out. For example, there is the track "March 18th" by an artist named September 21st, which is simply a recording of a voice saying "December 2nd." In some cases, the titles and artist names are the best part—take, for example, the song "Paul Blart 2" by How's Your Meat, which is simply a chop-up of M83's "Midnight City." Elsewhere, there are brief snatches of YouTube videos, distorted samples of familiar songs, intense spurts of noise, and little snippets of pop songs, often featuring a choice vulgar lyric—like Fingers McGee's "There's a Reason They Call Me Fingers McGee," wherein the words "fuckin' shit" are crooned over melancholy piano notes. Like a scroll through 4chan, through which Stemshorn and Padaver solicited contributions, you get brief essences of each moment, inside joke after inside joke, with minimal foothold.

Interestingly, they were not the first ones to come up with the idea of a crowd-sourced compilation of second-long compositions. In the late 2000s, Eugene, Oregon's Obscurica Records[22] attempted a compilation of second-long songs, which was going to be called *Sloppy Seconds*. Obscurica's owner, Patrick Neve, also solicited contributions from far and wide using the internet, aiming to fill an entire CD-R, at 4,800 tracks overall. Submissions were sourced online, with people emailing Neve their one-second opuses; Neve would

---

21 It can be streamed online at crnvrv.bandcamp.com/album/the-second-album-the-first-of-its-kind-vrv05

22 Obscurica was a neat little label which put out a slew of noise releases between 2004 and 2007. They released albums by noise music middle- and heavyweights like Government Alpha (Japan), Knurl, Richard Ramirez, and Stimbox. They also did several compilations of local Oregon noise acts, including a compilation in which the track listing did not specify which track was composed by which artist, meaning the listener was left to guess. Two later CD-R releases, exploring this concept in more detail, featured no artist or title information whatsoever, such that the identity of the artist was completely unknown—instead, all the listener got were blocks of freeform noise and artfully crafted covers composed of old picture books and assorted bric-a-brac. Sadly, it is all out of print now.

then add them to an archive hosted on the Internet Archive. Several big names in experimental music contributed, including R. Stevie Moore, Cock ESP, and Government Alpha. Unfortunately, Neve never reached his goal. Falling short of the dream of 4,800 tracks, the project ended at nearly twenty-nine minutes of single-second submissions. And then the label folded before the physical release could be prepared.

I tracked down Patrick Neve, now working as a systems specialist at the University of Oregon, and he told me that punk was a central influence, citing the direct music of the Minutemen and the Dead Kennedys' song "I Like Short Songs," which was dedicated to Yes keyboardist Rick Wakeman and intended to skewer progressive rock's long-windedness. Neve also acknowledges the inspiration of the Residents' *Commercial Album*, which comprised forty individual one-minute songs, each one intended to distill the essence of a pop song into the space of an advertising jingle. Finally, he credits his indoctrination into noise music, which inspired him to start up Obscurica, named in homage to noise music's willful obscurity.

Sloppy Seconds was slated to be the crowning achievement of Neve's career releasing noise records. After putting out nearly fifty releases on Obscurica, he was ready to close up shop, but there was one project he had been pondering for a while. "I wanted to see what the logical extension of compositional efficiency would be if I collected pieces in their smallest practical format," Neve explained to me by email. "There had been plenty of comps of tracks one minute or less in length. Amazing one-minute lock-groove LPs and all kinds of experimentation in the field of short form collections. I wanted to field submissions from everyone I could reach and collect into one massive comp, in the smallest reduction of form that was practical."

He solicited tracks on online experimental music discussion boards and reached out to a few friends and dream collaborators. "To my encouragement, submissions came flooding in." One appeal of the format was that "the investment was slight...just one second. This allowed me to get submissions from artists I normally couldn't afford to work with, or had no business approaching."

He spliced sixty individual pieces together to each CD track, since CDs can only handle ninety-nine tracks per disk. Initially, he assembled the compositions in the order they were submitted, but after finding the results somewhat jarring, he started sorting them according to their sonic characteristics.

In the end, minor logistical glitches accounted for most of Neve's labor on the project. "Though the requirement was specific, easily half of [the submissions] were something other than precisely one second in length," he explains. "Thus began my quest not only to edit these tracks into a cohesive project, but to individually trim hundreds of audio files, zoomed in to the 1:1 level, to fit exactly to 44,100 samples."

The work was exhausting, and the project's central ambition was blinding. "My original intent was to extend the project until A) submissions fell off, or B) the 80-minute theoretical limit of a CD-R had been met," he recounts. But life got in the way. "The label was no longer the most important thing in my life, and neither was this most labor-intensive project to date. The number of submissions were overtaking

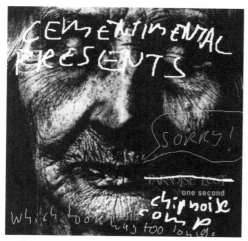

The *Cementimental presents 1 second chipnoise comp which took way too long* compilation. Image courtesy of Tim Drage a.k.a. Cementimental.

my inbox faster than I could process them, I wasn't filling web orders of the other 50 CD's efficiently enough, job and family life were changing, and I needed to pull the plug." Feeling as though his label had served its purpose, he decided to publish it on archive.org for anybody to enjoy.

Listening to what exists of the *Sloppy Seconds* project, it is obvious that a major goal was to experiment with the unpredictable effect of tightly queueing so many sonically diverse tracks. In one passage, grindcore snippets, piercing digital bleeps, decontextualized speech, lo-fi guitar fuzz, synthesized beats, a pornographic moan, and noise of various timbres all float by in an unyielding procession. The ideas come and go so quickly that the listener experiences them but cannot *process* them—it's almost as if each second-long bit remains on the edge of perception, heard but not listened to.

These days, Neve is rather ambivalent about the central detail of *Sloppy Seconds*. "Honestly if I had it to do it over again, I would have chosen a sample length other than one second. There's nothing magical to me about a mechanical by-product of medieval clock construction, creating a 1/60th minute structure as a means of turning gears in a cuckoo clock. I could have calculated an oscillating sample length based on moon phases of the Mesozoic, or an indeterminate pattern graph showing the rate of meteorite impacts on the earth's surface around the time of the planet's first microbial activity."

Tim Drage, who has been creating noise, chiptune, and chipnoise music as Cementimental since 2000, was responsible for coordinating another one-second-song compilation, although at only 259 songs, it was significantly less ambitious than *Sloppy Seconds*. The collection, *Cementimental presents 1 second chipnoise comp which took way too long*, was released digitally in 2011 through Bandcamp. He solicited submissions via the 8bitcollective message board, a forum for chiptune enthusiasts that's since gone down in flames.[23]

Drage identifies the song "Fingertips" by They Might Be Giants as the reason he got into short songs. It is a goofy suite of twenty-one songs squeezed into four and a half minutes, the band's idea being "to write a bunch of choruses and nothing else."[24] Armed with an enthusiasm for brevity, Drage and his band, Gymnastic Decomposition, invented

---

23 'The 8bc Scandal: Hex, Shrugs, and BleepBloop | CHIPFLIP,' *CHIPFLIP*, 2010 <chipflip.wordpress.com/2010/01/18/the-8bc-scandal-hex-shrugs-and-bleepbloop/> [accessed 7 July 2020].
24 Bill DeMain, *In Their Own Words: Songwriters Talk about the Creative Process* (Greenwood Publishing Group, 2004). (As cited by: tmbw.net/wiki/Fingertips)

**Gymnastic Decomposition's *Egg is Magnetic* three-inch CD-R.
Image courtesy of Tim Drage a.k.a. Cementimental.**

two subgenres as jokes, "happy grindcore," described as "either a notional combination of happy hardcore or just incongruously combining positive/fun/'nice' subject matter with the extremity of grindcore," and "haikore," which was grindcore "in haiku form."

"Our arbitrary rule for Gymnastic Decomposition was that songs should be under a minute in duration," Drage explains. "But most were just a few seconds long. When we put together our three-inch CD-R album *The Egg is Magnetic*, I actually had to extend some tracks once I discovered that the minimum length track possible to burn on a CD is four seconds. We played one gig with actual songs as opposed to pure improvisation and made several recordings."

Gymnastic Decomposition's three releases were all put out on tiny formats—a business card CD-R, a mini video CD-R, and the three-inch *Egg is Magnetic* CD-R.[25] After networking with several other short-music fanatics, Drage eventually hatched the idea of a one-second compilation.

He took initial inspiration from a call for submissions to a proposed compilation of one-minute chiptune tracks. "I was surprised by how many people working in this limitation-centric and 'cute' genre were so aghast at the idea of recording such an absurdly short song," Drage recalls. "It seemed to me that the minimal nature of 8-bit music and the use in video games soundtracks of very short loops and abrupt noisy sound effects perfectly lent itself to creating short songs using the same technology, and that making something interesting to fill a whole minute shouldn't be hard at all. Finding this amusing in the light of how much ridiculously short music I knew of, and had made, by that point, I responded that one minute was way too long, and semi-trollishly created a spinoff thread requesting chipnoise tracks of one second duration. This was also part of my interest in at the time in the crossover between chiptune and harsh noise, and a desire to combine these sounds and aesthetics and increase communication between the two scenes."

25 Tim Drage, 'Gymnastic Decomposition Releases - CD, VCD - Happy Grindcore, Haikore, Noise, Very Short Songs,' Cementimental <www.cementimental.com/gymnasticdecomposition/releases.html> [accessed 7 July 2020].

The main problem Drage faced, like Neve, was contributors' refusal to conform to the compilation guidelines. The chiptune artists tended to submit tracks that were not exactly a second long, while the noise artists tended to contribute pieces that weren't sufficiently 8-bit. "I allowed most submissions even if they went a little over length, mainly because it seemed much less effort than trying to explain to people how long a second was, or editing or rejecting tracks myself."

One contributor, a mail-artist who went by the name Rain Rien, submitted a silent YouTube video of a whale surfacing. Drage included it in the compilation as a text file containing the one-second video's URL. "Out of respect for our years of correspondence, and because it would further confuse people downloading the compilation," he adds.

The project went live in February 2011; both Drage and listeners saw it as a big success. One forum dweller, who originally assured Drage that the project "just will not work," eventually conceded, "I eat every word I said about this not being capable of working. So so so awesome."

The entire thing is up on YouTube in a video that laboriously lists each song as it plays. In some ways, it's similar to *Sloppy Seconds*, but because the artists are focused on chip music, it feels somewhat more cohesive. Whereas Neve's compilation seemed to exist on the level of perception but outside the realm of cognition, several moments on this compilation can be mentally processed.

There is a historical precedent to these short-song compilations. Slap-A-Ham Records, a record label run by Chris Dodge, put out several compilations that collected droves of miniature tracks. Dodge was the bassist and vocalist for a Bay Area band called Spazz, and Slap-A-Ham was a key player in the scene known as powerviolence: an ultra-fast and often structurally complex sub-breed of hardcore punk.

In 1991, Dodge decided it was time for Slap-A-Ham's first compilation, and he assigned it the marvelous title, *Bllleeeeaaauuurrrrgghhh! - The Record*. Pooling the efforts of a bunch of bands, this record squished sixty-four tracks onto one seven-inch. The next year, Dodge put out *Son of Bllleeeeaaauuurrrrgghhh!*, which advertises "52 bands! 69 songs!," again all in the space of one seven-inch. Finally, in 1998 Dodge capped off the series with *Bllleeeeaaauuurrrrgghhh! - A Music War*, the title a reference to the iconic 1982 post-punk video compilation *Urgh! A Music War*. This rendition of *Bllleeeeaaauuurrrrgghhh!* upped the ante further, housing a series-topping eighty-four tracks by a litany of grindcore artists on one single.

The second in the series is an exemplary choice: seconds-long spurts of guitar, bass, and drums, often sounding like they've been recorded on a broken tape player with a broken mic, expend their energy and then disappear. Each track occupies a different spot on the continuum between hardcore and extreme metal, and political allegiances can be gleaned in the names of some bands (Slave State, Capitalist Casualties, Disrupt, Dicktator), though for others, the joy is more visceral (Arse Destroyer, Putrid Offal, Cum Dumpster).[26]

26 *Son of Bllleeeeaaauuurrrrgghhh!* also features a track each from the seminal sludge-metal act Melvins and, arguably the most important powerviolence band of all time, Man is the Bastard.

The *Bllleeeeaaauuurrrrgghhh!* comps have attracted a dedicated following that continues today. They have even attracted bootleggers—a Mexican grind label whimsically called Goatsucker Records collected all three singles and compiled them as an unofficial CD release, which has seen three separate releases, none of which were sanctioned by Chris Dodge.

The tradition of short-song compilations established by *Bllleeeeaaauuurrrrgghhh!* has persisted, and there are several examples to be found in the grindcore, powerviolence, and extreme metal/punk canons.[27] A Polish noise label named Keep it Frozen (a.k.a. kifrecording) put out two compilations of ten-second songs, one featuring fifty-eight contributions and the next featuring seventy.[28] The Death Tones netlabel, based in Kuala Lumpur, Malaysia, put out three ten-second compilations and an eight-second compilation, featuring a variety of noise and grind sounds. Those four releases each contain between fifty-four and one hundred bands, a monumental feat of collation![29] And a label called Ratskin Records put out (*Triskaidekaphobia*), a compilation of thirteen-second songs that features 215 different contributors![30]

In 2006, Legion Sudan, a Danish label run by Eli Gudnason, entered the fray by proposing the *coup de grâce* of short-song compilations. With a working title of "*the reaction speed of a human at the blink of an eye twice the cycle time for the lowest audible tone,*" the record was to feature sixty minutes' worth of 100-millisecond songs, totaling 36,000 individual tracks.[31] When I caught up with him years later, Gudnason revealed that the project was a joke, a parody of the fact that two labels at the time were soliciting recordings for one-second compilations—neither of which saw the light of day.

In my quest for short music, I eventually came across the work of an anonymous Californian who records under a litany of aliases and runs the Tsundere Violence label. His most prolific alter ego is Himeko Katagiri, named after a minor character in an anime series named *Pani Poni Dash*. In one interview he notes that he started making music in 2009, at which point he was "like thirteen." This might help explain the youthful exuberance that pervades his online footprint, which comprises lo-fi noise and breakcore compositions inflected heavily with anime and manga references.

Katagiri takes short music to the next level. He once put out a split release titled *Under One Second Split*, which squeezed thirty tracks into less than one second. "Majority of the tracks are inaudible," he tells me. Because his discography is a labyrinth, I asked him to pinpoint the album that fits in the most songs in the shortest amount of time. He points me to a netlabel release put out under his Ninja McTits moniker, titled *Fellatio,*

---

27 Some examples: Various Artists, *100 Bands 7"* Vol. 1 (2010, France, NYDIYSTREC); Various Artists, *Earache: World's Shortest Album* (2013, USA, Earache)—13 tracks totaling 1:27, released on 5" vinyl for Record Store Day, including "You Suffer" by Napalm Death.

28 Details from Discogs.

29 '10 Seconds Compilation Vol. 2 (2014) | DEATH TONES RECORDS,' Bandcamp, 2014 <deathtonesrecords.bandcamp.com/album/10-seconds-compilation-vol-2-2014> [accessed 7 July 2020].

30 'V/A : (TRISKAIDEKAPHOBIA) 13,000 MilliSeconds. .', Ratskin Records <www.ratskin.org/thirteenseconds.html> [accessed 7 July 2020].

31 This was previously documented on the industrial.org website at industrial.org/news.php?t=27576

You Say; the title is a line from a manga book, which is reproduced on the EP's cover. It contains eighty-three tracks in the space of two seconds!

Katagiri describes his technique, which involves using sound production software to separate larger sound files into microscopic bits. "The first album I did of these was actually just really, really tiny samples of a Venetian Snares song," he tells me. "But all of the ones since then have been original. I record and make a small bit of noise; what I do exactly is different every time. I then open it up in Audacity to cut and export tracks out of it. Audacity is great for this, as it lets you cut, edit, and export insanely tiny clips of audio very easily. The inaudible ones are weird; they actually are sound, but they're so short you can't hear them. I'm not sure what's happening there exactly; is it some new discovery that humans can't hear sounds that short? Did it enter some weird frequency? Or is it just an issue with the computer? Whatever it is, when they're incredibly short, they do run the chance of becoming 'silent.'"

For Katagiri, one imperative is to take things to their conceptual extreme. "Lots of people make long songs, and lots of people think that the 'one second' song that every grindcore band does a cover of is the shortest song ever," Katagiri explains by email. "But no, things get sooooo much shorter. I've made songs so short that you can't even hear them."

He sees his work not just as the apotheosis of short music but also as an exploration of the concept of musical minimalism. "Instead of making a 20-minute lowercase track that's barely audible, why not take it in the other direction and make it so short that it either can't be heard or is so short it becomes minimal by default—so that there's no room for any real sound to happen? Micro-tracks are basically minimalism with a grindcore mentality, then released as experimental."

And he will freely admit that bragging rights are involved. He stakes his claim on "micro-tracks" as its very own genre, although I suspect he's being somewhat satirical. "[Micro-tracks] very much can be a new genre entirely on their own," he says. "So, yeah, claiming that now, Micro-track is a genre of songs that are 0:00 in length."

A two-second digital release is an impressive conceptual achievement, but it takes far more commitment to extend this approach to physical media. Even so, at least three separate sources have put out cassettes that last mere seconds.

Michael Ridge, who records experimental music under the moniker Zebra Mu and runs a record label called Quagga Curious Sounds, released a one-second tape loop in 2015. Unlike commercially available tapes, it is designed to play on a loop indefinitely until you hit stop. The tape, titled *One Second / One Heartbeat*, came out on NONE Records, which is quaintly described as "an anti-label for static and ephemeral anti-releases by musicians and artists." The sole audio is one of Michael's heartbeats, and when it loops, it reproduces the sound of a heart beating continuously. In a sense, it could be argued that it is indefinitely long.

EXTREME MUSIC

Ridge lives in Norwich, England, with his wife and several pets, and works at the local museum. He explained that *One Second / One Heartbeat* was inspired by the Dada and Fluxus movements, in particular Yoko Ono's *Snow Falling at Dawn*, a loop of reel-to-reel tape that captured the sound of, yes, snow falling at dawn.[32] Released in 1965, Ono sold it at twenty-five cents per inch of tape.

In order to record *One Second / One Heartbeat*, Ridge attached a sensitive contact microphone to his chest. "Before recording, I ran on the spot in my studio for about five minutes to get my heart rate up," he explains. But that was the easy part. "I managed to capture about 30 seconds

Packaging for Needle Factory's *One Second Tape*, featuring only one second of audio.

directly to cassette—very lo-fi, but it worked quite well. The magnetic tape was then carefully removed from the shell and meticulously spliced into one-second segments, ensuring each one contained a heartbeat. Creating each loop was incredibly fiddly and time-consuming but definitely worth the effort."

Freda Wallace, a Manchester artist who builds custom synth modules and records abstract music using sewing machines, self-released her cassette under the pseudonym Needle Factory.[33] She made ten copies, selling them at £25 per copy—which adds up to a steep 2.5 pence per millisecond!

"The main concept behind this was to do with subverting the idea of a money value for music," she says. "I had talked to musicians who complained about the fact they got almost nothing for a 40-minute album via digital download sales and then bemoaned the days of selling CDs at £10 each. It struck me that the problem wasn't the music...only the format. If you can create a desirable object to carry the idea and make it original, it could still sell."

"I made the tapes from a batch of ten blanks," she says. "I recorded a few minutes of random noises on to one, then cut that up. After taking the unneeded tape from the cassettes, I re-spooled them all with the 20-centimeter pieces. I edited each tape and subtracted any unwanted noise with the recording head to get each as close to one second as possible. They were not looped. The tape just plays for one second and then stops. It's quite amusing."

She adds, "I think it's important to point out that a lot of my work has a knowingly satirical edge."

In 1986, a Japanese punk band named Nira Kodomo released a tape called *Global Domination*. It contained only a one-second track on each side. Each copy was created by taking a regular-length cassette and then manually cutting out almost all the magnetic tape.

---

32 'Yoko Ono | Snow Falling at Dawn,' *Artists' Books and Multiples*, 2013 <artistsbooksandmultiples.blogspot.com/2013/05/yoko-ono-snow-falling-at-dawn.html> [accessed 7 July 2020]. Also referenced in: Yoko Ono, *Grapefruit: A Book of Instructions and Drawings by Yoko Ono* (Simon and Schuster, 2000).

33 'Info,' Needle Factory <www.needlefactory.info/Bio> [accessed 7 July 2020].

Before *Global Domination* came out, the band had yet to release a demo, and their growing local fan base was getting antsy. So Nira Kodomo launched a promotion at a record store, where folks could submit their names for an opportunity to buy one of ten copies of their very first release. They promised that the lottery winners could buy their copy for a mere one yen—equal to less than a penny. Though that may have still seemed too expensive for a two-second long tape, the cost-benefit ratio has improved over time, since a surviving copy is now quite the collector's item. Following *Global Domination*, the band did eventually release a real demo the next year. Snippets of that tape can now be enjoyed on YouTube, revealing a raucous, lo-fi document of the late-eighties Japanese punk scene.

But doctored tapes are not the only releases that stand alone as ultra-brief audio documents. Some short albums are short because their formats have a limited capacity, e.g., the small scene of individuals who put out music on floppy disk. These producers ironically developed their preferred format long after the crest of the floppy heyday. In fact, according to data on Discogs, there were only fifty-nine floppy disk releases during the floppy disk salad days of the 1990s, the vast majority of which were simply electronic press kits for major label releases by Michael Jackson, Radiohead, and other big acts. In the first decade of the 2000s, 161 floppies were released, whereas the 2010s saw no fewer than 991 released! Many of these releases, apart from those containing music recorded at a very low bitrate, offer less than a minute of audio.

There has even been a floppy disk compilation. In 2011, the previously mentioned Toxic Industries, an Italian noise label run by Fabrizio De Bon, put out *Floppylation 1.0*.[34] Much like the mini-song compilations discussed earlier, De Bon limited submissions to one second of sound. He collected these over four months and then sequenced them into one fifty-second collage, pooling fifty artists' best efforts. Each of its seventy-seven copies comes in a square white envelope, with a shred of a destroyed CD glued to the front, representing the victory of obsolete technology over somewhat less obsolete technology.

On November 20, 1971, Sly and the Family Stone put out their fifth studio album, *There's a Riot Goin' On*. After establishing a reputation for upbeat R&B music and helping pioneer the hybrid genre of psychedelic soul, leader Sly Stone alienated audiences with a darker, political album that was largely his solo work. Though it divided critics and fans at the time, *Riot* is today recognized as a seminal work that expanded the boundaries of R&B.

At the end of the A-side, the album's title track is listed, with a duration reported as "0:00." Some figured it was a tongue-in-cheek nod toward those who falsely blamed Stone for inciting a riot in Chicago. But it was not until 1997 that Stone himself weighed in, explaining to writer Jonathan Dakss why he included this zero-minute, zero-second non-song on his band's classic album. "I did it because I felt there should be no riots," he said.[35]

---

34 *Floppylation 1.0* is long out of print but can be found on YouTube. Unsurprisingly, there are many segments of harsh noise, but interspersed are various disparate textures, from dissonant glitch acrobatics to fuzzy snatches of drone.

35 Jonathan Dakss, 'My Weekend with Sly Stone,' Sly and the Family Stone, 1997 <web.archive.org/web/20001118011300/http://www.slyfamstone.com/weekend.html> [accessed 7 July 2020].

III.1 LATHE-CUT

For years, New Zealand's Peter King worked as a session drummer for TV New Zealand, providing the rhythm section for advertising jingles.[1] While exploring the dusty corners of the station's studio one day, he discovered some old equipment that he initially mistook for sewing machines. Looking closer, he determined they were record-cutting machines, used in the recording studio to convert live performances to vinyl records in real time. King bought these machines and repaired them, but the biggest challenge was to find an ideal material for the records themselves. After multiple failed experiments, he discovered a transparent polycarbon plastic that performed optimally, and started offering his record-cutting services to independent bands and record labels.

Because each record must be etched in real time, it is a slow process, so he stuck to editions of under one hundred copies, perfect for small bands looking to release something unique on a budget. Artists would mail in their master tapes, then wait up to a year before their custom job got back to them. For many, the wait was worth it, given that they could see their music released on record without breaking the bank, often in interesting shapes and sizes. He even figured out how to create picture discs.

For the most part, Peter King's records were small-scale affairs done for independent artists and labels. In one notable exception to this rule, he was commissioned by the Beastie Boys' label to press 1,500 copies of a single—a monumental task, given that each disc needed to be etched in real time. According to the Peter King website, "surprise partial payment for this came in the form of a mustard-yellow Ford Mustang that arrived at the Port of Timaru, addressed to P. King."

In 2001, King moved out to Mount Somers, a small town in Canterbury, New Zealand—population 2,307—where he has lived ever since. He has also expanded his operation to keep up with demand, building several new lathes from scratch using washing machine motors. His web presence, including a website that offers current rates and submission information, is run by a friend, and King himself will only discuss jobs by phone or snail mail.

The principle behind lathe-cutting records is relatively simple. As outlined by the owners of Smalltown America, a recording studio, record label, and custom lathe-cutting company[2]:

1. *Buy bulk, transparent polycarbonate sheeting (essentially clear plastic).*
2. *Cut that sheeting into circular discs.*
3. *Lubricate the discs using a lubricant spray (they recommend Turtle Wax Matte-Finish Cockpit Cleaner, a product intended to be used on vinyl and plastic car interiors to prevent fading and cracking).*

---

1 'Peter King Lathe Cut Records' <peterkinglathecutrecords.co.nz/history.htm> [accessed 4 January 2021].
2 Anton Spice, 'A Beginner's Guide to Lathe Cutting Your Own Records,' The Vinyl Factory, 2016 <thevinylfactory.com/features/a-beginners-guide-to-lathe-cutting-your-own-records/> [accessed 4 January 2021].

4. Put the disc into a machine designed for cutting records. (Smalltown salvaged a couple of Atom A-101 machines from a Tokyo karaoke bar that was shuttering—presumably the machines were there so people could record themselves performing. These machines came built into a briefcase and were part of a wave of portable record-cutting machines popular in Japan in the seventies.[3])

5. Fit the record-cutting machine with a strong needle. These come in a variety of shapes and include expensive crystal and even sapphire needles.

6. Master the audio, usually by means of digital audio software.

7. Channel the audio into the record-cutting machine. The machine will rotate the record as the needle etches the surface and the audio will be transformed into vibrations, which will be carried through the needle and etched into the record, creating grooves.

8. Play it back! But be mindful that, compared to commercially pressed records, the grooves are much shallower. As a result, it can be hard to find the run-in groove, the needle can skitter across the record if the tone arm isn't heavy enough, and you may need to increase the volume to get good audio.

Lathe-cutting a record is, mechanically, an elegant and simple process. The real challenge is taking these old machines and getting them into functional order. This often requires mechanical knowledge and creative solutions are often required to fix defunct parts. Additionally, to obtain a quality final product, one must find a way to adapt old equipment to accept digital input.

In recent years, several newcomers have invested in equipment and figured out how to produce their own lathe-cut records. Many have followed in King's footsteps, selling their services to small bands and record labels. There are four for-hire lathe cutters in Tucson, Arizona, alone!

There is even a message board, "The Secret Society of Lathe Trolls," where lathe cutters share tips and tricks, offer custom jobs, sell technical equipment, and root out scammers. One vendor from Poland has been selling a custom-built lathe-cutting apparatus to gullible buyers, even falsifying customer reviews to generate credibility. After one forum member splurged on the machine, they received a broken, nonfunctional apparatus in the mail, only recouping some of his money by launching a PayPal dispute. Another German scammer stole a bunch of equipment from a French pressing plant he used to work for, sold some of it, then collected thousands of dollars in orders for more equipment before supposedly fleeing the country for the Philippines with his wife and child.

The man to know when it comes to innovative lathe-cutting is Michael Dixon, who has operated the cult label People in a Position to Know (a.k.a. PIAPTK) since 2006, and who considers many of his records "vinyl art." He released a whole series of records that were cut into plastic picnic plates; in 2016, he estimated that he has cut at least 2000 of them.[4] "They sound surprisingly good considering the circumstances of

3 'Japanese Portable Lathes of the 1970s - Page 2,' The Secret Society of Lathe Trolls, 2013 <www.lathetrolls.com/viewtopic.php?f=8&t=4434&start=20> [accessed 4 January 2021].

4 Aaron Cooper, 'The Art Of Vinyl: Interview—Michael Dixon,' 50THIRDAND3RD, 2016 <www.50thirdand3rd.com/art-vinyl-interview-michael-dixon/> [accessed 5 January 2021].

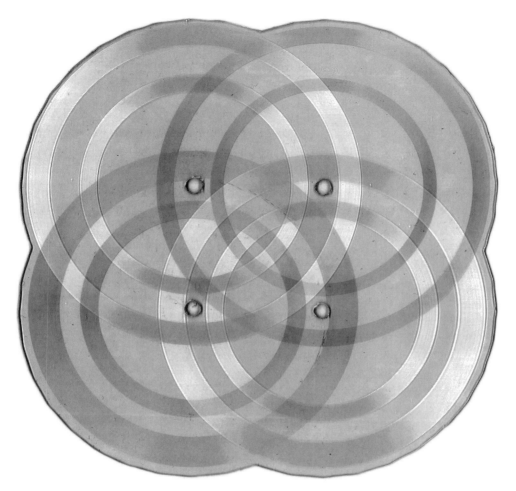

One of PIAPTK's Eulerian discs. Image courtesy of Michael Dixon.

their birth," he observed. He has also done a series of hybrid CD-R records, which have CD-R data on one side and record grooves etched on the other.

For Dixon, the appeal of these oddball records is that they allow him to contribute something creative to a release, instead of just being the financial backer. "I want to make impractical things that make the physical object as important as the music," he explains.[5] "The music is obviously very important, but that is the creation of the band or songwriter. With my labels, I want to be as much a collaborator as a curator. I don't want to just be the money behind the release; I want to put some of my own personality and creativity into it."

His ingenuity is also motivated by a familiar competitiveness that seeps into extreme and conceptual music. "There are plenty of other labels doing cool and innovative things," he says. "There is somewhat of an arms race for the strangest record happening

5 Cooper.

III.1 EXTREME RECORDS: LATHE-CUT

now. And each time something new comes out that I haven't seen, it pushes me to try to one-up them."

One of Dixon's most inventive concepts was a series of releases known as "Eulerian discs," records with multiple holes and multiple sets of concentric grooves. Listeners can place the record on their turntable at one of any of the holes. Occasionally, the circular grooves intercept, and there is an audible sound.

One was with the Flaming Lips, featuring three holes. Mike Watt's *Watt: On Bass* has two intersecting circles. SpaceFace's *Up in the Clouds* features three circles and is cut into the shape of a cloud. The University of Arizona's Planetary Sciences Department even commissioned a series of them for their annual art show, each limited to twelve copies.

The pièce de résistance so far, however, is Dimitri Manos' *American Monoxide*, a five-holed Venn diagram of a record composed of a sixteen-minute sound collage, which "chirps" every time the grooves cross. In a marvel of planning, Dimitri designed the audio such that the chirp is strategically incorporated into each piece.

Dimitri Manos' disc can be yours for $35 USD, plus shipping. In a 2017 interview, Dixon explains that several of PIAPTK's releases, originally produced in sub-100 editions, command exorbitant prices on the secondary market.[6] PIAPTK's clear, triangular lathe single of "lost tracks" from nineties indie rock act Poster Children has sold for over a hundred dollars. "I released the Flaming Lips *Good Vibrations* Eulerian Circle disc at Psych Fest in Austin, and literally an hour later, one popped up on eBay for $500—somebody posted it from the festival on their phone minutes after they bought it," Dixon explains. "The muddy field that the festival was thrown in was the background of the photo!"

A full discography of Peter King discs does not exist, although there is a Facebook group where enthusiasts mingle and share acquisitions. Some collectors have accumulated small hoards of these discs, many of which were assembled by a University of Canterbury lecturer named Luke Wood for a recent exhibition, *A Short Run: A Selection of New Zealand Lathe-Cut Records*.[7] But many of these limited-run records are now lost to the annals of time, and a comprehensive list will likely remain elusive. The main website dedicated to Peter King does include a very partial discography, including a sub-list of "Mystery Lathes."[8] The listing for one record includes no artist or title, but instead merely "blue crossing lines on black label/dense blue specks on black."

---

6 'Interview: People in A Position To Know Records,' New Commute, 2017 <www.newcommute.net/feed/2017/3/22/interview-people-in-a-position-to-know-records> [accessed 5 January 2021].

7 'A Short Run: A Selection of New Zealand Lathe-Cut Records, Curated by Luke Wood,' The Dowse Art Museum, 2020 <dowse.org.nz/exhibitions/detail/a-short-run> [accessed 5 January 2021].

8 'Lathe Cut Record Discography,' Peter King Lathe Cut Records <peterkinglathecutrecords.co.nz/mystery.htm> [accessed 5 January 2021].

III.2 LARGE

In 2014, in a massive waste of money and materials, the company that owns Madison Square Garden installed a 4,884-inch record atop an arena in Inglewood, California.[9] The size of four and a half football fields, it was a massive replica of the Eagles' *Hotel California* LP, and actually rotated at a linear velocity of seventeen miles per hour. So big it could be seen by those on airplanes arriving at LAX, it was used to help promote a series of six concerts by the band.

It was almost the biggest record ever created, but the development company could not figure out how to make a massive stylus and tone arm to play it, so it remains a record in theory only. But it wouldn't have been the only record to exceed the diameter of the standard 12-inch LP.

In the recording industry's early days, records did not come in standard sizes, nor did they play at standard speeds. As scores of companies jockeyed for market space in a growing market, each one manufactured and distributed its own gramophone player. Most proprietary devices were calibrated to play only their own records, designed to fit only records of a specific diameter and to play at one particular speed. As a result, before the now standard 7, 10, and 12 inches, there were some interesting variations which emerged. Some were a lot larger than today's LPs.

If you comb through enough antique shops and estate sales, you may come across records that are a whopping sixteen inches in diameter, which were quite common at one point. Dr. Walter J. Beaupre, a music historian who used to work at a local broadcasting station that utilized these large discs, provides an informative history in an article titled "Music Electrically Transcribed!"[10] He explains that these oversized records were initially produced for early "talkie" films, the first movies to follow the silent era. At a movie theater, they would be played simultaneously with a film to create a coordinated audiovisual experience. Eventually, film studios figured out how to include audio on the film reels themselves, and these large records were instead used to deliver prerecorded content to radio networks. These premade radio discs were referred to as electrical transcriptions. According to Beaupre, by 1935, there were four transcription companies, each with their own retinue of radio shows and musical selections; radio stations could lease the libraries for periods of time. Originally, acetate and vinyl records were both used, but vinyl eventually became the industry standard. There were apparently even a few 17-inch electrical transcription discs, although the 16-inchers were far more common. Furthermore, despite 78 RPM being the typical speed for consumer records, the 16-inch discs were played at 33 RPM to maximize their duration. Even so, each record could only manage around fifteen minutes per side.

Electrical transcriptions remained the industry standard for about a decade and a half, with the 16-inch variety most commonly used for syndicated and government-

9 Ben Kaye, 'The Eagles' "Hotel California" Turned into the World's Largest Vinyl Record,' Consequence of Sound, 2014 <consequenceofsound.net/2014/01/the-eagles-hotel-california-turned-into-the-worlds-largest-vinyl-record-2/> [accessed 5 January 2021].
10 Walter J. Beaupre, 'Music Electrically Transcribed!', The Vintage Radio Place <www.otrsite.com/articles/artwb006.html> [accessed 5 January 2021].

issued programs, including military recruitment shows. However, two developments ushered in the demise of electrical transcription records in the late 1940s. For one, record stores and labels started sending their new music records to radio stations to play on air, providing an alternative source of content for radio program directors. More importantly, reel-to-reel tape recorders began to appear at stations. As a result, the typical radio format evolved into a mix of commercially available singles and tape-recorded content.

Believe it or not, there are a few rare records that extend beyond the 17-inch barrier. Neophone, a short-lived British record company, is credited with developing the first long-playing records way back in 1904.[11] The company was founded by a German Inventor, Dr. William Michaelis, who created a supposedly indestructible record made of pristine white plastic with a backing of compressed cardboard and, according to rumor, straw. These durable records were a gargantuan twenty inches in diameter!

According to lore, Dr. Michaelis would demonstrate the indestructibility of his records by throwing one off a four-story building, and then having his assistant run down, pick it up, and bring it back to be played, good as new. Yet despite the novelty and long running length, these discs did not sell well. After a rapid expansion into America, Canada, France, Belgium, Germany, Australia, and Japan, Neophone was acquired by the General Phonograph Corporation after only four years, and in 1908, that company closed.

According to Joe Batten,[12] a concert accompanist and recording manager for Columbia, one of the factors involved in Neophone's decline was that the records, sitting in shop windows, would curl up in the sun and "[assume] pathetic surrealistic shapes." The outcome was that many recordings—of "military bands, banjo soloists, concertina players, and singers, both comic and serious"—were lost to the annals of time. Today, Neophone's giant white records seldom turn up, although some collectors have amassed small quantities, and there are even YouTube videos of people playing their records on Neophone's proprietary oversized gramophones.

In 1906, a French record company, Pathé, seized on Neophone's idea. In their early days, they put out a variety of discs of varying sizes, intended to be played at speeds from 60 RPM to a blistering 120 RPM. Like Neophone, they had a series of 20-inch records. These discs played from the inside out; because of their speed, the tone-arm was prone to go flying when the record ended![13] Interestingly, because these records play at such high speeds, and because their grooves are especially wide, each record itself could only fit three minutes of audio on it. Even more remarkable, a Pathé 20-inch disc weighed approximately five and a half pounds—on a two-sided record, that is nearly a pound per minute![14] Like Neophone's 20-inch discs, Pathé's big records were a failure and were discontinued soon after.

11 'Neophone 20 Inch Disc,' ROMFI --- World Repository of Manufactured Items <web.archive.org/web/20200806170007/http://www.romfi.com/news.cfm?CFID=226341&CFTOKEN=866> [accessed 5 January 2021].

12 Adrian Hindle-Briscall, 'Neophone,' The 78rpm Record Home Page <78rpmrecord.com/neophone.htm> [accessed 5 January 2021].

13 '20 Inch Pathé Record,' The Talking Machine Forum, 2012 <forum.talkingmachine.info/viewtopic.php?f=3&t=11317&sid=66eaf78eaeae885401f9e3234c0414f7&start=10> [accessed 5 January 2021].

14 'Really Old Records,' Facebook, 2013 <www.facebook.com/permalink.php?story_fbid=658766594144429&id=113492545338506> [accessed 5 January 2021].

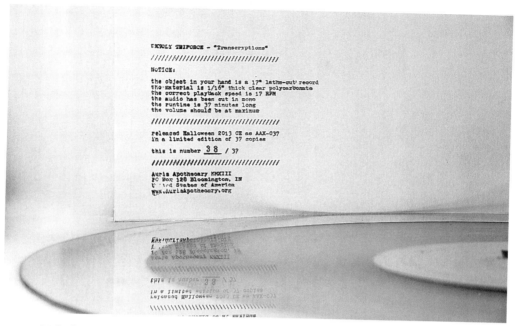

Unholy Triforce's 17" *Transcryptions*. Image courtesy of Auris Apothecary.

Since those early days of warring gramophone companies and fly-by-night entrepreneurs, there has been minimal experimentation in the realm of oversized records. After all, record players capable of playing these large records have not been manufactured for decades, meaning any record larger than twelve inches is functionally an anti-record.

With that said, a couple of intrepid experimenters have managed to defy these obstacles. The White Stripes' Jack White somehow got a pressing plant, United Pressing, to produce a series of thirteen-inch records to celebrate the 2010 South by Southwest music festival in Austin, Texas. The idea behind the oversized record was that "everything is bigger in Texas," so they also pressed up some eight-inch records to serve as oversized 45s. The 13-inch LPs were special editions of White Stripes and Raconteurs albums and were produced in limited quantities, so they today command correspondingly oversized prices.

Then there is the Bloomington, Indiana, label Auris Apothecary, whose conceptual work will turn up over and over in this book. Devoted to "the quest to bring physical interactivity to the listening experience," the label, run primarily by the enigmatic Dante Augustus Scarlatti, creates releases that require great effort to play.[15] In 2013, they pulled off a single-sided, 17-inch lathe-cut record that plays at 16 2/3 RPM. The album, limited to a mere thirty-seven copies, is named *Transcryptions*, a tribute to the electrical transcription records of yore.

Scarlatti filled me in on some of his record's finer details. "The name *Transcryptions* is a made-up word that alludes to the fact that a lot of the voices and broadcasts

---

15 'Auris Apothecary ::: Info,' Auris Apothecary <www.aurisapothecary.org/info/> [accessed 5 January 2021].

recorded onto old transcription discs are people long dead, so the physical discs containing them are in essence an audio crypt containing waveforms of the deceased," he tells me. "Or something like that. Their crazy size, 16 inches, coupled with the fact that most people don't have a way to listen to them inspired us to make *Transcryptions*, but we also wanted to give it a twist, so we made it 17 inches just to further push the envelope of absurdity."

Placing "giant sheets of polycarbonate" on an antique lathe cutter that "that very well could have been used to cut real transcription records in the 1950s," he cut each record manually. Though the disk is seventeen inches in diameter, the grooves do not start until the 15-inch mark, and the audio itself does not start until the 13-inch point. "Meaning the disk is always one inch bigger than it's supposed to be."

III.3 SMALL

Seven inches is the smallest standard size for a vinyl record, although five-inch records, which are roughly the same diameter as a CD, are not terribly uncommon. In 1980, UK pop band Squeeze issued their single "If I Didn't Love You" on a record of this size,[16] and there are many other examples from the underground noise and punk scenes.

But there also exist records that fall below the five-inch threshold. In the late sixties, a few record companies started to put out miniature singles, limited to approximately three and a half minutes per side, under the marketing rationale that they were more portable than standard 45s. These were somewhere between three and four inches in diameter. Philco, an electronics company that got its start in the late nineteenth century by manufacturing carbon arc lamps, named their version "Hip-Pocket Records," and manufactured a shoebox-sized turntable to play them. Americom Corporation, meanwhile, made four-inch records they called PocketDiscs, which they sold out of vending machines.[17] They licensed contemporary songs from approximately twenty-eight record labels, even striking a deal with Apple Records to issue Beatles singles on their format.[18]

Ad copy from a Hip-Pocket Record sleeve demonstrates that convenience was the goal: "Take them to parties or to the beach or picnic . . . they are the most portable form of music... Don't let the small size fool you . . . the sound is amazingly big."[19]

The public was not impressed; production of these mini-records ended in 1969, just a couple years after they entered the market. One problem was that the amount of music contained on each side was severely restricted by the format. Secondly, to fit, the grooves could only be rendered in mono. Most importantly, however, was a consideration that whizzed by Philco and Americom: Do people care about being able to bring their records to the beach?

But that was not the end. In no time at all, the tiny record concept took on another, even smaller form. In 1970, Ohio Art, makers of the Etch-a-Sketch, introduced a new toy called the Mighty Tiny Record Player. This was a colorful plastic box containing a rotating platter, which was powered by one AA battery. On the platter the owner would place a *2.25-inch* record, and when the box was closed, the disc would rotate and a steel needle would play the grooves. There was no electronic amplification; instead, the box simply transmitted and amplified the contact sound of the needle running against the grooves. Apparently, approximately sixty different records were produced, each containing a few seconds of audio.[20] These included contrived studio musicians like Banjo Pete, Mundo and His Steel Drum Band, and The Tijuana Tigers, and even a

16 According to Discogs, to squeeze the song onto the small disc, it played at 33 RPM.

17 'PocketDisc (1967–1969),' Museum of Obsolete Media <web.archive.org/web/20200612122136/https://obsoletemedia.org/pocketdisc/> [accessed 5 January 2021].

18 Chuck Miller, 'Hip Pocket Records: Lighter Than Air,' *Goldmine*, 1 January 1999 <www.rarebeatles.com/photospg/flexiad.htm> [accessed 5 January 2021].

19 'Hip Pocket Records,' Dead Media Archive (NYU Department of Media, Culture, and Communication) <cultureandcommunication.org/deadmedia/index.php/Hip_Pocket_Records> [accessed 5 January 2021].

20 Larry Waldbillig, 'The Ohio Art Mighty Tiny Record Player,' *History's Dumpster*, 2014 <historysdumpster.blogspot.com/2014/03/the-ohio-art-mighty-tiny-record-player.html> [accessed 5 January 2021].

fake garage rock band called The Mad Men, responsible for songs called "Rock in the Afternoon" and "Pussycat Looks Up To Go-Go."

The next development in miniature records occurred in the Kingdom of Bhutan in 1972, where a new type of record was developed to sell postage stamps. The idea came from the mind of Burt Todd, an American businessman who visited Bhutan in 1951 and somehow became a trusted advisor to the Bhutanese government. When the country's request for a loan from the World Bank was denied, he was enlisted to develop a postage stamp agency for Bhutan, with the goal of creating stamps to appeal to collectors, which could then be sold to raise money for the country's infrastructure. Todd relied on gimmicks, which in their day were frowned upon by philatelists but have since then, ironically, created valued collectors' items. Among the creative products were stamps meant to be viewed with 3D glasses, stamps embossed with textures, stamps layered with gold foil, stamps printed with perfumed ink, and, most incredible of all, postage stamps that were little records, available in two sizes: 4 inches and 2.75 inches.

A set of these record-stamps was created featuring a variety of recordings, including a brief educational lecture about the country, a rendition of the Bhutanese national anthem, and a number of traditional folk songs. They were pressed onto vinyl and came in yellow, purple, white, red, and blue varieties. Although they sold out quickly, for years they were regarded with skepticism by collectors. In 1993, the listed value of a complete set was only seventeen British pounds. Since then, perhaps because curiosity extended beyond philatelists to record collectors, their value has skyrocketed. Chris May, writer for online blog *The Vinyl Factory*, explained in an interview for NPR that a complete unused set of the record stamps can now command between $400 and $600 USD!

Chris Dodge's Slap-A-Ham Records label was described in the chapter on brief songs, when we discussed the *Bllleeeeaaaauuurrrrgghhh!* series of powerviolence compilations, featuring dozens upon dozens of extremely short songs collected onto seven-inch singles. But Dodge had numerous gimmicks up his sleeve, many of them intended to lampoon the punk scene's ravenous collectors' market, which had inspired, and financed, countless novelty releases.

Around this time, Dodge had taken to teasing audiences with weird records in Slap-A-Ham ads. The first issue of *Monkeybite* zine, published in 1996, mentions a "test pressing of the Gordon Lightfoot/ Los Crudos split 1" one-sided picture disc," presumably a joke. But that same year, he put out an actual novelty record by his own band, the seminal powerviolence outfit Spazz. It was a one-inch record entitled *Funky Ass Lil' Platter*, which was assigned the catalogue number Slap-A-Ham #34 and released in an edition of fourteen copies. Because of its size, the record is unplayable and does not include any actual audio. The hole apparently doesn't even fit on a standard turntable, and legend has it that the records were toy records from a dollhouse that were repurposed and repackaged in Slap-A-Ham sleeves. Each one is approximately the size of a quarter and is dwarfed by a copious acknowledgments list that was folded multiple times and included in each sleeve. The tiny center label lists the disc's supposed songs: "Hemorrhoidal Dance of Death" and "Patches Are For Posers."

According to information accompanying an auction of *Funky Ass*, the original plan was to make fifty copies of this release, but because of the time-intensive process required to hand-craft each one, they stopped at fourteen. Given the scarce quantities, it is even more surprising that two have turned up for sale online, leading to bidding wars that capped at $204 USD and $208 USD.

Two years later, Slap-A-Ham put out a tongue-in-cheek best-of compilation for the Japanese powerviolence band Slight Slappers, this one a two-inch record that, like Spazz's disc, was also unplayable and contained no music—although it came with liner notes listing twelve tracks. *Very Best of Slight Slappers* was produced in a 666-copy edition and looks more like a record than the Spazz disc. It even includes a listening speed, 45 RPM, although the back cover fairly warns: "If you wanna break the needle, go ahead, put this on turntable!!"

The trail again goes dead for a while until the mid-2000s, when the White Stripes introduced a novelty product for their 2005–2006 tour: A Triple Inchophone, a small record player designed to play custom-made three-inch records. The turntables themselves were originally created by a Japanese electronic company, Bandai, and marketed as the "8 Ban" in Japan. Supposedly, only three thousand units of that product were made,[21] although there are several Japanese three-inch singles that were pressed to be played on the machine.[22] This includes reissues of old British and American singles, including such classics as the Drifters' "Save the Last Dance," Connie Stevens' "Sixteen Reasons" and the Monkees' "Daydream Believer."

The White Stripes' Jack White contacted Bandai about the record player, making plans to buy them, although by the time arrangements were made, only four hundred units remained, the rest having been sent to the landfill. Undeterred, the White Stripes bought them, and they quickly sold out. They also rapidly sold the handful of three-inch records they had pressed to play on it, many of them White Stripes singles, including "Fell In Love With a Girl," "Seven Nation Army," and—rarest of all—"The Denial Twist."

In 2011, a label known as Bastard Tapes got into the action. Self-described as "one person and one tape duplicator based out of Philadelphia, USA, putting out records/tapes for and by friends," Bastard Tapes put out a two-inch lathe-cut split single between +HIRS+ and Cocaine Breath. +HIRS+ is the label owner's band, an obscenely prolific grindcore duo who write songs about far-left politics and LGBT rights, often using samples. Cocaine Breath, meanwhile, is the noise project of Dylan Wells, notable for adorning his album covers with images of celebrities like Kim Kardashian and Lindsay Lohan.

Unlike the Slight Slappers record, the +HIRS+/Cocaine Breath 2" split indeed contains music and can be played if you can get your turntable arm to "bend that way." Because of space constraints, there is only room for roughly 15 seconds of audio per

---

21 'BANDAI 8 Ban Triple Inchophone Portable Record Player,' Shop Tokyo, 2013 <web.archive.org/web/20141217234211/http://shoptokyo.wordpress.com/2013/12/13/bandai-8-ban-triple-inchophone-portable-record-player/> [accessed 5 January 2021].
22 'The White Stripes Inchophone Player and Complete 3" Record Set - Auction Details,' Popsike.com, 2016 <www.popsike.com/The-White-Stripes-Inchophone-Player-and-Complete-3-Record-Set/191948970303.html> [accessed 5 January 2021].

III.3 EXTREME RECORDS: SMALL

side, enough time for one track by +HIRS+ and six by Cocaine Breath. The record itself is a clear, square record that was released in an edition of fifty and comes with colorful collage cover art.

In January 2013, the large indie label Razor & Tie issued suburban Atlanta metalcore band Norma Jean's new single, "Ahhh! Shark Bite! Ahhh!" as a novelty 3.5-inch single. Apart from Jack White's gimmickry, this is probably one of the highest-profile miniature records, clearly aimed at building up buzz for the band's *Wrongdoers* album, which came out a few months later. At thirty-two seconds total, it was not much to listen to.

The year 2013 also saw the arrival of two separate 1.5-inch records. The first one, out in August, was an unnamed record by Gorgonized Dorks, an extremely prolific grindcore act from Culver City, California. It was created by recycling old 45s: the band merely took old records, then cut a 1.5-inch circle out of the middle. This central circle was then put into a plastic slip along with some cover art. As a result, the records contained no grooves or audio, instead representing an amalgamation of contemporary art and collector bait. After the Dorks mentioned the release on their Facebook page, they had to shut down a slew of collectors begging for ordering information.[23]

Gorgonized Dorks' 1.5-inch record.

Esion's playable *For The Shit Hits the Fans* 2-inch record.
Images courtesy of Wolfe Padawer.

The second miniature release from 2013 likely holds the record for the smallest publicly available, playable record. While the Gorgonized Dorks 1.5" and the Spazz 1" contained no audio, Esion's *For the Shit Hits the Fans* contains a theoretically playable locked groove on each side. The man behind Esion, Mike "Sludgesicle" Stock, died in 2014, but his misanthropic brand of noise and grindcore lives on, both in his multitude of releases under various pseudonyms and in his prolific database of recordings purveyed by his Sludgesicle Records label and distro.

Two forty-eight-copy editions of *For the Shit Hits the Fans* were produced, one with blue labels and one with white labels, and both were released on the one-off Esion Industries label (catalog number EI-01), presumably a sub-imprint of Sludgesicle Records created

---

23 Gorgonized Dorks, 'Untitled,' Facebook, 2013 <www.facebook.com/gorgonizedXdorks/photos/a.222407067842402/505854712830968> [accessed 5 January 2021].

**Split 3-inch record by Hades Mining Co. and Colostomy Baguette?.
Image courtesy of Mortlock of Hades Mining Co.**

to frame the significance of this unique release. There isn't much information about the record online, although a Facebook post in July 2014, shortly before Mike Stock's death, suggests that only a fraction of the original pressing remained.[24]

The year 2014 saw the release of what is likely the smallest vinyl compilation ever, a six-artist comp called the *ADHD EP* that came with the third issue of a miniature zine called *Pea Brain*. Compiling a handful of obscure hardcore and grindcore acts, the disc is only two inches, featuring mere seconds of content from each band.

In 2015, two bands, Hades Mining Co. and Colostomy Baguette?, put out a split three-inch lathe record on the former band's own label, Continuum. Hades Mining Co.'s bassist, Mortlock, recalls that it was actually the members of Colostomy Baguette? who suggested the release. Mortlock specifically identifies Slap-A-Ham as an inspiration. In fact, Mortlock's old band, Tomsk 7, had a track on Slap-A-Ham's seven-inch compilation of ridiculously short songs, *Bllleeeeaaauuurrrrgghhh! - A Music War*.

Mortlock lives in his hometown, Rochester, New York, and has been performing in Hades Mining Co. since 1999. He works "a crappy day job to pay the bills and help fund band adventures," and considers HMC his focus. "It just seemed like a cool idea at the time," he says. They got the split record done at Perthectionist, a Perth, Australia-based lathe-cutting company.

"I'm pretty sure there were people who bought it because it was a three-inch record and had no interest in the bands," Mortlock surmises. "Having said that, it did move well to the established fan base, again probably due to the novelty aspect of the release."

Although most people seemed to like it, Mortlock mentions that there were a few negative reactions. One blog critic skewers the release for being unplayable on their turntable, complains about the short running time (around fifteen seconds per side),

24 Mike Stock, 'Untitled,' Facebook, 2014 <www.facebook.com/mike.sludgesicle/posts/788630244504800> [accessed 5 January 2021].

laments that "If I payed [sic] money for this I would be so mad," and concludes that "this is for true noisefreaks and lovers of all that is dumb."[25]

In September 2014, a newcomer started a thread on the "Experimenters' & Innovators'" subforum of The Secret Society of Lathe Trolls' message board, where specialists who create lathe-cut records congregate to compare notes. This commenter, graeme06, was looking to commission an 18mm record—seven-tenths of an inch!—that could be worn as a pendant but was also playable.[26] Another member named Flo offered his services, and by April 2015, it was done. A follow-up post, linking to a YouTube video showing the pendant being played on a special turntable, came in late 2016.[27] In that video, graeme06 revealed that the pendant featured a brief recording of his own heartbeat, which was given to his then-girlfriend as part of a marriage proposal. By the time the video was released, he was happily married.

25 'Death Rattle Hummer,' *Built to Blast*, 2015 <builttoblast-vii.blogspot.com/2015/09/death-rattle-hummer.html> [accessed 5 January 2021].

26 Graeme Bow, 'Looking to Commission a Very Small Record (13mm Diameter),' The Secret Society of Lathe Trolls, 2014 <www.lathetrolls.com/viewtopic.php?f=15&t=5255> [accessed 5 January 2021].

27 www.youtube.com/watch?v=XvZjT1KPse8

III.4 SHAPES

While disc-shaped records are most materially economical, this has not stopped innovative record companies from experimenting with different approaches. There is not much theory or philosophy to cover when it comes to the world of oddly shaped records. They are also relatively common, with countless examples in the realms of popular, underground, and novelty music.

As far as I can tell, the first uncommonly shaped records were done in the late 1940s. Before this, there were several companies producing record postcards, which tended to be small circular records glued onto square or rectangular cardboard. These either came with prerecorded audio or allowed the sender to record a custom message via specialized equipment. German record postcards date back as far back as 1903, but the format really took off in 1929, when the Raphael Tuck Company, a postcard producer, introduced a line of Gramophone Record Postcards to the American market.[28]

Voco's "The Ringmaster of the Circus" disc. Image courtesy of Dan Berkman of Jump Jump Music, Portland, OR.

The first truly unusual shapes came in 1948 or so, when Voco, a former greeting card service turned children's music label, put out a string of unusual records, many credited to an obscure singer named Bob Kennedy. These records were picture discs featuring colorful cartoon images of animals behaving like humans, shaped around the contours of the pictures. "Rover the Strongman" features a muscular dog lifting a dumbbell with what looks like lipstick on his cheek. "Tom Cat the Tightrope Walker" features a gussied-up kitten traipsing along a tightrope, its ear, paw, and tail protruding out from the record's circular core. "The Ringmaster of the Circus" features a rabbit holding his top hat in one hand, a whip in the other.

Following the Voco discs, the shaped records trail goes cold. I turned to a collector of shaped records named Nightcoaster, né Tim Murphy, to guide me through the next part of the story. Murphy is as expert as you can get on the topic; he maintains an exhaustive listing of all known shaped vinyl records. The earliest entry on his list is a 1971 release of Gil Mellé's score for *The Andromeda Strain*. Murphy confirms that this was the first shaped vinyl record, the Voco discs having instead been made of cardboard.

Released on Kapp Records, which folded a year later, the score for *The Andromeda Strain* was hexagonal in shape and came in a unique fold-out cover. According to an article on *Idolator*, the record was only pressed in an edition of 10,000 copies,[29]

---

28 Rainer E. Lotz, 'Phonocard and Phonopost History,' *Antique Phonograph News* (Toronto, 2016), pp. 16–20.
29 Andy Beta, 'The Oscillations And Pulses Behind "The Andromeda Strain,"' Idolator, 2007 <www.idolator.com/334101/the-oscillations-and-pulses-behind-the-andromeda-strain> [accessed 7 January 2021].

and its design was overseen by the film's director, Robert Wise, in collaboration with graphic designer Virginia Clark. The famous sculptor Joel Shapiro helped conceive its innovative cover.[30]

It is not until 1978 that another shaped disc emerges, after which a flurry of differently shaped records follows. These shapes run the gamut, but a few commonalities emerge. Records shaped like hearts are ubiquitous, although there is only one shaped like a *human heart*—specifically a 1987 version of Bon Jovi's "Edge of a Broken Heart" recorded by the British melodic metal band Briar. Square vinyl, though boring, is also commonplace. Triangles, too, tend to recur frequently, even though they are geometrically suboptimal for accommodating record grooves. Interestingly, hexagons and octagons are abundant, yet there are only a few pentagons, and only one nonagon—courtesy of the cult psych-rock band King Gizzard and the Lizard Wizard, on their 2016 LP *Nonagon Infinity*. Heptagons and decagons, meanwhile, remain elusive.

III.4.1 Places

Geography is also a recurring theme. For their 1984 single, "Warsaw in the Sun" b/w "Polish Dance," the legendary synth act Tangerine Dream pressed a special UK version in the shape of Poland, the edges extending to an 11-inch diameter at their extremes. These tracks were pulled from larger suites on the band's live *Poland* album. Meanwhile, Toto's enormous 1982 soft-pop hit "Africa" came in a special shaped version featuring a map of Africa and part of the Atlantic Ocean. It was released as a promotional single in both the U.S. and UK markets, and now sells for over thirty dollars on the collectors' market.[31] Also in the eighties, Men At Work's Outback anthem "Down Under" was pressed onto Australia-shaped wax, and Aussie synth-poppers Icehouse released the UK version of their "Crazy" single on a shaped map of the continent.[32]

In 1985, Celtic punk act the Pogues put out a limited version of their sublimely melancholy "A Pair of Brown Eyes" single, which includes band photos superimposed on a map of Ireland; in a cosmic tribute to that country's fondness for a morning cup of Barry's, copies now all appear "tea-stained" due to the manufacturing process used to press the image onto vinyl.[33] Meanwhile, thrash metal behemoths Megadeth, in 1988, pressed their surprisingly stiff cover of "Anarchy in the UK" onto vinyl contoured around a map of the United Kingdom.[34] And the Scots known as Big Country fashioned a limited-edition version of "Fields of Fire" into the shape of Scotland.

The United States also looms large in the world of shaped vinyl. For the 2015 iteration of National Record Store Day, the immensely popular Columbus band Twenty One Pilots threw three live tracks onto a seven-inch that was shaped like the state of

---

30 '20,000 Vinyl LPs 121: Gil Mellé — The Andromeda Strain (Original Electronic Soundtrack),' *The Styrous® Viewfinder*, 2017 <styrous.blogspot.com/2017/12/20000-vinyl-lps-121-gil-melle-andromeda_71.html> [accessed 7 January 2021].

31 www.popsike.com/TOTO-AfricaRosannaNEW-1982-Africa-Shaped-Pic-Disc-Columbia-8C838685/230774609717.html

32 'Icehouse - Crazy / Completely Gone 7 Inch Picture Disc Shaped,' Totally Vinyl Records <shop.totallyvinyl.com/record/13229-icehouse-chrysalis-7-inch-picture-disc-shaped> [accessed 7 January 2021].

33 'The Pogues A Pair Of Brown Eyes UK Shaped Picture Disc (Picture Disc Vinyl Record) (420128),' Eil.com <eil.com/shop/moreinfo.asp?catalogid=420128> [accessed 7 January 2021].

34 'Megadeth Anarchy In The U.K. UK Shaped Picture Disc (Picture Disc Vinyl Record) (43695),' Eil.com <eil.com/shop/moreinfo.asp?catalogid=43695> [accessed 7 January 2021].

Ohio. St. Paul and The Broken Bones also paid tribute to their home state for RSD 2015, releasing a live single on maroon-colored, Alabama-shaped vinyl.[35] Meanwhile, the iconic hip-hop single "Int'l Players Anthem," by UGK & Outkast, was issued for RSD 2016 on Texas-shaped vinyl, patterned with the Texas flag.[36] The choice of shape is doubly apt; the great 2007 single is based around a sample from "I Choose You" by Willie Hutch, a prolific singer, songwriter, and Motown associate who grew up in Texas. Finally, singer/songwriter Chuck Ragan, a member of the Florida punk band Hot Water Music, put out a 2012 single called "Saw Blade" that takes the shape of California superimposed over a saw blade, with a hammer running perpendicular to the state—seemingly a nod to the hammer and sickle symbol. It was sold as a bundle with concert tickets and came in several colors.[37]

American regionalism may end there, but national pride does not. They Might Be Giants' John Linnell put out a single, "Montana," which was pressed onto green marble vinyl and shaped like the continental United States. A fan site points out that, because of America's irregular shape, "the grooves are so far in to the center that some automatic record players lift the tone-arm off the record before the needle ever reaches the actual recording."[38] Taking a less nationalistic tack, the Canadian hardcore band Ruination, whose members would go on to play in acts like Fucked Up, Charles Bronson, and Los Crudos, also did a USA-shaped record for their self-titled 2001 EP, which is sometimes referred to as *Let the Motherfucker Burn*.

III.4.2 Sawblades

Another recurring shape is the circular saw blade; records taking this form are also sometimes called buzzsaw vinyl. One reason this shape is popular is because the teeth of the blades are only found on the record's circumference, barely encroaching on the space for the record's grooves. As a result, it is easy to fit a full album onto one disc.

As far as I can tell, the first buzzsaw record was released in 1986. A 1984 special edition of hair metal band W.A.S.P.'s single "Animal (Fuck Like a Beast)" does come on a shaped picture disc, and its cover does depict the pelvis of a man wearing a thong fitted with a circular blade. But that record is not shaped like a buzzsaw—instead, it is contoured around the pelvis itself, crossed through with a bolt of lightning.[39] The first truly buzzsaw-shaped record seems to be one of several differently shaped editions of California thrash metal band Dark Angel's 1986 single, "Merciless Death," its art depicting an unfortunate man strapped to a medieval torture wheel.[40] The song, fittingly, is a frenzy of blast beats, rapid-fire riffs, and ecstatic vocals, perfectly suited to the vinyl's sharply toothed edge.

---

35 'St. Paul and The Broken Bones Live Recording Set for Alabama Shaped Vinyl Release on Record Store Day, April 18th at Mellow Matt's Music and More!', Buy Local Bowling Green, 2015 <buylocalbg.com/2015/04/14/st-paul-and-the-broken-bones-live-recording-set-for-alabama-shaped-vinyl-release-on-record-store-day-april-18th-at-mellow-matts-music-and-more/> [accessed 7 January 2021].

36 Elijah C. Watson, 'UGK & Outkast To Release "Int'l Players Anthem" On Texas Shaped Vinyl,' Okayplayer, 2016 <www.okayplayer.com/news/ugk-outkast-to-release-intl-players-anthem-on-texas-shaped-vinyl.html> [accessed 7 January 2021].

37 'Chuck Ragan - Saw Blade 7'' (2012, Red, Vinyl),' Discogs <www.discogs.com/Chuck-Ragan-Saw-Blade-7/release/3585272> [accessed 7 January 2021].

38 'Montana (Single),' TMBW: The They Might Be Giants Knowledge Base <tmbw.net/wiki/Montana_(Single)> [accessed 7 January 2021].

39 'W.A.S.P. - Animal (F**k Like A Beast) (1984, Vinyl),' Discogs <www.discogs.com/WASP-Animal-Fk-Like-A-Beast/release/1448189> [accessed 7 January 2021].

40 'Dark Angel - Merciless Death (1986, Sawblade, Vinyl),' Discogs <www.discogs.com/Dark-Angel-Merciless-Death/release/10975554> [accessed 7 January 2021].

MT Undertainment's casting mold, used in the process to create their sawblade records, and one of its products. Images courtesy of Joe Raimond of MT Undertainment.

The next year saw a few different saw blade records, most notably the obscure single "You Can't Get No Pussy" by a one-off female rap group named LS Fresh, which was a response to 2 Live Crew's "We Want Some Pussy."[41] Released on clear buzzsaw vinyl, it narrates a series of sexual humiliations subjected to the members of 2 Live Crew.[42]

From 1988 through to 1991, a suspicious label operating out of an English village called Shrewton released several picture discs with buzzsaw edges. This label, Tell Tales, specialized in recordings of interviews with popular heavy metal bands, among them Def Leppard, Alice Cooper, Bon Jovi, and Helloween. But the origin of these interviews is dubious. As one release noted:

"Each interview is presented independently and without collaboration of the artists. This enables us to produce items without artistic or management censorship, which means we can often present a wider view of the artists and their opinions."[43]

MT Undertainment, a German label specializing in punk, experimental, and industrial music, started a sub-label called Saw Blades in 1992 that was dedicated to saw-blade-shaped singles. Their first release was a split single between the Seattle grunge act Mudhoney and fellow Washington State garage band Gas Huffer, each contributing a cover song. Two different versions of that clear saw blade record were produced—one sharper than the other!—in a total edition of 2,000. The label would continue the series into the twenty-first century and then sporadically thereafter, with the most recent record coming out in 2015. Singles included underground stalwarts like Circle Jerks, Sonic Youth's Lee Ranaldo, White Flag, and Controlled Bleeding. In a remarkable feat of licensing, Jimmy Page, Alice Cooper, Ace Frehley, Cher, and even Frank Sinatra are all paired with punk bands.

41 'LS Fresh - You Can't Get No P--Sy! (1987, Vinyl),' Discogs <www.discogs.com/LS-Fresh-You-Cant-Get-No-P-sy/release/6490447> [accessed 7 January 2021].

42 Sample lyric: "When you pulled down your pants, the odor made me sneeze!"

43 'Picture Covers - Stylized Bats,' Caveinspiredmusic.com <web.archive.org/web/20190303040239/http://caveinspiredmusic.com/rubriques/22_pic_covers_bats/pdf/22i_Bat_Shaped_Discs.pdf> [accessed 7 January 2021].

Joe Raimond, who co-founded MT Undertainment in 1984, tells me that the idea for sawtoothing the Mudhoney/Gas Huffer split came from the mind of Florian Schück, who at the time was one of the people running the label. Since the Mudhoney record was also being released in the USA, they wanted to set their version of the single apart, so European audiences would be interested.

Raimond tells me they were able to license the nonexclusive rights to famous artists like Jimmy Page and Alice Cooper due to an unexpected windfall. Earlier, they had released an album called *Explizite Lyric* by the James Blast Orchester, a metal band who did parody covers of famous pop songs. That album was a big success, staying on the German charts for over half a year. The money helped fund Saw Blades. As Raimond explains, licensing the tracks was not nearly as difficult as it seemed. "It is usually just a question of not giving up, asking the right person, and then faithfully providing accounting and keeping the whole release very transparent for the artists involved. After we had done several of the releases, it got easier to get permission for the next releases."

He tells me that Cher was a tricky one to put together because the licensor's default position was that labels could not license individual tracks from her, only full albums. "Not wanting to give up, we supplied her manager with copies of the saw blades," Raimond recalls. "And according to what the licensor claimed, the manager showed the records to Cher, and she then, liking the concept, gave permission for us to license one track."

Raimond explains that the saw blade records all started out as normal, circular singles, which were then cut into their buzzsaw shape using a stamping machine. Originally, this was done by the pressing plant, but when that business closed after a few Saw Blades releases, MT Undertainment bought the machine. "The machine itself was ancient, and was dangerous to operate," Raimond says. "I came close a few times to losing a finger when the machine was in operation." They learned they had to order the records released on thin vinyl, and that certain colors were easier to cut into shape, whereas others tended to crack. After using that machine for several years, they got fed up with its hazards and contracted a local company that specialized in laser-cutting large sheets of plastic.

"Originally," Raimond says, "we had planned to put out, as our perhaps last saw blade single, a split single between the Beatles and the Tater Totz (famous for their Yoko cover songs!), but the laser company raised their prices by about 300 percent shortly before production, which effectively killed the series instantly. So *The Beatles* was released as a normal single a few years later." A couple of other ideas, aborted for different reasons, were a split between SF noise-rock/punk band Flipper and a "German band that your grandma would have loved" named The Flippers, as well as a split between the James Blast Orchester and the James Last Orchestra, "which shortly before had threatened to sue J.B.O. for their name."

Raimond recalls hearing about an Australian customer who was told by the customs office that they had to declare the records as dangerous weapons. And at least two individuals complained to the label that the records damaged their record players, apparently because they had used automatic turntables, which dropped the needle into the bladed part of the record.

Numerous one-off saw blade records came out through the nineties and beyond, including a 1996 twelve-inch by the minimal techno artist Steve Stoll, combining two mixes of his lively "Elastic," and an LP called *8 Cuts* by noise artist Lockweld, which was released in 2003 on an experimental label called Noise Control Corporation, five hundred copies produced in total.[44]

In 2011, two death metal bands, Machetazo from Spain and Marrow from Baltimore, put out a split sawblade 12-inch with a special edition on silver vinyl with red "splatter," approximating the appearance of blood.[45] In 2005, Havoc Records released a fifty-copy edition of Finnish hardcore punk band Riistetyt's "Tuomiopäivä" single which was an actual used saw blade, with a record glued to each side.[46]

III.4.3 Beyond

In 2013, punk band Anti-Flag released a shaped picture disc for their song "Bacon." It featured an image of a big glob of raw bacon strips. The members of Anti-Flag are apparently vegan, which explains why they made this hulk of smoked pork look decidedly unappetizing. Chris Stowe, who runs Anti-Flag's own label, A-F Records, tells me the idea behind the single was to find "a tongue-in-cheek way of putting out a 7-inch with two songs about police and police brutality on them."

To get the gross raw bacon image, Stowe had to be creative. "I actually bought a package of bacon and assembled that in a bunch of different and disgusting ways and took photos of it," he told me. "So that pile of bacon you see there is exactly how it appeared on my kitchen floor." Stowe was impressed by how they pulled it off and says that fans seemed to agree. "We sold out pretty fast, maybe in a week or so. It was such a small run of records, I think 500? You can snag one on eBay now for a mint," he laughs.

Along similar lines, in 2015, J Dilla released an update version of his 2001 song, "Fuck the Police," on vinyl in a picture disc shaped like a police badge. (The song itself protests the British new wave band, not law enforcement officers.) Elsewhere, among reams of Madonna collectibles, one might find a bootleg interview picture disc featuring a topless image of the pop queen, the record shaped around her contours. Its provenance is unclear, but it was supposedly pressed in Germany.[47] And there's even a Pee-wee Herman novelty picture disc that came out when his *Big Adventure* film was in

44 'Lockweld: 8 Cuts,' NCC: Noise Control Corp. <web.archive.org/web/20040106204545/http://ncc-records.com/detailstest.cfm?SKU=lockweld> [accessed 7 January 2021].

45 'Album Artwork of the Month: Machetazo/Marrow Split 12",' Invisible Oranges, 2011 <www.invisibleoranges.com/album-artwork-of-the-month-machetazomarrow-split-12/> [accessed 7 January 2021].

46 'Havoc Limited Edition Records,' Havoc Records and Distribution <web.archive.org/web/20080802113525/http://havocrex.com:80/photos/image/11/36> [accessed 7 January 2021].

47 'Madonna - Interview 80 (Vinyl),' Discogs <www.discogs.com/Madonna-Interview-80/release/1969048> [accessed 7 January 2021].

Anti-Flag's shaped *Bacon* picture disc. Nestled within its plastic package, it looks like something lurking in the corner of the reduced-to-sell section of the grocery store. Image courtesy of A-F Records.

theaters—it features Pee-wee crouched in front of a swirling vortex, the record's edges traced around him.

An even more unconventional shaped record was *Ja Soa Schmarm* by Vegetarian Bavarian In Exile, which was the project of Elke Skelter, wife of the Legendary Pink Dots' Edward Ka-Spel. This hundred-copy 12-inch was a single-sided record that was circular but had a small, handcrafted mountain sitting atop its center. Each copy had its own unique mountain, replete with miniature people and cabins fixed among the cliffs. René Heid, who runs the Rund um den Watzmann record that put out the release, tells me that he proposed the record to Elke, who at that time had done some mixing but had not released her own music on record. She called her project Vegetarian Bavarian In Exile because she was a non-meat-eater in the very carnivorous region of Bavaria.

EXTREME MUSIC

Heid explains, "If you think about Bavaria, besides the music, it's mountains, meat eaters, wearing lederhosen, eating huge tarts. We tried to integrate these elements into the release." For him, the idea to transcend the third dimension is integral to its charm. "Mountains realized on a record seems a contradiction in terminis. Playing a record means the record needs to be flat. Like a hat, I thought, maybe it's possible to combine. My releases always try to sit on the edge of the (im)possible. This project really reflects this."

First, they tried melting vinyl records to produce the mountain shape in the middle of the disc, but that did not work out. They next went to the pressing plant to ask if they could find a way; they were told it would be achievable but cited an "astronomical" estimate. So Heid went to a friend at his local art academy, and she tried out several prototypes. "The results of these experiments were mountains made of Styrofoam," he recalls. "Light, easily 'adjustable' piece by piece. A good basis to carry Alp scenes in the style of model train scenery." Over several sessions, they laboriously created all one hundred copies. "Coloring these figures, thinking of diverse apocalyptic Alp scenes, playing with the possibilities to tell a story by creating a miniature mountain to the music," he recalls.

Despite the miniature mountain at its center, these records were playable. But they had a quirk, Heid tells me. "At a certain moment, the needle of the record player will touch the mountain and that normally results in a jump of the needle to the outside, back into the 'music.'" He regards this as a positive feature, because not only is every copy unique, but the music itself ends up distinct with each play. "No need to stop the record after the track, but let it continue while coincidence decides how it develops."

Such an unusual release resulted in a few unpredictable outcomes. For one, the LP "sleeve" was a bona fide cake box, with photos silkscreened onto them. Heid needed to sell them quickly, since they took up a lot of space. He also recalls that all copies shipped to customers in Israel arrived at their destinations "cut into pieces" for some reason. And though they sold out very quickly, there were mixed reactions. "Collectors of the Legendary Pink Dots and all stuff linked to them sometimes begged for a regular flat copy. Sometimes the postal system shook the mountains and forced the customer to reassemble some figures. Some people hate the idea of incidental looping, fearing for their stylus. Some people argued about the volume of the release... But overall, it was very well received. It garnered interest from galleries, museums, and collectors of extraordinary record releases. Got many reviews all over the world and was shown at several exhibitions about art records."

III.5 PICTURES

No vinyl variation has commanded as much attention from record fetishists as picture discs. What few know is that the story of picture discs goes way back to the early phonograph era.

III.5.1 Picture Disc Prehistory

To better understand the earliest precedents to picture discs, I got in touch with Dr. Rainer E. Lotz, a German academic whose PhD is in economics but who has become an institution in jazz history. He has published a slew of articles and reference texts on early recorded music, and in 2014 was even nominated for a Grammy award for compiling *Black Europe*, a monster of a boxed set comprising forty-eight CDs and two hardbound books, which documents the history of black music in Europe up until 1927.

Probably the first predecessor of picture discs was a series of "audio postcards" produced in France as early as the first decade of the twentieth century. These were cardboard postcards that had a small, translucent celluloid record glued to the front, containing music intended to accompany the image visible behind the grooves. Dr. Lotz has traced this practice back to a label known as E.P.I. ("épis de blé"), which was first registered in December 1908. Four E.P.I. postcards have turned up, including one bearing a color image of two foxes wandering through a snowy forest. [48]

In 1932, the Victor recording company put out a series of circular picture discs, constructing them like a sandwich. In the middle was a sturdy core disc made of shellac. Attached to each side of this core were sheets of paper illustrated with the record's desired image; then the whole thing was coated in clear plastic, which was imprinted with the audio grooves. Considered by some to be a marketing gimmick designed to stimulate sales during the Great Depression, this series was not successful, only lasting a few years.

Collector Tim Brooks has identified thirty of these Victor pressings.[49] They include a rare and now incredibly valuable Jimmie Rodgers record, perhaps country music's first picture disc. Featuring a black-and-white photograph of Rodgers sitting at his guitar, dressed in a suit, sun hat, and polka-dot bowtie, it was released on June 27, 1933, just a month after Rodgers died of tuberculosis—and was apparently recorded a mere nine days before his death! Today, because only a few hundred records were ever produced, even cracked copies fetch over a thousand dollars in auction.[50]

---

48 With that said, a Berlin patent filed in October 7, 1904, by a phonographic machine manufacturer, Max Thomas, makes an earlier mention of translucent gramophone postcards: "I prefer to employ disc records of thin transparent celluloid, first, because the small weight of this material does not cause any appreciable increase in the cost of postage, and second, because such records can be mounted over a picture or other representation without obscuring the same." According to a *Daily Mirror* article from March 17, 1905, Thomas had marketed a whopping eighty 'singing postcards' in England by then! Dr. Lotz tells me that he believes these records existed. "I have no reason not to believe this, except I cannot identify any. The patent was quite clear about images under the grooves." He also found advertisements between 1904 and 1908 that reference them.

49 Tim Brooks, 'Review: Lindsay, Picture Discs of World,' Television and Record Industry History Resources, 1990 <timbrooks.net/review-lindsay-picture-discs-of-world/> [accessed 7 January 2021].

50 'RCA VICTOR 18-6000 JIMMIE RODGERS PICTURE DISC **RARE** - Auction Details,' Popsike.com, 2005 <www.popsike.com/RCA-VICTOR-186000-JIMMIE-RODGERS-PICTURE-DISC-RARE/4073236429.html> [accessed 7 January 2021]; Ronnie Pugh, 'Country's First Picture Disc: A Jimmie Rodgers Rarity Goes Up for Auction,' CMT, 2003 <www.cmt.com/news/1472180/countrys-first-picture-disc-a-jimmie-rodgers-rarity-goes-up-for-auction/> [accessed 7 January 2021].

Regrettably, another very early picture disc is credited to none other than Adolf Hitler, who commissioned a now extremely rare 78 RPM in 1934, its grooves superimposed over a Godzilla-esque jumbo image of the dictator towering over a massive crowd of Germans. Another picture disc, Mel Brooks' 1983 single, "To Be or Not To Be (The Hitler Rap)," featuring Brooks dressed up as a goofy Adolf knock-off beneath its grooves, is a nice counterpoint.

According to an online auction listing, there was a series of picture discs produced by Hitler's Ministry of Propaganda, featuring speeches from Hitler and Joseph Goebbels, as well as at least one collection of military marches. There apparently were never sold, but instead given to loyal supporters of the Nazi regime.[51] These discs were created by coating an illustrated cardboard core in vinyl and then pressing the audio grooves onto them. Due to the flimsiness of this production method, over time the cardboard has desiccated, causing creases to form in the exterior layer of vinyl.

III.5.2 Vogue Records

It was not until May 1946 that the next chapter in the picture disc story arrived in the form of the legendary Vogue Records label. Run by a Detroit inventor and entrepreneur named Tom Saffady, Vogue designed a new way of pressing picture discs that featured vivid images and an "indestructible" design. Saffady, described in 1944 as "a broad-shouldered, slim-hipped Detroiter with the somber, brooding eyes of a musician and the calloused but sensitive hands of a good mechanic," was responsible for a laundry list of inventions, including a plastic beer-bottle cap, a razor that only needed to be sharpened every five years, and "a housewives' butter slicer run by a flashlight battery." At age twenty-seven, he was the owner of Sav-Way Industries, a bustling business allegedly raking in $400,000 per year and employing six hundred people.[52]

Billboard ran several articles chronicling the label's formation and announcing its imminent first release. The March 1946 issue proclaims "First Vogue Glamour Disks Reach Press; On Market in Month,"[53] and in October of that year, one article offered "A Look at Vogue's Glamour Puss Disk Plant and Vinyl Fabricators."[54] Saffady's new record-making process resembled that of RCA Victor's early picture discs but generated a sturdier product: it involved placing paper illustrations around an aluminum "core" record, then coating the sandwich in vinylite and pressing the grooves using a mold.

Vogue's story is well told in a seminal article by Tim Brooks, published in 1977.[55] One of the first records, "Sugar Blues" by Clyde McCoy and His Orchestra, sold terrifically, likely facilitated by the novelty factor—that song, released in its first version in 1931, had already been an enormously enduring success for McCoy for over a decade. But the

---

51 Ted Staunton, 'Patria 1,' Ted Staunton's 78 RPM Label Gallery <www.tedstaunton.com/labels/1930_1939/pages/Patria_1/patria_1.html> [accessed 7 January 2021]; 'NAZI - German Picture Disk - Patria Spezial 2017 - Auction Details,' Popsike.com, 2006 <www.popsike.com/NAZI-German-Picture-disk-Patria-Spezial-2017/250018236818.html> [accessed 7 January 2021].

52 'MANAGEMENT: Young Tom Saffady,' TIME, 27 March 1944 <content.time.com/time/subscriber/article/0,33009,803257,00.html> [accessed 7 January 2021].

53 'First Vogue Glamour Disks Reach Press; On Market in Month,' The Billboard, 30 March 1946, p. 26 <books.google.ca/books?id=JBoEAAAAMBAJ&pg=PT25&lpg=PT25&dq=First+Vogue+Glamour+Disks+Reach+Press;+On+Market+in+Month,"&source=bl&ots=cpBrGflNFE&sig=ACfU3U1N1YOCSISDDetaihJXkoFFPd9zLg&hl=en&sa=X&ved=2ahUKEwj26trc14ruAhWIQcOKHfOpCqIQ6AEwAHoECAEQAg#v=onepage&q=First Vogue Glamour Disks Reach Press%3B On Market in Month%2C"&f=false> [accessed 7 January 2021].

54 'A Look at Vogue's Glamour Puss Disk Plant and Vinyl Fabricators,' The Billboard, October 1946, p. 36.

55 Tim Brooks, 'No Title,' Record Research, July 1977, pp. 1–8.

Early Vogue picture disc "Sugar Blues" by Clyde McCoy and his orchestra.

initial excitement died down quickly. One reason was because Vogue records were relatively expensive to produce, and thus had to be priced at a premium—the discs' $1.05 price tag was 50 percent higher than most comparable records of the day. Even more significant was the lack of star power on the label, apart from McCoy.

A *Billboard* headline in January 1947, just three months after the inside look at their "Glamour Puss" pressing plant, asked: "Vogue Label Up For Sale?" Then production ceased in April 1947, not even a year after Vogue's first record went to market. In that time, Saffady's company released an estimated seventy-four distinct records, although the exact figure is not known because no existing catalog or master list has survived. Sav-Way itself went into receivership four months after the production line shut down.

But Saffady's name has lived on in the form of a devoted collectors' niche specializing in Vogue discs. Tim Brooks' authoritative history includes interviews with former employees of Sav-Way. Through scrupulous research, Brooks explores the many reasons why the label failed, including the high prices, the lack of a hit record, and the intense competition between independent labels at the time. For many years, there was an entire organization dedicated to chronicling the label's history, The Association of Vogue Picture Record Collectors (AVPRC). Their website remains a key resource, offering detailed information and color images of most known Vogue discs. And no fewer than two books have come out chronicling the label's history and discography.

According to the AVPRC, the market value of Vogue discs varies widely between records. The most abundant discs, such as Clyde McCoy's "Sugar Blues," sell for thirty to forty dollars apiece. On the other hand, a copy of Art Kassel's Orchestra's exquisitely rare "Queen For A Day" single once sold for over $11,000 following a bidding war between two collectors.[56]

III.5.3 Red Raven Records' Zoetrope Discs

In 1956, a label named Red Raven Records put an interesting spin on the picture disc concept. Red Raven discs were printed with a series of animation frames and sold with a mirrored ornament, which sat in the middle of the record as it played. As the turntable would spin, the mirror would show a brief, repeating animation using a zoetrope effect. Initially issued as six-inch cardboard discs, the label eventually started pressing them in an expanded eight-inch version, manufacturing the product into the 1970s. Unfortunately, while the original product was a bona fide picture disc, later versions

---

56 Lisa Wheeler, 'It's the Real Thing - Collector Finds Rare "Rum and Coca-Cola" Vogue Picture Disc,' *Goldmine* <www.isleofwrite.com/stories/Vogue.pdf>.

were just colored records with the animated sequence glued on as a label. Red Raven's music was almost beside the point; generic in a charming way, it was performed by an anonymous studio band dubbed the Red Raven Orchestra and composed by George Salisbury Chase, a library and film music composer whose compositions were used in the notorious B-movie *Plan 9 from Outer Space*.[57]

Children's music is a bit of a black box when it comes to record collectors, and as a result, the Red Raven label has accumulated far less of a following on the collectibles market than Vogue Records. Its history is also poorly documented. A collectors' organization called The Wolverine Antique Music Society has compiled a brief history on their website, including some animated GIFs of the animations in action.[58] Assorted Red Raven facts can also be cobbled together through scattered mentions online: Red Raven's zoetrope records were not just produced in the U.S. but also in Sweden, France (where they were known as Teddy Disks), Italy (where they were called Moviton Mamil), and apparently several other countries.[59] The most comprehensive listing of Red Raven records comes from Peter Muldavin's exhaustive *Complete Guide to Vintage Children's Records*, which reports that the label's American branch put out twenty releases in total, including renditions of old standards "Rudolph the Red Nosed Reindeer" and "Mary Had a Little Lamb," as well as more esoteric tunes like "Tootles the Tug" and "Peewee the Kiwi Bird."[60]

More recently, a contemporary duo named Sculpture, composed of British musician Dan Hayhurst and New Zealand animator Reuben Sutherland, have revived the zoetrope concept. They put out a slew of twelve-inch picture discs that feature a similar framed animation under their grooves. But this record does not come with a mirrored apparatus; instead, the effect is revealed by setting up a camera to record at a specific frame rate and filming the surface of the record as it spins. This may lack the parsimony of Red Raven's movie records, but Hayhurst's experimental electronic compositions are more adventurous than the efforts of the Red Raven Orchestra, and Sutherland's abstract images offer a more vivid feast for the eyes.

III.5.4 Picture Discs in the Rock Era

The first rock music picture disc has traditionally been thought to be 1971's *Air Conditioning* by the English progressive rock band Curved Air. Manufactured in an edition of 10,000 copies by Metronome Records, it was produced using a five-layer process analogous to the 1930s Victor Records picture discs, as conceived by graphic designer and upstart band manager Mark Hanau. In the center was a black vinyl core, to which paper decals were attached to each side. These sheets were "kiln-dried," presumably to solve the desiccation and warping problems that cursed the Victor discs. Then an outer layer of clear vinyl film was applied, which contained the grooves.[61]

57 Bob Clampett, 'Red Raven Records and Creepy "Teddy Bear" Themes,' Cartoon Research, 2013 <cartoonresearch.com/index.php/red-raven-records-and-creepy-teddy-bear-themes/> [accessed 7 January 2021].

58 'Red Raven "Movie Records,"' Wolverine Antique Music Society <www.shellac.org/wams/wraven1.html> [accessed 7 January 2021].

59 'Animated Records 78rpm,' Vinyl Engine, 2013 <www.vinylengine.com/turntable_forum/viewtopic.php?f=41&t=56666> [accessed 7 January 2021].

60 Peter Muldavin, 'Childrens Records, Children's Records, Record History, 78 Rpm, Vintage,' Kiddie Rekord King <www.kiddierekordking.com/index.html> [accessed 7 January 2021].

61 This information comes from a Wikipedia entry originally written by Mark Hanau himself.

Bubbles of air ended up trapped between the layers, leading to flawed playback, which audiophiles still complain about.[62]

Since Curved Air became established as the first rock picture disc, collectors have discovered that the Metronome label put out an earlier precedent: an obscure 1969 compilation called *Off II - Hallucinations (Psychedelic Underground)*, released in Germany and featuring bands like Love, the MC5, and the Holy Modal Rounders. This

record uses the same process as *Air Conditioning* but predates its release by two years.

As more and more bands and record labels experimented with the format, there ensued many elaborate variations upon the theme, ranging from beautiful *objets d'art* to gaudy gimmicks to vivid discs that are truly gross.

One particularly nasty picture disc is Vomit Lunchs' *Violent Clash Between Killer Bastards of Eardot Remix* (Hot Air, 1998), which features a smorgasbord of cuts of meat on one side, and an overhead shot of a pot of boiling oil on the other. Sizzling in the oil are several objects that look

Off II—Hallucinations (Psychedelic Underground), a strong contender for the first rock picture disc.

like entrails but are apparently just banana and pineapple fritters.

I got in touch with Hot Air honcho Matt Wand, also a member of the seminal plunderphonics act Stock, Hausen & Walkman, who tells me about the congruence between the music and the imagery. "Something about that high pinging sound of hot fat reaching the right temperature and then the violent white-noise sizzle when the fritters go in, plus the general overall feeling of danger when standing too close to a huge pan of boiling oil... I don't know why... It just felt very connected to Mr. Lunchs' sound work!! Also the garish colors and the general idea that too much fried food usually would make me feel sick..."

But taking a photograph above a pot of boiling oil and dough was not easy. "Handheld photography, very quickly, of course, and with the neck strap ON. You don't want a deep-fried camera... though maybe the Scots would disagree." The raw meat picture on the other side, meanwhile, was a found photo, chosen because "it connected with the food thing and also I liked the idea of making vegetarians nauseous."

Sadly, this colorful Vomit Lunchs picture disc was not a hit among record buyers. "I thought it was the BEST thing in the world, but nobody else did. I think I maybe sold a hundred of the picture disc." Most tragically, Wand was forced to destroy a few hundred copies of the release to clear up space!

---

62 'Curved Air - Airconditioning (1970, Vinyl),' Discogs <www.discogs.com/Curved-Air-Airconditioning/release/1709548> [accessed 9 January 2021].

Another striking picture is the grindcore band ZEUS!' self-titled album, whose picture disc features the inside of a mouth on one side. Paolo Mongardi, who is one half of ZEUS!, explains that when the first run of LPs sold out, he wanted to do something different for the second pressing, so he proposed a picture disc pressed with the original cover's vivid picture of his throat. It was an image he had taken years earlier using his first compact digital camera, a Nikon—illustrating the fact that everyone took the same photo when they got their first digital camera. He cropped out the teeth to "make it more ambiguous" and pressed three hundred copies through a now-defunct pressing plant called MicroWatt, which all sold out.

Meanwhile, a reissue of Abscess' *Urine Junkies* put out by the grotesque Horror Pain Gore Death Productions label features, beneath its grooves, two sets of hands syringing urine from a urinal—which was essentially the album's original cover transposed to the picture disc. As Mike Juliano, who runs HPGD (and who also works for Relapse Records, who originally put out *Urine Junkies*), says, "This Abscess album needed to be a picture disc for obvious reasons."

One last remarkable picture disc is a split release titled *Rough Skin*, released on Little Mafia Records. On one side is Smell & Quim, a macabre UK noise act who once got an entire noise festival shut down when he brought out a pig's head during a performance, slammed it with a jackhammer, coated it with paraffin wax, and set it on fire. On the other side is Priest in Shit, one of many pseudonyms of U.S. noisester Richard Ramirez, who has produced an innumerable quantity of harsh noise records, tapes, and CD-Rs throughout his career. The picture disc itself was designed by Tony Roberts, an illustrator and visual designer from Norman, Oklahoma, who did a few records for the Little Mafia label.

The Priest in Shit side features a close-up photo of an older man's face that's been cut up into bars and recycled. The flipside features what looks like discolored and misshapen flesh, again rendered in macro view.

"I knew of S&Q and [Priest in Shit] so I had a good idea of the kind of thematic territory they were working in," he explains. "I thought of the images as psychological illustrations of body mania and destructive obsession. I look at noise releases—especially on vinyl—less as traditional records and more like sound-generating objects with an important physical presence. The presentation was intentionally minimal. I didn't want it to look like a record of music . . . all the release info is on a vinyl sleeve that was a bit like sanitary wrapping, more to protect fingers than the disc."

The Priest in Shit side's source image was a news photo of a priest who had just been convicted of child molestation. The fleshy side is described as "a photo collage of stains, bruises, and fetishized vascularity." Reflecting now, he is satisfied with this grisly-looking picture disc, particularly the sense of menace it evokes. "A bit like something you don't really want to touch. I don't know what else I could ask for."

THE MADONNA *EROTICA* DEBACLE

In 1992, Madonna released "Erotica," the title track to her album of the same name. It was a racy single that flirted with S&M themes and was accompanied by a controversial music video. It also spawned one of the most notorious and expensive picture discs of all time.

To match the song's taboo subject matter, a picture disc was commissioned which had a close-up of Madonna sucking on someone's toes; the foot was rumored to belong to Naomi Campbell. In a letter to *Record Collector* magazine,[1] a former Warner Brothers employee told the story. Apparently, thousands of copies had been pressed when Rob Dickins, the company's managing director, took one look and decided they were too pornographic to be released. The discs were sequestered for a while, and eventually all but a few were destroyed. There's a rumor that only 138 copies survived, matching the disc's catalogue number, but it's suspected that this is apocryphal. With that said, most believe that fewer than 150 evaded ruin.

This disc has become the Holy Grail for Madonna collectors, with copies fetching several thousand dollars apiece in auction. As the Madonna memorabilia website Madonna Decade explains, a bootlegged version was released in 2008, intended to sate collectors' taste for the original; for many fans, it has been a sufficient substitute, and the value of the original has dropped—to just over a thousand dollars.[2]

---

1   Alex Harris, 'My Erotic Madonna 12" Regret,' *Record Collector Magazine*, 17 December 2010 <recordcollectormag.com/letter/my-erotic-madonna-12-regret> [accessed 9 January 2021].

2   'Erotica,' Madonna Decade, 2013 <www.madonna-decade.co.uk/erotica3.html> [accessed 9 January 2021].

NUDIE DISCS

First there were picture discs. Then there were nude *picture discs. The progression was inevitable. Here is a doubtlessly incomplete list of several such items. Unfairly, these records only feature women in various states of undress, as I could find no instances of the undressed male body pressed to wax.*

Jonathan King, "You're the Greatest Lover" (UK Records, Apr 1979) In 1979, the now-disgraced English singer Jonathan King released a cover of a song released a year earlier by a Dutch girl group named Luv. It peaked at #67 on the UK Singles Chart but was especially notorious for its marketing gimmick. According to a *Billboard* magazine article from the time, the first 5,000 copies came accompanied by the world's very first picture flexi-disc. That disc included an image of a topless Sian Adey-Jones, the former Miss Wales, holding a miniature Jonathan King in her hand. In an interview, King said, "I want to reach the marketplace of the pocket-money kids who no longer can afford a single a week, and I want to give them an eye-catching picture plus a reasonable price tag."[1] In a dark coda, King was convicted of child sexual abuse in 2001.

Throbbing Gristle, *Live At Death Factory*, May 79 (No Label) This bootlegged picture disc captures a live set by this seminal UK industrial band. It features a topless woman bent over in front of a fridge, seemingly taken from a German pornography magazine.[2]

Savage Grace, *Ride Into the Night* (Flametrader, 1987) The L.A. speed metal band Savage Grace are considered canonical today, despite only putting out a handful of recordings. This picture disc EP came out in only one edition, a rare Dutch pressing. The disc depicts the band standing above two topless women (one of whom was frontman Chris Logue's girlfriend, Rose Vito). The cover of their debut featured a nude woman ball-gagged and cuffed next to a police motorcycle, so this is actually on the tame end for them. The band's original name was Marquis de Sade; go figure.[3]

Samantha Fox, Limited Edition Interview Picture Disc (Baktabak, 1987) This one features a topless image of glamour-model-turned-eighties pop star Samantha Fox, as released by a bootleg label known for picture discs of interviews with popular artists.

Gert Wilden & Orchestra, *Schulmädchen Report* (Crippled Dick Hot Wax!, 1996) This is one of several picture discs featuring nude women released by the German label Crippled Dick Hot Wax! Subtitled "German Schoolgirl Report & Other Music From Sexy German Films (1968–1972)," this record collects the score music from several sexploitation

---

1 'King Claims First Picture Flexi-Disk,' *Billboard*, 1979, p. 91.
2 'Throbbing Gristle - Live At Death Factory, May 79 (1982, Vinyl),' Discogs <www.discogs.com/Throbbing-Gristle-Live-At-Death-Factory-May-79/release/1236165> [accessed 9 January 2021].
3 Toine van Poorten, 'Savage Grace: The Master Of Disguise Reveals......', Truemetalfan.org, 2010 <www.truemetalfan.org/savagegrace2010int.htm> [accessed 9 January 2021].

movies, including such hits as *Was Männer nicht für möglich halten* (released in English as *Swinging Wives*) and *Die fleißigen Bienen vom Fröhlichen Bock* (released as *Sex Is Not For Virgins*). Both sides of this disc feature lurid stills from the movies in question.

Splash, "Got 2 Have Your Love" (Nu-Trax Records London, 1992) German house duo Splash managed several dance hits, including their 1990 anthem "I Need Rhythm." "Got 2 Have Your Love" was a Mantronix cover that did not achieve the same level of success as their earlier work. But it did have the honor of being pressed in a picture disc edition featuring a black-and-white shot of a topless model.

Kevin Wet, *Wet* (Visual Vinyl, 1982) Originally released as a clear vinyl record in  1980 with the image on the album cover behind it, this record was then issued as a true picture disc by Visual Vinyl in 1982. Kevin Wet was a Portland, Oregon glam rocker who hired some session musicians to play backup for him, then put out this controversial disc.[4] Its cover features one nude woman pressed up against a clear shower door (reportedly Kevin's girlfriend), with another crouched in front of her (reportedly her sister!). The music itself is somewhat subpar, but the visuals helped him score a profile in *Kerrang!* magazine, issue five.[5] His follow-up EP, *Hard Attack*, also was pressed as a picture disc featuring two nude women; it was released on Kevin's own Wet World Records.

Drugface, *Cunt Masters* (Remixes) (Überdruck Records, 2003) A close-up of someone sniffing cocaine off a woman's bare crotch graces this hard trance single, which blends an iconic sample from *Pulp Fiction* into the mix. This eye-popping image was no doubt intended to soak up attention, and in a 2003 interview for the website HarderFaster, Dirk Northroff, one half of Drugface, remarks that the single was one of their most successful releases. "Remember the *Remixes* on picture disc? David (Rzenno) told this to me: at that time, he couldn't show his grandma the picture disc."[6]

C-Base, "In The Beginning" (Dirrty Budapest, 2003) This 12-inch picture disc features two women captured in an erotic pose. It's the first of a handful of explicit picture discs put out by this label. *Gates of Eden* by Markus F and *I Cry* by Akira Yamamoto share a similar aesthetic, and copies of these records today command between $50 and $150. Even their least pornographic record (Markus F's *Turn the Page*) depicts two beetles in *flagrante delicto*. Despite the racy content, C-Base were the very average-looking duo of Christian Zikeli and Jörn Oelschlägel. The A-side of this single, dubbed the "'Fuck Me I'm Famous' Mix," is an improbable blend of fast-paced trance and Gregorian chant-style vocals.

---

4   Explorer, 'Wet, Kevin - 1982 Wet/Hard Attack,' Glory Daze Music, 2019 <glorydazemusic.com/vf/discussion/9382/wet-kevin-1982-wet-hard-attack> [accessed 9 January 2021].

5   Strappado, 'Kevin Wet - The Dreamer [EP] (1981),' *Rare and Obscure Metal*, 2011 <strappadometalblog.blogspot.com/2011/02/kevin-wet-dreamer-ep-1980.html#axzz6E9aWUJTk> [accessed 9 January 2021].

6   Latex Zebra, 'Interview with Uberdruck,' *HarderFaster*, 2003 <www.harderfaster.net/?sid=&section=features&action=showfeature&featureid=10527> [accessed 9 January 2021].

III.6 ADULTERATED

Pressing plants have produced vinyl records in many different colors. An Israeli punk band named MooM advertised a special edition of their third single as being on "puke green" vinyl—a marbled mixture of yellow and green, to be precise.[63] And Lobotomized, a death metal band from Oslo, Norway, proffered a "shit-brown" edition of their 2013 LP *Norwegian Trash*.[64]

Others have not been content to limit themselves to mere simulacra of bodily fluids. Eventually, people experimented with adding things to the vinyl medium—both human by-products and not.

New York noise-rock band Perfect Pussy, led by charismatic vocalist Meredith Graves, were challenged by the owner of their record label, Captured Tracks, to come up with an original design gimmick for their debut album *Say Yes to Love*. When she joked about soaking the record in blood, Captured Tracks' Mike Sniper took her seriously. She used menstrual blood for practical reasons. As she explained in an interview: "It wasn't like I went and got blood drawn . . . I don't have health insurance!"[65] As a result of the blood, the clear vinyl is tinted a light pinkish purple, veined with dark pink threads.

Two years prior, the Flaming Lips released ten copies of their double LP, *The Flaming Lips and Heady Fwens*, with the blood of their collaborators contained in a hollow layer inside it. For a mere $2,500, you could own a record filled with the lifeblood of Chris Martin, Ke$ha, Erykah Badu, and Sean Lennon, among others—20 mL to be exact. Because the vinyl is clear, you can see the blood moving around inside it as it spins. Before it sold out, buyers had to pay an additional two hundred bucks for the record to be delivered to them by hand—perhaps to avoid accidental damage, or perhaps because it's illegal to mail body fluids through the post.

The idea goes back to the late seventies, when Mark Hanau, the man responsible for the earliest rock picture discs, pioneered a variety of different filled discs in a product line he called "Han-O-Discs." According to a *Cash Box* article from January 31, 1981, he devised this format by bonding together two clear vinyl record halves using "a non-ionizing radiation process," allowing for the space in between to be utilized. That reverent article provides a list of different design models. The "Liquid Disc" contains intermingling colored liquids, while the "Liquid Crystal Disc" changes color when the record is pressed or viewed from different angles. There is a disc filled with glitter, a record dubbed "the world's first holographic record,"[66] and something called a "Diffracta Disc," which "splits light into a moving spectrum." The most

63 'MooM - Third 7 (Puke Green Vinyl) [TLAL154puke],' To Live A Lie Records Webstore <tolivealie.com/store/index.php?main_page=product_info&products_id=2175> [accessed 9 January 2021].
64 'Lobotomized - Norwegian Trash (2014, Brown, Vinyl),' Discogs <www.discogs.com/Lobotomized-Norwegian-Trash/release/6399765> [accessed 9 January 2021].
65 Cam Lindsay, 'Perfect Pussy's Meredith Graves Talks Blood-Infused Vinyl and Debut LP,' *Exclaim!*, 2014 <exclaim.ca/music/article/perfect_pussys_meredith_graves_talks_blood-infused_vinyl_debut_lp> [accessed 9 January 2021].
66 However, a special edition of Saturnalia's *Magical Love*, produced in 1973, may actually take this honor—it featured "detachable holographic centers" on both sides, and is considered the world's first 3D picture disc.

extreme model mentioned is "a record containing live alfalfa sprouts that grow inside the two LP halves."[67]

It is not clear that any of these tantalizing Han-O-Discs reached the marketplace, although there was apparently an attempt at realizing the "Liquid Disc." Commissioned to produce a novelty pressing of the soundtrack to the Disney film *The Black Hole*, Hanau filled a record with differently colored aniline dyes. However, the effort had to be scrapped because the prototypes kept leaking.[68]

In 2012, Jack White put out an LP replete with a bubble of translucent blue liquid as a special release for Record Store Day. It came with a sticker: "Third Man Records and United Record Pressing make no guarantees as to the longevity or integrity of this revolutionary liquid-filled record." The warning was better off heeded; as one online commenter warned: "My friend brought one of these to my place and it leaked while playing it. beware!"[69] Regardless, despite selling for $100 initially, copies would subsequently sell for over seven times that amount on eBay.[70] There is also an entire message board thread with multiple users griping about their copies of the disc, which had leaked their blue contents into the plastic sleeves. There, repair tips are exchanged, including instructions to seal the inlet hole with a layer of Krazy Glue, as well as suggestions for replacement liquids to inject into the record via syringe.[71]

Others have taken up this craft with more success. Curtis Godino is a Brooklyn-based artist and musician who has become skilled at designing custom liquid-filled records. He has produced a reissue of the score for the film *Aliens* for Mondo Records that contains green slime, or "Xenomorph Blood," and a vinyl version of the *Friday the 13th* score filled with fake blood for Waxworks Records. Even more spectacular are the liquid records he produced for his own psych-rock band, Worthless; their *Greener Grass* single features intermingling liquids of different colors.[72]

To design these multicolored records, he used technology that was developed in the sixties to stage liquid light shows. These were parties that combined music with psychedelic visuals achieved by projecting light through a glass container that contained two liquids that repel one another—like oil and water—each one dyed a different color. The resulting blobs could be manipulated by rocking the container in time with music, filling the room with shifting patterns. Godino had been making "oil wheels" for his own light shows—self-enclosed, sealed containers that are readymade to be placed on a projector—so it was not a stretch for Godino to adapt this approach to records.[73]

He tells me that his old loft used to have a "light show" running 24/7 in the main

67 'Hanau's New Picture Disc Process Features Superior Sound Quality,' *Cash Box*, 31 January 1981 <worldradiohistory.com/Archive-All-Music/Cash-Box/80s/1981/CB-1981-01-31.pdf> [accessed 10 January 2021].

68 evad, 'Craft Blog / Unusually Colored Vinyl Records,' COLOURlovers, 2010 <www.colourlovers.com/craft/blog/2010/03/30/unusually-colored-vinyl-records> [accessed 10 January 2021].

69 'Jack White - Sixteen Saltines (2012, Liquid Filled, Vinyl),' Discogs <www.discogs.com/Jack-White-Sixteen-Saltines/release/3556751> [accessed 10 January 2021].

70 'Jack White Sixteen Saltines LIQUID FILLED 12" Inch Single RSD Third Man Records - Auction Details,' Popsike.com, 2012 <www.popsike.com/Jack-White-Sixteen-Saltines-LIQUID-FILLED-12-inch-single-RSD-Third-Man-Records/280867919320.html> [accessed 10 January 2021].

71 'Leaking Liquid Filled Records - Page 10,' White Swirl, 2012 <www.whiteswirl.com/forum/viewtopic.php?t=5916&start=135> [accessed 10 January 2021].

72 Curtis Godino, 'Liquid Filled Records,' Curtis Godino Artist <web.archive.org/web/20160910141126/http://www.curtisgodino.com/oil-wheels-and-liquid-records> [accessed 10 January 2021].

73 'An Interview with Curtis Godino,' Vertical Grooves, 2016 <floatingrecord.com/blogs/posts/interview-with-curtis-godino> [accessed 10 January 2021].

**One of Curtis Godino's oil wheels.
Image courtesy of Curtis Godino.**

room. One day, it occurred to him that the wheel itself looked a lot like a record. "I just looked at my oil wheel and looked at my record, and it was like, oh, they're the same thing. I could do this," he says.

His first record was for his own band, Worthless, and was intended as a tiny pressing. "We knew a guy who did lathe-cuts so I was like, oh, I'll give this a try on lathe-cut. We can make a few and see if it works... An oil wheel is just two six-inch circles and they're sealed together with a millimeter space in between, so I just did the same thing with the records."

Godino tells me the process itself is, in fact, quite complicated, and he considers some of the finer points to be trade secrets. Maintaining the right space between the records is no simple feat, and ensuring a good seal is the true test.

After making the Worthless "Greener Grass" discs, Godino didn't know what kind of interest to expect from fans. "I think I did this when I was 21 or 22 and didn't really have knowledge of how to sell stuff on the internet too well. So I put up a website and I said I was going to sell them at noon. I put them up at noon, and after I made the website live, I had like 500 orders in one refresh. So I had to email everybody back and say, there's only twenty-five records. I had no idea that everybody would be interested in this!" He refunded everyone their money and ended up doing a second pressing to fulfill the demand of those who missed out on the first one. That was no simple task: At first, it took over an hour per record to create them—"a really delicate process," he explains—but he has since perfected the process and gotten the time down somewhat.

After all the hubbub, Godino started getting requests from companies to do special, limited-edition records. One email came from Waxworks Records, asking to do the special *Friday the 13th* record filled with blood. *Aliens*, filled with green slime, followed. He then did a run of sixty-six red-and-black liquid-filled records for a reissue of hardcore band Integrity's album *Humanity Is The Devil*. And a soundtrack reissue label called Enjoy The Toons Records commissioned him to fill a seven-inch of music from the *Teenage Mutant Ninja Turtles* cartoon with green liquid, with four small plastic turtles floating inside.

There really do not seem to be many others who have mastered his art of liquid-filled records. The Swedish metal band Ghost has done their own liquid-filled lathe records, including one with black oil and golden glitter, as well as one filled with red wine. Godino tells me he is aware of them—his experiments with fluids like wine have been less than stellar, so he wonders if they used a wine substitute. He hints that he may have a new filled-record project in the works, but these days, he is occupied with his own music, his first album having come out a few months prior. Here's hoping Mark Hanau's alfalfa-sprout concept may be revived one day.

Blood is not the only human by-product that's found itself incorporated into records. In 2014, Pittsburgh label Velocity of Sound, which specializes in limited-edition seven-inch singles sold "AT COST!," put out a record by weirdo VoS house band Eohippus, titled *Getting Your Hair Wet With Pee*.[74] Described as an "epic Beefheart psych jam" by vinyl fetishist blog *7 Inches*,[75] the music is almost beside the point: the principal gimmick is its billing as a "piss-soaked, hair-filled" record, meaning that actual human hair was incorporated into the vinyl, and that it was pressed onto transparent pale yellow vinyl. I refused to believe that the record itself was dipped in urine—although I suspected many folks gave this disc a rinse before dropping it onto their turntable—so I shot the VoS folks an email through the online form on their website.

Darren Little got back to me within a day. "I'm so glad you asked me this," Little responded. "And the answer is no. Believe it or not, you are the first person to ever ask that question. The 'piss-soaked' aspect is all part of the 'legend' of the record. I believe that stems from the description that Velocity of Sound used when the record went on sale. I think we said something like 'on piss-soaked colored vinyl,' meaning yellow, but the description was taken very literally."

Apart from this, I wanted to understand where the idea came from to put hair in a record. Little explains that it was an intuitive response to the song itself. "I had the idea one day while driving. I wanted to release another Eohippus single and decided on the song 'Getting Your Hair Wet With Pee.' I remember laughing to myself, thinking, 'We could put hair in it and release it on piss-colored vinyl.'"

With inspiration on their side, the VoS folks connected with Gotta Groove Records, a pressing plant, who gamely agreed to press the records. "When I placed the order, they told me not to expect them to play. I was so obsessed with the idea of putting hair in a record that I was willing to risk failing."

From there, it was a matter of execution. "The hair was added to all 100 copies by hand, meaning whomever was running the press had to sprinkle the hair on the vinyl before it was pressed, one 7" at a time." The hair came from Little's sister's hair salon. "They laid down the A-side center label, then a warm puck of vinyl, then put hair on the warm vinyl, then add the B-side center label and then finally pressed it all together!" Remarkably, the hair did not end up clumping together or charring in the process—the strands are disseminated evenly and artfully throughout each copy.

---

74 '(Black) Eohippus "Getting Your Hair Wet With Pee" (VOS010)', Velocity of Sound <web.archive.org/web/20180311105954/http://www.velocityofsound.com/product/eohippus-getting-your-hair-wet-with-pee-vos010> [accessed 10 January 2021].
75 Jason, 'Eohippus "Getting Your Hair Wet With Pee" Single Sided 7" from Velocity of Sound Records,' *7 Inches*, 2014 <7inches.blogspot.com/2014/10/eohippus-getting-your-hair-wet-with-pee.html> [accessed 10 January 2021].

Eohippus's hair-adulterated *Getting Your Hair Wet With Pee* record. Image courtesy of Darren Little of Velocity of Sound.

Does the hair have an effect on the audio? "Yes, it certainly does. The single has plenty of 'pops' and surface noise, but the music drowns most of that out when played."

Still, there was a big question: Was anyone going to want to buy these hair-filled records? "I honestly didn't know if we'd sell ten copies," Little admits. "The whole project was under wraps until the day we released it. I could appreciate the fact that we were running the risk of the release being too weird for most people. With that being said, it sold out in a little over an hour, and we were getting orders from ALL over the world. Orders were going to countries that had previously showed zero interest in our releases. I could tell that more people than just our email subscribers knew about the release. After a Google search, I was amazed to see music blogs from all over the world talking about it. It was an amazing feeling knowing that people could dig it."

If blood, hair, and urine weren't enough, there is a company named And Vinyly that offers a unique opportunity: to have your remains cremated and pressed into vinyl. The audio itself is up to the client's discretion, as is the cover art, meaning your memory can be associated with Ke$ha's 'Tik Tok' for all eternity. The cost of the procedure will run you $3,000 USD.

But how about that Holy Grail of bodily fluids, diarrhea? Way back in 2004, techno artist RA-X put out a twelve-inch EP, *The Opium Den (Parts I–IV)*, on brown vinyl. For some reason, a rumor spread soon after that the artist's "hemorrhoid-infected diarrhea" was mixed into the vinyl when they were being pressed. This appeared to stem from a couple of comments left on the record's Discogs page. As one commenter put it: "When chopping this up on the ones and twos . . . a subtle but detectable odour of human faeces emanates through the air around the DJ."[76] This rumor was accepted as fact in separate articles by *Vice* and the Discogs Blog, though the fact that hemorrhoids are not infectious should have been a hint. I was skeptical, so I sent Vincent Koreman, the man behind RA-X, an email to confirm whether or not the rumor is true. It is not.

But with all the other ideas floating around, it seems inevitable that someone will attempt it at some point, pressing plant permitting. Keep your eyes—or your nose, as it were—peeled.

---

76 md, 'Ra-X - The Opium Den (Parts I–IV) / User Reviews,' Discogs, 2005 <www.discogs.com/release/354620-The-Opium-Den-Parts-I-IV/reviews> [accessed 10 January 2021].

III.7 NON-VINYL

In 2012, Stephen Coates was in St. Petersburg performing with his band, The Real Tuesday Weld, when he came across a strange object in a flea market. It appeared to be an X-ray of two hands, but was disc-shaped, with a center hole and grooves like a record. The stall owner was reluctant to provide any information, but Coates bought it anyway.

As Coates dug deeper, he realized this record was one of many contraband records produced during the Cold War, when Soviet authorities outlawed all but state-sanctioned music. He learned there was a whole community of individuals bootlegging recordings and distributing them, including classics like Bill Haley & His Comets' "Rock Around the Clock." They would obtain X-rays from hospitals in exchange for money or liquor, then cut grooves into them using a homemade lathe record cutter. These distinctive records were named *roentgenizdat*, but were also known as "bones" or "ribs," after the images that graced them. At times, the authorities hunted down these illegal operators and more than one was sentenced to time in the gulags. But as soon as they were released, they would return to cutting pirated records.[77]

Coates was able to connect with many of these former bootleggers, compiling his findings in a book called *X-Ray Audio: The Strange Story of Soviet Music*. These bone records are an early example of record-cutting ingenuity, born of necessity, but this was not the only time innovators have used unconventional materials to produce records.

III.7.1 Records That Melt

But first, let us review some information about the material used in normal records.[78] The "vinyl" of vinyl records is polyvinyl chloride, or PVC, which is a polymer of vinyl chloride—a material made of many molecules of vinyl chloride bound together in chains. It is these long chains that give vinyl its sturdy structure. PVC as we know it was invented in the 1920s by a chemist named Waldo Lonsbury Semon. At the time, he was working for B.F. Goodrich, a tire company, assigned to develop a synthetic rubber that could be used to coat metal. After exhausting the prototype rubbers of the day, he started experimenting with other substances, including PVC, which had been first synthesized in 1838 by the French physicist Henri Victor Regnault (one of the many names engraved on the Eiffel Tower). Prior to Semon's experiments, PVC was considered a nuisance, a stiff white solid that would slowly accumulate on the inner surface of vials of vinyl chloride gas, generally considered useless itself. Semon, though, was curious about whether it could have applications beyond clogging up lids, and started to tinker with the substance. He tried heating it to its boiling point

---

77 'X-Ray Records 1946–1964,' Garage <garagemca.org/en/exhibition/bone-music/materials/onlayn-tur-po-vystavke-muzyka-na-kostyah-online-tour-around-bone-music-with-the-exhibition-s-curator-stephen-coates> [accessed 10 January 2021]; Stephen Coates, 'No Title,' in *The Story of X-Ray Audio: What Would You Risk for the Sake of Music?* (Kraków: TEDxKraków, 2015) <tedxkrakow.com/archive/en/videos/223-the-story-of-x-ray-audio-what-would-you-risk-for-the-sake-of-music.html>.
78 Karel Mulder and Marjolijn Knot, *PVC Plastic: A History of Systems Development and Entrenchment*, Technology in Society, 2001, xxiii <www.elsevier.com/locate/techsocDiscussion> [accessed 10 January 2021].

and eventually combined it with a plasticizing solvent to create a readily elastic and moldable product that was easy to work with.

At the time, B.F. Goodrich was hardly jazzed about the new plastic. Its initial application was in shoe heels, and over time, its use expanded widely, eventually to such ubiquitous items as water pipes and credit cards. In 1944, he was awarded the Charles Goodyear Award, which, according to Wikipedia, is "the highest honor conferred by the American Chemical Society, Rubber Division." There is even a Waldo Semon Woods Conservation Area in Ohio.

Though vinyl has been the standard record material for nearly a century, after they replaced shellac records in the 1930s, some enterprising record producers have made records out of things other than vinyl. For example, in 2008, Mercury Records put out a special, limited-to-300 edition of Gonzales' "Working Together" on records made entirely of chocolate—meaning they could be played or eaten. Because of chocolate's meltability, these discs must be kept at a cool temperature and can only be played a few times before they break down.

The origins of the chocolate record date way back to 1903, when Germany's Stollwerck Chocolate company produced a series of tiny chocolate records, sold with a miniature gramophone designed to play them.[79] The machines themselves were designed by a clock company, who created an intricate mechanism for playing the teensy discs. Unfortunately, these devices were far from perfect. For one, the gramophone made a lot of mechanical noise, which often drowned out the tinny sound coming from the records themselves.

The records themselves were 3⅛ inches[80] and were indeed made of chocolate. The gimmick was summarized in the French magazine La Nature, which did a feature on them: "when a song no longer pleases, oh well! just savor the disc like you would a simple snack, and eat it."[81] A more permanent version of these discs was also produced by Stollwerck, made of a special wax named "karbin." The company would later issue a slightly larger, sturdier version of the mini-gramophone, with small records made of wood coated in wax; however, these were a commercial failure, barely selling 5,000 copies.

I contacted René Rondeau, a retired watch repairman living in California who collects antique gramophones, who tells me he owns many records but has never considered himself a record collector. For him, it is the phonographs that matter most. "I occasionally like to listen to the music on old records," he explains. "But by and large, they are more for demonstration than entertainment."

He mentions that the old Stollwerck records are elusive. "I have never seen a surviving chocolate record. I have heard rumors of some that supposedly survived, but I've never found anyone who actually has one." Instead, it is the "karbin" wax records that persist today; he owns about half a dozen of them.

79 René Rondeau, 'Stollwerck and Eureka Chocolate Phonographs,' René Rondeau's Antique Phonograph and Photography Site <www.edisontinfoil.com/stollwercks.htm> [accessed 10 January 2021].
80 'Tiny IMPERIAL Record... What Is It?', The Talking Machine Forum, 2016 <forum.talkingmachine.info/viewtopic. php?p=159359&sid=cd6d779cbe4f4f25b8e102dab5738ea8#p159359> [accessed 10 January 2021].
81 Rondeau.

One of the phonographs designed to play Stollwerck's chocolate records. Image courtesy of René Rondeau.

Rondeau tells me there has even been an attempt to recreate the chocolate records. "Several years, ago a friend worked with a chocolate maker to try to find a suitable chocolate to cast reproduction records by making a mold from a karbin wax record. Despite extensive efforts, with many different types of chocolate, he never was able to make one that would not melt easily. He gave me one during a visit to L.A.; it had largely melted by the time I drove home, despite being in an air-conditioned car. It tasted great, however."

Information is minimal about the actual content of the records. Rondeau says that the majority were, unsurprisingly, children's songs, though there were a few more serious records—including one of France's national anthem, "La Marseillaise." The provenance of the recordings themselves is lost to time. "None that I have seen mention a performer's name," Rondeau notes. "They are simply labeled as 'song,' or 'orchestra,' et cetera."

Despite their predisposition to decay, a handful of other individuals have taken up the idea of chocolate records. A French DJ named BreakBot released a special edition of his 2012 album, *By Your Side*, on chocolate, limited to 120 copies. Because of the production process, the record had to be single-sided, meaning customers only got the A-side of the first disc, whereas the standard release was a double LP.

Innerpartysystem, an electronic pop band from Mohnton, Pennsylvania, released the UK edition of their debut single "Don't Stop" as a chocolate record in 2008; the non-chocolate version hit #35 on the *Billboard* Modern Rock chart, making it the highest charting release to have a chocolate release. (Sadly, the chocolate version was capped at one hundred copies.) The Edinburgh band Found, meanwhile, collaborated with a baker to put out a chocolate version of their "Anti Climb Paint" single in 2011. In a short news item shown on local TV, a baker is shown pouring the chocolate onto an original metal master of the single, then chilling it in a fridge and peeling it off.

**Shout Out Louds' record made of ice.
Image courtesy of Ted Malmros.**

Chocolate can melt, but another band took the principle to a whole new level. In 2012, Swedish indie pop band The Shout Out Louds came up with the idea to create a record made of ice as a promotional strategy for their new single, "Blue Ice." To create this product, they designed a boxed set, which included a rubber mold of the record imprinted with the inverse of the single's grooves, as well as a bottle of distilled water. Users were instructed to pour the water into the mold, throw it in the freezer, then peel the frozen disc from the mold. There is a video online that documents the process of creating and playing a frozen "Blue Ice" disc. Though the sound is warped and riddled with imperfections—and skips every so often—it plays a lot more clearly than you might expect.

The "Blue Ice" record was primarily a promotional product, released in anticipation of the band's upcoming album *Optica*. Though nifty, this is hardly a meaningful method of music storage and dissemination—the sound quality is mediocre, and as the record melts, it can destroy the turntable cartridge as well as the insides of the record player itself. As far as I can tell, nobody has repeated the concept, although I suspect it is only a matter of time. In a charity auction run by Radio Sweden, a copy of the "Blue Ice" boxed set sold for a reported 4,758 Swedish kroners, equivalent to roughly $730 USD.[82]

III.7.2 Project Dark

In 1995, Kirsten Reynolds and Ashley Davies were on a five-week tour of continental Europe with their band, Headbutt, when an unusual idea came to them—one that would eventually form the basis of a sprawling experiment in unconventional turntablism. "We were most often the two in the front of the van, navigating and playing cassettes and keeping the driver awake," Reynolds tells me. "Each day was predictable in that we always drove, got

82 Boston Blatte, 'Innovative Sweden: Playable Frozen Record,' *The Local Se*, 2013 <web.archive.org/web/20151129033512/https://www.thelocal.se/blogs/bostonblatte/2013/01/24/innovative-sweden-playable-frozen-record/> [accessed 10 January 2021].

Project Dark's "Logging a Dead Horse" b/w "Chip Off The Old Block" single. Image courtesy of Kirsten Reynolds of Project Dark.

lost, found a venue, unloaded a van, did a sound check, ate vegetarian food, drank beer, did a gig, packed down the equipment, chatted to the locals, sold a few records and T-shirts, drank more beer, slept in some weird dormitory often above the venue, slept, got up, loaded a van and did it all again.

"After a while, the conversations became quite free-thinking. We were feeling very creative, we didn't have to worry about gas bills or boring stuff, just playing the shows and everything connected to that. I think we must have seen something, possibly a round object, and remarked that it could be a record. The next logical step was to imagine making records out of all sorts of materials. They would look like a gold disc, but perhaps made of something worthless—like sandpaper. With all the spare time, we developed the idea and realized you could make records out of pretty much anything."

"It started just passing the time on ten-hour drives to the next venue," Davies adds. "Kind of 'wouldn't it be funny if...' conversations that for some reason kept recurring and developing. It was probably about the context of putting everyday life objects that nobody really pays attention into a gallery context, a bit Duchamps-like."

Their idea turned into D.A.R.K., an ABBA-esque moniker composed of their initials spelled backward, and later took the name Project Dark. The premise was to create 7-inch singles out of unconventional materials, released in small editions as part of a Singles Club. The first one was made of etched glass; one hundred more would follow, made of a variety of media: several different grains of sandpaper, blackboard and chalk, a mirror, a slice of a Douglas fir trunk, a grinding wheel, and even Edam cheese! One whimsical record made from a Dutch biscuit was the focus of several media articles—though they released several biscuit records, featuring several brands and varieties.

The promoter of the final show of their European tour liked the concept and offered to set up some events on their behalf, so they quickly whipped up a series of records using materials they had collected on their travels. These early exhibitions did not feature the records actually being played: in fact, many were showcased in wooden cases, intended ironically to look like the gold records awarded by the recording industry. But attendees were curious about what these unusual discs would sound like through a stereo. "So, when we got back to London and were invited to exhibit in a Cinema in the West End, the idea expanded to playing them on discarded record players," Davies recalls.

EXTREME MUSIC

"Things escalated pretty quickly after we played live with some of the 7-inches at the opening. That event got a review, and then we were invited to play in New York at the Turntablism Festival." In addition to write-ups in *The Wire* and *Record Collector*, Project Dark's gambit garnered titillated stories in mainstream publications like *The Face* and *The Independent*, the latter of which remarked upon their "antiestablishment values, day-glo locks, and predilection for blowing things up." In a surprisingly contentious interview in *Sound Projector* magazine, writer Ed Pinsent repeatedly tries to get Reynolds to admit that the point of the records was not about sound at all, but instead merely a provocative conceptual ploy—to which Reynolds patiently reflects that all music objects have both a visual and auditory aspect to them, with their unusual records focusing to a greater degree on the latter.

Today, Reynolds feels that Pinsent may have been put off because "we were deadly serious about the whole project and yet found humor in it." A record made from a mirror ball is titled "Ballroom Bits" b/w "Come Dancing." The tree cross-section features "Logging a Dead Horse" b/w "Chip Off the Old Block" (meanwhile, a record made of woodchip paper features "Woodchip Off the Old Block," and another made of a circular saw blade features "A Rip Off the Old Block"). A stylus-tickling disc made from the fake grass that is used for model train sets is dubbed "Graze Anatomy" b/w "Gritty, Gritty, Bang, Bang!"

Reynolds and Davies designed other concepts primarily for performance purposes. As described in the article in *The Wire*, they used to conclude their shows by attaching a firecracker to the edge of a record on a turntable; once ignited, the record starts to spin, causing rapidly building noise to rumble through the stylus. Eventually, the rocket explodes and the turntable lid blows off in a cloud of smoke.

In that *Wire* interview, they balk at attempts to intellectualize their efforts. However, other interviews reveal more about their intentions. In *The Independent*, Reynolds explains that they take joy in upending the reverence typically bestowed upon disc jockeys. "The DJ has become this hallowed figure with ridiculously expensive equipment," he reflects. "We pay a couple of quid for our decks at flea markets, and then we blow them up." They specifically cite the influence of Einstürzende Neubauten, the German industrial band whose name means "collapsing new buildings" and whose music often boasted the destructive clatter of scrap metal and construction tools.

Today, Kirsten notes that the project democratized the stuffy world of sound art. "It was a great project at its peak, in the sense that it captured imaginations and engaged people who weren't really from that noise/sound art/avant-garde world. I think the visual introduction and humour helped with that."

Davies agrees: "I think we embraced all manner of attitudes and nuances from Dada, surrealism, Fluxus et al., without having the tired, over-studious attitude that so often seems to come with the territory. Every day seemed to produce another thing to marvel at—we simultaneously looked backwards and forwards with great joy at all the things we unearthed. We discovered that we'd accidentally gone down many of the thought processes of Edison and his sound-recording-world predecessors."

The Project Dark singles catalog survives today, albeit barely. Davies and Reynolds tell me they distributed the records informally at parties and shows and sometimes sold framed editions to support themselves. Sampled audio from the records also survives in the form of the multiple-edition *Excited by Gramophones* album series, along with various unreleased recordings of live performances. They also did some limited-edition releases on the Phono Erotic label, which today survive as curious artifacts. For their *Magnetophone* EP, they took a turntable and replaced the stylus with a cassette tape head, then prepared a record that had ¼" tape instead of grooves; the results were captured on that CD-R release. Their *Plate of Biscuits* EP, meanwhile, contains recordings of their biscuit records being played on a turntable.

Reynolds also explains that they were able to preserve the noxious sound of their infamous sandpaper records for posterity. "Somebody said that they really wanted to hear what sandpaper sounded like but didn't want to damage their stylus, so we recorded sandpaper on a deck and then pressed that sound onto a picture disc, with the image of sandpaper on the A-side and the reverse of sandpaper with corresponding sound on the B-side. These were made in very short editions of twenty or thirty and were pressed as lathe-cut discs by Peter King in New Zealand. He makes clear vinyl, so the picture discs are actually two color prints sandwiched between two clear discs."

Their most ethereal disc, meanwhile, is one that nobody owns. Housed inside the liner notes of *Excited by Gramophones Vol. 4* is an early discography of their Singles Club, which contains a listing for a "Virtual Reality 7" Single," catalog number SIN023. Reynolds explains, "The virtual reality single was literally virtual: it exists because we say it does."

Davies adds, "We were testing the theory of Zeno's paradoxes with that one!"

III.7.3 Other Unusual Materials

Bloomington, Indiana label Auris Apothecary also joined the nonvinyl party. Under the name Unholy Triforce, the label's Dante Augustus Scarlatti created an innovative record named *Brahms Destroys Haydn*, which is a one-sided, ten-inch record made of white glue, dried into the shape of a record. Designed to play from the inside out, the premise of the record is that the glue provides an irregular surface, resulting in an unpredictable cacophony of sound.

By email, he explained the genesis of this peculiar record. "Over the course of researching the technology of lathe cutting and the history of pressing records, we were in awe of the variety of materials that were tried/tested/used over the past 150+ years of record pressing. Even modern-day compounds differ from those used just 30 to 40 years ago!"

After discovering an online video of the chocolate records, Scarlatti and company were emboldened to try their own feats of record-making. "We performed tests using multiple materials and came out with some winners. The *Brahms Destroys Haydn* records proved to be incredibly inconsistent to produce, despite meticulous care, so we embraced it for what it was—an experiment."

EXTREME MUSIC

Though the Auris Apothecary website warns of the stylus-destroying possibilities of the glue record, Scarlatti assures me they had their own quality-assurance process. "We've played the glue records many times, as every copy was tested before selling. The record indeed holds the potential to be stylus-damaging—there are imperfections in the grooves that will make the tonearm jump around erratically or get caught, but every copy is different, so results may vary."

Other materially unique records owe their existence to technology. An MIT graduate student named Amanda Ghassaei

Unholy Triforce's *Brahms Destroys Haydn* glue record. Image courtesy of Auris Apothecary.

has developed a method for producing custom records by laser-cutting the grooves; she has used this process to create records out of wood, acrylic, and paper. She also designed a method for creating 3D-printed records. She used some of her favorite songs, including "Idioteque" by Radiohead, to demo her methodology. In addition to posting detailed instructions about how to create one's own custom discs, Ghassaei has also released high-resolution videos of her creations being played on a turntable. Both 3D printing and laser-cutting are digital methods of etching record grooves, and the resolution they can produce is much less than the direct process of carving a record from the vibrations of a needle on a lathe. As well, the media that she uses wood, paper, et cetera—feature far more surface irregularities than vinyl, and these aberrations contribute to the background noise.

But despite the method's technical shortcomings, the songs are still undeniably recognizable. And the records themselves are often beautiful to behold—particularly the wooden record, in which the rings of a tree follow the record's circumference. Ghassaei's least-pretty record was a version of "The Mexican Hat Dance" that she laser-cut into a tortilla—which she followed by renditions of Los del Rio's "Macarena" and Taco's "Puttin' on the Ritz."[83]

Interestingly, Ghassaei's wooden record was not entirely unprecedented. Back in 2011, the Munich-based conceptual artist Bartholomäus Traubeck devised a novel turntable that, while spinning, used visual sensors to analyze the surface of a cross-section of wood, particularly its rings. The visual details of the surface were then sent through a computerized algorithm, which generated a custom piano score. Traubeck's

---

83 'Make a Working Playable Tortilla Record With a Laser Cutter : 6 Steps (with Pictures),' Instructables <www.instructables.com/Make-a-Working-Playable-Tortilla-Record-with-a-Las/> [accessed 10 January 2021].

remarkable work has been released as a vinyl LP, with ten special copies glued to a circular slab of wood. The wood glued to these records was responsible for the music itself, and came in various varieties: birch, pear, ash, beech, maple, and so on.[84]

In a 2012 interview, Traubeck says that he does not connect his artwork with a particular conceptual framework, although he does recognize that it is a form of generative art—pseudo-improvisatory artwork that is created automatically under the parameters of a given system, in this case using an algorithm that reads natural data.[85] He also sees it as rooted in dendrochronology, which is the science of gleaning historical information by analyzing tree rings. In an interesting reflection, he remarks on the fact that the wooden record itself takes around half an hour to play from start to finish, whereas each tree has taken decades to grow into its full diameter. In a sense, then, each time Traubeck converts a cross-section of tree into music, he is condensing that organism's extensive natural history, collapsing decades into minutes.

84 Bartholomäus Traubeck, 'Years,' Bartholomäus Traubeck <traubeck.com/works/years> [accessed 10 January 2021].
85 Joe Patitucci, 'Interview: Bartholomäus Traubeck on "Years,"' Data Garden, 2018 <www.datagarden.org/post/2018/9/18/interview-bartholomus-traubeck-on-years> [accessed 10 January 2021].

III.7 EXTREME RECORDS: NON-VINYL

SECTION IV

TECHNOLOGICAL QUIRKS

IV.1 CHIPTUNE

On August 17, 2009, an unusual album was released to commemorate the fiftieth anniversary of Miles Davis' *Kind of Blue*. The album in question was named *Kind of Bloop*, a note-for-note remake of *Kind of Blue*, done in 8-bit style to sound like a videogame soundtrack. The album was produced by a programmer named Andy Baio and featured five different musicians doing versions of *Kind of Blue*'s five songs. Ironically, it was the cover art—a pixelated version of the original *Kind of Blue* cover—that attracted legal attention, in this case from the photographer who shot the original photo. Baio was forced to settle, paying out $32,500 and agreeing not to use the image again.[1]

But how did we arrive at an 8-bit version of *Kind of Blue* in the first place? To start our tour of technological quirks, many of which are rooted in a nostalgia for primitive electronics, let's start with chiptune, a colorful musical subculture in which artists use the hardware from old arcade and video game systems to make 8-bit music.[2] In their excellent 2009 article for the journal *Transformative Works and Cultures*, Kevin Driscoll and Joshua Diaz outline the history of the scene. According to their account, early home computers and game consoles featured primitive sound systems that were difficult to program. In 1982, however, the Commodore 64 was released. It contained an audio chip called the SID, or Sound Interface Device, which was designed by an electronic engineer named Bob Yannes, who apparently cites Emerson, Lake & Palmer's "Lucky Man" as his greatest sonic influence.[3] As Driscoll and Diaz explain, the SID contained three oscillators, each of which could churn out four different waveforms: square, triangle, sawtooth, and noise waves. The device would send these waves through an "envelope generator," which could alter the sounds' timbre, varying from short stabs to sustained drones. Modulation effects could also be applied using a series of programmable filters. Because there were three oscillators, the chip could only play three things at once—for example, a three-note chord, or a composition with three simulated instruments playing simultaneously.[4] Still, the result was a profound step up from previous audio chips.

This audio hardware was eventually hacked by tech-savvy programmer-musicians who wrote code that allowed them to create their own original compositions, played through the SID. Early programs developed by hobbyists, including SidMON, Future Composer, and JCH, were unwieldy, requiring users to program their songs as text, and only accessible to those armed with technical knowledge about how the SID worked. That changed with The Ultimate Soundtracker, a rudimentary but influential program designed for the Commodore Amiga computer in 1987 by a programmer named Karsten Obarski. Technically, The Ultimate Soundtracker does not work by allowing users to program sounds from the ground up. Instead of generating each note in code, this

---

1 Andy Baio, 'Kind of Screwed,' Waxy.org, 2011 <waxy.org/2011/06/kind_of_screwed/> [accessed 10 January 2021].

2 Kevin Driscoll and Joshua Diaz, 'Endless Loop: A Brief History of Chiptunes,' *Transformative Works and Cultures*, 2 (2009) <doi.org/10.3983/twc.2009.096>.

3 B. Bagnall, *On the Edge: The Spectacular Rise and Fall of Commodore* (Variant Press, 2006) <books.google.ca/books?id=4TgeAQAAMAAJ>.

4 'The Sound of SID: 35 Years of Chiptune's Influence on Electronic Music,' The Conversation, 2017 <theconversation.com/the-sound-of-sid-35-years-of-chiptunes-influence-on-electronic-music-74935> [accessed 10 January 2021].

program used prerecorded tones, like a sampler, which the musician could play using the keys on their keyboard. Marketed to computer users, The Ultimate Soundtracker itself was apparently quite buggy and, as a result, sold poorly. But some hackers later cracked open Obarski's code and created improved (if illegal) versions like Soundtracker 2; it was these iterations that led to Soundtracker's outsized influence. Nowadays, this entire class of audio production software is known as "tracker software," a reference to Obarski's pioneering creation and its various bootlegged exponents.

As Driscoll and Diaz point out, despite the ability of tracker software to digitally sample any source, many producers were drawn toward the basic, synthetic sounds that were employed by early game computers out of necessity: "the triangle waves, noisy percussion, and synthesized bass tones that characterized the SID chiptunes." It was these nostalgic, primitive sounds that became the purview of chiptune music.

The short songs that composers created found a venue on the demo scene. In the eighties, the computer game industry figured out that many gamers were not paying for their games but were instead sharing them with each other by copying the files. As a result, the companies began adding copy protection code to their products to circumvent this practice. But committed gamers would stay a step ahead, rapidly developing counter-software to defeat each iteration of copyright code. This cracking software was shared over BBS, the early bulletin board system that composed much of the internet before the advent of the World Wide Web. Soon, there were groups of BBS users who competed to be the first to release cracking software for each newly released game. To bolster each group's identity, these groups would add little promos to their cracking programs that identified who had created the software. Through the eighties and nineties, these promotional materials evolved from simple title screens to elaborate introductions replete with vivid graphics and music created on tracker software. These intros were called demos, and the scene that spurred them was—and still is—referred to as the demo scene.

Demo scenes existed for many early computer systems and video game consoles. Online, you can browse extensive archives of demos created on the Commodore 64, ZX Spectrum, and Atari ST. To this day, there continue to be international demo competitions, some of them large live events, where programmers compete to create demos on these ancient platforms, often restricted to a small file size to encourage innovation.

Through the nineties, tracker music separated from the demo scene, and songs started to be traded on their own, without the visuals. Entire packages of songs would be offered up online. Around 1998, this tracking scene gave way to a network of netlabels dealing in chiptune music. This music was modeled on the early 8-bit sounds of those video games but was often composed using digital software on contemporary computers.

In the nineties, the Nintendo Game Boy emerged as a popular piece of equipment to create chiptune music. Its 4-bit sound chip was a hit with chiptuners, who would devise their own custom game cartridges to compose songs and store them. *Little Sound DJ* was one popular cartridge; its developers no longer produce physical cartridges, but they do sell their software, which can be used on Game Boy emulators to recreate the experience.

One of the seminal chiptune netlabels is 8bitpeoples, which doubles as a collective of 8-bit composers. It was formed in 1999 by Nullsleep, a.k.a. Jeremiah Johnson, an early member of the Game Boy scene. Now in his late thirties, Johnson, who grew up in California, cites Giorgio Moroder's score for the 1984 sci-fi film *Electric Dreams* as an early influence. The film featured "Together in Electric Dreams," a collaboration between Moroder and Phil Oakey, a founding member of Human League, the seminal synth-pop band whose sounds evoke pixelated eighties memories.

As outlined in a 2012 interview, Johnson first got into chiptune as a university student in the late nineties.[5] By then, he'd cultivated interest in early Nintendo music and the songs that accompanied demos. "My brother and I used to watch demos that we downloaded on PCs over slow modem connections," he explains. "This was 1997, so we were downloading on a modem, watching demos and using MS-DOS to write music for the PC speaker." And yet he is careful to emphasize that video game music was not the heaviest influence. Instead, his sound was predicated on the synth pop of Depeche Mode, the shoegaze of My Bloody Valentine, and the intricate IDM of Aphex Twin. That last artist, incidentally, used the pseudonym Power-Pill to release a 1992 EP called *Pac-Man*, featuring a breakbeat-lacquered mash-up of the music featured in two arcade games, *Pac-Man* and *New Rally-X*.

Johnson's early work was made using tracker software on his computer to create 8-bit sounds that emulated the tones of earlier systems. Eventually, he discovered *Little Sound DJ* and a similar product, Nanoloop. His music, primarily released online via his label 8bitpeoples, piles melodic loops over each other, crafting an intricate network of sounds, often at a frenetic pace. The sound is somewhat akin to an IDM Game Boy score, as on the 2008 *Unconditional Acceleration* EP, whose "Supernova Kiss" fluctuates in tempo, pacing up explosively to very un-Nintendo rhythms.

There is also Bit Shifter, a.k.a. Josh Davis, one of the elder statesmen of the Game Boy scene. Born in 1973, he is among the oldest practitioners, and he still records today from his home in New York City. His *Information Chase* EP, released free on 8bitpeoples, is considered a classic of the genre.

Davis resists the interpretation that his music is nostalgic. In a 2006 interview, he comments on a few downsides of being a chiptune composer, including "people misunderstanding the motive as retro-fetishism" and "people yelling 'play Contra' from the audience."[6] On the flipside, he espouses his "less-is-more philosophy." As he explains, "From a composing standpoint, I think it presents a really perfect mixture of built-in guidelines and challenges. And I think it's probably pretty eye-opening from a listener/audience perspective for similar reasons, seeing a familiar and fairly humble device being made to surmount its apparent limitations."[7]

Information Chase, his seminal EP, is available for free online through several channels. It is a quick listen, squeezing six songs into a mere sixteen minutes. The opener is "Case

5   'Blip Tokyo Q&A: Nullsleep Interviews Manabu Namiki,' Indie Games Plus, 2012 <indiegamesplus.com/2012/01/blip_tokyo_nullsleep_namiki> [accessed 10 January 2021].

6   Bob Gourley, 'Chiptune Pioneer Bit Shifter Discusses the Game Boy as a Musical Tool,' *Chaos Control Digizine*, 2006 <www.chaoscontrol.com/bit-shifter/> [accessed 10 January 2021].

7   Tristan Burfield, 'Bit Shifter Interview,' Tristanburfield.com, 2005 <tristanburfield.com/Main/Bit_Shifter_Interview.pdf> [accessed 10 January 2021].

Init_", a delicate smudge of woozy synths, following which Bit Shifter jumps into the zippy pop of "Activation Theme," a jubilant jig that might accompany the payoff of defeating a final boss and rescuing the princess. "Particle Charge," meanwhile, is the invigorating battle scene, while the title track is the toe-tapping theme song. Despite its brevity, however, its reputation is broadly recognized. A tribute album was even released in 2011, comprising twenty-three tracks by twenty-three different artists—and boasting a runtime several multiples longer than the original.

Eventually, chiptune grazed the mainstream. 50 Cent's hit, "Ayo Technology," with Timbaland and Justin Timberlake, sets hip-hop beats to a bed of 8-bit synths. And Ke$ha's monstrous hit, "TiK ToK," would be nothing without its gluttonous chiptune tones. A memorable intersection between pop and chiptune occurred in 2007, when Timbaland produced a song called "Do It" for Nelly Furtado, which was discovered to have sampled parts of a 2000 Amiga module called "Acidjazzed Evening," by a Finnish demoscener named Janne Suni.[8] This led to legal proceedings, although the outcome was not publicized.

In a 2014 article for the journal *GAME*, a Madrid-based researcher named Israel Márquez argues that the chiptune scene is about far more than nostalgia. For one, chiptune is strongly tied to hacker culture, particularly the playfulness and creativity that characterize that world. As he points out, "There is a passion within the chiptune subculture—especially during its early days—of forcing a limited machine to make unexpected things and create new types of sounds." This ethic of experimentation transcends mere nostalgia. Secondly, Márquez highlights the commonalities between the chiptune subculture and the punk scene, particularly the do-it-yourself aesthetic and the way people who aren't indoctrinated into the 8-bit sound often complain that it is unlistenable noise. He sees chiptune as far more than a music genre, and instead as a "cultural phenomenon that lies at the intersection of technology, music, art, and politics," dedicated to exploring "how old, obsolete, and 'dead' gaming devices can be sources of innovation and creativity in contemporary digital society."[9] And while its brief references in pop culture may reduce 8-bit music to its immediate influences, it is hard to imagine that the droves of people who operate within the chiptune paradigm are all in it solely to reminisce.

---

8 Hassan Ghanny, 'Was Timbaland's Skillful Sampling a Cultural Crime?', *Medium Cuepoint*, 2016 <medium.com/cuepoint/was-timbalands-skillful-sampling-a-cultural-crime-e756da16f095> [accessed 10 January 2021].

9 Israel Marquez, *Playing New Music with Old Games: The Chiptune Subculture*, G|A|M|E Games as Art, Media, Entertainment (Ludica, 29 March 2014), <www.gamejournal.it/3_marquez/> [accessed 10 January 2021].

THE ELECTRIC FAMILY'S *MARIOPAINT*

In 1995, a group of artists affiliated with the Irdial Discs record label billed themselves as a supergroup called The Electric Family and recorded a concept album, *Mariopaint*. This album was composed entirely using the Super Nintendo game *Mario Paint*, which, in addition to allowing you to create art, also had a sub-game in which you could create songs by placing mushrooms, Game Boys, hearts, and other symbols on a musical stave. For the individuals behind The Electric Family, the idea was to create something innovative despite a restricted set of tools. As the Irdial website points out, "Modern recording studios, and even those found in the bedrooms of musicians the world over are full of equipment that affords the composer a huge range of sonic possibilities... *Mariopaint* strips all of that away and deliberately puts the artists in a straitjacket."

Each of the artists on *Mariopaint* were further limited to only one audio effect for their track, which was then recorded onto cassette. The goal was to prove that "less is more." The strange compositions are at their best when they use the program's otherworldly timbres to craft off-kilter melodies, as on tracks by Ray Tracing and Anthony Manning.

Mariopaint is available for free online via the Irdial Discs website.

IV.2 LOBIT

Chiptune is about reinventing antiquated technology to create new music. It holds as its Platonic ideal the severely limited 8-bit microprocessors contained inside early computers and game consoles, capable only of producing rudimentary graphics and sound.

In the 2000s, a new movement emerged, one that absorbed many chiptune producers. This was lobit, a.k.a. low-bit, a scene in which music is produced at deliberately low bitrates.

To understand this phenomenon, it is helpful to review the technical background behind digital music. The bitrate of an audio file, for example an MP3, is the amount of data contained within one second of sound. It is measured in kilobytes per second (kbps) and therefore tells you how many kilobytes of data there are in each second of that file. So, if an MP3 were encoded at 1 kbps, that would mean there is one kilobyte of data contained in one second of sound. The higher the bitrate, the greater amount of data per second, and thus the clearer the song will sound. When MP3s first came out, the standard bitrate was 128 kbps, although several standards emerged over time, particularly as average internet speeds increased. These included 160, 192, 256, and 320 kbps, the latter of which is where MP3s generally top out; for higher-quality audio, most music snobs will turn to other types of files.

The average music listener may, with close attention and good speakers, detect a difference between 128 kbps and higher bitrates, although for most casual audiences, the 128–160 kbps range is acceptable. Conversely, many audiophiles would consider even 320 kbps insufficient and will often turn to FLAC, a lossless cousin to MP3s, to get their fix.

Below 128 kbps, audio quality drops precipitously, quickly acquiring that fuzzy, distorted quality that plagued early online audio streams—a shoddy, echo-chamber-cum-loose-wire sound that you hear intermittently on internet calls.

Lobit artists revel in low-bitrate audio. Within their world, 64 kbps is the absolute upper limit of audio quality. The majority of lobit releases are encoded at rates well below 64 kbps, some as low as 1 kbps! For reference, there are YouTube videos that take popular songs and demonstrate what they sound like at different bitrates. Once you get down to 8 kbps, they sound entirely unrecognizable—like bleepy sonic pixels that somehow sound wet. Take that and halve the quality three more times: that will bring you to 1 kbps—an absurd figure, like the Mona Lisa reduced to four pixels.

Lobit evokes the early days of the internet, when now-ancient modems restricted transfer speeds to a trickle. Streaming audio was often supported by the now-defunct RealPlayer, which today evokes nightmares of incessant buffering. MP3s were encoded at low bitrates to facilitate rapid transfer, and, even so, it would take an hour to download a three-minute Offspring single.

The first lobit label was 20kbps Records, formed in December 2002 by Mathias Aeschlimann, then a high school student in Switzerland. His simple idea was that every release had to be encoded at 20 kbps. For Aeschlimann, the reasons were more pragmatic than ideological. "While I started the first lobit netlabel, I don't think I was the first person to use lobit for aesthetic purposes, but I don't know anything about these precursors," he tells me. "I arrived at lobit more or less by accident. In the early 2000s, I was part of the scene, ripping CDs and vinyl from the record store I was working at in order to get access to FTP servers with music releases. Typical hard drives in that time had a capacity of about 100gb and, being an art student, I couldn't afford many of them. Downloading stuff from the FTP servers, I'd eventually run out of space. So I had the idea to encode my own productions in lobit, in order to save space. They kinda sucked anyway. As this still used space, I thought to myself, 'I could simply move that stuff to the internet and call it a netlabel.' That's how it got started."

Eventually, he involved collaborators. "A friend of mine, Laub, liked the idea so much, he offered to redo the web design, which is still in place now. Erhalder contributed a lot of releases, as did artists I got acquainted with at the Babydoll record store. One of them, Willoc Babbyz, is still active today."

Over time, Aeschlimann came to attribute multiple meanings to his kilobyte-deficient tracks. In a 2005 interview, he acknowledges the theme of nostalgia, referring to it as "a pseudo-retro thing."[10] He recognizes that lower file sizes facilitate access for people in countries where high-speed internet access is not a given. He cryptically references media theory: "To really understand 20kbps rec. you should read Marshall McLuhan's *The Media is the Message* [sic]." He also likens lobit music to fast food at a time when his label was putting out releases several times a month. And as he astutely points out, someone can have the most expensive sound production equipment in the world and still produce lackluster music: "Bullshit still sounds like bullshit at 96khz and 24 bit." Good music shines through regardless of bitrate, just as a Big Mac is a classic, even if it costs just a few dollars and is ready mere minutes after you place your order. "I love fast food," Aeschlimann opines in a 2004 interview for a Russian webzine.[11] "I do not think that it is worse than ordinary food."

By now, Aeschlimann has been releasing lobit music for over fifteen years, a startling figure. The pace has slowed down as of late, but his total stands at over three hundred releases—all available online as ZIP files—and he continues to link up with new artists to this day. The emphasis is on electronic music, particularly in the realms of techno, ambient, and bleep, but he also puts out noise and some dub. He tells me he has recently been unwell with a rare form of cancer, but continues to host a monthly electronic music radio program called *Slackjackerz* with his friend Erhalder, broadcast on the Swiss radio station Kanal K.

What Aeschlimann might not have realized when he kicked off his label "by accident" was that lobit music would amass a cult following, spawning an array of labels and artists that has persisted even as high-speed internet became commonplace. Many of the scene's practitioners, like Aeschlimann, come from Europe.

---

10 N.E., 'Netlabel Profile: 20kbps Rec.', *Dozer*, 2005 <dozerblog.blogspot.com/2005/05/netlabel-profile-20kbps-rec.html> [accessed 10 January 2021].

11 Dmitry Bogdanov, '20kbps Records,' Experiment.ru, 2004 <web.archive.org/web/20060219064012/http://experiment.ru/articles/132> [accessed 10 January 2021].

Microbit-Records was run by Russia's Evgenij V. Kharitonov, who holds a doctorate in literature and whose day job is to oversee all the literary projects at a state library for young adults. Born in 1969 in Moscow, Kharitonov has been immersed in music his whole life. In the eighties and nineties, he played guitar and sang in several rock groups with fantastical names, like The We and Kharitonov's Fuck Orchestra. Near the turn of the millennium, he got interested in experimental electronic music, which was a gateway to the litany of genres he has dabbled in since.

As Kharitonov explained, his initial interest in low-bitrate sound occurred independently from the then-nascent lobit movement. "My interest in lobit sound occurred in 2001–2002," he tells me. "At this time, I turned toward electronic and Fluxus experiments. I experimented with voice, with sound poetry, [and] was passionate about the experiments of the great French experimentalist Henri Chopin. I was looking for a new sound. Once, [while] rendering another audio experiment, I accidentally put the wrong values of frequency characteristics, and the track was preserved in 32 kbps. When I heard this, I just fell in love with the new sound! Of course, some time later, I learned that there are a number of musicians who also make lobit sound, and in 2005 or 2006, I found two or three of the labels producing this kind of music."

Evgenij V. Kharitonov. Image courtesy of Evgenij V. Kharitonov.

He quickly immersed himself in this network of netlabels, enthusiastically downloading everything in sight and, eventually, recording a prodigious quantity of music under his moniker Microbit Project. Amid the exuberance of newly discovered possibilities, the quality control was questionable: "I think it's kind of ruined my taste in music (ha-ha!), because in the flow of the lobit movement, [there was] a huge number of blatant nonsense and garbage! I have created a large amount of bad music. The only justification for me: I was a real hungry wolf, [and] in the menu of the electronic underground all the dishes seemed delicious."

In 2007, Kharitonov started his own lobit label, Microbit-Records, which he ran until 2014, ending the journey at release number two hundred (excluding a one-off release in 2016). He believes the label's end was an inevitable outcome of lobit's global decline. "The decline of interest in the aesthetics of lobit has occurred simultaneously in all countries after 2013. I think this recession is a temporary phenomenon."

EXTREME MUSIC

Kharitonov notes that the enormous boom in lobit sound also exhausted much of the low-hanging fruit, describing the movement's current hiatus as a "pause to find new interesting ideas." Kharitonov, himself, has released only a trickle of releases as Microbit Project as of late, instead moving toward more hi-fi ambient music, which he releases under the name EugeneKha.

There have been other European lobit outposts. Italy's Unicode Music limits releases to a maximum of 32 kbps; it is run by Polus, a hyper-productive experimental electronic artist who has started five different labels,

Cover for Starpause's *Lucy Lefty*. Image courtesy of Jordan Gray.

not all of which fall under the lobit frame. He also records harsh noise prodigiously under the pseudonym Astral Vomit. A German netlabel called Abulia Concepts, run by someone named Hertzcanary, also devoted much of its early work to lobit music, though later releases diversified. They billed themselves as "dependent on an escape that makes the lowbit seem beautiful and the reality of byte seem unnecessary."[12] The now-defunct Dex and the City label out of Latvia, which at one point threatened "DEATH TO CONSUMERISM! DEATH TO MAINSTREAM" on its exuberantly decorated website,[13] represented another cog in the European scene.

Beyond the continent, an active lobit scene also creeped up in America: mp3death is run by the chiptune artist Starpause, a programmer named Jordan Gray who lives in San Francisco. Gray's own music as Starpause is lo-fi but accessible; 2016's freely available *Lucy Lefty* is a collision between chipper videogame melodies and more off-kilter, IDM-inspired tendencies, constantly underscored by plodding analog rhythms.

Gray recalls being given a drum kit as a toddler, then trashing it and reverting to banging pots and pans. As a teenager, he started a band while working at a big chain toy store, using defective merchandise as instruments. Though they only played a few "renegade" shows, this inspired Gray to start a solo project, recording feedback noise onto four-track, and trading cassettes with other hometapers.

But the appeal of making music and running a lobit label has its origins in circumventing copyright. "I don't know if I would have gotten into writing music and running labels if I wasn't a pirate first," he reflects. "It showed me how easy it is to copy and distribute media. Getting on a tangent, but artists aren't poor because of circumvented

---

12 Max Dolor, 'Abulia Concepts,' 2011 <gorehole.org/abuliaConcepts/index.htm> [accessed 10 January 2021].
13 'Dex and the City Records,' 2008 <web.archive.org/web/20080719022154/http://dex.neirothe.net/index2.htm> [accessed 10 January 2021].

Cover for K9D's *JPEG SEKZ.*
Image courtesy of Jordan Gray.

distribution channels. Artists are poor because society doesn't value creativity." He recalls trading anime fan subs "along with even less savory materials" by mail, and parlaying access to a photocopier into a zine.

In 2000, in an early foray into lobit music, Gray wrote some 1-bit tracks on a Macintosh SE, which were released the next year by the Floppy Swop label, which released music exclusively on floppy disks. He eventually started making 4-bit music using a *Little Sound DJ* cartridge in his Game Boy, at which point he stumbled upon the 20kbps label. At this point, he was recording under the name k9d.

"Releasing on 20kbps was super easy," he tells me. "I emailed Mathias, the label boss, and he put the material up without any hesitation. That first k9d release got reviewed by *De:Bug* magazine,[14] which felt huge and encouraging. A month later, I dropped another 2-track EP on 20kbps. Like a lot of noise music, the packaging mattered. I enjoyed writing up a text file and finding extra art goodies to go in the zips.

"I was living with either Overthruster or Jonkie at that time," he expands. "Overthruster had his first release on 20kbps in December 2003. I put out a second k9d release with 20kbps that month and also started the mp3death netaudio label. Jonkie was the first release on mp3death. We were all part of the same crew, which was gaining notoriety in Minneapolis. Our main instruments were Gameboys, PVC didgeridoos, and wrestling. Sometimes car alarms in rubber trash cans so we could throw them around. Anyway, this tight-knit rowdy noise crew was all in on lobit."

He identifies 20kbps as the "TRUE CREATORS" of the lobit scene, but also shares a few other milestones. In 2004, archive.org rose to prominence as a platform on which netlabels could freely upload MP3 releases, which was a boon to many producers. A Japanese chiptune review website called VORC, which ran from 2001 to 2008, also provided extensive coverage of the lobit scene.

A chiptune producer who has overseen twenty-two releases on his own lobit label, Gray sees the two scenes as linked—and not just because lobit music was often produced by the trackers used by chiptune producers. "Sonically, lobit and chiptune have a similar effect. Initially, both sound like crunchy noise, but as your psychoacoustic sensibilities warm up, there's a lot of expression and detail to savor. Both genres are also attractive

---

14 De:bug is a German review site; their review of k9d's debut EP, *Jpeg Sekz*, describes it as "computer game music that sounds like the Atari is still rubbing the crash sleep out of its eyes."

in that their limitations force you to focus on the core as a producer. You're not going to be worried about fine details of mixing, compression, et cetera, when you don't have access to those effects or know that those subtleties will be lost to encoder crush."

Toledo, Ohio's 4m@-records imposed a 1.44-megabyte limit on its releases, such that each release could be downloaded and copied onto a floppy disk. Its owner, Adam Crammond, is a shortwave radio enthusiast and operated 4m@ as a sub-label of his Proc-Records netlabel, which was not restricted to lobit music. However, he considers lobit his "heart and soul" in a 2016 interview.[15] For Crammond, his allegiance to lobit boils down to aesthetics. As he explains, his music seems to sound best when encoded as 32 kbps mono MP3s.

Minneapolis' NORTHAMERICANHARDCORE label released records from artists across the globe, spanning noise, hardcore, and a disturbing release called *My Dad Beats the Shit Out of Me* by one-and-done moniker Nick, billed as "a live recording of verbal domestic abuse."

There was also a Bangkok label called Top of the Flops whose focus was on "dance music and avant garde experimental stuff only." Top of the Flops, which ran from 2010 to 2012 (plus a one-off revival in 2013) is an interesting label, not least because of the man who ran it. Kai Nobuko is a Dutch man who lived in Thailand for many years, and who records as Toxic Chicken.

If you search for information on Toxic Chicken online, you will find a whirlwind of far-fetched and seemingly conflicting information, most of it originating from Nobuko himself. After a wild and productive several years in Thailand, he currently resides in London with his "creative sister," singer Bloom de Wilde, "creating things but also being an uncle for her kids." He describes himself as being guided by his art, maintaining his existence through a combination of minimalism and ingenuity. He does not have a "normal job," nor does he receive government benefits. He explains that he typically volunteers his time and talents. "I don't believe in the concept of money but rather [to] replace it with love," he explains. "I don't need a lot. Food, a roof, and some electricity would be all I need in exchange for love and creative things, which crazily had kept me alive all these years."

This romantic but pragmatic approach to life parallels his pathway to lobit music. He started with some early experiments using music composition software on his childhood Atari ST, then moved to recording "cutlery, voice, household equipment" with a faulty microphone, manipulating the sampled sounds with a program called *Fast Tracker 2*.

Civil disobedience has been a feature from the start. "Once, I took the telephone book and called random numbers and recorded what was on the other side of the line, making a song in which a confused lady was saying, 'Hello? Hello? This is Tiny... hello?' My friends liked it, and as a joke, I sent it into a competition because I thought it would be funny if some important bozos in the Dutch music industry would hear it.

15 'Interview - Graffiti Mechanism / C4,' Sirona-Records Blog, 2016 <www.sirona-records.com/blog/interview-graffiti-mechanism-c4> [accessed 10 January 2021].

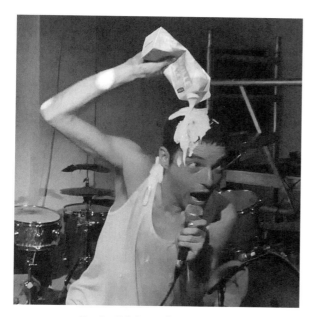

Toxic Chicken playing live.
Image courtesy of Frank Janssens.

But instead of getting a laugh, they actually took it serious and asked me to play. I brought an entire metal band and had demands for a big drum kit and gear, we had to pretend to play at the sound check, and once it was time to perform, the band was standing still and I made sandwiches for the audience."

Banned from big venues, Nobuko staged various performances and anti-performances at squats, festivals, and demonstrations. His pathway to lobit was incidental, since he was already recording at low fidelity by the time he discovered the scene. This came after the release of his first album, a CD-R release called *Lo-Fi* which came out on the esc. rec. label, said by one reviewer to "breath [sic] the good, raw, and untamed energy of elektro punk."[16] After that release, he discovered a network of lobit netlabels like Floppy Swap and 20kbps. Several elements appealed to him. For one, he could quickly download "all kinds of mysterious music" due to its compact format. And the low-bitrate sound, which "gave the music an extra warm layer of coziness" was part of the charm, as was the challenge of making music that was pleasurable when heard at limited kbps. As Nobuko puts it, "It was the ideal 'fuck you' against the snobbish world of the rich big-time producers that enjoy making everything sound squeaky clean and lifeless." He thinks of it as a digital-age punk music, a comparison that makes sense given the shared aesthetic of primitivism. And, like three-chord punk, he warns of lobit's addictive properties, threatening that "once you are completely inside it, there is a high chance that you won't really enjoy high-fidelity music anymore, and the hunger for lobit becomes unstoppable."

Today, Nobuko continues to create art, but at this moment, he is toying with high-fidelity music. He also runs a hyperactive monstrosity of a blog called *Yeah I Know It Sucks*, which churns out review after review of esoteric new albums, most freely available via online channels, in his distinctive, stream-of-consciousness writing style.

Of the many lobit labels discussed, none are currently active, apart from Unicode. Some retain their archives, while others have been replaced by stock websites. Most petered out between 2010 and 2014. One netlabel that continues to maintain a consistent strain of lobit releases is 8 Ravens, which churns out experimental releases exclusively

---

16 Frans de Waard, 'TOXIC CHICKEN - LO FI (CD-R by Esc Rec),' Vital Weekly, 593 <www.vitalweekly.net/593.html> [accessed 10 January 2021].

in 8 kbps, each packaged in a small ZIP file and made available for free download. Nobuko, convinced that lobit will live on eternally, pointed me toward a new lobit label called sub65, which mandates that all releases must be encoded at 64 kbps or less. Started in 2018 and already thirty releases deep, it is the work of Adam Sigmund, an electronic musician from New Jersey who records under the name Origami Repetika.

What to make of lobit, conceptually? The obvious analogy is to think of it as a digital age version of lo-fi music, the strain of tape-hiss-infused indie rock pioneered by bands like Guided by Voices and Pavement and promulgated by a network of independent labels in the eighties and nineties. Those artists could not afford access to real recording studios, so they instead churned out droves of bare-bones recordings done on four-tracks or worse. Once the capacity for better recording conditions arose, many bands and labels continued churning out shoddily recorded tape and vinyl releases, embracing the aesthetic for its own merits. Contemporary lobit, similarly, continues to employ paltry bitrates, even though internet speeds have improved. But the parallel is curiously inverted. Whereas lo-fi artists record music at low fidelity, lobit artists typically compose their works rendered at regular bitrates, then down-convert them to lower file sizes.

Lobit can also be regarded as a punk-style response to audiophiles' obsessiveness with sound quality. Punk rebelled against the indulgences of progressive rock; lobit sends a big middle finger to the snake-oil stereo systems that deplete audio snobs' wallets. A hyper-lossy 20 kbps OGG file can be considered a counterreaction to a lossless 24-bit FLAC vinyl rip. Echoing this, The Cryovolcano, the lobit producer behind the 8 Ravens label, issued a manifesto of sorts in April 2010, listing a handful of lobit raisons d'être, among them: "A cultural stance against technological snobbery."[17]

The Cryovolcano also considers the lobit ethic as "an aesthetic choice for an artist who enjoys the warm, raw, and somewhat unpredictable nature of Low Bit sound," bringing to mind the familiar "warm sound" argument that vinyl purists often make. For many, that argument may seem difficult to accept, since the tinny quality of lobit sound is customarily synonymous with *bad audio*—poorly rendered YouTube videos, early MP3s downloaded off peer-to-peer networks, et cetera. Like many fringe music scenes, lobit privileges a sound that rubs most people the wrong way, drawing a line between lobit devotees and everyone else.

---

17 The Cryovolcano, 'WHAT IS LOW BIT?', 8 Ravens, 2010 <8ravens.blogspot.com/2010/07/what-is-low-bit.html> [accessed 10 January 2021].

IV.3 FLOPPIES

In 1983, New Order released their iconic "Blue Monday" 12" single in a special sleeve that was designed to look like a 5¼" floppy disk. Designed by a graphic artist named Peter Saville, the package was apparently so expensive to produce that Factory Records' owner, Tony Wilson, used to claim that the label lost five pence on each copy that was sold—which really added up once the song, unexpectedly, became a huge hit![18]

"Blue Monday" may have been the first reference to floppy disks in the world of mainstream music, but the format has since become an object of fascination on the experimental music's fringe. Before we get into that, however, let us first review the history of the now-antiquated digital storage medium.

IV.3.1 Early Floppy History

It was 1967, and people were still using punched paper cards to store computer data. An IBM team led by engineer David L. Noble imagined an alternate form of data storage that relied on magnetic material. They considered magnetic tape, which was already being used in other industries, but instead opted for a Mylar disc coated in magnetic material and enclosed in a protective plastic envelope. This was the first floppy disk, so named because it would flop back and forth if shaken. First marketed in 1971, its eight-inch diameter dwarfed the floppies that would follow, but it changed the digital storage industry. As the IBM website explains, this single disc could contain 80 kb of data, the equivalent to 3,000 punched cards, and as a result, those paper cards quickly became obsolete.[19] Subsequent versions of the 8-inch disc would hit 500 kb, and there was even a double-sided 1 MB version.

In the late seventies, computer companies began complaining that the 8-inch discs were too large and too expensive. A 5¼-inch floppy was created in 1977, which could store up to 110 kb of data; further revisions to the format would raise this to 1.2 MB. It was this floppy disk that would inspire the New Order single. In 1978, Apple introduced the Apple II personal computer, which came with two 5¼-inch floppy drives, signaling the death knell of the 8-inch disks, which are now a largely forgotten relic.

In the early eighties, several manufacturers introduced competing floppy disk formats into the market, ranging from 3½-inch models all the way down to two-inch discs. Eventually, the companies convened and agreed on a 3½" as the new industry standard. This is the square, un-floppy floppy disk that we recognize today. It contains a black plastic disk coated in magnetic material, buffered by a thin polyester sheet, all locked into a plastic shell. There is a sliding metal shutter that protects the disk when it is not in use; this mechanical sheath retracts when the disk is in a drive. This industry-standard 3½" floppy stores 1.44 MB of data.

---

18 Dave Simpson, 'How We Made: New Order's Gillian Gilbert and Designer Peter Saville on Blue Monday,' *The Guardian*, 2013 <www.theguardian.com/culture/2013/feb/11/how-we-made-blue-monday> [accessed 11 January 2021].

19 'The Floppy Disk,' IBM100, 2011 <www.ibm.com/ibm/history/ibm100/us/en/icons/floppy/> [accessed 11 January 2021].

EXTREME MUSIC

Floppies were the portable data storage format of choice before CD-Rs, flash drives, and eventually cloud-based data management took over. In 1996, it was estimated that there were five billion floppy disks in use—almost one per person on Earth![20] But as the nineties progressed, people turned to other means of data storage. Tellingly, in 1998, the iMac came out with a CD-ROM drive but no floppy drive, even though the floppies themselves sold two billion units that same year.[21] Instead, floppy lovers were forced to buy an external floppy drive and connect it by USB to get their floppy fix. In 2003, Dell stopped including floppy drives in their line of home computers. A 2007 article in *The Telegraph*, cleverly titled "Floppy disks ejected as demand slumps," notes that only 2 percent of new PCs and laptops contained floppy drives by then.[22] In 2011, Sony stopped manufacturing floppy disks altogether.[23]

Floppies never caught on as a practical option for distributing music for obvious reasons. When music moved from analog to digital, it needed a format with a greater storage capacity, a function served by compact discs. Floppies, at 1.44 megabytes apiece, can only accommodate music that is encoded at very low quality or that is very short. An MP3 encoded at just 128 kbps would run approximately a minute and a half before exceeding a floppy disk's capacity.

Floppies were sometimes used to disseminate early demos during the demoscene days, as described in the chapter on chiptune. For a time, floppies were also used to house electronic press kits (EPKs): the packets of band photos, press releases, and media clippings that labels and PR houses would include with promotional CDs sent to radio stations and music magazines. Some of these are documented online and have been even sold to gratuitously completist fans. For example, an EPK for Pulp's *Different Class* sold on Discogs for $44.66 USD in 2011.[24]

In 1995, meanwhile, Sony Records attempted to exploit the floppy format for a new cash grab. Music Screeners were a short-lived gimmick aimed at the growing PC market. They were floppies containing screensavers that were thirty- to forty-second video clips of an artist's current single. They also came with simple computer games. A contemporaneous *Billboard* article notes that the list price for Music Screeners was a steep $12.98—one of many examples of the major-label hubris that presaged the Napster age.[25]

In 1996, Brian Eno released *Generative Music I*, a floppy release that offered listeners the opportunity to listen to music that was created algorithmically. Eno's disk contained files that were intended to be played on a computer program called Koan. Instead of containing predetermined music, Koan took the data in the files and created entirely

---

20 Andy Reinhardt, 'Iomega's Zip Drives Need a Bit More Zip,' *Business Week*, 1997 <web.archive.org/web/20080706151833/http://www.businessweek.com/1996/33/b3488114.htm> [accessed 11 January 2021].

21 David Derbyshire, 'Floppy Disks Ejected as Demand Slumps,' *The Telegraph*, 2007 <www.telegraph.co.uk/news/uknews/1540984/Floppy-disks-ejected-as-demand-slumps.html> [accessed 11 January 2021].

22 Derbyshire.

23 Charlie Sorrel, 'Sony Announces the Death of the Floppy Disk,' *Wired*, 2010 <www.wired.com/2010/04/sony-announces-the-death-of-the-floppy-disk/> [accessed 11 January 2021].

24 'Pulp - Different Class Interactive Presskit (1995, Floppy Disk),' Discogs <www.discogs.com/Pulp-Different-Class-Interactive-Presskit/release/2506388> [accessed 11 January 2021].

25 Catherine Applefeld, 'Sony Acts Putting A Stop To Computer Burnout,' *Billboard* (New York, September 1995), p. 81 <books.google.ca/books?id=9A0EAAAAMBAJ>.

I.2.3 Ambient
A Robert Rich sleep concert

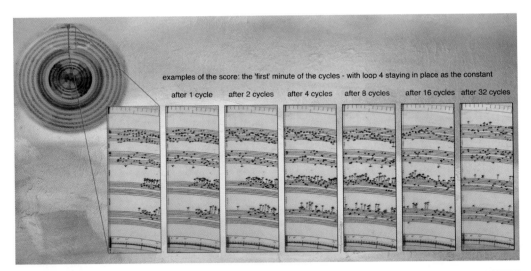

examples of the score: the 'first' minute of the cycles - with loop 4 staying in place as the constant

after 1 cycle   after 2 cycles   after 4 cycles   after 8 cycles   after 16 cycles   after 32 cycles

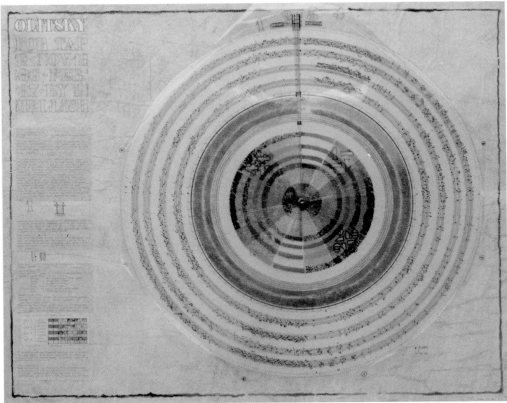

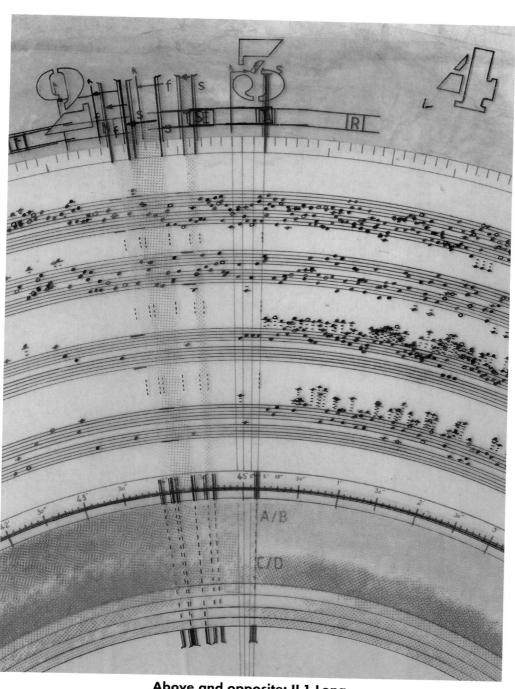

Above and opposite: II.1 Long
Score for *Olitsky* by Ian D. "Mel" Mellish

III.4.2 Sawblades
Two sawblade records from Musical Tragedies/MT Undertainment
Top: MT-222, 1994, Doc Wör Mirran, "Screaming for Titties"
Bottom: MT-370, 1997, Ace Frehley, "Take Me To The City"

III.5 Pictures
Top: Hot Air Records EP4 LUNCH, 1994,
Vomit Lunchs "Violent Clash Between Killer Bastards Of Eardot Remix" 10"
Center: Horror Pain Gore Death Productions HPGD044, 2016,
Abscess *Urine Junkies* LP
Bottom: Little Mafia Records LM066, 2010,
Priest In Shit/Smell & Quim *Rough Skin* split LP

Top: III.7 Non-Vinyl
Quagga Curious Sounds QCS_121, 2019, Michael Ridges *Dreams In Vintage Hairy Latex* LP. Latex record pressed with the artist's pubic hair.

Bottom: V.1 Elaborate
Destroyed 7″ record that served as packaging for
D.L. Savings T.X.'s *Thank You Urine Doll* cassette (American Tapes).
Created by John Olson, image courtesy of Henry Rollins.

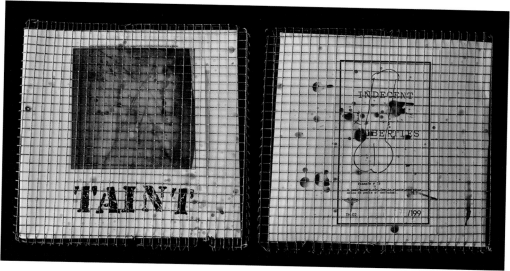

V.2 Bodily Fluids
Top: Pale Horse Recordings PHR002, 2007, Senthil *Septisemesis* cassette
J-card with razor blade and band members' blood
Bottom: Praxis Dr. Bearmann TH-02, 1995, Taint *Indecent Liberties* LP.
Cover smeared in animal blood and wrapped in metal wire

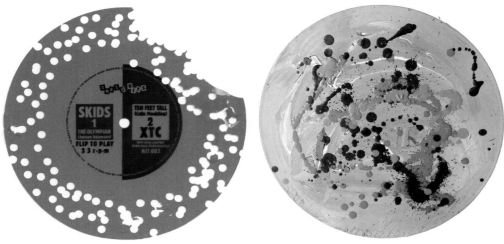

VI.2 Damaged
Top: Silver Blue Records, 1997, Cock E.S.P. "As If" single

VI.3 Unplayable
Bottom left: Michael Ridge, hole-punched flexi-disk
**Bottom right: Jill Lucas *Wax on Wax*, LP decorated
with melted candles and paint**

new music using the parameters dictated by the code, a sort of improvisation via digital randomization. Eno famously bandied his generative sound as the future of music, imagining that future generations would "look at us in wonder and say: 'You mean you used to listen to exactly the same thing over and over again?'"

IV.3.2 Floppies as Subculture

The first in Synesthetic Recordings' FLOP series, FLOP 001. Image courtesy of Petter Flaten Eilertsen.

At first, floppies were used sporadically as gimmicky add-ons to vinyl or CD releases, but the idea of releasing music on standalone floppy disks emerged as an explicit aesthetic in the mid-2000s, around the time they were being phased out of the software market in favor of CDs and flash drives. This timing adds credence to the idea that it is the defunctness of the format that fuels interest in them as musical objects.

It was Petter Flaten Eilertsen, then a twenty-nine-year-old archivist living in Oslo, who set the precedent for floppy music in 2002. Involved in music from an early age, Eilertsen had recorded individually and as parts of several bands, particularly in the areas of noise and drone music. In the year 2000, he started a record label called Synesthetic Recordings, through which he released experimental music on CD, CD-R, and vinyl. But things changed in 2002 with the start of a special series called FLOP. Over the space of thirteen months in 2002 and 2003, Eilertsen released one floppy disk per month, each one containing a one-minute MP3 file. Each disk came out at the top of the month and was deleted from the catalog at the end, at which point the file was put up on the Synesthetic website for anyone to enjoy. They have since been made available on Bandcamp.

Via email, Eilertsen tells me that FLOP was "meant as a bit of a joke," the name intended to imply that the floppy disk was an impractical music format. Not only was there very limited storage space on each disc, but, because floppy drives were too slow to play the MP3 file in real time, the file had to be copied to the person's hard disk before it could be played! "Yet," he reflects, "I liked the physical format of the floppy disk, as it felt slightly arcane and archaic even back then."

Eilertsen bought the floppy disks from a hardware store and made them to order, printing the labels on a barcode printer at the company where he worked. Only a few people ordered copies, so a complete set is, today, a rarity. "It was meant to go on for longer," Eilertsen says, "but after a year, I just couldn't be bothered to make them anymore…"

In addition to Eilertsen's FLOP series, the year 2002 also saw several floppy releases come out on other labels. The PurePainSugar label of France put out a split of thirty-second tracks by two French emo bands, Overmars and Iscariote. A mysterious IDM artist from Sweden named Sovtek put out a triumvirate of floppy releases, about which there is barely any surviving information. Kosksidose, a small cassette label out of Haugesund, Norway, run by Vidar Evensen, put out a floppy disk by Evensen's solo act, Marakel. And the iconoclastic noise act Cock ESP put out their own ode to the format, *Three and a Half Inches of Floppy Cock*.

These days, there are a handful of labels who put out floppy disks, most of them the 3½" variety. Sergiy Fjordsson runs the Depressive Illusions label out of his home in Ukraine. He started the label in 2009 to put out black metal and related genres and has somehow amassed nearly eight hundred releases on that imprint alone. In 2013 he started up a sub-label of Depressive Illusions named Floppy Noise Records, billed as a conduit for releasing "raw black metal and noise on 3½" floppy disk ONLY." Fjordsson is very dedicated to his concept. When I reached out to him for an interview, he declined to participate, on the grounds that I could not promise my book would be published exclusively in print—for him, it was analog or nothing!

Floppy Kick is a label formed in 2013 by a secretive character in Hungary. Offering their floppy disk releases for a slim three Euros a pop, they have assembled a discography of singles, splits, compilations, box sets, and special ultra-limited editions (five to ten copies each!) that trends toward noise and otherwise abstract sound. As the Floppy Kick owner shared in a brief interview: "Well, I like to release music on strange formats; also I had some old diskettes at home, so I just made one. I think this is an almost unused small gap between the analog and digital world, but it's rarely seen as a carrying format for musical releases. Also it's a kind of recycling too."

From 2012 to 2013, Davide Femia, who ran the experimental label SantoS Productions, released a series of fourteen floppy disk releases by noise acts like Richard Ramirez, Maurizio Bianchi, and the Mauthausen Orchestra. He used short digital tracks designed to be played on loop. The series was a matter of opportunism. "I found a box full of blank floppies in my office," Femia recounted. "And I really didn't want to trash them, so I thought about what I could do with those prehistorical pieces of magnetic disc. So I decided to start a floppy series for my label."

Femia considers himself an "average 36-year-old guy from Italy" who lives with his wife and young son. He has since shut down the label, but continues to be involved in fringe art, creating glitch-influenced visuals which he disseminates on Instagram. He also loves tattoo art and is heavily inked. To pay the bills, he owns and runs a hot-dip galvanizing plant, a process which involves dipping steel products like car parts, corrugated roofing, and metal pails into molten zinc to prevent corrosion.

For Femia, there was no grand philosophical vision behind releasing music on floppy. Instead, it was a combination of eighties nostalgia and an appeal to collector

Anla Courtis' *Kayrophonics* box set on Floppy Kick Records. The disks come in a custom box decorated with floppy disk innards. Photo courtesy of Mark Windisch of Floppy Kick.

fetishism. "I've loved them since I was a kid at the end of the eighties," he explains. "Floppies were the only way to get games and other stuff on PC, so they remind me of those days. I also chose the format as [a] collector item, more than an effective useful format for music."

Although early releases, such as the Maurizio Bianchi floppy, relied on Femia's already established network of collaborators, the novelty ended up drawing others to ask Femia about releasing their own work on floppy. "Oh, I loved those days so much, big experimental artists asking me to be released on my tiny label."

The floppies were, interestingly, the "best sellers" on SantoS, and their tiny, limited-to-twenty editions immediately sold out. Amusingly, some folks made the purchase seemingly without realizing what they were getting into. "I clearly remember people asking me how the fuck should they play music out of floppies, so I had to explain that they could easily download the track from a protected internet archive and listen as any other file." Others embraced the defunct format. Someone even wrote Femia to tell him that they had bought a used floppy drive simply to listen to his releases. "I'm so proud of it," Femia reflects.

Diskette Etikette, run by Neil Jennings of London, is a well-regarded floppy label perhaps best known for a series of compilations cleverly called *Now That's What I Call Retro-Futurism*, of which there have been four editions.

Jennings, now thirty-three years old, works for a charity and emphasizes that he does not make any money from music, although it is his main interest apart from soccer. In the 2000s, when he was attending school in Birmingham, there were plans for a floppy label called My Little Floppy, with four releases planned, but it folded before any of them came out. Several years later, in 2010, he recalls "a chance encounter at work with a pack of floppy disks. No one wanted them, so I decided to make use of them—and Diskette Etikette was born! After a couple of weeks of planning and research, and some encouraging chats with lobit heroes like Adam Crammond from Proc, I put out the first release."

Diskette Etikette's *Now That's What I Call Retro-Futurism Vol. 4* floppy disk compilation. Image courtesy of Neil Jennings.

For Jennings, there were several appeals to floppy releases. "I guess I love the retro-futurist element—using obsolete technology to release digital music on a physical format," he opines. He also sees the appeal of challenging artists to "maximize what you can fit on 1.38MB of disk space! Having such a restrictive format really helps with creativity—as the wonderful lobit scene attests to!"

He sourced second-hand floppies from friends' workplaces, eBay, and Freecycle, a website where people give away items to be reused. As computer technology progressed, he had to move from using a built-in floppy drive to a USB-connected one. Despite the increasing effort required to obtain blank floppy disks, Jennings considers the hobby well worth the effort because it has allowed him to connect with a tight-knit community of floppy lovers. One floppy, by a UK hardcore band named Pariso, unpredictably sold out all fifty copies within the first few hours, requiring a frantic change to his website to avoid selling more disks than existed. He also once DJed a three-hour floppy-only set at the Floppy Totaal festival in the Netherlands, using a box of floppies and four USB drives!

Rob Michalchuk from Brantford, Canada runs Poor Little Music, a noise/experimental CD-R and tape label that has also put out a handful of 3½" floppies on special occasions. He even managed to put out three limited-edition releases on 5¼" floppy disks: one by himself, and others by Zebra Mu and Trous. Zebra Mu is the stage name of Mike Ridge, who has also put out a few 3½" floppies on his own Quagga Curious Sounds label.

Perhaps I am repeating myself, but floppy disks are an immensely inconvenient means of disseminating music. They accommodate only small slivers of data. In terms of per-megabyte value, they are extremely heavy and therefore expensive to ship. Few people still have the means to play a floppy disk, unless they are holding on to an ancient desktop computer or willing to invest in a USB floppy drive (which, in fairness, can be obtained for a mere twenty dollars online). Beyond these hurdles, companies no longer produce new floppy disks, so obtaining them means hunting down people who are selling old stock. Even though billions were originally manufactured, it is a slowly dwindling supply.

Some folks, perhaps inspired by New Order's "Blue Monday" single, have participated in floppy nostalgia from one step removed. The breakcore producer Toecutter nestled his 2001 CD-R release *Punk Snot Dead* in the shell of an old 5.25" floppy disc. It was the perfect size for a standard compact disc, which is five inches in diameter. In 2012 a German electronic artist named Sascha Müller tracked down some very old-school 8" floppy disks from the 1970s, packaging his untitled 7" single in their shells.[26]

Despite its limitations, the floppy disk evokes a positive reaction in a subset of especially nostalgic folks. One contemporary label named Strudelsoft utilizes a distinctly nineties graphic aesthetic and releases music in the most nostalgic of contemporary genres, vaporwave. The sound rehashes and reimagines the synthetic, dawn-of-digital sounds of the eighties and early nineties. Strudelsoft, run out of Ottawa by a thirtysomething named Sterling Campbell, has been issuing floppies since its inaugural release, even catching the attention of *Rolling Stone* magazine, who profiled the label along with the vaporwave floppy scene in general.[27] In that interview, Campbell says he was inspired by a limited-to-twenty-five-copy floppy disk release called *Culture Island*, self-released by an obscure and now-defunct producer named Miami Vice. It is now considered the first vaporwave floppy and is exceedingly coveted.

In that interview he explains that he "discovered, after playing around, that you can actually release about 11 minutes and 38 seconds of 8-bit audio MP3 on a floppy disk." Strudelsoft's floppies are sold via Bandcamp and can be obtained for approximately eight Canadian dollars, plus shipping. Produced in quantities of around twenty copies per release, they typically sell out rapidly. He has produced around twenty-five different releases in under two years.

26 Floppy habits tend to stick. Müller has also released a number of one-off releases on 3.5" floppy disks, including a special "cover/bootleg version" of Michael Jackson's "Billie Jean" named "Booty Flop," described by one reviewer as "pretty raw and unprocessed but quite charming in a way." (www.discogs.com/Sascha-M%C3%BCller-Booty-Flop-1/release/3723872)
27 Christopher R. Weingarten, 'Revolution at 3.5': Inside Vaporwave's Mini-Boom of Floppy Disk Releases,' *Rolling Stone*, 2018 <www.rollingstone.com/pro/features/vaporwave-floppy-disk-trend-666085/> [accessed 11 January 2021].

EXTREME MUSIC

The floppy furor has even inspired the creation of an International Floppy Disk Day by Poor Little Music's Rob Michalchuk, a lampoon of the annual Record Store Day and the lower-profile Cassette Store Day. The first day came and went on October 18, 2016, without much fanfare (Michalchuk put out several ultra-limited editions to celebrate, of which there are still remaining copies), though a Facebook account has continued to trumpet the approach of that date each year.

The scene has even produced a self-published book of reviews and interviews compiled by Kai Nobuko, the person behind the *Yeah I Know It Sucks* blog, a 337-page tome titled *Yeah I Know It Sucks: Floppy Diskette Reviews Vol. 1*, available both digitally and as a print-to-order physical edition. The product description warns the customer not to buy the book unless they know what they are getting into, promising a volume "full of poor grammar, highly irregular spelling, and pointless descriptions of terrible music on an outdated medium."

IV.4 MICROCASSETTES

"Normal" cassette tapes—the music medium that takes the form of magnetic tape spooled within a 4 x 2.5" plastic rectangle—first hit the market in 1963, under the name Compact Cassettes. It took a while for the format's sound quality to improve to a degree that consumers considered acceptable, but they eventually became an appealing, portable format that supplanted the 8-track and even outsold LPs.

But before Compact Cassettes emerged as the industry standard, many different companies jockeyed to push their own magnetic tape cartridges onto the market. Olympus, a company best known for manufacturing optical equipment, unveiled their own format in 1969, releasing an even more condensed competitor to the Compact Cassette called the *microcassette*. Much smaller than its rival, it was designed for convenience: microcassette recorders could fit into a trouser pocket.

Dr. Gough's Techzone, a blog that explores technology in detail, has a great article exploring the format's technical specifications.[28] Dr. Gough notes that a microcassette's magnetic tape is thinner than that of a cassette, and because there is only room for a short length of tape within each tiny cartridge, microcassettes record at a lower speed than regular tape. As a result, the microcassette is best suited for reproducing the frequency range of the human voice, as it poorly captures the broader sound spectrum of music. Still, a handful of experimental artists have explored microcassettes as a medium for recording or disseminating audio, seeing the format's sonic limitations not as restrictions but instead as creative opportunities.

IV.4.1 Microcassettor

In 2001, Sounds From The Pocket, a label run by Justin Waters, released a CD-R compilation called *Microcassettor*. To assemble it, Waters put a call out for contributions, specifying that all compositions had to arrive on microcassette. Aware of the format's miniature dimensions, he urged submitters, on his Earthlink-hosted Microcassettor website, to "WRAP & SEAL THE TAPE UP IN BUBBLE WRAP OR SOMETHING TO DULL THE EDGES OR IT WILL CUT THRU PAPER AND SLIP OUT INTO THE DEPTHS OF NOTHINGNESS THAT IS THE US POSTAL SYSTEM." The thirty-six microcassettes he received were transferred to audio files and burned onto CD-R, resulting in a fuzzy sonic mosaic that he limited to a mere ninety-five copies, each one coming in a hand-assembled package that used a recycled LP cover as its base. Most tracks were noise tracks and field recordings, including contributions from tape-trading veterans like Big City Orchestra and Ernesto Diaz-Infante.

Fanfare for this release was limited. Frans de Waard, who runs an email newsletter called *Vital Weekly* that reviews experimental music releases every week, aptly identified that the medium was the message, reflecting that "The sound quality is usually not that good, so I guess that's what is so appealing for the compilers of this

---

28 lui_gough, "Tech Flashback: The Microcasette — Part 1: The Tapes."

compilation."[29] Still, interest was strong enough that the compilation became a series, and volumes two and three followed in the next couple of years.[30] These releases, despite coming out in minuscule editions, are often invoked as seminal moments by other artists working in the microcassette medium.

IV.4.2
One-Touch Recordings

Around the same time as *Microcassettor* came out, Russian noise artist Philipp Wolokitin's Monopolka label put out a series of microcassettes on a sub-label intended for conceptual odds and

Cover of *Microcassettor*, constructed from a cannibalized LP cover. Image courtesy of Justin Waters of Sounds From The Pocket.

ends, One-Touch Recordings. The surviving One-Touch website is a colorful, Fluxus-inspired cornucopia with skronky formatting and off-the-wall language that might be part intentional obfuscation and part lost-in-translation. His microcassette releases, which he dubbed "Midgets," are advertised thus:

"Our Midgets are everybody' necessary items. High consumer characteristics and modern design make our Midgets very competitive."[31]

Wolokitin offered me some context behind One-Touch as well as his musical career. Living in St. Petersburg, he works as a theatrical technician to pay the bills, and with his free time he travels through Europe, practices alto saxophone, and performs occasional noise and free improv as a "family band" with his wife and daughter. He tells me he performed in one of the first Russian noise groups, drawing early inspiration from the irreverent and DIY activities of RRRecords and *Bananafish* magazine.

Wolokitin's collection of microcassette releases, known as the "microcassette serie" [sic], represent one of many experiments with novel permutations of cassettes, which include highly ornamented but playable tapes, as well as anti-cassette experiments like tape cartridges filled with rice and, on one dubious occasion, liquid hydrogen.[32] The idea to release microcassettes came after Wolokitin acquired an answering machine that used the format. He initially tried to record directly onto that machine, but after this turned out to be "just a disaster," he switched tacks and connected a portable microcassette recorder to an ordinary tape deck. The result was the ability to dub music onto microcassettes, which he then sold as limited-edition releases.

29 Justin Waters, "Microcassettor Vol. 1" <web.archive.org/web/20130602110903/http://soundsfromthepocket.com/ps1r.htm> [accessed March 19, 2022]

30 Vol. 3 was a split release between just two artists, Tore Honoré Bøe and Reynols.

31 "Safety Midgets," Monopolka <trilobit666.narod.ru/s_midgets/s_midgets.htm> [accessed March 19, 2022

32 "Antirecords," Monopolka <trilobit666.narod.ru/antirec/antirec.htm> [accessed March 19, 2022]

Interestingly, this process was not without its curveballs. As Wolokitin recalls, "At the time the microcassette series was started, there was the first herald of what we now have—control and censorship [like it was in the] Soviet times." According to him, postal authorities would open parcels and listen to the music contained inside. "[Microcassettes] were illegal to send because customs [didn't have] appropriate equipment to listen." At times, Wolokitin had to trek out to Finland and Estonia to mail his packages.

When asked about the conceptual motivation behind his choice to release microcassettes, Wolokitin is surprisingly pragmatic. "Call it postal rationale. We all were far too mingy when dealing with postal expenses, and microtapes were cheaper to send because of the weight of the parcel." With that said, he also recalls pontificating about reducing the swanky, "high-end sound of some Japanese noise artists into utter rotten crap" by subjecting them to microcassette's thin frequency band and low granularity. Yet there was only ever one Japanese artist released as part of the microcassette series, namely Toru Kai of Zensuko Grind. "But his music was brilliantly utter shite in itself," Wolokitin jokes.

Kicking off near the start of this millennium, the One-Touch microcassette series spawned a handful of releases, including one by NAPALMED, a long-running noise act led by Radek Kopel that has since transformed into an Einstürzende Neubauten tribute band. For Wolokitin, the most interesting release was a sixteen-minute tape by an obscure Californian artist named Yinkolli, which is officially self-titled but sometimes referred to as *Forest of Labandi*. Yinkolli also appears to have put out one self-released CD-R called *Mem Kalzac* and performed live at a few iterations of the Northern California Noisefest (according to archived listings, he played the opening slot at an 11 a.m. show in 2000, as captured on that year's compilation CD).[33]

Wolokitin recalls receiving Yinkolli's tape in the mail. "The music was superb. Just brilliant in my opinion. Lo-fi-ish impro kitchen junk noise with some alien sounds and blurps in the language he called 'yuillonki-jibberish.' Each track was accompanied by a pompous story on how he is visiting the planet Yullonki (every night!) and making new friends there." Wolokitin never met him and has not heard from him since. "Hope he made it to stay on the Yullonki planet finally," he reflects.

For Wolokitin, it was eccentrics like Yinkolli that made the noise tape scene of that era so delightful, a dynamic which has since dissipated. He sees microcassette releases as an extension of that whimsy.

IV.4.3 dirgefunk's microcassettes

From 2005 to 2011, electronic artist Christopher Jion put out a series of four microcassette releases on his dirgefunk Records label, assigning them the catalog codes *tape 000–003*. Via email, Jion explains that the fact that microcassettes are not *intended* to transmit music was the point unto itself. "I just wanted to do something weird on a format not meant for music. It completely changes the sound and mood of the music because it has a very specific-to-the-format lo-fi quality that sounds like nothing else."

33 Lob Instagon, "Our History," Norcal Noise Fest <www.norcalnoisefest.com/NF_history.html> [accessed March 19, 2022]

To produce the releases, he transferred digital recordings to the miniature tapes using the line-in jack on the microcassette recorder. He says he was not aware of the work of Wolokitin and Justin Waters' Sounds From The Pocket label, and was mostly driven by the joy of experimentation and the novel possibilities of the strange medium. "People I gave them to really seemed to like them though," he recalls.

IV.4.4 Dictaphonia

Working with obscure formats, particularly those unintended for mass reproduction, comes with its share of technical challenges. The trouble with putting out microcassette releases, as long-running hometaper Hal McGee points out in an interview, is in duplicating recordings onto the format.

Christopher Jion's *Building Skyscrapers On Frozen Seas* microcassette. Image courtesy of Christopher Jion.

McGee started out by connecting the output port of one microcassette player to the microphone port of another. However, the results were distorted because the mic input had a built-in pre-amp to boost the signal. A friend then built a little tool to attenuate the signal and counteract the effects of the pre-amp.

McGee has been recording experimental audio and distributing homemade tapes since the 1980s, running the long-running HalTapes label, which has amassed an enormous discography over the years. After releasing on cassette for many years, he eventually transitioned to CD-R, then moved online to Bandcamp for simplicity. But in 2009, he stepped back into the realm of the physical, soliciting submissions for a compilation called *Dictaphonia*. All contributions needed to come on microcassette, and it was preferred (though not required) that the audio was recorded live to microcassette.

Originally intended as a standalone compilation, *Dictaphonia* sprawled into a ten-volume monster, each one released on microcassette itself but also made available on his website, where they can still be accessed.[34] This was an remarkable feat, one that McGee expounds upon in his "Microcassette Manifesto," which articulately lays out the joys of microcassettes in as much detail as I've found.[35] Surprisingly, in his manifesto, McGee remarks that he judges the current cassette tape revival, popular in underground music circles, to be "a sort of preciousness, a fetishistic clinging to physical objects," though he emphasizes that he also admires its spirit. Consequently, his decision to release music on microcassette may seem hypocritical on first pass. But he offers several counterarguments.

For one, given the limited frequency spectrum, narrowed to just the range of the human voice, he finds the format's sound to be somehow *human*, and consequently

34 Hal McGee, "Dictaphonia Microcassette Compilations," HalTapes <www.haltapes.com/dictaphonia-microcassette-compilations.html> [accessed March 19, 2022]

35 Hal McGee, "Hal McGee's Microcassette Manifesto," HalTapes, January 2010, <www.haltapes.com/hal-mcgees-microcassette-manifesto.html>

very direct. He also likes the fact that microcassette devices are utilitarian—often used by professionals and students to record lectures and notes, he calls them a "kind of portable notebook," one that isn't "tainted by being an art object, like a standard-sized cassette." Since McGee believes that "life and art should be as close together as possible," microcassettes seem real because their use is most closely associated with everyday life.

Lastly, McGee deflects the complaint that the audio quality is too poor. He counters that "the sounds that we hear in daily life, and our perceptions and memories and sensations aren't all high-definition. In fact, far from it. Most sounds are small or in the distance or muffled or indistinct." He laments that advertisers sell us a message that "shiny and new" equals good, reflecting that decay is a natural process, and one that can add character and appeal. "Microcassettes sound like relics of a future past that never existed," he concludes.

Listening to *Dictaphonia Microcassette Compilation #1*, what is immediately striking is the tinny sound. Each track starts with a moment of silence; when the audio kicks in, it leads with a dense haze of tape hiss. Sometimes you can hear the record button being pressed. The foggy audio quality lends a homogeneity to otherwise widely disparate recordings—be it the juxtaposition of trailer-park chatter and combustion engine din on Otolathe's "Unorchestratable," the improvised strings of Mike Khoury's "Solo Violin," or the byzantine computer-music synth patterns of "Liquid Glass" by Dave Fuglewicz. Then there's Krysten Davis' "BBBBBAD," which is just a tape-submerged chop-up of "Bad to the Bone" by George Thorogood and the Destroyers. All have in common the medium's distinctive thumbprint: a limited sound spectrum. *Dictaphonia #1* takes extremely varied source material and makes it sound like a coherent whole. Yet it also helps underscore that microcassette audio is more interesting than alluring.

IV.4.5 Dictafawn

As far as I know, there has only ever been one label to devote itself solely to producing microcassettes: Dictafawn, founded in early 2011 by noise artist Chris Reierson, released music exclusively on the format. Reierson, who recorded noise music under pseudonyms like My Lovely Figment and FAP, recently returned from a hiatus with the album *Sensitive to Textures*, his first release under his own name.

Even though many artists have made the transition to releasing their music online, for Reierson, there is a constant "urge" to create releases by hand. Indeed, his early experimental music memories include recording "output that could generously be described as 'noise'" on a tape recorder with his friend, who introduced him to a lot of underground music. Eventually, he discovered the matrix of noise artists posting their productions on MySpace and had his first release put out by extreme Australian label Smell the Stench.

Around the end of 2010, Reierson bought a Quasar microcassette recorder/radio at a garage sale simply because he thought it looked cool. Since it came with a bunch of blank tapes, he decided to put out a microcassette release as a one-off, pooling the efforts of his HNW project, Zenith, with fellow noise artist Junkie Scum. He solicited help with engineering the microcassette releases from an online message board, only to be accused of ripping off Hal McGee's *Dictaphonia* compilations and being told his idea was stupid. He tells me some of the impetus for forming Dictafawn was to thumb his nose at those online doubters. An Irish noise artist named Bipolar Joe contributed the name—other proposed names reportedly included TinyTapes, Small Tapes for Small People, and Female Dudes Microtapes—and he constructed the logo out of a public domain drawing of a fawn.

Over his first seven or eight Dictafawn releases, Reierson fiddled with the technical process of transferring audio to his microcassettes, "a combination of a direct box (essentially an attenuator) and a low-voltage portable CD player for playing the master recordings." (He apologizes to those who bought the label's first, lower-fi releases.) Reierson has since read Hal McGee's *Microcassette Manifesto* but says he did not have any lofty conceptual goals for Dictafawn. "I just thought a tiny tape collection would look adorable," he explains.

In total, there were twenty-three Dictafawn releases. Early on, Reierson notes that there was a lot of enthusiasm for the releases, but as things went on, it seemed that more people were interested in submitting releases than actually buying copies. There were no limits to any Dictafawn edition, and he would typically dub a minimum of ten copies before announcing a release, then be lucky to sell half of those.

Eventually, Reierson's enthusiasm for running the label fizzled due to a variety of reasons. Dubbing microcassettes is slow and laborious work, and the tapes themselves became increasingly scarce and expensive over time. Besides, Reierson was in college and had more important things to do with his time. Near the end, he recalls turning down various submissions for arbitrary reasons, principally because the effort was no longer worth it. He told me about one remarkable missed opportunity. "I told [legendary Argentine experimental artist] Anla Courtis his submission wouldn't 'translate well' to the format . . . it was only years later when I learned who Anla Courtis was that I realized my mistake. D'oh!"

Today, Reierson no longer releases music on microcassette, but he has a soft spot for the format and an appreciation for the effort that goes into physical media. "I can go over to my own personal collection of tiny tapes, pick one out, and hold it in my hand. And then I can say with conviction, 'Yeah, I did this.'"

IV.4.6 Lavender Sweep

Chris Reierson pointed me toward the contemporary face of microcassette music, perhaps the only turn-of-the-decade purveyor of this miniature format—a label known as Lavender Sweep, run by a friendly curator named Ant Jones. For the past couple of years, Jones has put out several microcassette releases, as well as CD-Rs, regular tapes, a lathe-cut 7", and a couple floppy disks.

Jones explained to me that he started the label in 2017 to reissue old eighties and nineties demo tapes he had collected. His first release was a cassette edition of the California shoegaze band Ozean's 1992 demo, which channeled the thrill of bands like Ride and Pale Saints.

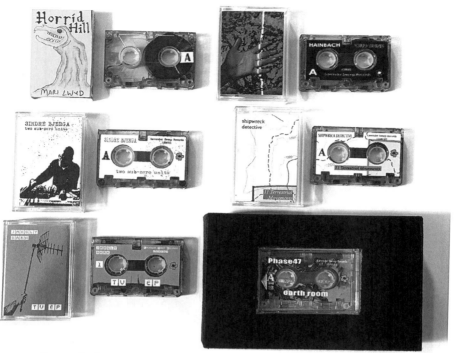

**Several of Lavender Sweep Records' microcassette releases.
Image courtesy of Ant Jones of Lavender Sweep Records.**

Around the time, he was watching a YouTube channel called Techmoan, in which host Matthew Julius Taylor explores obscure old technologies. "It made me think to release music on some of these more obscure formats, which were pretty much all long deleted," Jones told me via email. "I then began to look for existing releases and stumbled across Dictafawn, who to this day are the only label ever exclusively dedicated to releasing microcassettes. It was seeing these guys that inspired me to work on a series of microcassette releases for 2019 by Sindre Bjerga, Shipwreck Detective, Hainbach, Jangly Mark and Phase47."

"There are only certain types of music that work on microcassettes," he explains. "For example, I find that lo-fi electronic music and field recordings seem to work quite well. I know for some people this is an awful format."

One successful release was 2019's *Old Suns*, a microcassette by Hainbach, a German experimental electronic producer who posts popular videos on YouTube. Its first run of fifty-eight copies sold out in just under five hours, which Jones figures is the fastest-selling microcassette release ever. "Each tape was hand-dubbed in real time, and I went through two dictaphones in the process. Always have spares if you are going to do a lot of dubbing."

In 2019, to celebrate his fifth and final microcassette release of the year, Jones organized an online event called Microcassette Day on November 23rd. "Nowhere on the scale of Record Store Day or even Cassette Store Day but a very miniature version, quite like the actual tape itself," Jones humbly remarked.

IV.5 8-TRACKS

Eight-track tapes were invented in the fifties but became indelibly associated with the seventies. In a book about The Kinks called *You Really Got Me*, authors Doug Hinman and Jason Brabazon tell the story of this oft-maligned format,[36] which was designed as an improvement on the less-popular four-track cassette. Eight-tracks took four-track technology and multiplied the tape by two, resulting in more tracks per cassette. As a result, listeners could switch conveniently from track to track if they wanted to skip ahead on an album; unlike a regular cassette, which has two sides, 8-tracks had four sides—referred to as "programs." The dividing of magnetic real estate meant a decrease in sound quality, but customers enjoyed the convenience. They were even willing to forgive the fact that record labels had to rearrange the track listings of their favorite albums to fit the four programs of an 8-track tape. In fact, sometimes a song would be cut down the middle and separated over two programs, an affront to those who cherish the purity of classic albums. But the largest factor in 8-tracks' popularity was a boost from Ford Motors, which offered players in their full line of 1966 model cars. Indeed, in its early days, the 8-track format was principally sold at auto shops and truck stops, though their availability would later expand as home players reached the market.

Eventually, the advent of Compact Cassettes eclipsed 8-tracks. These new tapes were less expensive and could be played on machines that were magnitudes smaller than the chunky 8-track players. Eight-tracks petered out as the seventies progressed, barely clinging to life into the eighties. The last mass-produced 8-track was believed to be Chicago's *17* album, released in 1987, though there are rumors that small quantities of 8-tracks are still produced in Nashville for truckers with old decks.

Despite the format's protracted death, a group of collectors emerged in the late eighties and nineties, as epitomized by the efforts of a Chicagoan named Russel Forster, who published a zine called *8-Track Mind* through the nineties. In a 2014 interview, Forster described becoming endeared to the "ugly duckling" quality of 8-tracks, a quaint identity resulting from the tapes' clumsy design and proneness to breaking. His fascination with this defunct technology shares features with the anti-audiophile position staked out by some of the lobit producers profiled in Chapter 5.2. In the interview, Forster remarked on "poking the purveyors of music technology in the eye by eschewing their barely veiled attempts at making people re-buy their music collections on a 'new, improved' format to boost corporate profits."

In 1990, having amassed an enviable collection of 8-track cassettes, Forster and his pals started a Disco Bowling night at the local bowling alley in Chicago, where he would play 8-tracks as people bowled. In the interview, he recalls Meco's disco-fied rendition of the theme to *The Wizard of Oz* as one memorable throwback. He then doubled down on his obsession, starting his zine, *8-Track Mind*, in 1990. He began at issue number 69, Forster explained,[37] because "we were told that there were 68 issues published

---

36 Doug Hinman and Jason Brabazon, You Really Got Me: An Illustrated World Discography of the Kinks (Douglas E. Hinman, 1994).
37 Mark Maynard, "The Untold History of Zines.... Russ Forster on the 8-Track Mind," They're All Going to Laugh at You, January 16, 2014, <markmaynard.com/2014/01/

in the 1970s and early 1980s by an unbalanced gentleman by the name of Gordon Van Gelder," only later concluding that Van Gelder was "a master manipulator who used a bogus story about the prehistory of 8-TM to become a contributor to our version." The zine's pages were replete with interviews with 8-track collectors, pieces on 8-track history, guides to 8-track equipment, and profiles of neat finds.

8-Track Mind delivered enough content to sustain thirty-two issues before concluding in 2001, though a couple of revival issues were published in the past few years. It also found kinship with a network of 8-track collectors from across the USA, culminating in a feature documentary named *So Wrong They're Right*[38] which was produced by Forster and his friend and chronicled a cross-country hunt for fellow fans of the esoteric format.[39]

IV.5.1 Malcolm Tent's 8-Track Obsession

While the world of 8-track collectors was growing, a handful of 8-track fiends were channeling their enthusiasm into creating *new* 8-tracks. The first new 8-track since the format's last mass-produced release may have been a special, limited-edition version of *Rock Against Spindlers*, an album by the Danbury, Connecticut hardcore band Violent Children.

The TPOS label would eventually put out several special editions of their releases on limited runs of 8-track tapes, including albums by GG Allin, Bunny Brains, and Anti-Seen—most padded with exclusive bonus tracks to get collectors' blood flowing.[40] "Lovingly handcrafted from virgin tape stock (when possible)," they were sold at a premium, because, as the TPOS website emphatically puts it, they are "A PAIN IN THE BUTT TO MAKE."[41]

I had the opportunity to speak with Malcolm Tent, the long-standing owner of TPOS and former owner of a Danbury record store called Trash American Style, via telephone in 2017. Tent has been making a living from music his whole life. Previously a member of messy garage-punks Bunny Brains, he now divides time in several bands, including They Hate Us, noise act Ultrabunny, and a project called B.B. Gun, which he reserves for "when I want to get out anger."

Via Skype, Tent told me a bit about how he got into non-mainstream music. "I remember when I was in fifth grade, I read a newspaper review for what was supposed to be the worst band in the world. And I was automatically attracted to that, because I wanted to hear what the worst band in the world sounded like. Unfortunately, it turned out to be Rush, who were the worst band in the world but for all the wrong reasons," he laughs. Years later, when he heard about punk rock, supposedly "music for degenerates and subhumans," that was where he found his calling.

Tent is grateful that he has been able to eke out a life subsisting on art and music, laughingly telling me he is driven by a "lack of desire to ever work a regular job." Besides his income dealing records, he also reflects that a lack of "bad habits and expensive vices" has permitted a fiscally lean lifestyle. Danbury, notable for its cheap rent and persistent cultural underground, has been a fertile ground for Tent's experiments with fringe music.

---

the-untold-history-of-zines-russ-forster-on-the-8-track-mind/>

38 Russ Forster and Dan Sutherland, So Wrong They're Right (USA: Other Cinema, 1995).

39 Russ Forster, "So Wrong They're Right," 8-Track Heaven <www.8trackheaven.com/archive/doc.html> [accessed March 19, 2022]

40 There's even a ninety-minute 8-track version of Charles Manson's *Saints Are Hell On Earth*, an acoustic folk album recorded in prison.

41 Malcolm Tent, "TPOS RECORDS," Trash American Style <www.trashamericanstyle.us/tpos.htm> [accessed March 19, 2022]

8-track on TPOS.
Image courtesy of
Malcolm Tent of TPOS.

When an old 8-track recorder showed up at the Trash American Style shop in 1987, it got him thinking. "There'd been a number of punk rock 8-tracks in the seventies, but 8-track never made it to the age of hardcore. So I just thought it would be amusing to pick up the baton and do a hardcore release on 8-track."

Tent was familiar with the format, having bought his own recorder back in 1979, after which he would buy cheap 8-tracks to record things off the radio. As a result, he understood how he could make new tapes.

There were technical challenges with dubbing music onto old 8-tracks. Because of their age, they were prone to falling apart, necessitating many failed attempts. He showed me a garbage bag filled with failed 8-tracks that had not withstood the process. He ran down the painstaking process, a finicky method which requires re-splicing the tape due to the 8-tracks' affinity for tangling in the recorder and gumming up the capstans. "I buy lots of old, sealed tapes. I crack one open and have to manually pull the tape out of the shell a few feet until the point where it splices together. Provided it doesn't fall apart when I try to pull the tape out, I re-splice it, manually put the tape back in the shell, and then I hit it with a bulk eraser to get rid of all the signal on it. And then I manually thread it back, at which point it may or may not completely unspool in the recorder. If it does finally go ahead and record from start to finish, I then stick the label on the front."

The first couple copies of the Violent Children release were meant only for display at the store. He also gave a few away to other record store proprietors. He did not expect people would want to *buy* them. But people kept asking if they could purchase his store copy. When another store called to say they had sold theirs and wanted more, he relented. "I thought, 'Well, it looks like the cat's out of the bag. I'm kind of obligated to keep it going now.'"

When he reflected on the merits of the format, the gusto was evident. "I've always loved 8-tracks. I think they're a very romantic format. Very evocative of a certain time and place." He described the distinctive plastic smell that arises when 8-tracks play, which he associates with listening to music on his father's hi-fi. He tells me that he thinks the smell has stayed the same all these years, even as the format has aged.

But it is more than nostalgia that motivates Tent's 8-track fixation. "A lot of it was a big F you to the major labels, and digital in general," he pointed out. "Because when I was doing 8-tracks in earnest it was at the height of the CD era. CDs were overpriced. They all had exclusive bonus cuts. So just as a reaction to that, I thought, 'If you're going to play that game with your cheap aluminum bits, I'll play the same game with an obsolete format with exclusive cuts and all that.' It was my veiled statement on the condition of the record industry at that time, and the way it is now."

All his 8-tracks feature exclusive content, and he has done a couple that are only available on 8-track. One is a collection of live recordings by Charlie Pickett and the Eggs called *8-Track Fever*. Another was a live recording by Atom and His Package, the cult synth-punk act helmed by Adam Goren. "A lot of time people will ask me, 'Hey, man, can you make a CD of that Atom and His Package?' And I'm like, 'Nope, if you want to hear it, you've got to hear it the way it's meant to be heard, and that's on 8-track!'"

IV.5.2 8-Tracks in the Nineties

In the years that followed Malcolm Tent's first foray into the format, a number of other 8-tracks appeared on the underground music scene. There was a poorly documented 8-track label named Tosk Worldwide, run by a Canadian radio personality named Nardwuar the Human Serviette. Starting in the early nineties, Tosk Worldwide put out a series of 8-tracks by Canadian bands like Superconductor (AC Newman's band before he co-founded the New Pornographers) and the Evaporators, Nardwuar's band. Catalog numbers suggest at least thirteen 8-tracks were released, although little information remains beyond that,[42] and messages to Nardwuar went unreturned.

There were also a handful of one-off 8-tracks that came out in the nineties, several of which are profiled in a guide published on the 8-Track Heaven website.[43] A 1996 CD compilation of surf music from Michigan, *Surfin' the Spillway*, was accompanied by a special twenty-copy limited edition on 8-track. Interestingly, the album cover's (doctored) image of people surfing on Ann Arbor's Barton Dam led to complaints from the City of Ann Arbor's Attorney's Office that this would incite trespassers to attempt to surf the dam. As a result, Rees says no more copies can be made. Besides, he sold the duplication equipment on eBay.[44]

Meanwhile, in 1993, a strange 8-track named *Copy Cat Suicide* appeared courtesy of a band called Surface Noise. It billed itself as an "Exclusive Franchise Opportunity" and could be purchased for ten dollars on the condition that it was destroyed after being listened to once. As the press copy explains, "Any further listening mandates the FURTHER commitment of starting your own Surface Noise franchise wherever you are."

Then there were the Wildbunch, the progenitors to the Electric Six, the Detroit band most popular for the hit single "Danger! High Voltage." In 1996, they put out their first release, a full-length album exclusive to 8-track called *An Evening With The Many Moods Of The Wildbunch's Greatest Hits... Tonight!* It came out on their own vanity label, Uchu Cult, and is incomprehensibly rare at this point—sought after by 8-track enthusiasts and Electric Six completists alike.

IV.5.3 The Twenty-First Century

In the 2000s and 2010s, a miniature boom of 8-track revivalists emerged, many based around Dallas, Texas. In Arlington, Kathy Gibson has been running Kate's Track

---

42 "Tosk Label," Discogs <www.discogs.com/label/389435-Tosk> [accessed March 19, 2022]

43 Russ Forster, "'New' 8-Track Releases," 8-Track Heaven <web.archive.org/web/20210107043035/https://8trackheaven.com/the-big-questions/new-8-track-releases/> [accessed March 19, 2022]

44 Jim Rees, "Surfin' the Spillway," Jim Rees <jim.rees/happy-hour/> [accessed March 19, 2022]

Shack, an online business specializing in used 8-tracks since 1998. In the late aughts, however, they delved into producing new 8-tracks, offering their services to bands and record labels under the umbrella of KTS Productions. In 2009, Cheap Trick used their services to release a special (thirty-dollar) edition of their new album, *The Latest*, as a marketing gimmick. Not to be outdone, eighties hard rock band Tesla commissioned a special 8-track run of their covers record, *Reel to Real 2*, on which they perform songs by Bachman-Turner Overdrive, Bad Company, and Peter Frampton.

There were others who dabbled in the 8-track format around this period. An ambitious but short-lived Canadian label named Scotch Tapes, run out of a remote fishing community in northern Ontario, issued a couple of 8-tracks during their run. In an interview, label runner Al Bjornaa describes being gifted an 8-track recorder by a family friend and eventually modifying it to record onto pre-recorded tapes—a big plus, given the rarity of blank 8-tracks. This allowed him to work with bands that were otherwise too big for a tiny DIY label. "They love the idea of throwing out a few copies of an 8-track on their merch table," he said at the time.[45] One such catch was veteran psych act Plastic Crimewave Sound, who released an exclusive three-track tape titled *Extended Haze* on the label.[46]

Auris Apothecary also got into the game with a homemade 8-track edition of garage-rock band Apache Dropout's self-titled album, which was meant to supplement the band's other CD, LP, and cassette editions out on other labels.[47] There's a very recent label called EmoCow Records that does small runs of 8-tracks for interested bands and also makes one-off reissues of classic emo records. And the Denton, Texas, duo RTB2 released their album *We Are a Strange Man* exclusively on 8-track as a friendly (and no doubt polarizing) gesture to their fans. In an article for *D* magazine, writer and RTB2 enthusiast Dick Sullivan documents his efforts to play the darned thing, concluding that the effort was worth it.[48]

The Dead Media, the 8-track label and duplication service that released RTB2's album, is one of the more notable contemporary examples of 8-track revivalism. It was founded in 2006 by Nathan Brown, who has argued that the sound quality of the 8-track is superior to that of other formats. According to the *Arkansas Times*,[49] Brown cottoned onto 8-tracks when his wife, Tara, explained the difference between digital photographs and real film. He quickly drew a parallel to audio and arrived at the conclusion that magnetic tape is a more veritable reproduction of music than digital methods. He then started collecting 8-tracks, linking up with a veteran collector who sold him tapes on eBay.

I connected with Brown online to clarify a few concepts. An audiophile with a deep knowledge of the technical aspects of music recording and reproduction, he has perfected the laborious art of recycling old 8-track cassettes. As he details in

---

45 Michael Tau, "20 Questions: Scotch Tapes' Al Bjornaa," Indieville, October 2009, <www.indieville.com/articles/interviews/scotchtapes.htm>

46 Another act to put out a Scotch Tapes 8-track, Green Mist, was a now-defunct but prolific figure on the underground noise scene who has released tapes with charming names like Semen Grit (Loveless Tapes, 2007), Poo & Wee (split with BBBlood; Turgid Animal, 2008), and Drinkin' Lighter Fluid (rundownsun, 2006).

47 "Apache Dropout — Apache Dropout (2011, T40, 8-Track Cartridge)," Discogs <www.discogs.com/release/3307740-Apache-Dropout-Apache-Dropout> [accessed March 19, 2022]

48 Dick Sullivan, "Does RTB2 Sound Better on 8-Track? - D Magazine," D Magazine, April 14, 2011, <www.dmagazine.com/arts-entertainment/2011/04/does-rtb2-sound-better-on-8-track/>

49 Sam Eifling, "Raising an Audio Lazarus - Arkansas Times," Arkansas Times, July 3, 2008, <arktimes.com/entertainment/ae-feature/2008/07/03/raising-an-audio-lazarus-2?oid=862680>

Above and opposite: Two of Dead Media's recent 8-track productions: a reissue of the Cramps' *Bad Music for Bad People,* and a reissue of Com Truise's *Galactic Melt* on Ghostly International (which reportedly sold out in one hour). Images courtesy of Nathan Brown of Dead Media.

another interview: "After the exterior is polished, I open it up, detail the inside clean, and relubricate the hub posts. There are some parts that need replacing as well. I can eyeball whether there is enough tape on the reel but time it anyway to get the precise length, then cut the excess amount off. Occasionally I have to add tape. The tape is erased with a degausser, which resets it to a truly blank state. The recording is made, then it's labeled and packaged." His tapes often retail for thirty to forty dollars by the people who commissioned him to create them. But, as he points out, original 8-tracks sold for prices that today would amount to about $34 apiece.

Brown is a true believer in magnetic tape. He thinks it captures the presence of the original recording conditions that digital recording and reproduction are incapable of. "It's magnetic," he tells me. "Why wouldn't it pick up energy from people?" While digital audio can only capture frequency and amplitude, he reasons that magnetic tape captures part of the performer's aura or psychic energy. He dreams of scientific experiments involving test groups assessing double-blind conditions, "and even somehow seeing if dynamic physical gesturing onto a pure tape recording in silence can even be measured with advanced devices that I don't know exist.

"Have you ever noticed that if you acoustically, not amplified, hear someone playing or singing something live that you don't normally care about or maybe even dislike, it seems to have an electricity to it that affects or speaks to you differently?" he asks. "I have this crackpot instinct that some measure of that electricity can and did at one time make it onto tape recordings. That being especially during the fifties and sixties,

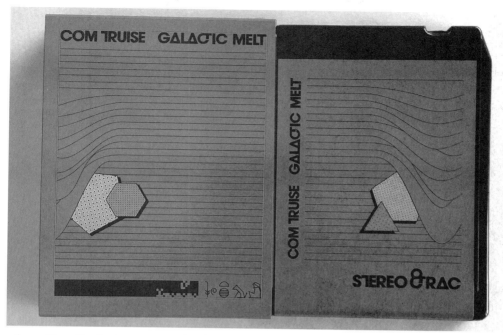

when all audio devices were tube-based and discretely wired high-quality components. Before integrated circuit chips. And when nice, well-made microphones were used." He figures that digital wiped this all out. "Digital can only be two-dimensional, regardless of how far it goes. That much we know. Dimension 1: Volume. Dimension 2: Frequency."

But 8-tracks, despite their appealing properties, have their drawbacks. Brown told me about a commission he did for the Swedish metal band Ghost, for one thousand copies of their album *Prequelle*. He was asked to do this seven weeks before they were due. "I knew that would never happen. A thousand tapes is a five- to six-month job. I was working sixteen-hour days but it ended up taking three months."

He still recalls the tedium of dubbing the tapes. "Going insane sitting there. Had a pallet next to the work bench to sleep at night." His and his wife's newborn baby would stay in a bassinet next to Brown, keeping him company as he worked.

Brown, whose wife also works, has managed a life where this is his full-time gig, from his home in Denton, Texas, just outside Dallas. These days, Brown's Dead Media Tapes and KTS Productions are the only two companies who can mass-produce 8-track tapes.

Both businesses are from the Dallas area, which was also once home to a museum dedicated to 8-tracks, run by local collector named Bucks Burnett, owner of a secretive record/8-track store called Cloud 8.[50] A few years ago, the Eight Track Museum in Deep Ellum, a Dallas neighborhood, closed after a five-year run. Yet this was not the first time someone conceived of a museum dedicated to the format. Before the Dallas museum was created, an 8-track collector named Bob Hiemenz, who had somehow

---

50 So secretive that its location is kept private, and it's only available by making an appointment via phone—and making an appointment apparently obligates you to buy at least one item, in cash only, of course. Jonathan Patrick, "Cloud 8 Is Dallas' Secret, By-Appointment-Only Record Shop ," Dallas Observer (Dallas, May 6, 2015), <www.dallasobserver.com/music/cloud-8-is-dallas-secret-by-appointment-only-record-shop-7181561>

accumulated over seventy thousand tapes and nearly six hundred players,[51] had spent years trying to get the municipal government of his hometown, Flora, Illinois, to pay for the electricity and plumbing for a proposed 8-track museum. They never agreed, despite his argument that it would draw in tourists.[52] He has since moved to Peoria, where he has taken his case to a different set of government officials.

There are a few other crafty individuals who have figured out how to record new music onto old 8-tracks. H8-Track Stereo, a mainly 8-track-only label run by Sean Beard, was formed in May 2013 and rapidly amassed an extensive discography of punk and noise releases before closing shop in 2019. Nathan Brown told me that he taught Beard how to create new 8-tracks after Beard had approached him, requesting an 8-track edition for his one-man power electronics band, Waves Crashing Piano Chords. Beard is a Juggalo—an enthusiastic fan of the band Insane Clown Posse—and is no stranger to subversion. He used to crash metalcore shows, alienating the adolescent attendees by showing up on stage in evil clown face paint, playing his eardrum-dissolving noise using only a microphone and amplifier.

H8-Track Stereo was a labor of love. "All the cartridges are rebuilt from old ones with new splice/foam pad, and all that essential stuff," he explains in a 2013 interview with *Musique Machine*, back when his operation had just gotten off the ground. "It's a long process, and each tape takes hours to complete." For Beard, the appeal boiled down to nostalgia. "It's just nostalgic for me because my parents listened to them when I was a kid. They're a classy format, and they sound amazing, honest!"

Another label, jujufrootcoop, puts out experimental music from its home in Providence, Rhode Island. It has gained a reputation for releasing music on unconventional formats like reel-to-reel tape, lathe-cut records, and floppy disks, and has also put out a handful of 8-tracks in profoundly limited editions. These are all issued in editions of five or fewer, apart from a compilation called *Noise Pollution*[53] that was capped at twenty.[54] Two of them are limited to one copy each, raising an important philosophical question: if a tree falls in the forest, and there is nobody there to hear it, does it still count as a limited-edition harsh noise 8-track cassette?

Eight-track fanatics exist on the fringe and share a passion for a format that is finicky and prone to frustrating feats of malfunction. Though they produce higher-fidelity sound than regular cassettes, they have a tough case to make when it comes to arguments for sound quality as compared to vinyl records and CDs—unless you buy into Nathan Brown's perspectives on the ability of magnetic tape to capture the electricity of a live performance.

Yet, much like fans of cassettes, floppy discs, and microcassettes, 8-trackers have established their very own National 8-Track Tape Day, intended to take place annually on April 11. And while their holiday may not have the mainstream appeal of Record Store Day, it has been databased by the website nationaldaycalendar.com, an equal-opportunity aggregator of National [Blank] Days.

---

51 Phil Luciano, "Luciano: 'Tracker Bob' Hopes to Open 8-Track Museum in Peoria," Peoria Journal Start, April 10, 2013, <www.pjstar.com/story/news/columns/luciano/2013/04/10/luciano-tracker-bob-hopes-to/42008311007/>

52 Pete Freedman, "More Than 20 Years After Their Death, Eight-Tracks Are Resurrected In Dallas," Dallas Observer, February 10, 2011, <www.dallasobserver.com/news/more-than-20-years-after-their-death-eight-tracks-are-resurrected-in-dallas-6421486>

53 There have been at least six compilations released under this title, among them collections of noise, grindcore, heavy metal, and garage rock.

54 "Noise Pollution (2014, 8-Track Cartridge)," Discogs <www.discogs.com/release/5659235-Various-Noise-Pollution> [accessed March 19, 2022

IV.6 CYLINDERS

Floppy disks, 8-tracks, and microcassettes are arcane formats, but they pale in comparison to the holy grail of niche formats, the wax cylinder. This, of course, is the *original* music format: cylinders coated with a wax surface, into which audio grooves are etched. Like records, a needle runs along the grooves—but unlike contemporary record players, the resulting sound was not electrically amplified, but instead boosted acoustically using a horn.

Developed by Thomas Edison in 1877, the format was initially a method for experimentation in sonic reproduction, and cylinders and their players were not marketed as a consumer appliance until years later.[55] They had their commercial peak at the turn of the twentieth century, after which cylinders and shellac records competed for the fledgling home music audience. Records eventually won out, and cylinders disappeared around the late 1920s after a period of progressively dwindling sales. These increasingly rare relics have been the focus of a tiny niche of collectors, among them Michael Cumella, who has hosted *The Antique Phonograph Music Program* on WFMU since 1997, playing both early records and plenty of cylinders. (The show's current tagline is "Guaranteed 100+ years old!")[56]

For many years, the thought of creating a *new* wax cylinder was unthinkable. Much like the 8-track and the microcassette, the equipment needed to duplicate cylinders is no longer being produced. But unlike 8-tracks and microcassettes, these devices are nearly a century old.

That fact has not deterred would-be cylinder purveyors from attempting to revive the format. Specialists worked out that there are essentially two options for making new cylinders today. One is to hunt for original cylinder recorders, which were designed primarily for businesspeople to record dictated notes.

The other option is, on first pass, even more far-fetched. It entails designing a completely new process to replicate the original technology for reproducing wax cylinders. Much like the methodology used to produce records, this involves creating a negative "master" mold and then pressing this into wax.

Yet it has been done. An engineer named Duncan Miller runs the Vulcan Cylinder Record Company in Sheffield, England. In an interview for *Nature*,[57] Miller explains that he has been producing new cylinders since 1981. To arrive at his specialized process, he had to dig through old archival documents, working out Thomas Edison's process for manufacturing cylinders. In the early days of recording, these methods were closely guarded, and Miller had to develop his own process based on a mere outline, sometimes examining court documents of the era to work out additional details. He learned that Edison stopped using wax in 1912, instead employing celluloid as a more

55 "History of the Cylinder Phonograph," Library of Congress <www.loc.gov/collections/edison-company-motion-pictures-and-sound-recordings/articles-and-essays/history-of-edison-sound-recordings/history-of-the-cylinder-phonograph/> [accessed March 19, 2022]
56 "Centennial Songs - The Antique Phonograph Music Program with Mac Playlists and Archives," WFMU <wfmu.org/playlists/AP> [accessed March 19, 2022]
57 Jascha Hoffman, "Q&A: The Inventor with an Ear for the Past," Nature 2009 461:7262 461, no. 7262 (September 16, 2009): 351–351, <doi.org/10.1038/461351a>

durable substitute. As a result, Miller created his own form of "adapted modern plastics" for his cylinders, the recipe tweaked for maximum durability and optimal audio quality.

Recording new audio onto wax is a complex process because it must be done acoustically. Instead of playing into a microphone, the performers need to be situated around a recording horn, each one located at a precisely calibrated distance in order to get an ideal volume mix. All recording must be done live; there is no opportunity for production trickery or post-recording tinkering. As Miller explains, he goes to all this trouble because he believes that cylinders sound better than most records. "The stylus can vibrate quicker without dissipating energy, so there is nearly another octave of overtones in the higher registers that you need for speech, strings and brass," he specifies. As well, since the grooves on a cylinder maintain the same circumference, the fidelity remains the same throughout.

A few record labels have dabbled in cylinders, mostly commissioned from a handful of companies that produce them, either by Duncan Miller's process or using a cylinder recorder. From 2015 to 2017, the British label Bughlt arranged for a company called The Victrola Guy to do some very limited editions of one-off songs by Red Martian, including a rendition of "Daisy Bell (Bicycle Built For Two),"[58] written in 1892 and featured in *2001: A Space Odyssey* as the song that HAL 9000 sings as it goes offline.

A handful of other artists and labels have joined the fray, offering pricey cylinders to those with enough disposable income to invest in impractical and esoteric audio formats. Noise label Baked Tapes did a three-cylinder run of Shingles' *Swarm of Pigs* to commemorate the shutdown of a New York concert venue.[59] At this moment, two of the three have sold. A group of "medieval space rock pioneers" that go by Gandalf's Fist released their single "The Waxwork Downs" on a cylinder along with "replica" pages from a faux old-timey newspaper called the *Daily Cog*.[60] A polymath named Thomas Negovan recorded an entire album acoustically and put out one of the songs as a cylinder single in 2011, which he claims to be the "the first single on wax cylinder in over half a century."[61] This is untrue; Tom Rodwell, once called "Sheffield's answer to Lightnin' Hopkins," put out a single called "Soldier in the Army of the Lord" in 2007 on Vulcan.[62] And in 2010, an electronic music label called Icasea put out limited-edition cylinders by experimental artists Ynys Enlli[63] and Collapsoft[64]; both are digital recordings ironically pressed on the most acoustic format imaginable.

Michael Ridge, who runs the Quagga Curious Sounds label, put out a special one-copy edition of "The Crank" in 2015. It is a recording of a device that was used as hard labor in Victorian-era prisons in the UK—inmates would hellishly rotate a crank against resistance all day as a form of punishment. The idea behind his cylinder, as

58 "Red Martian – デイジーベル (Daisy Bell) (2017, Yellow Cylinder, Cylinder)," Discogs <www.discogs.com/release/10639733-Red-Martian-デイジーベル-Daisy-Bell> [accessed March 19, 2022]

59 "Shingles – Swarm of Pigs (2012, Cylinder)," Discogs <www.discogs.com/release/8355042-Shingles-Swarm-of-Pigs> [accessed March 19, 2022]

60 "Gandalf's Fist – The Waxwork Downs (2019, Cylinder)," Discogs <www.discogs.com/release/13798404-Gandalfs-Fist-The-Waxwork-Downs> [accessed March 19, 2022]

61 "Music," Thomas Negovan, 2020, <www.thomasnegovan.com/music>

62 "Tom Rodwell – I'm A Soldier In The Army Of The Lord (2007, Cylinder)," Discogs <www.discogs.com/release/11782822-Tom-Rodwell-Im-A-Soldier-In-The-Army-Of-The-Lord> [accessed March 19, 2022]

63 "YGAM : YNYS ENLLI," Icasea <www.icasea.net/2010/05/ygam-ynys-enlli.html> [accessed March 19, 2022]

64 "△ UNIVERSAL BINARY : COLLAPSOFT," Icasea <www.icasea.net/2010/05/universal-binary-collapsoft.html> [accessed March 19, 2022]

Ridge explains on his website, was to showcase an obsolete means of punishment on an obsolete means of audio reproduction. The recording was sourced at the Norwich Castle Museum & Art Gallery, where Ridge works, and it is served up with black-and-white photographs of the loathsome device.

Then there is a Galician label called SOSOaudio, whose Luddite mission is to counteract modern "digital perfection" in favor of searching out "the analogue error, the bump in the plastic, the mechanical glissando." As their promotional-copy-cum-manifesto further explains:

"It is a tribute to the sound defects of plastic, to its residual noise and, above all, to the needle of discord: the one that gathers dust, the one that jumps, the one that wears out and is worn out, the one that suffers and with which we suffer—or have fun."

A handful of these cylinders were produced in 2010, and another followed in 2014, though limited information about these endures.

If some of these one-off releases seem like nothing more than novelty, then gird yourself for what became of New Zealand indie band Ghost Wave, who in 2013 had their single "Here She Comes" etched onto "the world's first playable beer bottle." Thanks to the patronage of Beck's Brewery, a special bottle adorned with grooves was designed in collaboration with "experiential marketing" firm Gyro Constructivists, no doubt at great expense. As explained by an esoteric academic article titled "Eat what you hear: Gustasonic discourses and the material culture of commercial sound recording," explains, "the Edison Bottle itself remains a consummate collectible, a mass commodity transformed into a quintessentially rare object." These bottles are unplayable on actual cylinder players, and instead can only be reproduced on a proprietary device created by Gyro.[65]

---

65 Shawn VanCour and Kyle Barnett, "Eat What You Hear: Gustasonic Discourses and the Material Culture of Commercial Sound Recording:," Dx.Doi. Org/10.1177/1359183516679186 22, no. 1 (January 10, 2017): 93–109, <doi.org/10.1177/1359183516679186>

IV.7 NONTRADITIONAL FORMATS

In 2007, the American toy company Tiger Electronics marketed a line of electric toothbrushes called Tooth Tunes. Listed at $9.99 USD apiece, they promised a musical experience while you brushed your teeth. Each brush issued a pattern of vibrations that is transmitted from brush head to tooth to mandible to inner ear. The brusher's cochlea would then interpret the vibrations as sound, so instead of the usual mechanical hum of a standard electric toothbrush, they would be treated to two-minute increments of pop songs like the Black Eyed Peas' "Let's Get It Started," the Beach Boys' "Fun, Fun, Fun,"[66] and even a song specifically recorded for Tooth Tunes by Devo, "Brush It." Two minutes, of course, is the recommended length of time someone is recommended to brush their teeth with an electric toothbrush.

Tooth Tunes were successful. These days, Tiger Electronics has gotten out of the game, but Arm & Hammer has picked it up and continues to market new songs.

Many bands and labels have experimented with new music formats, some nearly as innovative as Tooth Tunes. A 2002 article in *Stereophile* magazine proclaimed that "HitClips Are Hot,"[67] describing another Tiger Electronics product: tiny memory cards that contained one-minute blips of then-current pop songs, playable exclusively on a proprietary device. These got their start as a McDonalds Happy Meal toy but soon took on a life of their own and apparently became a part of the marketing strategy for new singles. The sound quality, characterized as "ultra-low-fi mono,"[68] found an audience amongst elementary students, aided by a parent-friendly $3.99 price tag.

Another strange format was something called a "super electronic removable MCD," a tiny plastic cartridge that could be inserted into a line of "singing dolls" marketed by Yaboom Toys. By pressing a button on their bellies, likenesses of Christina Aguilera, Britney Spears, and Elton John would then perform their own hit songs, albeit while remaining completely still.[69]

IV.7.1 USB & SD

In the era of high-speed internet, releasing music on USB flash drives seems redundant, but several artists have taken up this format, often putting an innovative spin on the format. In 2010, Lemonade, an alternative dance group from San Francisco, released a special edition of their *Pure Moods* EP. This was a direct reference to the as-seen-on-TV new-age/atmospheric compilation series that collected tracks by the likes of Jean-

---

66 Surely a hit with children in the year 2007—or perhaps intended for their parents?

67 Barry Willis, "HitClips Are Hot | Stereophile.Com," Stereophile (New York City, May 5, 2002), <www.stereophile.com/news/11335/>

68 For the technologically inclined, someone reverse-engineered a Jackson Five HitDisc, pulling the audio off the circuit board and into digital form (in its gleefully tiny form): "Reverse Engineering a Hit Clip," chOOftech Industries, December 31, 2013, <chOOftech.com/2013/12/31/reverse-engineering-a-hit-clip/>

69 "Christina Aguilera," Celebrity Doll Museum <www.celebritydollmuseum.com/325/christina-aguilera/> [accessed March 19, 2022]

Michel Jarre and Enigma. Lemonade made their EP wearable, releasing it in the form of USB bracelets engraved with the title, available in multiple colors.

Coincidentally, several folks have incorporated USBs into medically themed packaging. Three separate artists have used flash drives that look like red-and-white medical capsules, then packaged them in custom pill bottles. Dr. RxSonic, the progressive project of Albertan psychiatrist Dr. Andrei Poukhovski, put out his album *PRN Musications* with this packaging, and Tied To The Branches issued their *Tranqs For the Memories* EP the same way, exclusively sold by the now-closed San Francisco record store Aquarius Records. A band named Ginsu Wives put out their *Panic* EP on Thick Syrup Records using the exact same gimmick. Meanwhile, Oorlog Frankenstein's self-titled EP came out on a memory stick designed as a fake syringe.

Balkan Recordings released a retrospective compilation for their I Love Acid sub-label on a custom-made USB key resembling a miniature Roland TR-303, which is the bass synthesizer that gave rise to the acid house genre. Ragk's *Folder Run*, contained on a 1 GB memory stick, came packaged in a little metal tin and surrounded by recycled magnetic tape. A band named Synthetics put out a special edition of their *Synchronized Units* album on USB keys that double as robot figurines.

Alternatively, some folks have used SD cards to store audio files, incorporating them into whimsical packaging ideas. The ever-inventive Auris Apothecary label released a compilation called *Centum* as their hundredth release. It is an 8 GB microSD card that contains all the audio from their first 99 releases. Its compact size pokes fun at the fact that Auris Apothecary's strange releases are often recognized more for their physical manifestations than the sounds contained within. As the product description explains, each microSD is "attached to the underside of a cork used to seal a glass bottle filled with all sorts of debris, which includes broken glass, magnetic tape, pieces of tile, sunflower leaves, nails, cassette shards, scouring pads, sandpaper, wax seals, elk antlers, and pieces of broken vinyl records." SD cards are tiny and can be easily placed in tiny nooks—whether they are tucked on the underside of a cork or, in the case of Floridian experimental electronic producer Kyonpalm's *Easter Egg 2013* album, housed in a faux Fabergé egg.

IV.7.2 Self-Reliant Formats

Other innovators have designed their products to play music independently of any devices. Paul Morley teamed up with the cellist James Banbury to develop ServiceAV, "a kind of recorded music company," which put out a wacky release in 2010 by Banbury's Datahack project. *TAP3* was a cassette tape with a built-in SD card and MP3 player. Its multifaceted design meant it could either be played in a tape player or hooked up to headphones and played on its own.

Then there was the PlayButton, a series of wearable pinback buttons, each of which contained a full album. The front featured circular album art, while the back contained buttons allowing you to play and stop songs, skip tracks, and control the volume. By connecting headphones to the bottom of the PlayButton, you had a one-album MP3 player that you could wear. The product hit the market in 2011; within three years, their website was dead, and new PlayButtons were no longer being produced. An article in *Wired* calls the product "either a desperate attempt to incorporate all the annoyances of analog music into a digital package, or . . . a genius marketing move which will perhaps usurp the USB thumb-drive as the ultimate in corporate schwag giveaways."[70] Others have developed their own music-making machines without greedy corporate aspirations. The "Awesome Edition" of electronic artist Moldover's self-titled debut CD comes in a jewel case containing a custom-printed circuit board programmed to function as a light Theremin, meaning you can "play" it by varying the amount of light that reaches the sensor, the audio pitch shifting with the brightness.[71] Another artist, Tristan Perich, has also built circuit boards into jewel cases. His *1-Bit Music* has a headphone jack; you connect to it, and it will play a series of 1-bit compositions created by Perich. His *1-Bit Symphony*, meanwhile, uses the same principle but has built-in speakers, meaning no headphones are necessary.[72]

In a 2016 interview, Perich says he was inspired by early, pre-iPod MP3 players when he created his playable jewel-case circuit boards. "They were huge, and the batteries only lasted 45 minutes or whatever," he recalls of those early devices. With this form of player, music was no longer an object—it was more ephemeral. "So I can make a commentary [on that] by putting music out in the exact same packaging, but you open it up and it's its own player. That's the only way you can hear it—by jacking in and turning it on. As a listener, you're more aware of how the circuit is working and how it's powered and everything."

Perich includes the source code in the jewel case's liner notes, emphasizing the physical reality of the technology and trying to demystify the innards in a world in which much tech is proprietary—"making people aware that technology isn't magical," as he puts it.

Not so for the inscrutable Buddha Machine, which is a literal black box that produces sound loops. Introduced in 2005, Buddha Machines were the work of Christiaan Virant and Zhang Jian, two musicians living in China who call themselves FM3. The machines, which have been released in increasingly complex editions, contain a circuit board and built-in speaker, and play looped melodies which can be toggled by the user. They resemble a cigarette box.

In an interview for critic Marc Weidenbaum for his Disquiet website,[73] Virant describes the history of the Buddha Machine idea. While visiting a temple in southwest China in the mid-nineties, he noticed a machine that played a Buddhist chant on a never-ending loop. Surprised to learn it was not just a cassette player running a tape loop, he learned he could buy them from the gift shop and picked up two. Eventually, he thought it might be neat to create something similar that could play his own music. After much

---

70 Charlie Sorrel, "Play Button, an Annoying MP3-Player In a Button," WIRED (San Francisco, October 22, 2010), <www.wired.com/2010/11/play-button-an-annoying-mp3-player-in-a-button/>

71 Cory Casciato, "Backbeat: Coolest CD Case Ever Has Theremin Built In," Westword (Denver, August 20, 2009), <www.westword.com/music/coolest-cd-case-ever-has-theremin-built-in-5683584>

72 Tristan Perich, "Tristan Perich: 1-Bit Symphony," <web.archive.org/web/20190111134500/http://www.1bitsymphony.com/> [accessed March 19, 2022]

73 Marc Widenbaum, "Buddha in the Machine," Disquiet, December 17, 2005, <disquiet.com/2005/12/17/buddha-in-the-machine/>

technical tweaking and several prototypes, Virant and Zhang Jian contracted a factory to manufacture an edition of three hundred machines, which quickly sold out. (Brian Eno apparently bought six.) Three more editions followed, each with the technology tweaked, and there was even talk of developing it as a "format" that other artists could release on. Indeed, Throbbing Gristle had their own Buddha Box, and Philip Glass also released one for his eightieth birthday in 2017, but it is unclear if there are plans for more. While some see the box's lo-fi sound as the point, it also has its detractors.[74] Much like SD card releases, PlayButtons, and even Perich's circuit board jewel cases, the Buddha Machine is about concept over function.

As music increasingly moves online, there is still a subset of musicians and fans who are committed to enjoying physical manifestations of music. Even with CDs at their commercial nadir, there is room in the market for a variety of different formats, and ironically, much of this physical media is sold online, including on platforms like Bandcamp that are also responsible for facilitating digital distribution.

When I spoke with Ant Jones, proprietor of the Lavender Sweep label, about his microcassette releases, he told me about a project he was assembling as we spoke.

"A band that I am in called The Rusty Nutz will be releasing an album titled *We Tried To Make It Big But Something Somewhere Went Wrong And We Can't Work Out What That Something Is* on at least 25 formats, including CD, 12" vinyl, cassette, MiniDisc, Elcaset, DCC tape, metal microcassette, DAT, 8-track, USB in small box, Micro SD with mini MP3 player, ZIP 750 MB, Castlewood ORB, Rev Disk, Microdrive 340 MB, VHS Hi-Fi, VHS-C Hi-Fi, Sony NT60, reel-to-reel, Betahi-fi, Micro DV, Hi8/DTRS tape, S-VHS PCM audio, Beta PCM audio, and DVD-RAM audio."

"Well... that's certainly the plan anyway, I wouldn't quote all those formats in case it doesn't come off. But Elcaset, 8-track, reel-to-reel and MiniDisc are a certainty."

---

74 Larry Crane, "Christiaan Virant and Zhang Jian: Buddha Machine FM3 'Chan Fang' Buddha Machine IPhone App," Tape Op (Portland, OR, September 2011), <tapeop.com/reviews/music/85/buddha-machine-fm3-chan-fang-buddha-machine-iphone/>

V.1 ELABORATE

In 2012, the Residents put out the *Ultimate Box Set*, a career retrospective to mark forty years since they released their debut single, "Santa Dog." The set included 563 songs spread over forty LPs, fifty CDs, and scads of singles, EPs, DVDs and other goodies—their entire discography, including the original pressing of "Santa Dog" and four subsequent re-releases.

But there was a catch. Each copy of the *Ultimate Box Set* cost $100,000 in U.S. dollars and was packaged in a full-size refrigerator, the shelves stocked with all the records and CDs, plus a bunch of knick-knacks and goodies, including the band's iconic eyeball masks. A goofy infomercial was released to commemorate the release, with scraggly frontman Randy Rose shilling the product in a decaying Santa Claus suit.

The exact purpose of this prohibitively expensive item is a little unclear. On one hand, it was marketed, rather ironically, as the ultimate collector's item. On the other hand, the press release states that "the intended market for the box set lies within the realm of fine art." A copy of the set was even exhibited at the Museum of Modern Art in Manhattan.

Record covers are an art unto themselves. Hipgnosis, the design house that created legendary covers for Pink Floyd, Led Zeppelin, Genesis, and many others, has had its work collected in several art books. Other record labels established graphic themes across releases and would commission cover artwork, often at great cost, to grace their releases. British labels 4AD and Factory were trendsetters along these lines, and contemporary labels like Warp and Sacred Bones have since continued this tradition.

This tension is alive in the bizarre and elaborate forms of packaging discussed in this chapter. There are multiple threads that run through these innovative packaging designs. In some examples, the packaging is little more than a marketing gimmick. Elsewhere, the album artwork serves as its own *objet d'art* to complement the music contained within, particularly when it comes to ultra-limited-edition releases of noise records.

The examples in this chapter push several boundaries of reasonability, the Residents' *Ultimate Box Set* being an especially egregious example. A hundred grand for what amounts to a box set in a fridge? That is not just gratuitous; it prices out nearly the entire Residents fanbase. And even if there was a diehard collector with a trust fund and a soft spot for multidisciplinary avant-garde art collectives, you would think that even the most spendthrift multimillionaire should draw the line somewhere.

It turns out someone did buy the Residents' *Ultimate Box Set*. A news item from 2013[1] reveals that a fan from Bloomington, Indiana named Tripmonster pulled the trigger on the monstrous box, a purchase so noteworthy that it was filmed for an upcoming Residents documentary. I do not know who Tripmonster is, though a picture of him accepting the fridge is available online, and he also shares his name with a Scandinavian online travel agency. But he has staked his claim on an integral part of the Residents' discography.

You can too. There are still nine more available.

---

1   Josh Keppel, "The Residents' $100,000 'Ultimate Box Set' Sold and Delivered," NBC Bay Area, October 22, 2013, <www.nbcbayarea.com/news/weird/100000-ultimate-box-set-sold-and-delivered/1957152/>

EXTREME MUSIC

V.1.1 History of Elaborate Packaging

Packaging gimmicks have been a part of just about every entertainment medium since the beginning, and records are no different. I wondered what type of gimmicky packaging existed in the 78 RPM era, but information about packaging in the early era of recorded music was hard to come by. Most records seem to have been sold in featureless brown sleeves or, in their most elaborate incarnation, in heavy books resembling photo albums that would house a bunch of shellac discs. I suspect novelty packaging concepts did exist, to some degree, in the era of Edison cylinders and 78 RPM records, but, if so, this topic is not well compiled anywhere.

The rock era, on the other hand, was a golden era of packaging gimmicks, perhaps because it is when young people started buying records in large numbers. In one iconic example, the Rolling Stones' classic 1971 album *Sticky Fingers* was released in a special "zipper" edition. The cover, which features a close-up image of the fly on someone's jeans, was produced in a version with an actual zipper on the front. It was, at last, a chance to unzip Mick Jagger's pants, for the few who did not get the opportunity in real life.

Add-ons and visual gags were abundant in this era. *The Velvet Underground & Nico* (1967) came out in an edition with a peelable banana on the front.[2] A limited version of Alice Cooper's *School's Out* came in a cover that resembled a school desk; the actual record was wrapped in a pair of disposable paper panties.[3] These are a mere handful of the many examples of creative approaches to the record jacket which were concocted in the rock era. There is even a whole spectrum of records that explored the world of scratch-and-sniff.

In the post-punk era, John Lydon's Public Image Ltd set a new benchmark for album art with his band's sublime second album, which had a special edition housed in a gray metal canister. An interview with PiL's guitarist, Keith Levene, for *Perfect Sound Forever* outlines some of the background behind the making of the legendary metal box. To match the dense, inaccessible nature of songs like "Poptones" and "Albatross," the band spent $30,000 of their recording advance on the limited-edition metal box version, which they commissioned from a factory supposedly named Metal Box.[4] For maximum audio quality, they divided the album between three 45 RPM long-playing records, which necessitated an especially large metal container. Only in retrospect did they realize that the wide, circular metal box resembled an old film canister.

PiL's record label didn't share their enthusiasm. "They said, 'Forget any *Metal Box*, don't even go there,'" Levene laughed. "That was it, fuck it! 'Who do you think you are? You're lucky you're getting a cardboard box.'" As a result, *Second Edition* was the mass-produced, standard-issue-double-LP version of the record—leaving original copies of *Metal Box* to command hefty sums on the collectors' market.

PiL's *Metal Box* was a groundbreaking experimental album. Several tracks were composed principally of abstract dub rhythms and spindly guitar shards, which

---

2 The banana was a sticker which could be peeled from the surface. "The Velvet Underground & Nico — The Velvet Underground & Nico (1967, West Coast Pressing, Vinyl)," Discogs <www.discogs.com/release/371471-The-Velvet-Underground-Nico-The-Velvet-Underground-Nico> [accessed March 19, 2022]

3 "Alice Cooper — School's Out (1972, Panties Inner, Vinyl)," Discogs <www.discogs.com/release/11792624-Alice-Cooper-Schools-Out> [accessed March 19, 2022]

4 This likely refers to the Metal Box Factory in Southwark, which has since been redeveloped into a commercial office/studio building.

helped pave the way for the explosion of avant-garde bands that soon cropped up on the post-punk and industrial scenes. Those bands did not just borrow from PiL's dark and abrasive sounds, however; they also carried the tradition of innovative packaging forward. Future generations of industrial and noise scenesters would take these packaging ideas to their logical extremes as the century progressed.

Some were one-offs. German minimal wave artist John Bender released his second album, *Plaster Falling*, on his very own Record Sluts label, in a first edition that came in a sleeve dipped in white plaster. To access the record itself, a string embedded in the plaster had to be pulled, causing the case to crumble apart. I spoke with C.V. Mansoor, the artist who was commissioned to create the packaging for this unique release. "At the time I had done some works that were on paper and were layered with a coat of plaster, and then they were folded or cracked to expose what was underneath," she explains. "[Bender] liked them and wanted me to use this technology on his album. "I mixed the plaster with an Elmer's glue mixture, and I wanted it to open the way a Band-Aid wrapper used to, with a string. So, we used paper tape, the kind used in watercolor masking to seal the packages. Then we just had a lot of fun dipping them... Each one was different. At some point we put in found objects, such as Polaroids and other 2D objects in the album jackets before we sealed them. This idea was inspired by how they used to put surprises in Cracker Jacks." Mansoor, who also once designed a "reverse globe"—in which the world's countries and oceans are detailed on the inner surface of a sphere—remains friends with Bender to this day.[5]

V.1.2 American Tapes

When it comes to elaborate, handmade packaging, the story cannot be told without addressing American Tapes. It was a record label run by John Olson, a founding member of the seminal noise band Wolf Eyes, as well as over a hundred other bands and solo projects. American Tapes started in the early nineties and ran for over twenty years, closing up shop in 2015, accumulating an incomprehensible mass of approximately one thousand releases in total. From the perspective of packaging, the common theme behind many American Tapes releases was its *homemade* aesthetic. Utilizing pop-culture detritus in the form of found objects and collage work, Olson would handcraft limited-edition releases into pieces of art that were more akin to sculpture than album art.

American Tapes set a high watermark for design early in the label's history, drawing from Olson's parallel career as a visual artist. Befitting the name, most early releases were on cassette, a durable and relatively compact medium that worked well with the recycled materials Olson used to build his packages. Many of the cassette shells were closer to nests than traditional cases.

Olson tells me that the prehistory of American Tapes began in 1989 when he, then a college sophomore at Michigan State University, went to New York City with his friend, a freshman named Jeff Dunn, and their pal Becky for one of the *Village Voice*'s New Music Seminars. There, they attended a nearly empty noon show with sets by Blue Humans, Thurston Moore, and William Hooker.

---

5 "CV Mansoor Reverse Globe Sculpture," Everything But the House <www.ebth.com/items/754271-cv-mansoor-reverse-globe-sculpture> [accessed March 19, 2022]

EXTREME MUSIC

"The Blue Humans played and it just changed our lives, inside out," he tells me. "We had to drive home that night back to Michigan, and on the way home, we were so excited." They wanted to start a similarly adventurous sound project, but one that had a distinctive Michigan identity.

Relatively little is known about early American Tapes releases because most were issued in editions of around ten. From 1990 to 1992, Olson was living with Jeff Dunn and another friend named Bryan Ramirez (who joined them in the bands Plants and Universal Indians) in a place they called the Rocket Room—not a quarter-mile from where Olson lives now. He attended classes at MSU by day and taught drawing by night. He told me that they would "record nonstop" at the Rocket Room, experimenting with improvised guitar, sax, and drums. One of those recordings became the first American Tapes release, dubbed in an edition of thirty.

At the time, he was also working in an antique shop owned by a retired professor named Spud, who would scour garage sales for merchandise, some of which would sell, and some of which hung around. Olson had a fair amount of downtime at that job and, when Spud was not around, he would experiment with packaging ideas using things that were not selling, often combining them with lacquer. He kept these exploits from Spud to avoid being told to stop. Olson estimated that there were thirty early American Tapes releases before the officially numbered series began. These are not documented online and now mainly exist only as memories. He made these early releases from scratch using antique-shop materials and a stamp pad for lettering—part of an early fascination with fonts. One release was a rehearsal recording of his band at the time, Kill Devil Hill, which he gave out free at a show. He only knows of two people who still own copies: Max Mitchell and Jimmy Johnson from *Forced Exposure*.

Olson told me the "only person who would take" these releases was the Seattle distributor Anomalous Records, though he would often trade copies via mail with the then-booming underground network of small labels and tape traders. This is how he came across work by the Japanese noise artist MSBR, who would become a major influence. In particular, he recalls ordering a copy of MSBR's *Structured Suicide*, which came wrapped in a bundle of Japanese daily newspapers, solidified with a coating of wax.

The first release in the American Tapes numbered discography, which is where online discographies start, was *In Frozen* by Olson's own band, D.L. Savings T.X.[6] At the time, he had a job teaching a big classroom of ten-year-olds how to draw. On the day that daylight saving time turned over, the class was especially chaotic, and when he got home, he went to his basement and "started a band," recording a tape's worth of improvised music. He released this as AM-01, accompanying it with a zine that featured hand-drawn art and a short story. He estimates that he made thirteen copies in total, which he distributed for free to friends. "And no one said anything about them," he recalls, with a laugh.

Trying something new, he bought some cheap Kinko's envelopes and silkscreened them—this was the packaging for the several releases that would follow (AM-02 to AM-06). But subsequent releases became more complicated. Talking to Olson about his

6 Contrary to the online discography, Olson says he was still going by the name Daylight Savings Time at that time.

D.L. Savings T.X.'s *Cleopatra... Ruler of the Yard* on American Tapes, with tape removed from packaging. The peapod and organic matter have not survived. Image courtesy of Henry Rollins.

American Tapes is an experimental music trivia enthusiast's fantasy. During the interview, I had the 1,000-strong American Tapes discography open in front of me, bringing up releases that looked interesting based on photos from the label's now-defunct website.

D.L. Savings T.X.'s *Cleopatra... Ruler of the Yard*, release number 40, had a characteristically eye-catching package. The tape itself is cozied in a trash-nest composed of a crumpled Del Monte can, some plant matter, some rolled-up paper, ample "goop," and, the pièce de résistance, a pea pod. He tells me he put this together in the fall, when Lansing's abundant trees were shedding various organic bits. He assembled them into an irregular lattice, then strung them together with fishing line and coated everything in lacquer. The liner notes were slid into the pile in the form of a rolled-up scroll. Some customers even griped that the packaging was better than the music itself! Olson tells me that the pea pod itself lent the package a satisfying sound when shaken, so leaving the tape unheard was always a possibility.

American Tapes release number 43, a tape by E Ka (S) Boa titled *May You Be Joined By*, came housed in a ramshackle assemblage of metal junk and toy train tracks, all globbed together by dried glue and finished with silver paint. Olson says that the packaging for this release, which was an exhumed recording from 1990 of himself and Jeff Dunn, was built around the many model railroad tracks that the antique shop had accumulated but been unable to sell. For a uniform look, he used metal objects to

Above and opposite: E Ka (S) Boa's *May You Be Joined By* on American Tapes, model train tracks and all. Images courtesy of Henry Rollins.

augment the silver railroad tracks. Responding to the complaints that his packages had to be dismantled to be opened, he also made sure to fix the works to the cassette box so that customers did not have to destroy the package to get to the release.

The D.L. Savings T.X.'s tastefully titled *Thank You Urine Doll* was another novel concept. Reminiscing, he tells me that he named it after mishearing a friend saying to him, "Thank you, you're a doll." For the cover, he took a bunch of 7" records and coated the surface of each one with as many noxious chemicals as he could think of, including lacquer, enamel, acrylic, laundry detergent, Windex, oil, and paint remover. He then left the toxic stew for a month to react. Together, the chemicals were about half an inch thick, and by the end, the surface of each record looked a little like the surface of Mars. Each mutated disc was then fixed to the surface of one of the tape containers.

I challenge Olson to encapsulate his packaging aesthetic, proposing the term "junk" but wondering if it had too many negative connotations. For Olson, he prefers the term "homemade," borrowing it from an early American Tapes motto, "good thinking and homemade sound." Although there is a degree of chaos and repurposing to his aesthetic, he does not like the term destruction. "I got enough attention when I was a kid. I don't feel a need to destroy stuff," he reflects. "There's so much negativity in the tape world and underground; I don't want to be a part of that. American Tapes is a labor of joy rather than destruction."

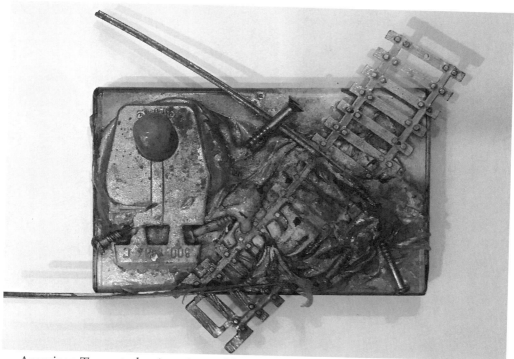

American Tapes, today, is an icon of the experimental music scene. While Olson may be better known as a member of Wolf Eyes, his commitment to releasing handmade, unique records with inventive design may be his most lasting contribution to the avant-garde underground. Many of the early American Tapes releases have surfaced on eBay, and a while ago, collectors started to notice that they were selling for astronomical prices to another musical legend, Henry Rollins. It turns out he was trying to build a library to archive the seemingly infinite remnants of the era's "great American underground sound art" scene.

V.1.3 MSBR Records

MSBR, short for Molten Salt Breeder Reactor, was the solo project of noise musician Koji Tano. He put out a seemingly endless string of releases from the early nineties up until his death in 2005 at only forty-four. Several of his releases are now classics of the harsh noise genre. Much of his work was issued on his own label, MSBR Records, which also put out releases by other artists.

Before starting his label, MSBR's first work as an artist, as documented on an archived version of his legendary website, MSBR.com, was more art exhibit than musical release. It was a sculpture built out of a gasoline tank, a pump, and "saveral junks [sic]." A speaker was nestled under the "stomach" of the tank, playing noise and vibrating the apparatus, "like a screaming beast."[7] Although MSBR claimed that the release had no meaning, it bore the thumbprint of the industrial-junk aesthetic that would pervade his discography.

---

7   Koji Tano, "Exhibition Works," MSBR Web Site <web.archive.org/web/20040606074357/http://msbr.com/inst/einst.html> [accessed March 19, 2022]

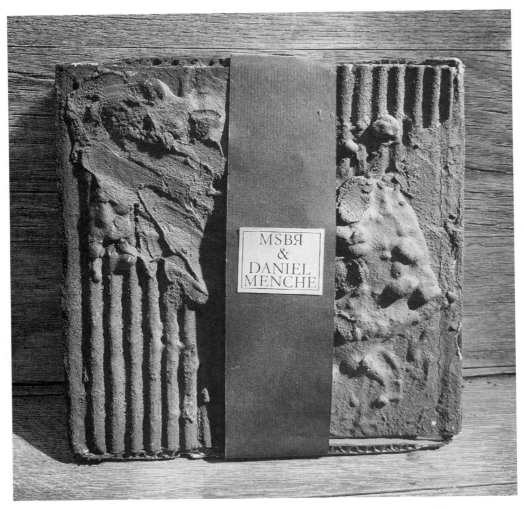

MSBR and Daniel Menche's *Multi Layering Termination* acetate 7" on MSBR Records. The packaging is a cardboard box covered in concrete. Image courtesy of Daniel Menche.

In 1992, MSBR put out his first record, an LP called *Ultimate Ambience* LP, which was also the inaugural release on his self-named label. Unsurprisingly, the *Ambience* in question is harsh noise. The first one hundred copies came in unique covers decked messily in glops of metallic paint, shreds of foil, and found images.[8] It was the prototype for many subsequent MSBR Records releases, which gained a reputation for their elaborate, handmade editions, partly inspiring the junk-art aesthetic embraced by American Tapes.

Ultimate Ambience is mundane compared to Tano's later exploits. A split between MSBR and Italian noise act Sshe Retina Stimulants comes in a custom-built case made of weathered sheet metal and wire. A split with Smell & Quim incorporates randomly lacquered wood pieces and fish bones. A split acetate 7" by Daniel Menche and Small Cruel Party was snuggled inside a mutant sleeve of cloth fragments and chunks of old

---

8   Copies now command over two hundred dollars apiece online.

stuffed animals. The "ingredients lists" of other releases are downright whimsical; among the components of MSBR packaging were flour, olive oil, rope, tissues, foam, leaves, socks, juice cartons, and a latex glove.

Each MSBR Records release is unique, but they often manage to embrace two aesthetics at once. On one hand, every copy is painstakingly handmade. Yet their qualities are also strangely industrial, often using miscellaneous scrap that might have been swept off a factory floor—things like sheet metal, wooden dowels, and concrete— evoking industrial art and ready-mades. Even the colors evoke machinery and mass production: sleek chrome, newspaper gray, rusty brown, faded orange. In some cases, as on a 1995 split between MSBR and L.A. artist Speculum Fight, the packaging must have been a headache to the postal service. This release is a lathe-cut 7" record mounted on a bizarre wooden frame that extends about three times beyond the diameter of the vinyl and would have likely been shipped from MSBR's home in Japan to all manner of international destinations. MSBR at one point claimed it was his favorite packaging project, preferred specifically because "it doesn't look like a record jacket."[9]

Today, all that remains of MSBR's legacy is his archived website, his entry on Discogs, and a smattering of online articles. In one archived interview for the *Angbase* zine, he describes being influenced by prog- and space-rock titans like King Crimson and Hawkwind[10] and is noted to love Japanese wrestling. In another cursory interview for a short-lived zine called *System Overload*,[11] he professes enthusiasm for the German industrial band Einstürzende Neubauten, who are known for recording densely abrasive albums using custom-built instruments made of tools and scrap metal. Neither interviewer asked Tano about his packaging.

The fact that Tano liked his split with Speculum Fight best because of its lack of resemblance to a typical LP sleeve tells us how important he considered the packaging of his releases. Tano has also said that he chose the name Molten Salt Breeder Reactor because it evoked a "heavy machinery image." MSBR's output both embraced and subverted the industrial manufacturing process. He references technology designed to bring consumers hundreds of thousands of identical items, but he warps and dismantles their by-products, hand-assembling them into broken and unrecognizable forms.

V.1.4 Toxic Industries / Very Toxic

The torch established by the likes of Olson and Tano has been carried on by a whole new generation of packaging experimentalists. One such practitioner is Fabrizio De Bon, who lives in Sospirolo, a small municipality in the northeast of Italy. He records noise as Fukte (pronounced ˈfukˈtɛ) and runs the Toxic Industries label, which has been putting out hand-designed limited-edition releases since 2009. De Bon's aesthetic is like a digital-age version of American Tapes' hand-assembled antiques and MSBR's penchant for industrial fuselage. Like those labels, De Bon maintains an affinity for things that are recycled and reused, reflecting a resource-conscious craftiness.

---

9 "Interview with Msbr and Govt. Alpha," sinkhole experimental music magazine, February 24, 1999, <www.angelfire.com/mi/sinkhole/intmsbrgovt.html>

10 "ELECTRO SUPLEX: An Interview with Koji Tano Aka MSBR," Angbase, 1998, <www.angbase.com/interviews/msbr.html>

11 "Interview with Koji Tano of Msbr," Information Overload Magazine <www.oocities.org/sunsetstrip/palladium/5854/msbr.html> [accessed March 19, 2022]

EXTREME MUSIC

He shared his conceptual leanings and the stories behind several of his unique releases, saying he discovered noise through black metal, taking a risk on an intriguing-looking record by black industrial band Mz.412, and then discovering a world of side projects. His first noise record was by the Mz.412 side project Hydra Head 9, buying the CD on a whim. And while his initial impression was that he had wasted his money, he forced himself to listen a few times and eventually saw the light. He started recording noise experiments in 2004, at first using a "very cheap microphone" and an old copy of Fruity Loops software. He eventually built his own contact mic and invested in distortion pedals and a proper mixer, preferring the analog sound for his noise.

In 2009, he started Toxic Industries to put out a split release between Fukte and the noise artist Escaton, a friend he originally met on a forum for horror film enthusiasts. This release was a tape that came in a cassette shell with a desktop computer's motherboard glued to its front. Using an angle grinder, he cut each motherboard to a precise shape, after which he spray-painted each one black.

De Bon told me about his reasons for starting a label that produces physical releases. "When you are listening to something and you have a release in your hand, looking at the package—the booklet or LP sleeve—is part of the experience itself. You can move the pages of the booklet, you can look at the package, you can study it. I feel that this is really important. I was influenced by some other noise labels and artists that were making packages with recycled material or with handmade stuff."

In particular, he mentions the Czech noise artist Napalmed, who uses recycled materials in his packaging, as well as several Japanese artists who put out handmade packages. "So I decided, okay, I can start a label to promote these kinds of artists and this kind of attitude in the packages. And at the same time, I was trying to use mostly recycled or trash material. Most of the releases that I've done so far are made with recycled material or stuff that people were going to trash. So I saved them and I recycled them in a creative way, as a kind of upcycling."

De Bon, who works in the IT field, had easy access to computer parts. As a result, his releases often employ computer detritus in their packaging, and the theme of gored PCs is one he explores in detail over his many releases. "Ninety percent of the computer parts that I reused are from my job... I still have boxes here at my place that are full of stuff that I'm waiting to think of how to match together and create new packages."

But his use of defunct computer parts does not reflect an underlying fetishism for technology. "There is a philosophy behind the label, which comes also to the name of the label," he explained. "Toxic Industries is a statement against the overproduction of industrialization. I work in IT, so I live it day by day that we are surrounded by a lot of stuff we don't need. There is mass industrialization of everything. I feel this is not really good for our life, but mostly it is not good for the environment itself."

He told me that he describes himself as an environmentalist, and that this is reflected in his aesthetic. "With the label, I decided to use packages, mostly from recycled stuff. I had a lot of computer junk that was destined for the trash, that was going to be exported to African countries to be burned. I thought, 'Wow, I don't want to take part in this process.'

**Fukte and Orgasm Denial's *Disk Failure* mini-CD-R, which
comes contained inside a defunct hard drive.
Image courtesy of Fabrizio De Bon of Toxic Industries.**

So if I can save something and recycle it, maybe in a creative way, why not? This is not just about computers, but more widely about recycling stuff that is going to the trash."

One of De Bon's most distinctive releases is *Disk Failure*, a 3" split CD-R that features both Fukte and the Hong Kong noise artist Orgasm Denial. It comes nestled inside a broken hard drive, stationed in the part of the drive where the magnetic data was stored. "It took a lot of time to disassemble the hard drive," he recalled. "You need a really tiny screwdriver, and it takes a long time to find the one screw and then the second one, and then you try to open it and you're like 'Where the fuck is the last screw that I can't find?' I had to extract the inner disk and remove it and put the three-inch CD-R in that place. It was really a lot of handiwork to assemble this release."

The music itself was noise that was collaboratively recorded via distance, each artist laying their noise on top of the other's. He explained that this is only the first in a planned trilogy of split releases between Fukte and Orgasm Denial, the conceptual focus being "different problems related to the reliability of data in the computer—even if you have top-notch technology and you rely on that, there is still something that can go wrong." Appropriately, the tracks on *Disk Failure* are named "Head Crash" and "Stuck Spindle." At a half-kilogram each, they were a challenge to ship but remain one of his label's most distinctive releases.

Most of De Bon's elaborately packaged releases are filed under a sub-label of Toxic Industries called Very Toxic, including both aforementioned splits. Many of them share his recycled-computer-parts aesthetic. His double-cassette split with Parisian harsh noise wall legend Vomir comes in a plastic box with pieces of a motherboard, and his very own *RAM* CD-R comes adorned with, you guessed it, a RAM stick, which has been coated in spray paint for good measure. Osskull's 2013 cassette release, *Con Tree 3rd*, includes a printed circuit board and a connection cable; the entire package is snuggled into one

**Fukte's *Longwaves* CD-R.
Image courtesy of Fabrizio De Bon
of Toxic Industries.**

of those anti-static bags that raw computer equipment is sold in. *Longwaves*, meanwhile, incorporates an antenna ripped from a Wi-Fi router.

Not all Very Toxic's releases are computer-themed, however. *Isolated Asylum*, a release by the Japanese noise duo Negative Climax, is a release that takes psychiatric illness as its focus. For this one, De Bon asked his friend, who worked on a psychiatric unit of a hospital, to collect old pill boxes. When they met in Turino, the friend brought a massive bag full of boxes, and De Bon selected some, flattened them, and glued them on the black cardboard that houses the cassettes. Images online show tape cassettes decorated with pill boxes for antipsychotic, sedative, and antiemetic medications.

In another example, De Bon spent two years painstakingly assembling the packaging for *Ritual* by Bangkok ambient artist Skulldust, wanting the full package to match the ritualistic tone of the music. To assemble this piece, he had to wait for his friend to smoke thirty boxes of a particular brand of cigarettes so that he could recycle the distinctive packages. He also asked another friend to collect hair from a local hairdresser, apparently by claiming that it was "for a contemporary art performance" so they wouldn't ask any questions. He then added iron dust from his father's work and pieces of incense from a trip to India. All those components were employed in the packaging to produce a distinctive final product. Ironically, by the time *Ritual* came out, Skulldust told De Bon that he had "completely lost interest in noise and experimental music," so the copies were instead distributed to friends.

What shines through when De Bon talks about his releases is how serious he is about his craft. He painstakingly conceives and realizes each release, allowing the time to make sure things come out right. His last Toxic Industries release came out in 2018 because lately he has had to devote more of his time to "real life" stuff. He and his girlfriend have moved into a new home, which they had to renovate, and they have become foster parents. Even that decision is consistent with his environmental aesthetic. "We decided not to have our own child, because we don't need to breed to express our parenthood. We can do it with people who need it."

He takes pains to emphasize that, while Toxic Industries is "in hibernation," it is not gone. He has several releases in various states of completion, including an upcoming boxed set that comes with custom-printed T-shirts. He is still committed to producing unique physical releases, though he also acknowledged the benefits of digital music in terms of facilitating access. "I believe digital music is good, because you have the support of technology, and if you use technology to promote music, that's good."

V.1.5 Others

There have been countless other innovatively packaged releases issued by other labels. Industrial titans :zoviet-france:'s 1985 double cassette *Popular Soviet Songs and Youth Music* comes in a custom ceramic pot, garnished with several accoutrements, including bird feathers culled from the shores of the Irish Sea, "the most radioactive area of seawater on Earth."[12] Hardcore band Tear It Up glued shards of broken glass to the front of their single-sided 7" single, "Zero to Suicidal...," complementing their aggressive blare with an appropriately hazardous physical manifestation. The label Auris Apothecary drew battle lines when it came to analog audio formats, encasing their cassette release of Little Orpheus and the Rogue Lions' *7th Grade is a Drag* cassingle in a hand-melted 45 RPM record. They also put out a microcassette, Deep Magic's *Illuminated Offerings*, that sits inside a scented candle. Noise act Luz Alibi's *Warm Marrow* tape, meanwhile, comes tastefully sandwiched between piano hammers, courtesy of the Resipiscent label.

And yet the most elaborate of all packaging gimmicks belongs to the Father of Noise himself, Merzbow, whose *Noisembryo* was honored with a one-copy-only special edition known as the *Merzcar*. The story has since become lore. As it goes, the owner of the Releasing Eskimo label, which put out the initial edition of *Noisembryo*, owned an out-of-commission Mercedes that police ordered him to move. So he decided to entice Merzbow fans to take his problem off his hands by rigging the car's CD player to play *Noisembryo* indefinitely, physically modifying the stereo to prevent users from turning it off or removing the disc. He then put the *Merzcar* up for sale as an ultra-limited-edition Merzbow goodie. You could debate whether this one-copy "edition" truly qualifies as a music release, but what this story illustrates is that even collectors have their limits. In the end, the *Merzcar* went unsold, and the enterprising label exec was forced to tow his own clunker to the dump.[13]

12 ":Zoviet-France: – Popular Soviet Songs And Youth Music (1985, C90 & C80, Cassette)," Discogs <www.discogs.com/release/100568-zoviet-france-Popular-Soviet-Songs-And-Youth-Music> [accessed March 19, 2022]

13 "The Merzbow Car," Eerie Materials <web.archive.org/web/20000902183436/http://www2.sbbs.se/hp/eerie/rcar.html> [accessed March 19, 2022]

SCENTED RECORDS[1]

Music is an auditory phenomenon. Album art is largely visual, but there is also a tactile element—lavish gatefold sleeves and infinite grades of cardstock. Some enterprising folks, however, have attempted to push records to a new frontier of sensory experience: the olfactory system.

Ernest Maxin and His Orchestra, *F#... Where There is Music* LP (Top Rank International, 1959)[2]

Considered the first scented record, this album came with a black felt cover imbued with the aroma of now-defunct cosmetics company Fabergé's then-new F# fragrance. A promotional release commissioned by the company, this featured classical selections from a fifty-five-musician orchestra "led" by Ernest Maxin, a British TV entertainer who ran a popular variety show.[3] In essence, it is like one of those scented perfume ads that come in fashion magazines, but in LP form. Released on a short-lived British label that was an offshoot of a film production company, this was an inauspicious beginning for scented records.

Laura Nyro, *Eli and the Thirteenth Confession* LP (1968)[4]

Nine years after *F#* came the sophomore album from NYC singer/songwriter Laura Nyro, a critically acclaimed record that was packaged with a lyric sheet whose ink was apparently perfumed. The pleasant aroma is said to persist to this day.[5]

Melanie, *Garden in the City* LP (Buddha, 1972)

The UK edition of this LP from American singer-songwriter Melanie Safka came with a cover sticker that asked owners to "rub gently to release the magic of Melanie's Garden." Scraping away the surface revealed an aroma of flowers; unfortunately, that was about the only compelling reason to purchase this record, a compilation of cover songs and scraps cynically marketed as an all-new album.[6] Another flower-scented novelty: Sylvester and the Hot Band, *Scratch My Flower* 1973 LP.[7]

Ben Atkins, *Patchouli* LP (Enterprise, 1971)

This obscure blue-eyed soul album, released on a subsidiary of the legendary soul label Stax, came

1 With thanks to some message board threads: <forums.stevehoffman.tv/threads/were-any-albums-released-with-a-fragrance.396718/>; <forums.stevehoffman.tv/threads/scented-vinyl-really.388821/>

2 "Ernest Maxin And His Orchestra — F#. . .Where There Is Music (1959, Vinyl)," Discogs <www.discogs.com/release/3645627-Ernest-Maxin-And-His-Orchestra-F-Where-There-Is-Music> [accessed March 19, 2022]

3 Naomi Musiker and Reuben Musiker, Conductors and Composers of Popular Orchestral Music: A Biographical and Discographical Sourcebook (Routledge, 2014), <books.google.ca/books?id=ipnrAgAAQBAJ>

4 Michele Kort, Soul Picnic: The Music and Passion of Laura Nyro, 1st ed. (New York: St. Martin's Press, 2003), <archive.org/details/isbn_9780312209414/page/57>

5 Andy Arleo, "Laura Nyro's Eli and the Thirteenth Confession: Transcending the Dichotomies of the Woodstock Years," in The Woodstock Years/Les Années Woodstock (Le Havre, France: Université du Havre, 2010), <halshs.archives-ouvertes.fr/halshs-00660090>

6 Charles Donovan, "Garden in the City - Melanie," AllMusic <www.allmusic.com/album/garden-in-the-city-mw0000837353> [accessed March 19, 2022]

7 "Sylvester And The Hot Band — Sylvester And The Hot Band (1973, Vinyl)," Discogs <www.discogs.com/release/941219-Sylvester-And-The-Hot-Band-Sylvester-And-The-Hot-Band> [accessed March 19, 2022]

with an inner sleeve spritzed with patchouli oil—the first of several records to take advantage of the now-iconic hippie scent. The album's cover features a photograph of an old-timey outhouse; back in the day, the fecal odor of outhouses was apparently smoothed over using patchouli oil,[8] which might explain the choice of scent. Better than the alternative, at least. A contemporaneous review in *Billboard* instructed the aspiring purchaser: "Smell cover before playing." [9]

Peter Tosh, *Bush Doctor* LP (Rolling Stones, 1978)[10]

The reggae star and noted cannabis enthusiast offered a unique gimmick for the cover of his third album: a scratch-and-sniff sticker that, once rubbed, exuded the smell of his favorite herb. Incidentally, it was also the debut album on the Rolling Stones' new record label. Predictably, this gambit was enough to get it pulled from the shelves of the British record store Boots; in an interview with *Melody Maker* at the time, Tosh himself disparaged the gimmick, which seems to have been the work of the marketing department of his record label.[11]

Raspberries, *Fresh* LP (Capitol, 1972)

Juicy power pop stalwarts Raspberries adorned their self-titled debut LP with a novel gimmick: a scratch-and-sniff sticker on the cover—though in many cases, the sticker was pasted to the shrink-wrap.[12] Once rubbed, it released a berry-like aroma. This was the first of several berry-themed scented records. Other berry-scented novelties: The Brothers Johnson, "Strawberry Letter 23" 1977 single (strawberry), The Damned, *Strawberries* (strawberry-scented lyric sheet) 1982 LP, Lightning Seeds, *Jollification* 1994 CD (strawberry).

Various Artists, *The Akron Compilation* LP (Stiff, 1978)[13]

Stiff Records, known for signing Akron, Ohio's most famous export, Devo, got really excited about the "Rubber Capital of the World," so named because it is home to several tire companies, including Firestone and Goodyear. *The Akron Compilation* was an attempt to chronicle the varying punk and new wave groups hailing from the city, though only a handful really became familiar names (the Rubber City Rebels and Rachel Sweet, who recorded the theme song to *Clarissa Explains it All*, were the most notable of the bunch). But the real treat is the cover gimmick: scratch the word "Akron" and you'll unleash the intoxicating aroma of rubber! Mmmm!

8   Andrew T. Burt, "Blue-Eyed Soul?: Ben Atkins' Patchouli and Jim Ford's Harlan County," Snobbin: Beautiful Trash in the Pop Culture Gutter, August 21, 2013, <indiegutter.blogspot.com/2013/08/blue-eyed-soul-ben-atkins-patchouli-and.html>

9   "BEN ATKINS- Patchouli," Billboard (New York City, November 13, 1971)

10 "Draft of Peter Tosh – Bush Doctor (1978, Stickered Scratch & Sniff, Vinyl) ," Discogs <www.discogs.com/release/3745741-Peter-Tosh-Bush-Doctor> [accessed March 19, 2022]

11 "Peter Tosh: The Bush Doctor Sessions," Midnight Raver, January 10, 2013, <marleyarkives.wordpress.com/2013/01/10/peter-tosh-the-bush-doctor-sessions/>

12 "The Raspberries - Scratch-and-Sniff Sticker?," Steve Hoffman Music Forums, September 19, 2006, <forums.stevehoffman.tv/threads/the-raspberries-scratch-and-sniff-sticker.91606/>

13 Rick Benedum, "Stiff Records Presents: The Akron Compilation," I Could Rule the World if I Could Only Get the Parts…, October 6, 2009, <akronness.wordpress.com/2009/10/06/stiff-records-presents-the-akron-compilation/>

Madonna, *Like a Prayer* CD/LP/cassette (Sire, 1989)

Madonna may have had little in common with Ben Atkins, but she did reprise his patchouli oil concept from way back in 1971, spritzing vinyl, LP, and cassette copies of her massive *Like a Prayer* with the stuff.

The County Medical Examiners, *Olidous Operettas* CD (Relapse, 2007)

A goregrind band formed by medical students, The County Medical Examiners took great pains to preserve their identities from the public. Their debut album, on the other hand, should not be missed: its gory cover features an ominous scratch-and-sniff panel, which releases the odor of rotting meat. As frontman Dr. Morton Fairbanks (a pseudonym) told *Metro* newspaper: "Most of the companies refused to work with me, but Sony has this technology that allows you to infuse scents into a CD, and they finally agreed to do one that smells like rotten meat... The album's gonna stink."[14]

Add N to (X), *Add Insult to Injury* 2xLP (Mute, 2000)

The cover of British electro-pop oddballs Add N To (X)'s 2000 album *Add Insult to Injury* featured plenty of greenery, so it came with four scratch-and-sniff panels that smelled like grass.[15]

Katy Perry, *Teenage Dream* CD (Capitol, 2010)

Befitting its candied cover, which features Katy Perry lying nude in a bed of pink cotton candy, both CD and 2xLP editions of her wildly successful *Teenage Dream* album came imbued with a cotton candy aroma. As shown in a brief documentary about the CD's production, the many copies of the CD booklet were taken to a special facility called MultiPKG, where a 50/50 mixture of cotton candy scent and varnish were rolled onto their surface, 8,000 units per hour.[16]

Black Moth Super Rainbow, *Dandelion Gum* 2xLP (Graveface, 2007)

The initial edition of this LP came with a scratch-and-sniff cover, suitably fitted with a bubblegum aroma.

Ray Parker Jr./Run-DMC, *Ghostbusters* (Stay Puft Edition) 12" single (Legacy, 2014)

This expensive reissue of two versions of the *Ghostbusters* theme included several odds 'n' ends, including a puffy, marshmallow-esque gatefold jacket, a Stay-Puft figurine, and several 3D images from the film. Best of all, the vinyl smelled like marshmallows.[17]

---

14 "This Album Stinks...of Rotten Meat," Metro, March 15, 2007, <metro.co.uk/2007/03/15/this-album-stinks-of-rotten-meat-187321/#ixzz4IKsDWr9p>

15 "Add N To (X) – Add Insult To Injury (2000, Vinyl)," Discogs <www.discogs.com/release/52433-Add-N-To-X-Add-Insult-To-Injury> [accessed March 19, 2022]

16 Chris Bauer, "CD Packaging: The Making of Katy Perry's Cotton Candy Scented Packaging," Unified Manufacturing, September 3, 2010, <www.unifiedmanufacturing.com/blog/cd-packaging-making-katy-perry-cotton-candy-scented-packaging/>

17 Ray Parker Jr. / Run-DMC – Ghostbusters (Stay Puft Edition) (2014, White, 6" Stay Puft Marshmallow Man, Vinyl)," Discogs <www.discogs.com/release/6243771-Ray-Parker-Jr-Run-DMC-Ghostbusters-Stay-Puft-Edition> [accessed March 19, 2022]

V.2 DISGUSTING

The music packaging discussed in the previous chapter tends to blur the lines between design and art, and many examples expand the parameters of album art into truly unique territory. There is also a subset of records whose artwork is designed to be as aversive as possible. Grotesque artwork tends to be the norm in extreme subgenres of metal and noise. For example, the genres of grindcore and goregrind, discussed earlier in this book, often make use of extremely violent images, sometimes real photos pulled from true gore websites. Pornogrind covers often combine explicit sexual imagery with violence to truly unsettling effect. Meanwhile, noise and black metal acts have mastered the art of menace, often using creepy, grainy images and serial-killer news items.

Many of these covers are designed to produce a visceral reaction, especially those with illustrated or actual images of gore and bodily decomposition. One of the hallmarks of small extreme music scenes is an affinity for testing the audience's mettle. Grindcore and death metal labels with artistic budgets will often commission this art from a network of illustrators who are experts in depicting ghastly phantasmagorias of offal and decay, many of whom bring their own distinctive style.

Some talented artists have mastered the art of rendering grotesque images as drawings or paintings. Mark Riddick is an illustrator who has done countless album covers. Most of his works are intricate black-and-white illustrations depicting human skeletons in various arrangements, typically dewed with a gossamer of rotting flesh. He tells me that he supports himself with his art, his achievements including composing artwork for the cartoon *Metalocalypse*, designing a collection for streetwear brand The Hundreds, and even helping design merchandise for Justin Bieber. He says he first got into heavy metal artwork as a six-year-old, having encountered Iron Maiden's *Killers* album at a record store. It is a striking cover, featuring the band's grisly mascot, Eddie, standing in front of a cityscape, holding a bloody hand-axe as someone's human hands struggle to resist his violence.

"I knew then that I wanted to make album covers, but it wouldn't come to fruition until 1994," Riddick explains. "In 1991, I was introduced to the underground death metal music scene and began corresponding with bands, fanzines, independent record labels, music distributors, and tape traders around the world via postal mail. I started getting my artwork published in underground fanzines, on demo tape covers, and by drawing logos for bands. After completing a demo cover and a T-shirt illustration for [the band] Torture Krypt, I was then asked to create the cover artwork for their debut CD release," the *Rotted Remains* EP.

He told me his concepts are largely directed by his customers, who will make requests with varying degrees of specificity. He derives influence from other artists' work. "I typically follow the work of other artists whose work I greatly admire, but I also find inspiration by simply being nostalgic and thumbing through some of the old underground metal fanzines in my collection."

His art can be quite grotesque. Scythelord's *Toxic Minds* depicts a human body stripped of everything but its skull, ribcage, brain, and abdominal viscera, its life cruelly sustained by lines and tubes. A 2017 EP by Cryptworm, *Verminosis*, depicts an uncomfortable-looking skeleton sitting in a grave full of worms.

I asked Riddick if he thought there was such a thing as art that is *too gruesome*. "Art is raw and often uninhibited expression," he

Mark Riddick's original artwork for the cover of Cryptworm's *Verminosis*. Image courtesy of Mark Riddick.

responded decisively. "It dwells in the realm of fantasy and subjectivity. Imagination should know no bounds; it's one of the most uniquely human qualities that separates us from the rest of the animal kingdom. Creativity moves our humanity forward—censoring this would stifle our ability to evolve."

Another common approach to gruesome cover art involves the use of real images. Carcass' *Reek of Putrefaction* is what many consider the very first goregrind album; its cover is a collage of images of body parts from medical journals in different stages of rot. Experimental music icon Lasse Marhaug discusses the cover in the August 2007 issue of *Wire* magazine, comparing the intricate nature of the collage, with its absurd number of components, to the Dada aesthetic. The cover was created by the band's bassist, Jeff Walker, under the name Gruesome Graphics, and was supposedly designed following the instructions of the record label, Earache, who had encouraged him to make it as disgusting as possible.

Reek of Putrefaction's gruesome graphics have become an inspiration for the many extreme metal acts that have followed in their wake. For the goregrind label on a budget, often tasked with putting out dozens of limited-edition releases per year, the most economical approach to cover design involves pulling images off the internet and Photoshopping them together. A cover may involve a close-up image of a gangrenous torso pulled from a medical compendium, or a crime scene photo of a shotgun-shattered face. Here, the goal seems to be to immediately provoke an extreme reaction, not unlike the music contained within, which often comprises sub-one-minute blasts of lo-fi grindcore with titles pulled from pathophysiology textbooks.

Mik Scum of Cadaveric Dissolution Records, a goregrind label, confirms that he has a subscription to a gore website called Documenting Reality, where he sources

Cover art for Chyme Licker's *Licking Up the Purulent Chyme,* on Regurgitated Stoma Stew. Note the *Reek of Putrefaction*-esque collage of autopsy images. Image courtesy of Bobby Maggard.

images for covers. Ivan Hermosa, who runs Viscera Records, another goregrind imprint, tells me he also sources images from online. Yet he insists these images deserve to be treated with respect. As he explains, "I spend a lot of time watching raw pictures of death, but I'm honest: I have respect for all the pictures I used to create cover artwork. We aren't hypocrites; life exists as death! Death is an obscure side of the life, and fascinates me in all her rotting colors."

If there is a king of lo-fi goregrind, it might be Bobby Maggard, who has recorded music under countless gruesome pseudonyms and who has put out over seven hundred different releases on his Regurgitated Stoma Stew Productions label. I asked him about where he finds the inspiration behind his covers. "It's nothing altogether spectacular really, quite honestly. It's really as simple as just doing a basic Google or Yahoo! image search online and hopefully finding something in the mix that's appealing/appalling enough to be used for potential album art. Every now and again, I may find something that's fairly gross but workable enough, in which case I may tweak it a bit on my end on the computer by turning it into a small collage or even adjusting the coloring hues to where it really brings the gore and grue a little more, y'know?"

Sometimes he will cut and paste various images digitally, but he also likes to print out images, assemble them with scissors and tape, then scan the resulting medley. He cites his 2018 Chyme Licker album, *Licking Up the Purulent Chyme,* as an example of this technique—it's a collage of autopsy photos that owes much to *Reek of Putrefaction,* albeit printed in black and white.

He cites some of the goregrind pioneers as inspiration. "Old school album artwork à la early Carcass, Dysmenorrheic Hemorrhage releases, Lymphatic Phlegm split releases, Regurgitate split releases, Autophagia cover art, early Dead Infection releases, et cetera. Basically, the ultimate deciding factor is my stomach. If at the end of coming up with suitable artwork for something it makes me go, 'That's fucked up!' then it's ready for production. Gotta go with that 'gut' feeling, right?"

I asked him about the appeal of these grisly images, which are wont to turn the average stomach. "There's just something so appealing to me about the gruesome side of life, I guess, but that's basic human nature, I think. That's in all of us. It's a sort of primal instinct that some of us just happen to have it stashed away deeper in their psyche than others, I suppose. Like when there's an accident on the road that's got traffic backed up something fierce, and when your ride finally starts moving closer to the scene of the carnage, a part of you doesn't want to look for fear of getting grossed out. But you feel the need to because you're in a sense facing a real raw, primal fear—you know what I mean?"

I asked Maggard the question I'd been dying to ask: whether there are any covers he's done that are too gross, even for him. He pointed me toward the cover for Hydrocephalus' *Unorthodox Examinations* EP, which he designed for the Running Through The Blood Productions label. It's an image of a man's mangled pelvis, his genitals dangling haphazardly. "[It] almost made me lose my lunch, haha... It still makes me a bit squeamish to look at, which is cool, because, dude, if it grosses ME out, then that's special! And I work as a butcher in a grocery store as my *job*-job too," he laughs. "There's just something so naturally disgusting about mangled genitals. And poop."

I asked Mike Juliano, the proprietor of Horror Pain Gore Death Productions, an extreme metal label responsible for Abscess' graphic *Urine Junkies* picture disc (discussed in the Picture Discs chapter), about whether some of his more vivid covers ever faced discrimination at the pressing plant.

He told me that he faced resistance for two recent projects. Lord Gore's *The Resickened Orgy* features a cartoon of multiple nude women being disemboweled, while Elbow Deep's *Sexually Offensive* is an illustration of a playground where a Transformers toy is positioned suggestively behind a child in a Tonka truck. "The ironic thing about these albums is that they are cartoon artwork, not actual nudity," he remarked. "I haven't had any trouble in the past releasing anything with the exception of one project, Fuck Face - *Assclown*. But that album cover was an actual nude photo of a woman, so that's understandable. The plant I normally use is owned by Christians, so they have cracked down on certain things. Seems like they have no problem with lyrical content but visually will not work with anything too extreme. In the end, I went through another plant that ended up channeling back to the original plant, so in the end they made it anyway," he said.

Ultimately, Juliano explains, there is always a way to get his records pressed, even if it means going to second-choice manufacturers. "Luckily, I have dealt with a few in the past. There are always plants that work with porn companies, so they are the last go-to. Cartoon nudity and violence should never be something censored, in my opinion. And I refuse to compromise for Horror Pain Gore Death."

For Juliano, who also works for the seminal metal label Relapse Records, gratuitous artwork can be great—if the music warrants it. "I don't seek out extreme art, but if it fits the music or album, then it's awesome," he reflected. "A lot of the time, it's the more simple art that fits a record. Over-the-top extremity needs to be warranted by an awesome album. It should set the tone for a release . . . there are some really good goregrind covers and also some really terrible [ones]."

V.2.1 Packs

Disgusting cover images are not where the story ends, however. Always keen to up the ante, the underground music scene didn't take long to move from images of disgusting things to *actual* disgusting things.

In 1987, Capitol Records put out a limited UK version of a new single by the controversial glam metal band W.A.S.P., known for irking the Parents Music Resource Center with songs like "Animal (Fuck Like a Beast)" and "Chainsaw Charlie (Murders in the New Morgue)." This special edition was their take on "I Don't Need No Doctor," an old song originally performed by Chuck Berry. The second single from W.A.S.P.'s third album, it was a relatively conservative pick by their standards. What was interesting about it, apart from the fact that the single itself was translucent red, was that it came in a clear plastic record sleeve which had an extra sealed-off layer built into it, containing a red liquid that looked like blood. It's unclear how many of these were produced; only a handful of copies have surfaced online, and all of those were miserably dried up, the red residue having reduced to stains on the plastic sleeve.[14]

The following year, Bay Area thrash band Vio-Lence put out a promotional 10" to support their *Eternal Nightmare* album. Seeking extra *oomph*, they also incorporated a special plastic layer to the package, this one filled with facsimile vomit, apparently made of sloshed-together vegetable soup and vinegar. The attention to detail is sublime, the chunkiness of vegetable soup augmented with vinegar's acidity.

Remarkably, this grotesque vomit pack was contrived by a major label. Mechanic Records was a sub-label of MCA, a major corporation that likely insisted upon the 'DO NOT EAT' label that came attached to the release. Twenty-one years on, all surviving copies of this record have apparently dried into a crispy crust, but this has not stopped collectors from paying good money for them.[15]

In 1990, Slayer adapted the W.A.S.P. blood pack compact for the digital age, putting out the "Seasons in the Abyss" CD single in a limited-edition jewel pack replete with liquid blood layer.[16] In 1993, industrial band Revolting Cocks put out their glorious rendition of Rod Stewart's "Do Ya Think I'm Sexy" on clear vinyl with a layer of K-Y Jelly; a CD single version was also released with its own "squishy pack." This goopy touch was a reference to a lyric in their version of the song ("He says, 'I'm sorry but I'm out of K-Y Jelly' / Never mind, sugar, we can catch the early movie"). Today, the lubricant in the remaining copies has liquified into a yellow fluid that resembles urine.[17]

The most fascinating anecdote in the pack saga was an ill-conceived record apparently inspired by the Slayer blood pack CD. Earache Records decided to do something

---

14 "W.A.S.P. WASP - I DON'T NEED NO DOCTOR - 7" BLOOD PACK - Auction Details," popsike.com - September 2008, <www.popsike.com/WASP-WASP-I-DONT-NEED-NO-DOCTOR-7-BLOOD-PACK/200256325338.html>

15 "VIO-LENCE*ETERNAL NIGHTMARE* 10" VOMIT PACK - Auction Details," popsike.com - March 2010, <www.popsike.com/VIOLENCEETERNAL-NIGHTMAREMEGA-RARE-10-VOMIT-PACK/300430326601.html>

16 "Slayer – Seasons In The Abyss (1990, Blood Pack, CD)," Discogs <www.discogs.com/release/3166715-Slayer-Seasons-In-The-Abyss> [accessed March 19, 2022]

17 "Revolting Cocks – Da Ya Think I'm Sexy? (1993, CD)," Discogs <www.discogs.com/release/201434-Revolting-Cocks-Da-Ya-Think-Im-Sexy> [accessed March 19, 2022]

special for Morbid Angel's fourth album, *Domination*; the idea was to create a clear plastic pouch filled with green slime. According to a thorough history of the debacle on Earache's own *Ask Earache* blog,[18] their big misstep was to assume that their chemical supplier was going to produce the same childproof green slime that came in children's toys. Shortly after the 1,000-copy order arrived in the Earache warehouse, problems began to arise. Some of the boxes were damaged in transit and were leaking, and they noticed that the dripping slime burned a hole in an employee's shirt. Elsewhere, an area of the floor was stained bright green and couldn't be washed clean.

Nervous, they looked at the packing slip, which included an extensive ingredients list as well as several warnings: "do not touch," "may cause neurological damage," "seek immediate medical attention if on skin." Earache immediately pulled the release from the market, but saved a few keepsakes for posterity. (They have, apparently, dried up into green and blue crystals over the years.)

According to Earache, the reason they ended up with the corrosive slime was because the recipes for the green slime in kids' toys were all proprietary; as a result, the chemical company was forced to develop their own slime. The company, assuming it was being used for industrial purposes only, did not bother to make it safe for commercial use. (Although one wonders what industrial process requires bright green slime.)

V.2.2 Body Fluids

It is sometimes said that artists give up a piece of themselves when they create art. Others speak of the blood, sweat, and tears that go into making artwork. For some, it is not enough to let these ideas stand as metaphors.

Keith Brewer, a power electronics producer from Texas who used to record as Taint, put out an LP in 1995 called *Indecent Liberties*, which was released in a quantity of just 199 copies on a German label called Praxis Dr. Bearmann. This cover of this LP was spattered with real blood and covered in wire mesh. The legend behind this release has inspired some chatter on the internet, and online accounts vary in terms of the exact provenance of the blood that was used—from "cat and dog blood"[19] to "WHAT I SUSPECT WAS SOME KINDA RANCH ANIMAL."[20] After hunting for Brewer's email address for some time, I tracked down the man himself to get an official clarification. He got back within a day, clarifying that "As far as I know, the blood came from a butcher."

Five years later, the Swedish black metal band Nifelheim put out "Unholy Death," a black metal single that came out in a fitting edition of 666 copies. One hundred copies of that beastly edition came hand-numbered and lovingly smeared in pig's blood, imparting the black-on-white cover with a reddish-brown hue. As far as I can tell, this band, who fired their first guitarist for having a girlfriend and also had a track included on the *Gummo* soundtrack, were the first to incorporate purely porcine blood into their packaging.

In 2003, a limited-edition reissue of French black metal band Mütiilation's *Remains*

---

18 Digby, "Morbid Angel- The Famous 'slime Pack' Fiasco," ASK EARACHE, September 10, 2009, <askearache.blogspot.com/2009/09/morbid-angel-famous-slime-pack-fiasco.html>
19 "Taint — Indecent Liberties (1995, Vinyl)," Discogs <www.discogs.com/release/182741-Taint-Indecent-Liberties> [accessed March 19, 2022]
20 "TAINT Indecent Liberties BLACK LEATHER JESUS SLOGUN - Auction Details," popsike.com, February 2008, <www.popsike.com/TAINT-Indecent-Liberties-BLACK-LEATHER-JESUS-SLOGUN-/190194286271.html>

of a Ruined, Dead, Cursed Soul compilation was released, the first sixty copies of which came smeared with blood. This special release was orchestrated by a low-profile black metal label called End All Life, which does not have a website but still puts out records on an intermittent basis. The special, blood-drenched copies of this reissue have since sold for over seven hundred dollars![21]

An obscure but infamous Texas "funeral doom" band named Senthil put out blood-coated records in 2005 and 2007. Their music comprises colorless, distorted guitar chords, and vocals that are intended to mimic the sound of torture—what one reviewer refers to as "demented schoolgirl-ripped-to-shreds shrieking."[22] They gained notoriety for both their nihilistic sound and the fact that their singer apparently chokes himself with chains during recordings to achieve a true *strangulated* effect.[23] Given that they have no web presence and have only put out three limited-edition releases, it is remarkable how many people have gravitated toward their racket. Their 2007 cassette EP *Septisemesis* apparently smells like an operating room and, in addition to being blood-soaked, also comes with a razor blade.[24]

Is it possible that the blood used on Senthil's records is human blood? There is no way of getting in touch with Senthil's secretive members, who go by the names Plague and Vomit (a third member, Wretch, apparently passed away several years ago). For now, the blood's provenance is likely to be shrouded in myth, though the sheer amount of it that would have to have been used for all these releases suggests that it might not be of human origin.

But that is not to say that human blood has never been used. In 2008, a Californian experimental musician named Christopher Jion issued a 7-inch single entitled *Abnormal Play For Collapsing Mentality*, which came with five special copies replete with verifiably human blood. According to Jion, he drew up his own blood using a "makeshift syringe," then splattered it on the release's white covers and sealed it in plastic. Whereas the main edition of 522 copies came with a mere image of his "blood and bone plasma," owners of those five special copies get droplets of Jion's own DNA.

In the vein of real human blood, in 2012 two artists, Ech(o) and Flat Affect, put out a split release washed in human blood. Ech(o), a one-woman noise act, collaborated with noisester Flat Affect for a CD-R release packaged in white cardstock that was smeared with an amalgam of her menstrual blood and Flat Affect's non-menstrual blood.

Flat Affect, a.k.a. Shaun Phelps, explains that this distinctly personal release came about as an attempt to capture something special. He met Ech(o) in high school, and their close friendship is one of a select few that endured over the years. As he tells me, "When I started recording music, I made it a point to record with any of my friends who were willing, especially if our time was limited by great distances. So when she said she would be in town, we stocked up on alcohol and the rest flowed from there."

Whereas the goal of the release itself was about "capturing the moment and the memory," the bloody touch made it "personal."

21 "Mütiilation — Remains Of A Ruined Dead Cursed Soul (2003, Blood Smeared Cover, Vinyl)," Discogs <www.discogs.com/release/4045755-Mütiilation-Remains-Of-A-Ruined-Dead-Cursed-Soul> [accessed March 19, 2022]

22 Noktorn, "Senthil Finds Their Niche," Encyclopaedia Metallum: The Metal Archives, June 29, 2010, <www.metal-archives.com/reviews/Senthil/Septisemesis/142397/>

23 Though I wonder if this is apocryphal. "Senthil," Ultimate Guitar (Forums), 2006, <www.ultimate-guitar.com/forum/showthread.php?t=329248>

24 "Senthil — Septisemesis (2007, Cassette)," Discogs <www.discogs.com/release/1060586-Senthil-Septisemesis> [accessed March 19, 2022]

Ech(o) also clarifies her intent behind the unusual packaging: "I remember feeling like I had given birth to something for the first time, and using my woman's blood felt right. It was a raw, visceral experience. I felt awakened and emboldened and quite calm painting menstrual blood. I remember being shocked that [Flat Affect wasn't] repulsed… The experience remains a singularly significant one."

There are practical considerations when it comes to using human blood. "I knew I would be shipping this internationally, and while I am a fan of gritty and real things, I also wanted to make sure people would be able to get, and keep, the product," Flat Affect explains. "So I 'laminated' the album art with a clear adhesive. As a result, there was not much of an opportunity for a smell. As for that night, the only odor was my leg burning from where Ech(o) set it on fire. She likes to maintain she didn't do that, but the scar is persistent evidence."

In the 2000s, a couple of extreme music producers with racist proclivities put out releases that came with a (reputed) mixture of blood and semen—one in a plastic pouch, and one in a "used condom." Both hinted at a fusion of sex and violence that was particularly unnerving. Semen is a particular fascination of many extreme music scenesters. Apart from album titles referencing the stuff (Hentai and Nordvargr's *Semen* split), there have been at least twelve record labels with *semen* in their name, including the likes of Regurgitated Semen Records, Purulent Semen Records, Speed Semen Clove Factory, and, to come full circle, a label called Semen and Blood.

Interestingly, the sanguine combination of seminal fluid and hemoglobin has a precedent in the world of fine art, namely the work of Andres Serrano, whose photos of cadavers were referenced earlier in this book in the section on vulgar music. Serrano's controversial body of work also includes *Blood and Semen II* (1990), in which cow blood and his own semen were interspersed and then squished between two plates of plexiglass, resulting in aesthetically pleasing whirls of color. The distinctive patterns arising out of that unholy amalgam were even used in the liner notes for Metallica's *Load* album.

Serrano's work is not unprecedented. Artist Antony Gormley completed a series of drawings entitled *Bodily Fluids* from 1986 to 1992, which employed blood and semen, either individually or in combination. As Anna Moszynska, author of *Antony Gormley Drawing*, writes, the first piece was just the outcome of a jet of blood that "spontaneously issued from a burst capillary on the artist's left middle finger to create an abstract trail across the paper." Elsewhere, "puddles or drips of blood and/or semen are allowed to fall upon moistened paper, creating an explosive, cosmic effect."[25] So Taint's *Indecent Liberties*, decorated with spattered animal blood, is in highbrow company.

There is, in fact, a whole world of biologically oriented fine art. There is even a Wikipedia entry titled "Body fluids in art," which includes a table of various works of art that incorporate human by-products. Filipino folk artist Elito Circa uses blood as a painting medium and has even done illustrations of his country's president. Marc Quinn took a mold of his own head, then froze blood inside it to create a chilly red cast in his image. Stelarc and Nina Sellars both had liposuction done on their bodies, then mixed the resulting blood and adipose tissue together and sealed it inside a machine that would

25 Anna Moszynska, Antony Gormley Drawing (London: British Museum Press, 2002).

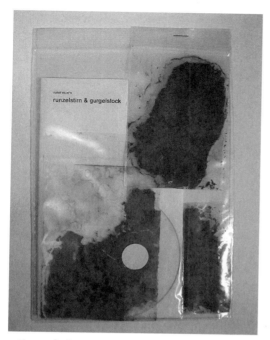

Runzelstirn & Gurgelstøck's *Hirnstamm, Kotloch Und Scheisse* **mini-CD-R, with dog feces enclosed within. Image courtesy of Rudolf Eb.er.**

automatically stir and aerate it every five minutes.[26] Artist Wenda Gu created a site-specific installation of beds and baby cribs, each one stained with either "human placenta powders (normal, abnormal, aborted, stillborn) produced according to ancient Chinese medical methods" or "blood and sperm from first episode of sexual encounter."

Can it get anymore grotesque? In 1997, the iconoclastic experimental electronic artist James Leyland Kirby, who then went by V/Vm, put out a satirical "reissue" of the seventies novelty song "Mouldy Old Dough" by Lieutenant Pigeon on his V/Vm Test Records label.[27] He gave it the subtitle "the official V/Vm ANTHEM" and also accompanied by a deconstructed version called "PIGEOn BiTS." To accompany the vitriol directed at Lieutenant Pigeon on the cover,[28] the 7-inch was accompanied by two Ziploc bags, one containing a feather and the other containing a dollop of pigeon poop.

Then, in 2004, another iconoclastic artist named Rudolf Eb.er, who records under the name Runzelstirn & Gurgelstøck, put out a mini-CD-R that was accompanied by three bags of "original shit by Eb.er's dog."[29] Over email, Rudolf recounted the concept and his methods. He explains that he created the packaging while living in Osaka, Japan. He collected the feces while walking his dog, then finished off the packaging and sent it to Björn Liebmann, proprietor of the Leipzig-based record label Scrotum Records, who added the discs themselves and put them up for sale. "It took me a while to collect enough dog feces," he recalled. "But then again, not forever. My dog Chi was a husky/shepherd mix, not a small dog and with a big appetite."

Rudolf tells me he was not aware of any other discs incorporating real feces, dog or otherwise, when he embarked on this release. Though he had heard of Andres Serrano's experimentations with body fluids, he denies taking inspiration from them. Instead, it was purely an aesthetic decision. "I do not understand this packaging as anything shocking or controversial (for healthy minded people—sick people may be shocked). It

26 "Blender," Stelarc <stelarc.org/?catID=20245> [accessed March 19, 2022]

27 "Pigeon — Mouldy Dough **the Official V/Vm Anthem** (1997, White, Vinyl)," Discogs <www.discogs.com/release/6682-Pigeon-Mouldy-Dough-the-Official-VVm-Anthem> [accessed March 19, 2022]

28 "Why not re-release the worst ever UK number one single and make it even worse on the B-side. Last seen offending children, beating up Keith Harris and orville duck whilst drinking enough Q.C. sherry to sink a battleship, PIGEON then spent the entire winter season at Butlins Bognor supporting BuCKs FIZZ and Boy George. After this success the PIGEON then disappeared to a life of crime and KEBABS to support his 27 siblings."

29 "Runzelstirn & Gurgelstøck — Hirnstamm, Kotloch Und Scheisse (2004, CDr)," Discogs <www.discogs.com/release/731403-Runzelstirn-Gurgelstøck-Hirnstamm-Kotloch-Und-Scheisse> [accessed March 19, 2022]

came from entirely aesthetic reasons. The contrasts of the brown-black-green-reddish colors and the form/structure versus the plain white paper and minimalist lettering."

Thinking back, he is proud to have disseminated this unique release, copies of which live on to this day. "It was my idea, and I am very happy to see several friends and collectors having this release still now displayed on their home walls," he tells me. "I was told they sensed a slight scent in their rooms but weren't bothered by it. The release was made thirteen years ago, and most copies I saw recently do still look pretty good. No scent left, I'd say."

V.2.3 Perishables

Records are meant to last. It is why they are called records. Their intended function is to store sonic information for posterity, to allow their owners to enjoy their contents over and over again. It is because of their permanence that many of the limited-edition releases that proliferated in the DIY music scenes of the eighties and nineties have appreciated steeply in value over time.

Then what to make of a record whose packaging *dares* you to throw it away? For example, who would want to store a tape attached to a decomposing boiled egg in their record collection, alongside their hard-earned collector's items and expensive boxed sets? This is the question raised by *Fuck*, a six-minute cassette by Coco & Fiend Friend and Mutant Love, two noise projects helmed by the duo of George Proctor and Nicola Vinciguerra. The tape itself comes in a plastic bag taped to a cardstock cover. Also taped to that cover is a sealed bag containing a boiled egg, which has been signed and summarily flattened. The autograph is a wink to the fundamental paradox here: this is an ostensibly collectable, limited edition release—in fact, only five copies were produced. Traditionally, a famous person's signature increases the value of an item. But here it has been scrawled on an egg, which is doomed to slowly rot.

Proctor and Vinciguerra run the Turgid Animal label collaboratively out of their separate home bases in Britain and Italy. Proctor's own noise act was named Mutant Ape, while Vinciguerra records prolifically under the name Fecalove. The duo are no strangers to perishable packaging and Vinciguerra especially seems to revel in the concept.

Another release was a tape by Frozen Corpse, limited to thirty copies, of which the first ten copies came with a chicken foot.[30] Then there was a split mini-CD-R between Fecalove and French noise act Ekunhaashaastack, which came with a piece of cooked beef. "I traded one copy of that mini CD-R, among other things, with an American guy called Levi," he tells me. "It turned out he was a militant vegan. It was summer, so when he got the package, the meat reeked really bad and he threw everything in the bin. I received some beautiful hate mail from a friend of his. Years later, Levi offered me a split with his band, so I guess we're good now."

In my opinion, Vinciguerra's crown jewel was Splinter vs Stalin's *Pasta Electronics II*, a sequel to the first volume of *Pasta Electronics*, which came in an otherwise unremarkable sleeve. Those who ordered *Pasta Electronics II* received, in the mail, a damp Barilla pasta box that was held together with masking tape, the band name and title scrawled

---

30 "Frozen Corpse — Hypnotized Animal (2007, C30, Cassette)," Discogs <www.discogs.com/release/939454-Frozen-Corpse-Hypnotized-Animal> [accessed March 19, 2022]

Splinter Vs Stalin's *Pasta Electronics II*, a CD-R that came packaged deep inside a box of rancid, cooked pasta. Image courtesy of Henrik Falck.

in marker on the front. Once the box was pulled apart, the owner was treated to a fetid surprise: Vinciguerra had cooked a bunch of pasta, portioned it into boxes, then buried each CD-R inside the mess. As he proudly explained, "I made the copies only to order, so the stuff didn't actually rot in my house. It rotted in postal offices, vans, planes, et cetera. On the way to my customers. Nasty, eh?"

Vinciguerra says he garnished the pasta with "fairly good commercial pesto sauce with the addition of some grated Parmigiano cheese and whatever else I had in the fridge. Ham, bacon, bresaola, pepper come to mind." Since they were made to order, each box was different, so you might consider them one of a kind.

According to the album's Discogs entry,[31] by the time *Pasta Electronics II* reached customers it was "covered with mold and smell[ed] awful." Only by digging through the mush would one reach the actual CD-R, which was thoughtfully sealed in foil to prevent contamination. Vinciguerra tells me the audio itself comprises two "long, repetitive, and not super noisy tracks," incorporating audio from television coverage of an Italian prime ministerial debate and some Japanese commercials for pasta toppings.

Vinciguerra explained the rationale for his distinctive packaging. "It was the epitome, the apotheosis of Italy," he says. "Rotten food thrown in a box of highly recognizable Barilla pasta, with a noise CD-R wrapped in aluminum foil. Pure tradition. I guess we don't think very highly of our country. I liked the idea that you had to break the box and actually touch rotten shit if you wanted to actually get to the music."

Vinciguerra has also done a couple of other gross things. He packaged a release in used panties, adorned another one with his pubic hair, and housed one release in a

31 "Splinter vs. Stalin — Pasta Electronics II (2007, CDr)," Discogs <www.discogs.com/release/983271-Splinter-vs-Stalin-Pasta-Electronics-II> [accessed March 19, 2022]

(mercifully unused) colostomy bag. There is apparently also a release that is merely a "Coco & Fiend Friend-labeled bag simply filled with (dried) cum." A release, indeed.

Vinciguerra recalls being inspired by a couple of other iconic record labels when he released *Pasta Electronics II*. "I was crazy about the extremely elaborate special packaging of legendary Japanese label G.R.O.S.S. and unique, disgusting, and bizarre relics from Lateral Agriculture Order. Knowledge of mail art had some influence too, I guess, but my focus was, and still is, the worship of industrial/noise music. I also simply always liked to make a mess."

G.R.O.S.S., despite its name, tended toward non-disgusting limited editions of experimental sound delivered in sleek packaging, sometimes incorporating metal. Lateral Agriculture Order was an obscure purveyor of micro-editions of noise releases under a variety of pseudonyms, often incorporating blood and medical supplies into the packaging. His releases were sometimes distributed by MSBR in Japan, typically in editions of two or three copies.

Vinciguerra's antics date from roughly 2006 and on, but the idea of putting together packages that will rot and attract pests into one's record collection dates back further. The Arbor label, run by Mike Pollard, put out an exemplary artifact as their debut album in 2004: *White Rye Bread*, a mash-up of the Skaters' *Dark Rye Bread* and the Beatles' *White Album*. It was a CD-R sandwiched between two pieces of bread, stored in a Ziploc bag. The images available online show splotches of mold. Multiple attempts to reach Mike Pollard went unanswered, but I was able to connect with Spencer Clark, who was one half of the Skaters (with producer James Ferraro). Clark told me that Mike Pollard was a Skaters fan who put it out as a "fan thang," though he doesn't know much about the release itself, having only been told stories about it at parties. "I don't know anything about it except that I hear they played Beatles music over our shit," he said.

The Japanese noise artist MSBR also dabbled in food. His 1995 CD, *Destructive Locomotion Dedicated to Chizuo Matsumoto* (PURE), saw a special limited-edition release with a cover made of chocolate, each one handmade by MSBR himself. It is hard to know if any of these have survived, twenty-five years down the line—all that exists today online is an image culled from MSBR's now-defunct website.

Taint, who was responsible for a blood-spattered release discussed earlier, also dabbled in perishables, putting out a tape called *B.A.T.* on famed British label Stinky Horse Fuck. It came attached to a genuine pig's ear via metal wire.[32] Stinky Horse Fuck also put out a Smell & Quim tape named *Chariot of the Cods*, which included several dried fish in its special oversized package.[33]

Several other releases have included different types of bone, including chicken and rat bones. One racist extreme metal band once put out a release that came with a very foul-smelling bag full of fragments of a dead rabbit, including flesh and viscera, that had been decomposing for half a year. Someone else covered the recorded side of a CD-R with dead worms and fish feed, rendering the release unplayable.

---

32 "Taint - B.A.T | Releases, Reviews, Credits," Discogs <www.discogs.com/master/1085179-Taint-BAT> [accessed March 19, 2022]

33 "Smell & Quim — Chariot Of The Cods (1996, C60, Cassette)," Discogs <www.discogs.com/release/716654-Smell-Quim-Chariot-Of-The-Cods> [accessed March 19, 2022]

Inventive and sometimes funny, these perishable releases make for compelling stories. But there is also something cruel about mailing a sopping packet of rotting pasta to someone who just wants to enjoy a noise CD-R. Then there are the casualties caught in the crossfire, the poor postal service workers and customs agents exposed to this organic decay. One wonders if any of Vinciguerra's rotting pasta boxes popped in transit?

V.2.4 A Final Anecdote

On September 11, 2006, at approximately 7 a.m., Adam Cooley and Kyle Willey, who performed together as a drone/doom act called Robe., embarked on a twenty-four-hour live set in Willey's living room. They invited friends to come jam with them, but Cooley and Willey were supposed to play the whole thing. They connected a microphone to Willey's computer and hung it from the ceiling. Every hour, they mixed the recording down and saved it as a WAV file.

It was a long day. Multiple people's fingers were apparently bleeding from nonstop playing, Willey's fingernail was split in half, there were jars of urine hanging around the room, and at one point, Willey was fed a hamburger in between greasy blasts through his saxophone. At 9 p.m., the police, who had apparently been staking out the house all day, showed up and informed Cooley and Willey that the noise was too much and they would be fined if they kept playing. They unplugged their amps and performed another hour as an acoustic set, but they were still too loud, so the police returned and told them they had to stop or they'd be arrested. Apparently, the next-door neighbor was a retired officer and had had it with their ruckus.

Cooley and Willey had to cut their set short at ten recorded hours, but they wanted to do something special to commemorate the occasion. Under the name Robe., they had released dozens of CD-Rs and cassettes, both self-released and issued on international labels. They decided to put this special recording out as a 10-CD-R boxed set, each collection entombed in a cigar box that had been decorated with collage artwork made of comic book scraps and newspaper cutouts from that very day. Only ten copies were made.

To commemorate the very physicality of their marathon performance, Cooley and Willey decided each box was going to come with a different bodily by-product. Someone got hit in the face with an instrument and lost a tooth; therefore, the tooth went in one box. Someone else cut their hair during the recording, and this hair went, loose, into another box, along with a burned Bible. You had to dig through the ashes and hair to get to the CD-Rs.

They sent five of these boxes out to record stores and review websites, and another five went to random people from a Sonic Youth message board that Cooley frequented. All copies were sent unannounced; the message board recipients were cobbled together from posts where they had posted their address in response to others wanting to send them something.

Willey believes that Aquarius Records got a box that had a medical waste bag filled with toenails. Thurston Moore and Byron Coley each got copies. A record store in Bloomington, Indiana named Landlocked Records received one with a Nintendo controller glued to the front; inside, nestled among the CD-Rs, was a sweat rag the band used for the performance. Other boxes included fingernails, a vial of tears, and a tissue soaked in blood. Another vial was filled with Cooley and Willey's intermingled saliva. One unfortunate person received Adam Cooley's pubic hair.

They saved what they thought was the most disgusting item for the author of an obnoxious and self-righteous message board post: a peeled-off scab wrapped in cellophane. They printed a copy of the post and included it in the box for posterity.

This remarkable story was told to me by Kyle Willey, who spoke with me via Skype. Cooley died in 2014; Willey credits his dynamic personality and zest for innovation as big factors in this release's inspiration. In fact, the idea for the release originated with Cooley's recollection of a Cock E.S.P. CD that was coated in the band members' semen and sealed in a picture frame.

Sending these mysterious boxes out unannounced was a calculated gamble, though its outcome was somewhat anticlimactic. A staff member at Landlocked Records told Willey that he had listened to and enjoyed all ten discs, though it is unclear if the box was ever sold. Thurston Moore acknowledged receiving a Robe. T-shirt that was included with the package but never mentioned the box of CD-Rs or their biological accoutrement. Byron Coley, who had previously reviewed a Robe. album for *Wire*, never wrote about the box.

Willey says he had not thought much about the *Live at Maniac Mansion* box until I reached out to him. He was thankful for the opportunity to reminisce, and it was obvious that he still misses his friend dearly. He says he is preparing to create a documentary about Adam Cooley's life for a course he is doing as part of a second degree in visual communications. He is going to be hired as a professor once he is done. He is also married now, and has two children, and thus has less time to record music—although he does intermittently jam in his home studio, releasing music under the name Apology on his Bandcamp.

The *Maniac Mansion* box exemplifies a homemade aesthetic that is shared by many of the innovators discussed in this chapter. It was created for deeply personal reasons, aiming to immortalize a one-of-a-kind performance by incorporating the participants' literal blood, sweat, and tears. But it is subversive in the same way as the many uniquely packaged releases discussed in this chapter are subversive. By converting their releases into limited editions, gross or not, these artists and label heads emphasize the difference between their music and music that is mass-produced and mass-consumed.

VI.1 SILENT

In 2014, an independent funk band named Vulfpeck put out their fourth album on Spotify. It was named *Sleepify* and contained ten tracks, each one comprising just over thirty seconds of complete silence. In fact, Vulfpeck was so committed to silence that they used sound production software to ensure that there was absolutely no signal on each digital file. As band member Jack Stratton put it in an interview, "It's not a recording of a still environment. It's an actual digital file full of zeroes."

Sleepify was not a highbrow conceptual project with art gallery ambitions in mind, although an article for the academic journal *Canadian Theatre Review* compared it to the work of John Cage and Marina Abramović. Instead, it was an attempt to make money. Vulfpeck had figured out that Spotify's royalty payments earn artists a fraction of a penny each time a listener streams one of their songs, one "stream" being defined as someone listening to at least thirty seconds of a given track.

To game this system, Vulfpeck called on their fans to stream *Sleepify* on repeat while they slept so that the band could earn money to fund a free tour. According to my calculations,[1] streaming *Sleepify* continuously during an eight-hour snooze would earn the band approximately $5.76.

After seven weeks, Spotify caught on to the *Sleepify* gambit and took the album down without providing any clear reason for their decision. But by then the band had already earned nearly $20,000 in royalties—which, to Spotify's credit, they paid out, allowing Vulfpeck to have their tour.

VI.1.1 Silent Pioneers

The best-known silent music foray is the 1952 performance of John Cage's notorious *4'33"*, wherein pianist John Tudor sat at his piano in a concert hall and proceeded to not play anything for four minutes and thirty-three seconds. The spontaneous noises in the room were intended to be the true performance—including, but not limited to, the sounds of people grumbling in their seats and walking out in contempt.

But *4'33"* was not the first kick at the silent can. That honor is thought to belong to a French humorist named Alphonse Allais, who devised a faux composition of twenty-four blank measures in 1897, which he titled "Funeral March for the Obsequies of a Deaf Man." This was exhibited in Paris at an art show put on by Les Arts Incohérents, a satirical and irreverent art collective perhaps most known for Eugène Bataille's portrait *Mona Lisa Smoking a Pipe*. Allais' silent composition, of course, was a gag and was never actually performed in concert.

The first silent piece composed for performance seems to be "In futurum" by avant-garde Czech composer Erwin Schulhoff, published in 1919. Working in the wake of WWI, he was inspired by the impact of Dadaism, the absurdist movement of the era

---

1 Using a figure of 30 percent of a penny per stream (the lower end of the estimate range specified on www.billboard.com/articles/news/6175358/vulfpecks-half-joke-silent-album-made-some-serious-cash), the calculation would be $0.003 x 2 (number of 30-second intervals in a minute) x 60 (minutes in an hour) x 8 (hours of sleep) = $2.88 per night.

whose penchant for chaos and randomness are reflected in the silent composition's irreverent score. Even though the piece is composed solely of rests (symbols denoting silent pauses in musical notation), they are organized into convoluted rhythms and subjected to bizarre time signatures.

In a brief piece for the *New Yorker*, writer Leo Carey describes the bemusement of a pianist rehearsing for a performance of "In futurum." He ponders at how to perform a meticulously notated span of silence:

Schulhoff's page is about as busy and frenetic as silence can be. There are long rests and short rests, triplet and quintuplet rests, and fast runs of thirty-second-note rests. There are fermatas, exclamation points, question marks, and, in the middle and at the end, enigmatic signs that look like a hybrid of a half note and a smiley face. Most challenging of all is the opening direction to play *"tutto il canzone con espressione e sentimento ad libitum, sempre, sin al fine!"* ("the entire song with as much expression and feeling as you like, always, right to the end!"). Bianconi wondered what to do. "Should I just sit there?" he asked.[2]

Schulhoff's silent work was followed, in 1941, by the exploits of a young Raymond Scott, a composer who would later score Bugs Bunny cartoons. That year, Scott assembled a thirteen-piece orchestra to put on a silent concert. He compelled each instrumentalist to go through the motions of playing, fingering their valves and making a show of blowing into their instruments, but instructed them not to produce any sound. Technically, much like Cage's piece, there was not a complete absence of sound. There were still the incidental sounds of trumpet valves sliding in their chambers and saxophone keys being fingered. A contemporaneous *Time* magazine described "a rhythmic swish-swish from the trap-drummer, a froggy slap-slap from the bull-fiddler, a soft plunk-plunk from the pianist."[3] The audience, much like Cage's, was not all that impressed.[4] As the *Time* reporter put it, the non-concert was "just provocative enough to make listeners wonder whether the silence of other bands might sound better than Scott's."

According to the Wikipedia page titled "List of silent musical compositions," there was also a 1949 composition created by painter Yves Klein named *Monotone-Silence Symphony*, a direct reference to Klein's own distinctive mono*chrome* art. This was not performed until March 9, 1960, when Klein staged a memorable show in which he smeared three nude models in blue paint and had them rub themselves onto giant pieces of paper while an orchestra performed a sustained chord for twenty minutes. Then, for the following twenty minutes, everyone was completely still and the orchestra remained completely silent. According to a fawning review by "M. Lewis" on a website dedicated to Yves Klein, the audience response was different than the contempt with which Cage and Scott were received:

> At the end of Yves' piece, everyone in the audience was fully aware they had been in the presence of a genius at work; the piece was a huge success! Mr. Klein triumphed. It would be his greatest moment in art history, a total success.

---

2 Leo Carey, "Sh-h-H," The New Yorker (New York City, May 16, 2004), <www.newyorker.com/magazine/2004/05/24/sh-h-h-5>

3 "Music: Silent Music," TIME (New York City, March 3, 1941), <content.time.com/time/subscriber/article/0,33009,851092,00.html>

4 Jeff Winner, "Shhh... John Cage & Raymond Scott," Raymond Scott Archives Blog, October 18, 2009, <raymondscott.blogspot.com/2009/10/shhh.html>

Images and video of the performance are available online, featuring Klein in a dinner jacket emphatically conducting a gaggle of cellists and violinists as young women covered in blue paint press themselves against canvases on the ground and walls. Meanwhile, well-dressed audience members look on impassively.[5]

Klein's piece was only *half* silent, which is an important distinction from works of pure silence. But it is an interesting sonic analogy to his monochrome paintings. Klein also once published a chapbook of blank pages, proving himself a master of content-free content.

VI.1.2 Silent Recordings

Bill Rabe was a native of Detroit who worked as a public relations man for both the University of Detroit and a tiny school called Lake Superior State University, located in Sault Ste. Marie, Michigan, just across the river from Canada. Over the course of his career, he was known for conceiving gimmicks to draw attention to the schools for which he worked. These included proto-viral stunts like an international stone-skipping contest and LSSU's famous "List of Words Banished from the Queen's English for Mis-Use, Over-Use, and General Uselessness," which has persisted since his retirement.[6]

In the late 1950s, Rabe developed the concept for the Hush Record Company, a record label that pressed special records whose grooves were completely silent. These quiet discs were then distributed to jukeboxes around town, allowing patrons at noisy bars and restaurants to buy a few minutes of silence amidst the usual stream of loud rock 'n' roll music. These silent jukebox records became big hits at the University of Detroit. In 1959, the first full week of January was apparently declared Silent Record Week. A year later, the newly annual Silent Record Week celebrated the occasion with a very-Cageian performance at the Cass Theatre, featuring a sixty-five-person choir uttering not a single sound. According to archived news accounts,[7] over a thousand people paid the steep five-dollar cover charge to attend a "silent parade" performing "When the Saints Come Marching In," each attendee receiving a nearly completely blank program with just a single ad to pay for printing costs. This type of gimmick was catnip for news wire services. An archived copy of the Camden, New Jersey *Courier-Post* remarks on the excitement surrounding the silent concerts, and notes that "students tried unsuccessfully to get a soft drink company to advertise its slogan 'The pause that refreshes.'"[8]

The Hush records were meant exclusively for jukebox use, not public distribution. But a whole panoply of bands and artists have since released silent pieces as parts of records, including the likes of Brian Eno ("Silence" on *Drums Between the Bells*), Korn ("[Silence]"), and John Denver ("The Ballad of Richard Nixon"). The purposes of these silent tracks range from parody ("The Ten Coolest Things About New Jersey"

---

5 Zeynep Kinli, "Yves Klein — Anthropometry Performance (1960)," Let's Fill This Town With Artists!, May 15, 2009, <zeynepkinli.wordpress.com/2009/05/15/825/>
6 2022 inductees include the terms "deep dive," "asking for a friend," and "you're on mute."
7 "Silent Concert With Non Singing Choir Will Highlight Observance," The Sacramento Bee, January 3, 1960.
8 "Don't Say a Single Word," Courier-Post, January 7, 1967, <www.newspapers.com/newspage/180839819/>

by the Bloodhound Gang) to politics ("The Sound of Free Speech" by anarchist punk band Crass) to snarky irreverence ("The Most Important Track on the Album" by Astronautalis; "Pure Digital Silence" by the Melvins).

There has even been a compilation of these silent tracks, licensed from various albums. Italian experimental label Alga Marghen's 2013 LP *Sounds of Silence - The Most Intriguing Silences In Recording History!*, trumpeted as "an anthology of some of the most intriguing silent tracks in recording history," sold out its first edition, warranting a repress in 2019.

Silent tracks are one thing, but fewer artists have put out entirely

Sounds of Silence LP, released on Alga Marghen. Image courtesy of Adam David.

silent records or albums, which, it turns out, are considerably less marketable. Throughout the history of recorded music, the phenomenon of the fully silent record shows up intermittently, each appearance a curious anomaly unto itself. Just more than a handful exist, but most seem to have emerged independently of other such silent works. They are random artifacts, created for different reasons, yet they all sound the same. One diligent Discogs denizen named *type* has helped compile many of these records.

One of the earliest silent artifacts is a bizarre 1957 record referred to as BunaB #5, which is advertised as the soundtrack to a silent film named *The Fatal Love* and subtitled "*Companion to T.V.*"[9] Long forgotten today, this bizarre item was one in a sequence of subversive products marketed in the late fifties. Branded BunaB, this series of "purposely useless novelty products" was designed by an Iowan radio host named Al Crowder. Much like Bill Rabe, the architect of the Hush Recording Company, Crowder was skilled at generating news stories, and his BunaB line of useless products ended up receiving national radio coverage and garnered a write-up in *Playboy* magazine. Crowder seems to have designed his products as an ironic dig at consumerism, designing a seven-strong line of numbered BunaB products that included a board game with impossible-to-play rules and a bottle of "Between Shave" cream that was empty. His biggest seller was the inscrutable BunaB #7, two short pieces of cable taped together along with an instruction guide that does not actually tell you how to use it. Forty thousand of these were made!

According to one source, the silent record, BunaB #5, was sold for $15, which would have been a remarkable sum at the time. The price was justified thus:

---

9 "1957- Soundtrack -Silent Film 'The Fatal Love' BUNAB #5 - Auction Details," popsike.com - December 2011, <www.popsike.com/1957-Soundtrack-Silent-Film-The-Fatal-Love-BUNAB-5/120821481546.html>

from the Original Sound Track of the Urban-Eclipse Silent film THE FATAL LOVE

COMPANION TO T.V.

BUNAB #5

The Fatal Love LP, BunaB #5, conceived by Al Crowder. Image courtesy of Adam David.

Mr. Crowder was once asked on a game show why it cost so much if it was only silence. Crowder defended the price well, saying that the production costs were tremendous. Imagine, he said, getting a full 40-piece orchestra into a studio, getting them all tuned up, and then asking them to remain silent for two 20-minute periods. Invariably, he went on, you'd be seven minutes into a take and someone's chair would squeak, or someone would cough, forcing you to start all over.[10]

Other silent records were more serious in spirit. In 1966, Fluxus-affiliated artist Ken Friedman put out *Zen for Record*, a disc whose grooves are completely silent. This record was an homage to *Zen for Film*, an endless loop of unexposed film that Nam June Paik, a fellow Fluxus artist, unveiled two years prior. In his book *No Medium*, poet and critic Craig Dworkin speculates that Paik and Friedman, inspired by John Cage, contrived their projects to make the point that the message can never be separated from its medium. Even when playing a silent record, you will hear the surface noise of the record—the hissing, crackling, and popping of imperfections in the grooves. Likewise, blank film will inevitably accumulate scratches, dust, and hairs whose silhouettes appear when projected. There will always be reminders of the means of reproduction.

As the century progressed, this sort of conceptual statement, formerly restricted to the fine arts scene, would become the purview of the contemporary noise and experimental music subculture. In 1985, a seminal noise act called the New Blockaders put out a forty-six-minute cassette of silent audio named *Epater Les Bourgois*, which translates, minus spelling errors, to *Shock the Bourgeois*. The New Blockaders' Richard Rupenus is not sure of the motivations behind this release, decades later. "I can't recall what the 'concept' behind *Epater Les Bourgois* was, if there even was a concept," he says. "Some reviews assumed that it must have been influenced by John Cage's (in)famous '4:33' but that wasn't the case. The *Pulp 7*" (recorded with Organum) had been described, by Paul Lemos in *Unsound*, as 'Relentless musical violence, the most savage aural attack ever committed to vinyl,' so perhaps I wanted *Epater Les Bourgois* to be the polar opposite of that?!"

He then provides some background on the title and its relationship to the concept. "'Épater les bourgeois' is a French phrase that became a rallying cry for the French Decadent poets of the late 19th century, including Arthur Rimbaud. It will not translate

---

10 Frank Lynch, "The Improved #7 Bunab," <www.samueljohnson.com/bunab/> [accessed March 19, 2022]

precisely into English, but is usually rendered as 'To shock the respectable classes.' As stated in the sleeve notes to the *Nonchalant Acts of Artistic Nihilism* CD: '...Volume isn't always the end game. Silence is often far more interesting.'"

Released on a short-lived eighties label and limited to merely twenty-five copies, the release has nonetheless attained a mythical status, leading to two separate reissues. The most recent re-release appeared in 2017, courtesy of a Swedish label whose lavish reboot included a special version housed in a handmade box with a T-shirt and sundry other goodies. As the venerable noise blog *Do or D.I.Y.?* opined: "If you listen to this collection of tape hiss for longer than ten seconds, then you are beyond pretentious, and beyond help......and probably Middle Class/bourgeois."[11]

Epater's absurdist uselessness as an audio object is consistent with the New Blockaders' credo. In 1982, they published a manifesto that was a rallying cry against art:

> *Blockade is resistance. It is our duty to blockade and induce others to blockade: Anti-music, anti-art, anti-books, anti-films, anti-communications. We will make anti-statements about anything and everything. We will make a point of being pointless.*[12]

Their extensive body of abstract noise tapes, records, and CDs stands as a testament to this philosophy of purposelessness, though by this metric *Epater* seems like the conceptual apogee of their body of work. How better to subvert the expectations of music than with forty-six minutes of silence on tape? It was an idea so good that they repeated it in 1991 with their blank tape *Simphonie In Ø Minor*, which much later was reissued on vinyl.

Then there is Reynols, an Argentine band whose name originates from a misspelling of Burt Reynolds. Fronted by their drummer, Miguel Tomasin, their exploits included orchestrating a symphony of chickens (released on red vinyl as *10.000 Chickens Symphony*) and nearly getting arrested after plugging a guitar into a pumpkin and playing an impromptu live concert on the street. Their 2000 release, *Blank Tapes*, is a CD recording of the audio from blank tapes. It was put out by the record label Trente Oiseaux, one of the highest-profile experimental music imprints of the era. Technically, *Blank Tapes* is not truly silent. Like *Zen for Record*, its focus is the incidental sound produced by the medium itself, which in this case is crusty old magnetic tape. There are no hefty conceptual statements accompanying the release, but within the context of the band's notoriety for conceptual hijinks, it appears to be a provocative statement about the nature of music itself—although one that, as a contemporaneous review pointed out, "yields surprising sonic pleasures amidst the indistinct analog fuzz of blank old cassettes."[13]

Silent records have also been used to make biting political comments: 1980 saw the release of a now-coveted silent album titled *The Wit and Wisdom of Ronald Reagan*, issued

---

11 Jonny Zchivago, "The New Blockaders - " Epater Les Bourgeois " - (Frux Records FC03) 1985," Die or D.I.Y.?, January 18, 2014, <dieordiy2.blogspot.com/2014/01/the-new-blockaders-epater-les-bourgeois.html>

12 "The New Blockaders," NoiseWiki <www.noisewiki.com/wiki/index.php?title=The_New_Blockaders> [accessed March 19, 2022]

13 "[R] Titles at Aquarius Records," Aquarius Records <archive.is/baCcE> [accessed March 19, 2022]

The Wit and Wisdom of Ronald Reagan and **The Wit and Wisdom of Margaret Thatcher.**
Image courtesy of Adam David.

by the "Magic" label, a phony stand-in for the iconic post-punk label Stiff Records. One side of the LP is dedicated to Reagan's Wit, and the other houses his Wisdom, and it was issued with the caution, "Warning: You may or may not hear something interesting on this record."

The joke has been repeated elsewhere. In 1983, several British equivalents appeared, of varying political stripes: *The Wit and Wisdom of Margaret Thatcher*; *of Michael Foot* (a Labour Party politician); *of the SDP* (the UK's centrist Social Democratic Party). Most recently came *The Wit and Wisdom of Nigel Farage*, a right-wing British politician. A Donald Trump version was issued for Record Store Day in 2019.[14]

In 1990, Virgin Records put together a less sarcastic political release. With a mouthful of a title, *Dance Hall of Shame: No Thinking. No Talking. No Music.* was a spartanly designed LP to protest censorship. It came in a white sleeve with little more than the title written on it, with a short and inexplicably capitalized essay on free speech being the only real piece of content: "If There Is One Lesson To Be Learned Through Our History, It's That Freedom Of Speech Has Inevitable Risks. But the Alternative Is Slavery Of Mind, In A Society Empty Of Thought." An email to someone who appeared to be the Bethe Austin responsible for *Dance Hall of Shame*'s liner notes went, sadly, unanswered.[15]

Beyond parody, other silent releases exist purely for novelty value, and are either cash grabs or good fun, depending on your perspective. Take, for example, 1970's *The Best of Marcel Marceao*. Marcel Marceao was a misspelled version of Marcel Marceau, a famous mime. The record is silent for nineteen minutes on each side, culminating in one minute of applause at each side's end. Its track listing reads as

14 "No Artist – The Wit And Wisdom Of Donald Trump (2019, Orange, Vinyl)," Discogs <www.discogs.com/release/13494960-No-Artist-The-Wit-And-Wisdom-Of-Donald-Trump> [accessed March 19, 2022]

15 "No Artist – Dance Hall Of Shame: No Thinking. No Talking. No Music (1990, Gatefold, Vinyl)," Discogs <www.discogs.com/release/2271671-No-Artist-Dance-Hall-Of-Shame-No-Thinking-No-Talking-No-Music> [accessed March 19, 2022]

follows: "1. SILENCE—19:00; 2. APPLAUSE—1:00" This tongue-in-cheek record was the brainchild of a young Michael Viner, who would go on to produce the music at the 1972 Republican National Convention and at Richard Nixon's Inaugural Ball,[16] and who assembled the Incredible Bongo Band before founding an audiobook empire in the eighties. *Marceao* is a novelty, and it is said to have been fodder for many a cutout bin before becoming a minor collector's item. The release's concept was echoed in 2007, when a tongue-in-cheek, completely silent single was released, credited to Hot Lixx Hulahan, the winner of the U.S. National Air Guitar Championship and an actor for the video game series *Rock Band*.

A 1980 German reboot of *The Best of Marcel Marceau*, entitled *Ruhe Im Spiegelbild*. Image courtesy of Adam David.

Another obscure silent record emerged in 1974, courtesy of a New Jersey anomaly named Jerry Cammarata. An article from the *Cincinnati Enquirer* dated November 24, 1974, provides some context about Cammarata and his record. Then a twenty-seven-year-old audiologist and speech-language pathologist, he was, at the time, attempting to set records to get his name into the *Guinness Book of World Records*. One successful feat involved singing continuously around New York City for ninety-six hours.

Garnering such "firsts" has become a secondary career for Cammarata. "They represent ambition, excitement and fun," he grins. "They offer that uncalled-for challenge that leads you nowhere but to the point of accomplishment."

His entry to the silent record pantheon is *Auditory Memory, or All You Wanted to Know About the Longest Silent Musical Composition*, which "pours forth 52 minutes and 10 seconds of pure silence." In the article, he is quoted as admitting that "It's a gimmick, and a conversation piece."

Cammarata is currently the chief operating officer and dean of student affairs at the Touro College of Osteopathic Medicine, where his biography makes no mention of his recording career, nor his world records. As it turns out, he has a lot to say about his silent album. He laments that there has never been a doctoral thesis on musical rests and offers his view on the different types of silence. Although largely undetectable by the human ear, when we record live silence, there is some sound on the audio spectrum: the sound of air moving through tight spaces, for example. It is this very live silence that Cammarata aspired to capture on *Auditory Memory*. It wasn't enough

---

16 Oliver Hall, "The Sound of Silence: The World's Only Mime Album," Dangerous Minds, June 2, 2016, <dangerousminds.net/comments/the_sound_of_silence_the_worlds_only_mime_album>

The Nothing Record.
Image courtesy of Adam David.

for Cammarata to simply unplug a microphone and hit *record*; instead, it's a true recording of live silence in a recording studio—meaning he had to pay for recording time and had to take pains to eliminate incidental sounds.

Cammarata's overarching goal was to expose the value of silence in music. Because silence forms the negative space of musical compositions, it is often neglected. But, as Cammarata reasons, musical rests have meaning, even if that meaning only occurs in relation to the sounds that border the silence. *Auditory Memory* is much longer than typical rests, he explains, mentioning the false ending on Joseph Haydn's "Opus 33," often referred to as "The Joke," as another example of an extended sequence of rests. But for Cammarata, that was the point. As its title suggests, *Auditory Memory* is meant to call attention to the sounds that precede it, which linger in one's memory like ghosts.

Like other media-savvy silent music pioneers, Cammarata stirred up a press event surrounding the release of his silent disc. He tells me his talent for media manipulation was enabled by the more playful media culture of the seventies, as well as the benefit of living in New York. He recounts a story of being interviewed about the record on the radio. At one point, the radio host instructed the producer to play the record—when only silence followed, the host proceeded to berate the producer, much to the poor technician's bewilderment.

Cammarata cited *The Nothing Book* as a key influence. This 1974 book "written" by Bruce Harris, the marketing director for Crown Books, was completely blank inside. In a contemporaneous interview with the *New York Times*, Harris suggested that the goal of the book was to "give people a book to write their thoughts in . . . to unlock the basic creativity in everyone."[17] This was a lot like Cammarata's use of his record as an imagination aid for schoolchildren.

The Nothing Book was a minor but significant novelty sensation when it came out, so much so that it inspired a budget label called Murray Hill to put out a companion release called *The Nothing Record* in 1978, which borrowed its cover formatting from the book and was apparently sold alongside its literary counterpart at discount bookstores.[18] Its cover loudly advertised "ONE FULL HOUR OF NOTHING!"

---

17 "Book Ends," The New York Times, 1974, <www.nytimes.com/1974/07/14/archives/book-ends.html

18 "Completely Silent but Grooved LP Side?," Steve Hoffman Music Forums <forums.stevehoffman.tv/threads/completely-silent-but-grooved-lp-side.720786/> [accessed March 19, 2022]

Likely inspired by *The Nothing Record*, in 1980, the Canadian label Solid Gold Records, known for putting out editions of albums by Canadian dinosaur-rock bands like Chilliwack and Toronto, issued a novelty album titled *The Nothing Record Album*, which, despite brandishing a full track listing, was entirely silent. There were even liner notes sardonically promising such exclusive treats as a "concert recording featuring Buddy Holly, Jimi Hendrix, Duane Allman, Brian Jones, Janis Joplin, Everett Dirksen, and the 'King' himself, Louis XIV," and a track sung by "the legendary 'sixth Beatle' Stu Sutcliffe." And there was a list of acclamations on the back cover, by the likes of Dolly Parton ("Fabulous. I have two of them."), the Dalai Lama ("An invaluable learning tool"), and the Rolling Stones ("...apocryphal...ethereal...ephemeral...at long last an answer to the musical question of being and nothingness...").[19]

Another intriguing record from this era was 1976's "Silent Knight" by Son of Pete, a single with two sides of silent grooves. Minimal information about this record's production persists, apart from the details gathered on a blog called *Steve's Curiosity Cabinet*.[20] Produced by Tom Lubin and arranged by Beserkley Records founder Matthew "King" Kaufman under the pseudonym "R. Bimber," there is no available information about its distribution and production.

Phil Brown, a mastering engineer from California who mastered "Silent Knight" while working for Columbia Records in San Francisco, explained that the record had two sides: one was 2:59 in length, and the other, "Disco Party, Part 2," was 3:01. They were made by cutting blank tape and mastering it. He told me that his boss, Matthew Kaufmann thought bars and restaurants might buy a copy for their jukeboxes in order to get a moment of silence every now and then, mirroring Bill Rabe's Hush discs from two decades prior. As a funny postscript, he explained that somehow the copies of "Silent Knight" that were initially sent to Beserkley Records by Columbia were actually pressed with "Beth" by Kiss, albeit with the "Silent Knight" covers and center labels. This problem was rectified for the final release (they may have just been the test pressings), though Brown suspects that, somewhere out there, there may still be some "Silent Knight" discs that actually contain Kiss' soppy ballad.

There are also silent records that fall within a conceptual category of their own. Conceptual artist Jonty Semper put out a single-sided 7-inch record in 2001 that contains one minute of silent audio, titled *The One Minute Silence From The Funeral of Diana, Princess Of Wales*. Semper has a specific interest in public silences, having also released *Kenotaphion*, a double-CD set of moments of silence from Armistice Day and Remembrance Day ceremonies. Semper justified this release in an article for *The Guardian*, explaining "I really don't think people will find it boring. All the silences are quite distinctive. What is remarkable is how different they are."

There are also a few true mysteries among the silent records pantheon. There is a bizarre promotional single from Telfort, a Dutch telecommunications company, whose cover promises Jimi Hendrix's "Are You Experienced?" on one side and Bob Dylan's "The Times They Are a-Changin'" on the other. A bizarre combination for sure, but

19 "No Artist – The Nothing Record Album (1980, Vinyl)," Discogs <www.discogs.com/release/2161017-No-Artist-The-Nothing-Record-Album> [accessed March 19, 2022]
20 Stevie, "Son Of Pete : Silent Knight," Stevie's Curiosity Cabinet, October 8, 2009, <steviecurates.blogspot.com/2009/10/son-of-pete-silent-knight.html>

**The mysterious *Glitter* LP.
Image courtesy of Adam David.**

what is stranger is that the discs are completely silent![21]

Then there is the mysterious *Glitter* record. A light-pink marbled LP given out as a promotional item at the Bellagio casino in Las Vegas for their end-of-2007 New Year's Eve party, it comes with a full track listing with such enticing song titles as "Beyond the Velvet Ropes" and "Bubbly is Better Doubly." Yet all its grooves run silent. The LP sleeve suggests that it was some form of gimmicky invitation to the event, possibly used as a giveaway.

In summary, silent recordings have been around for years, and they have been created for a host of different reasons. They have made artistic and political statements, served as novelty items, and poked fun at consumerism. If it is hard to imagine sitting down and *playing* these records and tapes, then gird yourself—because the story gets even more improbable.

21 Alan Fraser, "Singles All Formats International 2000-09," Searching For a Gem <www.searchingforagem.com/2000s/InternationalSingles2000s.htm> [accessed March 19, 2022]

REISSUING SILENCE

Kenny Johansson is a Swedish noise artist who records under the name Obskyr. He is also the owner of the Obskyr Records label, which in 2017 took on the extraordinary task of reissuing a silent cassette. That tape was the New Blockaders' 1985 album *Epater Les Bourgois*, a forty-six-minute track of silence originally issued by an obscure British label named Frux.

Johansson recalls obtaining the original tape years ago, only to be pleasantly surprised that the tape was blank. "I was like 'Oh, yeah, this is so great... oh, wait, there is nothing... even better!'" He has been a longtime fan of the New Blockaders' irreverent take on music.

Ten years ago, he emailed Richard Rupenus, one half of the New Blockaders, asking for his address to send some materials. "It felt natural to send gifts to a great guy like him. He and his younger brother Philip made 'noise' what it is today and I am forever grateful for their work." They ended up striking a friendship and have collaborated on many releases ever since, including a bizarre Kiss tribute album under the name Torpedo Girl.

In the late 2010s, Johansson was working on a reissue of a New Blockaders 7" single from 1992, "Epater Les Bourgeois," to be released on a Japanese experimental label called Siren Records. Though that single shares almost the same name as the tape (except properly spelled), it had more typical noise fare on it and was not silent. But it occurred to Johansson that the silent cassette *Epater* might be worth reissuing too, albeit on his own label.

"I asked Richard if we could do a reissue, as it is a favorite of mine," Johansson recalls. "Richard was very skeptical at first. But when I told him about my plans, he later agreed and we both had a blast working on it." Johansson requested the master of *Epater* from Rupenus and received one in the mail.

"When I sent the master tape to Tapeline, who made the tapes, they sent me an email saying, 'Sorry, but the cassette was empty, please send a new one.' Ha! I sent an email back, 'The tape is not empty, just silent, please proceed with the duplication!' I think they raised their eyebrows a lot!"

Johansson acknowledges that there is some tape hiss on the reissue, which means it is not entirely blank. The magnetic surface noise is the analog to the pops and cracks that appear on the surface of silent records—reminders of the medium itself.

VI.2 DAMAGED

In 1985, the experimental musician Christian Marclay released a record with no cover and no sleeve. He named it *Record Without a Cover* and, to ensure it lived up to its name, it was distributed with a warning to record shop proprietors and would-be purchasers: "Do not store in a protective package." As a result, each disc became progressively more dinged-up over its life cycle of production, storage, shipping, and sitting on a sales rack. The actual audio contained in its grooves, a collage of various other recordings mashed together, was beside the point.

Born in California but raised in Geneva, Marclay was exposed early on to the work of the irreverent art collective known as the Ecart Performance Group, especially its co-founder John Armleder. Armleder was interested in the role of the art gallery itself as a mediator of the artistic experience, doing wacky Dadaist things like incorporating the gallery furniture into his art, in turn toying with attendees' expectations of where to sit and of what art is supposed to be.

Marclay attended art school in Boston, where he was exposed to the New York punk and no-wave scenes and, most importantly, to hip-hop. Eventually, like the DJs he idolized, he became interested in the turntable as a musical instrument. Mirroring Armleder's fascination with the art gallery as a medium, he became interested in how vinyl records themselves impacted the musical experience. In an interview with the *Guardian*, he explained that his work explored "mass-produced objects as filters."[22]

Every record can be used in some way. If the music in a groove fits with what you're playing, then play it; if not, then you can play it backwards. If that doesn't work, you try it at a different speed. If it really doesn't work you just break it. The whole ritual to put a record on a turntable just to listen to it, I don't do that too often.

Record Without a Cover, then, came from Marclay's interest in the materiality of records as a medium. He wanted to highlight the record not as an accurate document of a performance, but instead as an evolving object that would gradually change over time as it accumulated more surface damage. "*Record Without a Cover* was about allowing the medium to come through," he explained, "making a record that was not a document of a performance, but a record that could change with time, and would be different from one copy to the next."

This would not be his only foray into the realm of damaged records. In 1988, he pressed 3,500 copies of a record that contained two recordings, one of footsteps and another of a professional tap dancer, Keiko Uenishi. He then used those records to line the floor of an art gallery in a warehouse in Zurich for over a month in 1989. Later that year, he pried one thousand of the scuffed-up records from the floor and released them on RecRec Music, a Swiss record label, irreverently dedicating the release to Fred Astaire.

From 1980 to 1986, Marclay also produced his *Recycled Records* series, which perhaps belongs more in the realm of visual art than music. For this project, he used a jigsaw to carefully cut apart differently colored records. He then glued them together to make

---

22 Rob Young, "Don't Sleeve Me This Way ," The Guardian, February 14, 2005, <www.theguardian.com/music/2005/feb/14/popandrock>

**The 1999 reissue of Christian Marclay's *Record Without a Cover*.
Image courtesy of Jan van Toorn.**

striking mutant discs. Since the vinyl was chosen for physical characteristics instead of sonic attributes, the resulting audio was a random outcome—an idea that is in keeping with the chance effects of shoe soles on vinyl records. It has been framed as a "revenge on the commercial picture disc," although at a deeper level, it furthers Marclay's interest in spotlighting the medium over the source audio itself.[23]

A PhD dissertation by Caleb Kelly, a senior lecturer at the University of New South Wales, titled *Cracked and Broken Media in the 20th and 21st Century*, explores the tradition of damaged records as art, but Kelly extends his study to tampered-with turntables as well as digital music. Specifically, he writes about "glitch" artists: producers who vandalize CDs to make them intentionally skip or who alter digital files to cause signal interruptions by overloading a computer's CPU. In both cases, the goal is to produce intentionally "cracked" sounds.[24]

Kelly's dissertation begins with a vignette of an experimental musician, Lucas Abela, performing a gig in a warehouse. He has built a rudimentary turntable using a meat skewer as the stylus and part of an industrial sewing machine as the engine. It is rotating at an absurd 2,850 spins per minute. Tiny shards of recognizable pop music, albeit played at ultra-rapid speeds, are audible between cavernous bursts of noise. Records are breaking on the turntable, and shards are flying out and lodging themselves into the walls of the performance space. The show ends with all the records in pieces and the meat skewer broken.

23 Simon Shaw-Miller, "A Complex Art," in The Art of Music, ed. Patrick Coleman (New Haven: Yale University Press, 2015), 32–59.
24 Kelly, Caleb. Cracked and broken media in 20th and 21st century music and sound. University of Canberra, 2006.

Kelly then extends the tradition of "broken media" further back. He explains that some theorists in the early twentieth century imagined hand-etching a record to produce custom grooves, theorizing that a talented etcher might carve out songs that defy human physiological limits, for example, simulating a singer with an unlimited vocal range. But Kelly draws a distinction between hand-carved records and what he considers "broken media." For Kelly, John Cage was the first to intentionally produce "broken" or "cracked" media by popping open turntable cartridges and replacing their innards with toothpicks and other junk, unpredictably altering the sound that was produced when they were then used to play records.

Prefiguring Marclay's music, Caleb claims it was the Japanese branch of the Fluxus movement that first truly explored the possibilities of altered or damaged records. Mieko Shiomi's 1969 *Amplified Dream No. 1* was an exhibit involving a record that had been damaged randomly with a soldering iron. For *Water Music* (1965), a record was lacquered with a special soluble glue that would dissolve when it encountered water. This record was played on a record player as water dripped over it and as a result, the audio would waver between the uneven surface of dried glue and the progressively exhumed source audio.

These pieces exist in the context of the Fluxus movement, a multidisciplinary group with several disparate ideas behind their art, one of which was destruction. For example, Nam June Paik staged performances where he smashed a violin over a table or dragged one along a road. And George Maciunas once destroyed a piano onstage by nailing down each of its keys. Kelly explains that this sort of destructive art raises several important questions:

It certainly calls into question the value of the targeted cultural artefacts, as all destructive acts tend to do. It also directs an audience to consider the new, post-destructive act. Does the very act of destruction create something new? Where does this new object lie? Is the new object fleeting—for example, the unique and singular sounds of the splintering violin? Or does the act of destruction actually create a new object that extends the possibilities beyond those intended for the instrument? Through the destruction of playback technologies, new instruments and sound possibilities are created.

This is a major crux of "cracked" music—the idea that even perhaps by using purely incidental methods, damaged media can produce entirely new art, often by drawing attention toward the media itself.

In the sixties and seventies, the Czech artist Milan Knížák produced a series of pieces called *Broken Music*, including a record cut into four pieces and then glued back together, which would cause an audible pop four times per rotation, only allowing snippets of music to occupy the space between. In the eighties, paralleling Christian Marclay, he became even more destructive: In one case, he covered records in paint, and in another stunt, he glued shards of one record to another before melting them together. When contacted by Kelly for his dissertation, Knížák explained that this was not mere wanton destruction, but instead a process of creating new art and new music, using a novel means of interacting with the medium of the vinyl record:

I don't understand my working with the records as a violence—it is just a different way of using them. Creating new, surprising, sometimes a bit aggressive, but sometimes also some kind of meditative sounds.

This idea of creating new art from the shards of old art is at the crux of Kelly's thesis. In his eyes, this process transforms the tenets of "old media" into the contemporary age. It used to be that records were static documents, intended to be listened to from start to finish in the comfort of one's parlor. But today's "new media" is interactive. Computers and the internet have transformed the way we consume art; now it is second nature for the experience to be customizable. You skip through a video to find the best part, or to replay a favorite interval. Collages and mash-ups are commonplace. For Kelly, these damaged or "broken" records take old media and make it new media, using an interactive process which creates something new.

As the twentieth century moved on, other artists adopted these ideas. Shiomi and Knížák, as compared with Marclay, restricted their work to art galleries. They were generally not producing multiple copies of their work for retail sale. (Though an LP of recordings of his mutant records was released in 1979, dubbed *Broken Music*, and has since been reissued.) Marclay, on the other hand, would issue hundreds of copies of *Record Without a Cover* using record labels and traditional approaches to music distribution. Yet Marclay always keeps one foot in the fine arts field; his background is in visual art and, despite collaborating with the likes of Sonic Youth, he is a fixture in contemporary art galleries.

In 1982, the New Blockaders, who were responsible for the silent tape called *Epater Les Bourgois* discussed in the previous chapter, included a destroyed LP with the first ten copies of their debut noise LP, *Changez Les Blockeurs*. That record, which is now extraordinarily rare, was covered in dirt, screws, and rusty nails and had segments cut out of it. It was an early salvo in the underground music scene's fascination with damaged vinyl.

In the late eighties, RRRecords, one of the most influential American record labels to put out and distribute noise music, got into the damaged record game. Run by Ron Lessard, a.k.a. RRRon, RRR is known for its expansive discography as well as its Recycled Music series, which features noise albums dubbed onto recycled pop/rock cassettes. In 1988, it released a compilation called *Colorado*, collecting the work of noise bands from the Centennial State. But one hundred of the copies had an unusual feature. The first track on side A, by Denver experimental ensemble Architects Office, was scratched out, with the words "FUCK ARCHITECTS OFFICE" carved into the vinyl. That track was also crossed out on the track listing, and the words "Anti Record" were scrawled in marker on the cover.[25] Lessard explained to me that this happened after the album came out, when one of the members of Architects Office contacted Ron and started complaining about the cover. In retaliation, Lessard took one hundred copies and scratched the words into the vinyl. "It was more of an emotional outburst than any sort of artistic statement," he explained.

---

25 "Colorado Anti Record (1988, Anti-Record, Vinyl)," Discogs <www.discogs.com/release/1102820-Various-Colorado-Anti-Record> [accessed March 19, 2022]

In 1995, experimental composer Otomo Yoshihide released a single called *Otomo + Mao* as the inaugural release on the F.M.N. Sound Factory label,[26] which specialized in improvised music from Japan. This single came accompanied by several odds and ends, including a cassette and a microcassette, and came packaged with a found LP that was defaced by a Kyoto-based art group called NAP.[27]

Although this may have been the only time he included a damaged LP as a physical component of a release, Yoshihide's 1997 LP *Memory Defacement* was an audio collage prepared using cracked vinyl.[28] At that stage in his career, Yoshihide's use of cracked records, often in tandem with improvised noise music with his band Ground Zero, was really about sampling. In a 1996 interview in *The Wire*,[29] he likens sampling to a "kind of virus of the memory, something which enters the memory and makes something new," similar to Caleb Kelly's idea of "cracked art" as generating new content from old media. Eventually, Yoshihide would remove records from the equation altogether, playing the turntable *without vinyl*—for example, by replacing the cartridge with a piece of metal and forcing it to drag along the turntable platter *sans* slipmat.[30]

In 1997, the iconoclastic noise and power electronics act Cock E.S.P. put out a single titled *As If* on a mystery label called Silver Blue Records, which was certainly not the disco label of the same name. The surface of each copy was scratched with a nail, rendering it damaged beyond recognition. Matt Bacon, who was a member of the group at the time *As If* came out, provides some background on this obscure release. "The idea was that we were getting set to go on tour, and I think it was one of my first with the band," he remembers. "We needed some extra product to bring along and, being a record collector, I came up with the idea to make an 'anti-record.' All I did was find a bunch of old 45s and gouged them with various sharp objects. This made them unplayable on most decent turntables... I believe I made about 25 of them. Half of them came on tour, and the rest we distributed through the old label/zine my pal Jason and I were doing called *Fever Pitch*."

I ask what attracted them to the concept of a damaged record. "It really had nothing to offer to anyone as far as sound and legitimacy, so it seemed like the perfect thing to do," Bacon told me, encapsulating the trademark Cock E.S.P. irreverence. "It had zero influence from any other record of its type, and the motivation was just trying to get products out to sell on tour so we could eat and put gas in the tank."

He told me that collectors have sporadically contacted him to inquire about spare copies, but that they are long gone, although he and co-member Emil Hagstrom have personal copies. "Plans for a 25th anniversary reissue are in the works though," he teases.

Dutch artist Mars F. Wellink created his *Anti-Record* single in 2001, using two separate records glued permanently together, then scratched up to the point of unintelligibility. He only made seven copies. Wellink tells me he created this scratched-up record as a way of using some 45s that accumulated in his "piles of stuff." A professional silkscreener

26 "Otomo Yoshihide — Otomo + Mao (1995, Vinyl)," Discogs <www.discogs.com/release/843163-Otomo-Yoshihide-Otomo-Mao> [accessed March 19, 2022]

27 "OTOMO YOSHIHIDE Otomo + Mao Reviews," Prog Archives <www.progarchives.com/album.asp?id=15026> [accessed March 19, 2022]

28 "Otomo Yoshihide 大友良英 - Memory Defacement," Noise Asia <www.noiseasia.com/products/otomo-yoshihide-memory-defacement-2lp> [accessed March 19, 2022]

29 Ed Baxter, "Benign Host," The Wire (London, 1996).

30 Caleb Kelly, "Cracked and Broken Media in 20th and 21st Century Music and Sound — University of Canberra Research Portal."

and collage artist, he sees it as an extension of his urge to recycle materials in the service of artistic creation. "All the stuff you collect is the inspiration for a self-taught artist. I've made collages all my life." He acknowledges being "a great fan of the Fluxus movement," which comes through in the records' artwork: each copy's cover was a unique collage of cut-and-pasted shreds of other LP sleeves, capped off with a rabbit's jawbone glued to its front.

Around 2005, Paul Nemeth, who now works as a professional double bassist, put out two bizarre records under the pseudonym Haruki Murakami. One was "Song b/w Song,"[31] a 7" single that had been spattered with paint and thus could not be played. The other was a split with a fellow noise act named Dance Wound, which was produced by creating a master record and using it as a mold by layering it with glue, then peeling the glue off. The resulting circle of dried glue was its own record.

Contacted for the book, Nemeth was pleased to hear that one of his records has survived to be catalogued online. He tells me most of his Haruki Murakami releases were tapes, but those two records were exceptions. They sprung from his adventures in the noise music underground, which he discovered online after downloading a Government Alpha track off the file-sharing program Napster. He sees his work in classical music as separate from noise, though he does recognize a relationship between "Song b/w Song" and the work of Christian Marclay and Nam June Paik. "The idea behind [both "Song b/w Song" and the glue record] was that the sound created by the 'record' is the performance itself," he explains. "The turntable trying to play something that would create mechanical interference is the performance instead of a record playing back a stored recording."

He sent me a recent video of Nam June Paik's "One For Violin Solo" being performed by the Los Angeles Philharmonic Orchestra as part of a Fluxus festival. In it, a violinist slowly lifts a violin over his head, then smashes it to pieces. In that case, instead of the recording being damaged, it is the instrument itself. "Cringe-inducing," Nemeth exclaims.

The idea of the damaged record lives on today. Quagga Curious Sounds' Michael Ridge, who has released droves of anti-records, shares the notion that damaged and otherwise modified sound media offer listeners another way of consuming music. In 2010, *Anti-Flex 1* was Ridge's first anti-record, released under his pseudonym Zebra Mu. He tells me he acquired 7" promo flexis and tried to repurpose them. "Firstly, an attempt was made to crudely lathe-cut my own recording over the existing grooves. This was an unsuccessful endeavour, so the playing surface was instead sanded down and spray-painted multiple times. The hidden and failed process behind this project is an appealing concept; all traces having been physically removed with sandpaper and paint. Essentially it is a noise record, playability is reasonable (there's a risk of damaging the stylus), and over time, it has become a useful sound source for recording harsh noise with."

His 2019 *Anti-Flex 2* flexi took things a step further. "My motive instead was exploring other ways to physically alter the playing surface of existing flexi-discs. Like

31 "Haruki Murakami — Song B/W Song (Vinyl)," Discogs <www.discogs.com/release/1949574-Haruki-Murakami-Song-BW-Song> [accessed March 19, 2022]

Zebra Mu a.k.a. Michael Ridge's *Anti-Flex 1* and *Anti-Flex 2*.
Images courtesy of Michael Ridge.

Anti-Flex 1 it was sanded and spray-painted; however, segments of the playing surface were shielded with masking tape, permitting fragments of the original recording to mix with the surface noise of the sanded/painted parts. However, the untouched segments are also hole-punched in places, opening interesting and risky playback possibilities."

All in all, artists who create damaged records and tapes are taking familiar sound media and expanding their artistic utility. Physical alterations to the playing surface of a record subvert the standard way in which music is reproduced, like a rudimentary version of the expertly hand-carved music records that were imagined in the early twentieth century. In some cases, like with Cock E.S.P.'s disc, the goal is simply to be irreverent. In other cases, the idea is to open new sonic possibilities, drawing attention to the unexpected features of a physical medium. And elsewhere, such as the hand-painted LP that accompanied Otomo Yoshihide's *Otomo + Mao*, the approach transcends modalities, expanding into the domain of visual art.

VI.3 UNPLAYABLE

Finally, there is a class of "recordings" that are not just damaged but, for various reasons, cannot be played. If a record that cannot be listened to sounds like a paradox, then you are getting the idea. The reasons that these seemingly functionless records were created will vary by artist, but it is helpful to consider them from the perspective of *anti-art*, an idea that dates to an art movement called Dada which emerged in the early twentieth century.

The art historian David Hopkins tells the story of Dada in his primer, *Dada and Surrealism: A Very Short Introduction*. He explains that, during the nineteenth century, fine arts were synonymous with bourgeois individualism. Art was an escape from "material constraints," an opportunity to transcend base reality. The resistance to this concept of art started in 1916, when a poet named Hugo Ball opened a bar called Cabaret Voltaire, which became the epicenter of the Dada art movement. This space was known for events called "provocations," subversive performances meant to upend art's conventions. For example, Ball constructed poems out of nonsensical syllables, calling the resulting anti-poetry "abstract phonetic poetry." One of the members of the group that revolved around Cabaret Voltaire was Hans Arp, who used provocations to express his hatred for art's professionalism, equating art with "egotism and a too-high valuation of humanity."

Marcel Duchamp is, perhaps, the best known of the Dadaists. He believed that art should prioritize ideas over technical skill. His most infamous testament to this belief was a piece called *Fountain*, which consisted of a porcelain urinal signed with the words "R. Mutt 1917." Duchamp sent it to the Society of Independent Artists, who had earlier promised they would accept all submissions for their first exhibition, so long as they came from due-paying members. Even though Duchamp was a bona fide member, *Fountain* was rejected, and Duchamp withdrew his membership in protest. This act of deliberate provocation was emblematic of the Dada spirit, which stood against the hoity-toity fine arts establishment.

As philosopher Stephen Hicks sees it, *Fountain* was doubly irreverent. On one hand, it is rebellious because it uses a mass-produced, industrially designed object, often referred to as a "ready-made," which challenges the art world's concept of art pieces as exalted objects. "But over and above that," Hicks points out, "Duchamp did not select just any ready-made object to display. In selecting the urinal, his message was clear: Art is something you piss on." Dada was a movement that used the absurd to make a mockery of the art world—they "waged war on the outworn rhetoric of art."[32]

The music scene's equivalent to anti-art is the *anti-record*, which is considerably less documented than anti-art. And while silent and damaged records both fall within the category of anti-records, truly unplayable records are the apotheosis of the style: anti-records at their purest.

---

32 "The Fascinating Tale of Marcel Duchamp's Fountain," Phaidon Agenda, May 26, 2016, <www.phaidon.com/agenda/art/articles/2016/may/26/the-fascinating-tale-of-marcel-duchamps-fountain/>

EXTREME MUSIC

The only history of anti-records available is an article by Ron Rice, originally published in a book called *unfiled* but now available online.[33] Apart from emphasizing that individual anti-records were created for eclectic conceptual reasons, it says little about the theoretical background behind them. It is primarily a chronology of art exhibits and record releases that fit the bill, most culled from the noise and experimental music scenes.

The list includes gems like Timm Ulrichs' *Schleifpapier-Schallplatten*, a collection of sandpaper discs exhibited in 1968 which, though technically playable, would result in little more than abrasive noise and would likely destroy your stylus. The sandpaper discs were produced with thirteen different grades of sandpaper, each with varying degrees of granularity, meaning you could customize your sound.[34] The earliest piece on the list that could be truly considered unplayable is Tomas Schmit's *Schallplatte*. A pioneering member of the neo-Dadaist movement called Fluxus, Schmit designed this work as a thin bar of wood with the letters "SCHALLP" written on it, playing on the fact that *latte* means "bar" in German.

You could argue that Yugoslavian conceptual artist Braco Dimitrijević's 1972 piece *His Pencil's Voice* is technically playable, though it would not make for a very substantial listen. It was a piece of white cardboard designed to look like a record, its "grooves" drawn onto its surface by Dimitrijević in pencil. It even came in its own record sleeve.

Dimitrijević tells me that this piece came about as he was seeking a more direct way of producing art, cutting out the laborious production process that would typically be involved in moving from concept to final product. "What bothered me always was the process of realization from the idea, the sketch to the final artwork," he explains. "This was not only in visual arts, but in music too. So I wanted to create a record with no score performed, but what is written is drawn to be played."

"I drew by hand the spiral on the paper and brought it to printers to make a zinc plate to emboss and print the label," he recalls. "In other words, unlike a classic record where the music is written as notes, which are then played by one or several instruments, recorded, and listened to, for my record what is written is played directly by the record player."

Dimitrijević points out to me that he has made analogous works using photographs and stone as media but does not elaborate. I suspect he is talking about the series of works from the start of his career that began life in 1968 as *Accidental Sculpture* and *Accidental Drawings and Paintings*, both projects he started while still in art school in Zagreb. On one occasion in 1971, he made a "portable monument"—a stone plaque that could be placed anywhere—which bore the inscription, "This could be a place of Historical Importance." This seemingly satisfies the same criteria as *His Pencil's Voice*, in that Dimitrijević is bypassing the creation process by designating any environment as artistically significant.

The other analogous project is his "Casual Passer-By" series of photographs, which is archived at the Tate Modern art museum in London and the Museum of Modern Art in New York. For that work, he took portraits of people he encountered on the street. His rules were simple: He took the first person he encountered that was willing to

33 Ron Rice, "A Brief History of Anti-Records and Conceptual Records," in Unfiled: Music Under New Technology, ed. Chris Cutler (London: RēR Megacorp, 1994).

34 Ursula Block and Michael Glasmeier, Broken Music, 2nd ed. (New York City: Primary Information, 2019).

participate, documenting the person's name along with the time and date. This image was then pasted, like a billboard, on a London bus for two weeks. By bypassing the usual selection of a formal "model," as well as the typical methodology done to prepare for a photo shoot (makeup, lighting, set design), he again skips the typical artistic production process in favor of something more direct.

VI.3.1 Anti-Records and Underground Music

Ron Rice's list of anti-records is extensive, but it is missing an important artifact in the anti-record canon. Post-punk band Gerry and the Holograms never put out an LP over their short existence, but their second single became a true classic. *The Emperor's New Clothes* is a 1979 7" single that came glued into its sleeve, so there is no way of recovering the record itself. They made five hundred handmade copies of this frustrating record, which might make it the most mass-produced unplayable record out there. Lawrence Beedle, the head of the Absurd Records label that put this out, claimed in an interview that it took most of a week just to paint and glue the records. The only way to recover the audio would be to find some solvent that could remove the paper and glue but preserve the vinyl, thereby destroying the packaging. And it would not have been worth it either, because the copies did not feature any Gerry and the Holograms music—they were just extra unsold singles from the Rabid Records catalog with a new center label glued on.

Around the same time, circa 1978–1979, John Morton, member of the Electric Eels, formed a band called Johnny and the Dicks who put out one self-titled album. The catch? Despite an eye-catching cover adorned with hand-drawn art, glitter, fiberglass, and polyester resin, there was no actual record inside. On his website, Morton tells a story of a woman who bought the record, then returned it, demanding a refund. Although she had torn her copy of the release, perhaps while trying to find the music, the record shop readily accepted it back, taped up the tear, and set it out for sale at a $1 premium.[35]

Christian Marclay, whose *Record Without a Cover* was a landmark in damaged records, put out *Secret* in 1988, a 7" master disc with a padlock through the center hole and no key to unlock it. It was a tantalizingly unplayable record arrested in the process of reproduction. According to electronic music critic Philip Sherburne, *Secret* was an homage to a piece by Marcel Duchamp in which an unknown object is trapped in a ball of twine, requiring destruction of the artwork to ascertain its identity.[36]

In 1993, Marclay further toyed with the idea of what comprises a record by putting out an "album" that consisted only of the center labels. Each one came in a white LP sleeve. Those labels were pure white with Braille writing on them, one side named "Invisible" and the other "Inaudible." The Braille listed Marclay's name and specified that the recording was in stereo and intended to be played at 8 RPM. They came with the catalogue to an exhibition in Cincinnati in which Marclay was featured, with fifty copies produced in total.[37]

---

35 John Morton, "Johnny & the Dicks: The Quick Fax !," Mortonia <web.archive.org/web/20160316135606/http://www.mortonia.com/dicks/fax.txt> [accessed March 19, 2022]
36 Philip Sherburne, "Christian Marclay's Cochlear Implants," Parkett (Zurich, Switzerland, 2004), <www.parkettart.com/books/p/70>
37 "Draft of Christian Marclay — Untitled [Braille Record ALabels] (1993, Conceptual Art, Vinyl)," Discogs <www.discogs.com/release/6505358-Christian-Marclay-Untitled-Braille-Record-Labels> [accessed March 19, 2022]

VI.3.2 RRRecords' Anti-Records

Let us return to the year 1988, which saw the release of Marclay's *Secret*. It was, it turns out, a banner year for anti-records overall. That was also the year that the record label RRRecords, whose "FUCK ARCHITECTS OFFICE" release was discussed in the section on damaged records, entered the fray. Ron Lessard, who runs the label, is a repository of information about anti-records. Though he knows the idea, he claims that he was the first to refer to these enigmatic music objects as anti-records. "Before [RRR's series of anti-records] no one used the term anti-record, they were always considered conceptual records or art objects—I started calling them anti-records and now it's the accepted phrase for such things."

RRRecords' first anti-record came out on February 16, 1988. Titled *Metastasis*, it was the lone record by Billboard Combat, the pseudonym of visual artist Andrew Smith. "I was visiting my friend Andrew Smith when he showed me these hand-painted LPs he made for the heck of it he painted directly on the vinyl and embedded them with dirt, grit, razor blades, thumbtacks, and whatnot. He also made hand-decorated covers to house the LP. I was immediately struck by their visual beauty and their potent noise possibilities, I knew if I played one of these they would make more noise than any LP ever recorded."

He recalls that Smith was able to produce one hundred copies of the disc in relatively short order, repurposing old thrift-store LPs as source material. He would sometimes incorporate some of the original artwork into his hand-altered designs. They were distributed principally through RRRecords' direct mail order, though he did disseminate a few copies to his Japanese and European distribution contacts. "Response was generally positive, but I do remember one of my customers sent it back for a refund—he was all 'WHAT THE FUCK!'!" Lessard laughs.

Satisfied with the results of his experiment, Lessard was quickly emboldened to attempt more anti-records, suggesting the idea to some of his musical contacts and asking them to develop their own anti-concepts. He thinks he may have sent them free copies of the Billboard Combat disc for inspiration.

Frans de Waard, who recorded under the name Kapotte Muziek from his home in the Netherlands, was one of those contacts. His interpretation of Lessard's request was 1989's *Heathen Muzak*, a 7" record in a 12" sleeve, whose "grooves" were merely random scratches etched into the vinyl using a lathe-cutting machine. Instead of having one hole in the center, there were multiple extra holes made by a drilling machine; owners of this rare, two-hundred-copy edition were encouraged to play it at any speed, through any hole, at maximum volume.

The year 1988 also saw the release of two anti-records on RRRecords by Due Process, a collaboration between Lessard and friends Thomas Dimuzio and John Wiggins. *Do Nothing* was a completely blank LP record: no grooves, no audio, no center labels. It came out in a one-hundred-copy edition in a white cover with nothing more than the title, artist name, and catalog number listed on front. *Do Damage* was nearly the same thing, but with "hand-cut grooves." As Lessard

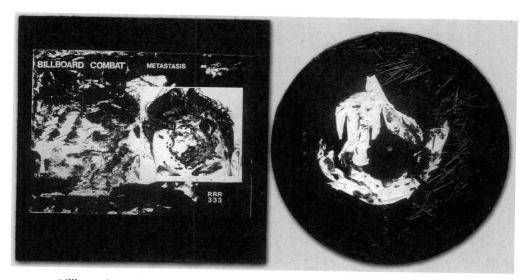

Billboard Combat's *Metastasis*, featuring a painted and junk-infused LP. Image courtesy of Ron Lessard of RRRecords.

explains, "I made a 'lathe' by pounding some nails into a plank of wood and then rotating the vinyl over the nails to cut grooves into the vinyl." Technically playable, it was not much to listen to.

Lessard recalls that the pressing plant didn't bat an eye when he requested two hundred blank records for the two releases. "I told them I wanted them for promotional purposes—they just quoted me a price and that was it," he recalled. As for *Do Nothing*, "I gave it a catalog number of RRR-433 because of course!" *Do Damage* was listed as RRR-CUT.

As Lessard was developing the idea for all these anti-records, he was contacted by Freek Kinkelaar, a Dutch experimental artist. Kinkelaar pitched him an idea of an especially poignant anti-record. This became *Manipulation Muzak*, released under the pseudonym Honeymoon Production. It was an amorphous blob of vinyl in a package, accompanied by instructions directing the owner to press their own record.

Kinkelaar tells me that he has been engrossed in the arts since he was young, through his college years, culminating in a master's degree of education in the arts. "My main interest has always been the concept, rather than the result. However pleasing on the eye, I always enjoyed the idea behind a piece best. Even when there seemed to be no idea—perhaps those pieces of art are the best. It allows you to make your own concept, form your own ideas."

Since the mid-eighties, Kinkelaar has been creating avant-garde music with Beequeen and under his solo project Brunnen, integrating concepts from the conceptual Fluxus movement. He recalls encountering RRRecords, a linchpin in the experimental music scene, and being impressed by their early anti-records. "Nothing new, of course, as there had already been a generation of anti-records artists," Kinkelaar recalls. "But Ron made it possible for a whole generation of new musicians, mostly noise and experimental musicians and artists, to release their anti-record on his label. I remember that one day Frans and I were discussing *Do Nothing* by Due Process—an anti-record that features no grooves at all. It made me think—this was an 'easy' anti-record to make; what is an anti-record? Just leave the grooves out and you got one. But what if you dig another step deeper? Start at the creation? Something that does not confront you with a finished anti-record but allows you to actually create one.

"Ron loved the concept but wasn't sure it would work," Kinkelaar recounts. "He sent me a test blob, which we heated in our household oven. It was quite exciting, as we had no idea whether it would melt, set the house on fire, explode, or whatever."

After the test run, production started in earnest. "Ron supplied the blobs from the pressing plant where he pressed up his RRR stock. I created the inserts and the title strip and sent these to Ron, who assembled the record." Lessard tells me that he approached his pressing plant for one hundred pellets of the vinyl they use to make records and was quoted a price.

Kinkelaar was attracted to the democratization of art that his release represented. "I like the anarchistic touch of it. What if you take a blob of vinyl and leave it up to the person who receives the blob? Ultimate freedom, away from 'what an anti-record should be.' Everyone is an artist—one of the most important statements ever made in art. By Joseph Beuys, of course."

At heart, Kinkelaar is attracted to Dada's irreverent perspective on art. "Art has no purpose," he tells me. "As such art is something of an anti-Aristotle teleology; there is no purpose other than to be... I have a soft spot for anti-records as they represent musical anarchy *avant la lettre*. They are punk before punk happened. They are sometimes creative, exciting, daring, funny, and sometimes they fall flat. As all art should—and actually does. They are the core of art and at the same time mock it. You gotta love the little buggers."

VI.3.3 The Haters

In 1988, RRRecords also put out *Wind Licked Dirt*, an anti-record by the Haters. Many artists cite this release as the most important moment in the history of anti-records. It was a blank LP with no grooves that came in a bag also filled with dirt. "I put each one in a plastic bag and then threw a handful of dirt in the bag," Lessard recalls. "When I approached various distributors, I would ask them if they wanted them with or without dirt haha!! I also remember getting letters from various customers, saying the dirt got on the other records they bought at the same time. Within my own record store, I put the LP in the racks without the dirt and kept a small bucket of dirt behind the counter whenever anyone would buy it, I would put the LP in the bag and then throw a handful of dirt in right in front of the customer. Most were highly amused, but a couple were kinda horrified." Purchasers of this record were encouraged to use the dirt to scratch the vinyl surface up and make it playable.

Ron recalls the idea being the brainchild of the Haters' GX Jupitter-Larsen, but he was tasked with the dirty work. "I should point out the dirt itself wasn't dark moist soil;

THE HATERS   "wind licked dirt"

THE HATERS
"Wind Licked Dirt"

**THIS RECORD IS
PLAYED BY
RUBBING DIRT
ON IT.**

**The Haters' *Wind Licked Dirt*.
Image courtesy of GX Jupitter-Larsen.**

it was basically dry sand," he says. "I got it from the neighborhood, sweeping it off the street and the empty lot next door. Now that I think about it, I think I may have scooped up a bucketful of sand from the city lot, the sand they use to spread on the streets after it snows."

Many have cited Jupitter-Larsen as the thought leader when it comes to anti-records, with *Wind Licked Dirt* as a seminal moment in the history of the format. He tells me he is surprised by the attention that *Wind Licked Dirt* attracted and takes care to explain that he does not consider it an anti-record, but instead a conceptual release. For him, an anti-record is one that cannot be played. *Wind Licked Dirt* is playable—so long as you play it according to its terms by rubbing dirt on it.

"I had used the term 'conceptual' years before I ever heard anyone call such records 'anti,'" he explains. "The first time I ever heard the term was when Ron Lessard invited me to do such a project on his label RRR. He specifically told me he wanted to do a series of 'unplayable' records. When I told him about my idea for *Wind Licked Dirt*, he said that was close enough."

It turns out that *Wind Licked Dirt* was not the Haters' first conceptual release. In 1983, he self-released an untitled EP with silent grooves, which had instructions that its owner should "first complete the record by scratching it before he can listen to it on his stereo."

"At the time," he explained, "I found myself enjoying the scratches on a record more than the recorded audio. So I wanted to do something that celebrated scratches, something that let me hear the scratches without the nuisance of having to have music on the vinyl. At the time, I was trying to listen to the surface noise of old records. Cheap vinyl gets scratched up just from normal usage. It was the entropy I was trying to hear, not the music."

By the time *Wind Licked Dirt* came out, his approach had progressed. "The thing with my first conceptual release was that you still needed a stereo for playback. Afterward, after thinking about it for a few years, I came to want to bypass the turntable altogether. I wanted to do a release that didn't need a stereo at all." He tells me he was also saddened by collectors who told him they could not bring themselves to scratch up the grooves on that silent EP.

In 1990, he self-released *Oxygen Is Flammable*:

> "A broken piece of plastic packaged in a small box. Enclosed are instructions which state that the broken plastic is a record. And that it's played by pouring water over it. The instructions also call attention to possible similarities between the sounds of water falling and fire rising. With the record as action, not object, the listener becomes the performer."

The following year saw the release of *Shear*, also put out by Jupitter-Larsen himself: "Ball of cotton batting packaged in a small box. Rapped [sic] around the contents are instructions on three thin strips of paper. Instructions which inform the holder that the cotton batting is a recording. And that this record is played by being squeezed. The sound this record gives being a 'sharp fluffy slightness' and a 'thin fluffy pressed.' Again, the record as action."

These releases did away with the records altogether, moving into the paradigm of "actions" performed by owners of the releases. "A big part of my motivation was economic," he

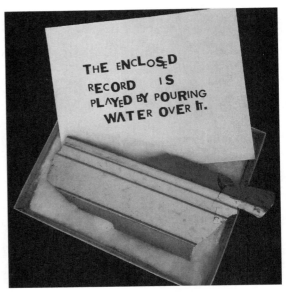

**The Haters' *Oxygen Is Flammable*.
Image courtesy of GX Jupitter-Larsen.**

explains. "There was a point in my life when I wanted to do releases but didn't have the resources to record audio or press vinyl. I didn't see why my poverty should stop me from doing whatever I wanted. So I redefined what a record could be. I wanted to redefine the concept of technology. At least for myself. Having the 'record' be a performance prop that people interacted with did just that."

He has been pleased with how people have embraced his peculiar Haters releases. "I'm very happy with the reactions I get from all the others. People seem to really get into the performance aspect of *Wind Licked Dirt*, *Oxygen is Flammable*, and *Shear*."

Given that his conceptual releases carry connections to the worlds of conceptual and performance art, I asked him about the conflict between his releases as artifacts of the underground music scene versus works of art related to the world of fine art. "The noise scene has always had this tension," he reflects. "About half involved see noise as a real part of the realm of art, while the other half see it as something completely outside such traditions or institutions. Some people take it super seriously, while some treat it as a casual excuse to hang out with friends. For me, it's all these things all the time."

He points me toward some recent conceptual/anti-releases that have piqued his interest. A record label called Mansfield Deathtrap Recordings spontaneously sent him a copy of their *Bronze Cassette*. "An actual solid bronze cassette done as a limited edition of twenty-seven," he told me. "You play it by dropping it on the floor." He also mentioned the visually stunning anti-records produced by Frau Unbekannt for the Psych.KG label, which has included them as add-ons to other releases, including a recent album by noise artist K2. Both examples, like Jupitter-Larsen's oeuvre, toggle between identities, being both objects from the world of underground music and works of conceptual art.

VI.3.4 Major Ego Produkt Objekts & Aktions

Founded in 1996, Major Ego Produkt was an unusual record label run by the mysterious Major Ego A777, a member of an extended network of experimental musicians and conceptual artists called Origami Republika. This collective was formed in 1990 and persists today, encapsulating countless music releases, manifestos, and live performances. Much like GX Jupitter-Larsen, their modus operandi is to simultaneously inhabit the worlds of underground music and the fine arts scene, often poking fun at both. Their work has been the subject of art galleries and respectable music outlets, but they have just as frequently undermined this from within by staging deliberate, Dada-inspired actions.

Major Ego Produkt's head honcho, Major Ego A777, has never emerged publicly, though he was said to be a man named Per Oscar Jørgensen. Looking for more information, I reached out to the folks behind the Origami Republika website. I was eventually patched through to Tore Honoré Bøe, who lives in a sparsely populated area in Norway a couple hours from Oslo. He explains that the idea for the Origami Republika emerged during his time running a small gallery in the back of a now-defunct record shop in Oslo called Debut. That shop was responsible for distributing experimental music and early Japanese noise to Norwegians via mail order, and it eventually became the base through which Bøe collaborated with various artists and assembled the Origami network.

Bøe reveals to me that the character known as Major Ego A777 was, in fact, nobody—just a fictional figurehead operated by Bøe and Lasse Marhaug. At the time, they had architected an online narrative that Major Ego had created his own subgroup called Origami Replika, which had split off from the rest of the Origami Republika crew. These "Replikants" were supposedly opposed to the overly serious experimental music produced by the mainstream Origami crew. Bøe and Marhaug staged fictional battles on early noise music message boards between the Republika and the subversive Replika agents, both Major Ego and his friend, Judge Replika. As Bøe explains, "Every time Origami did something serious, Judge Replika and Major Ego would slander it. 'Oh, come on, you serious artists.'"

Major Ego was the operator of the Major Ego Produkt label, which amassed a short discography of conventional CD, vinyl, and tape releases. The first release, put out in 1997, was a CD called *Ka/Skader* that compiled several Origami Replika recordings. But one of the most compelling aspects of Major Ego Produkt was an oblique separate discography of "Objekts & Aktions," described as a series of

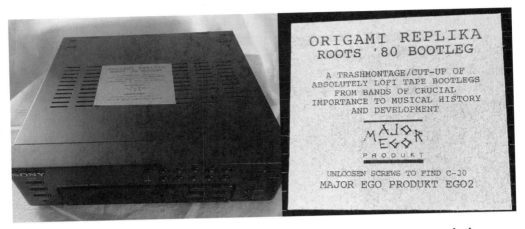

**Origami Replika's *Roots '80 Bootleg,* a cassette locked within a tape deck.
Image courtesy of Geir Yven.**

"ultralimited edition trashart objects, playable and unplayable," released in editions ranging from one to fifty copies.

The debut Objekt and/or Aktion was somewhat playable. It was a nineteen-copy edition in which an old 7-inch single by sound artist Lasse Marhaug, recorded under the name of serial killer Herb Mullin, was mounted onto a broken and painted LP. Bøe explained to me that the release was playable, although the base LPs, picked up from thrift stores, were so scratched that they would just skip meaninglessly. When the needle was placed on the LP right where the single was glued on, there was a satisfying locked groove which was unique to each copy.

The second release was a tape. Origami Replika's *Roots '80 Bootleg* came inside a fully functional tape deck that was screwed shut, requiring you to loosen the screws and pull it apart just to retrieve the tape itself. The audio is advertised as "a Replika rewreckording of lousy tape bootlegs" by several classic industrial bands. Two copies were made. Bøe explained to me that the tape decks were fully functional and came from a radio station where his ex-wife worked; he painstakingly took them apart, then cached the tape itself into a dead space inside the apparatus. It was grueling work for the owner to disassemble and then reassemble the whole thing just to listen to the cassette. When he, years later, told a member of Einstürzende Neubauten that they could sue him for bootlegging one of their concerts, they apparently gave their post-hoc approval with a laugh.

Dessert=Loops was a limited-to-ten tape suspended in a sealed jar of apple jelly, which Bøe explained was essentially unplayable, though he believes Lasse Marhaug dubbed actual noise music on it, only to include the master recording in one of the jars. Some of these were distributed to friends, though "the last few copies were thrown into the port of Trondheim, breaking through the ice," apparently captured in a short documentary about Origami done by some Trondheim film students. Bøe told me that a collector named Geir, who dutifully collected many of the Origami Replika releases, told him he still has a copy of *Dessert=Loops* in his refrigerator. The jelly has apparently

Origami Replika's **Dessert=Loops**, tape suspended inside a jar of apple jelly. Image courtesy of Geir Yven, who has preserved these preserves in his collection for over 20 years.

"turned into mushy water," but the release remains unopened and unplayed.

Origami Replika's *Ka/blod + Barad Dür* was a tape in a box filled with broken glass, and the potential for small fragments of glass within the tape makes it a dangerous proposition for one's tape deck. Bøe says this hazardous release included recordings of two uncharacteristically violent concerts staged by himself and Lasse Marhaug as Origami Replika. They typically liked to play what they called "happy noise," intended as a rebuke to the macabre antics of most noise producers of the era, but these shows, one an homage to Tolkien, and another staged right after Bøe was released from a jail stint for opposing military service, were angry and "cathartic." The broken glass, which came from one of the performances itself, was intended to reflect this.

Over half of the Objekts & Aktions discography is patently unplayable—for example, a box full of glass shards and broken vinyl records—and many do not even contain sound at all. One was just a chunk of hash and tobacco in a Ziploc bag, limited to ten copies, and "not available abroad due to customs regulations." My personal favorite is a release fittingly called *Food for Thought* and attributed to Origami Paprika. Advertised as "a statement that will make you laugh or freak out," it is a plastic box containing a rotten red pepper on pilaf. Bøe tells me that this release, "a statement on fine art," was distributed to attendees of a concert in Oslo. The pepper, which was "already rotten when it was published," came in a box with a nicely printed label, representing the conflict between exalted gallery art and underground "trash" art.

Bøe himself is ambivalent about record collecting. One release, *Vinyl=Matter=Enslavement*, was an "absolute trash object" in which an LP and CD were glued to cardboard, then spray-painted to remove any trace of playable grooves. "It was a statement about how, when an artist produces something, people buy it for a normal price, then they will resell it two years later with a much greater value. None of that money goes back to the artists in the first place. The collector thing is very capitalistic, in that the value does not go back to the producer. [It's driven by] the collector's addiction. A lot of people who don't have that money spend their money on second editions with slightly different serial numbers."

As Bøe explains, the entire Origami Republika movement makes use of ideas from the Dada and anti-art movements. He also mentions the auto-destructive art of Gustav Metzger, who would use acid and fire to stage destructions of his artwork in reference to the chaos of war. Much as Duchamp poked fun at the institution of fine arts, the Origami Republika network and the absurd Major Ego Produkt Objekts & Aktions took aim at the fine arts establishment. But as Bøe points out, there is also a logical trap in play. "On one side, you have the trash and the antiestablishment thing, but then this becomes part of the history of fine arts as well."

VI.3.5 One-Off Anti-Records in the Nineties

The year 1990 saw the release of a Finnish 7-inch single with no grooves. Hiljaiset Levyt is a Tampere-based record label specializing in independent indie rock and punk, run since 1986 by Jukka Junttila. For Christmas 1990, they put out *Totaalisen Hiljainen Levy*, translating to "Total Silent Record." Available images show an illustrated cover with several iterations of the label's trademark cartoon bear and a shiny black record devoid of grooves.

Junttila says that the idea was to put out a novelty release for the holiday season. "First there was an idea about doing a Christmas single with some of our bands, but because I don't like Christmas records, that sounded too stupid," he explains. "Then somehow, the idea converted to a silent record."

At first he considered putting out a record with silent grooves. "Then I thought that, because this is only, in a way, a Christmas card, why not have a really blank record with nothing on it? I phoned the pressing plant which I used at that time, Finnvox. They really liked my idea and wanted to be part of it by giving me a really low price, so it was a go. I asked a friend of mine to do the cover art and I made the labels."

Five hundred copies were made in total. He sent just under one hundred to the press, then hand-delivered them to media companies, studios, and record shops. He also included copies in packages that went out via the small Hiljaiset Levyt mail order from mid-November to mid-December. There were fifty copies left, so he gave these away to people who attended a show he was at, just a few days before Christmas.

There is an interesting technical footnote to this release. "Much, much later, I heard from one guy who had worked in Finnvox that my record caused a little bit of a headache for them," he says. "They had one mirror matrix (blank matrix) because every now and then, they would create a one-sided record. But they didn't have two mirror matrices, which they needed to make my record. They made another mirror matrix with their own expenses and never even told me that my record was a loss for them. They were such nice guys."

Today, Junttila reflects fondly on *Totaalisen Hiljainen Levy*. "I did receive some letters where people told me how wonderful the idea of the Silent Record was. And still every now and then somebody remembers it. So it was a good thing to do, I think."

The year 1991 saw the release of another intriguing blank record, the generically titled *Record1* by Telium Group released on the Magnatone label. Telium Group was a collaboration between Collin J. Rae and Damion Romero. Rae and Romero were both in an L.A. noise-rock band called Slug, and they ran Magnatone, releasing singles by bands like Unsane, Nels Cline Trio, and that dog.

Rae, who now works in the classical music industry and is a part-time foot fetish photographer,[38] told me that the record came about as Rae and Romero were involved in the late-eighties/early-nineties network of cassette labels. They released tapes via Romero's seminal label P-Tapes, and were also seeing their music come out on international labels. Surrounded by noise, they got the idea to create an "anti-sound" record, something that was more art object than music object. *Record1* came out in a limited edition, each copy hand-assembled at a local Kinko's, then distributed through noise distros like Anomalous Records. "We were trying to go beyond the music that Slug was doing and the noise that we were doing, and just looking at records in a different way," he tells me. "It was a response, being really anti-noise to the noise that we were making individually. What would be the opposite kind of project that we could do that would still maintain the same sort of pure integrity? We were not trained like classical musicians; we were self-trained punk rock and noise guys. We drew intellectual inspiration from things that sparked us artistically and not so much formally."

Getting the record pressed was really no different than putting out any other record. "There was a local pressing plant in L.A. that everybody used. We had a meeting with the plant manager one day and asked if they could make us a plate that has no grooves, then press the records with that. It's not something they could just do automatically—they did have to create a plate for it like they do for any record. But they said, 'Yeah, we could do that.'"

The record is interesting because of how little information it carries. Not just sonically. In addition to there being no audio data ("No grooves. You'd put it on the table and [the stylus] would just skate"), there were also no details about who the Telium Group were. This was part of the aesthetic; Rae says he wanted Telium Group to be "an abstract concept unto itself." The liner notes themselves included a disclaimer that the record was "the first in a series of phonographic endeavors conceived and funded by Telium Group. Telium Group operates as an exponent of nothing and/or no one," offering a sort of quasi-industrial facelessness that Rae says was part of the intent.

Record1 is a wonderfully executed anti-record, and the attention to detail in the final product is obvious. Rae recalls that he and Romero agonized over the Telium Group logo, wanting something appropriately slick and anonymous. They eventually settled on a lowercase letter 't.' Rae remembers this being a letter typed on a typewriter, blown up in size at Kinko's and surrounded by a circle. It comprises the entirety of the record's front cover and manages to be both intriguing and oddly generic. "We wanted to be pretty anonymous. And the Telium Group was just an entity that no one knew what names they were."

Rae also tells me that Telium Group did a limited-to-twenty-five-copy "LP" that was actually a Laserdisc, meaning it would just produce a "weird screeching noise" when played on a turntable. He no longer owns a copy, and he has never seen one

---

38 He published a book named *Carnival of Soles*.

surface since. He also put out a recording of the sound of destroyed records being played on a turntable with unusual speed settings under the name FAB.44—"a symphony of scratch noise," as he describes it.

In 1997, another unplayable record came out, this one from the field of electronic dance music. Sabotage Recordings was an electronic music label run by Robert Jelinek. Besides accumulating a significant catalog of dance music of various stripes, Sabotage also acted as a form of conceptual collective known for insidious pranks. Once, Jelinek and company concealed microphones in a private members

Matt Winch's grooveless *Will Not Be Playing Tonight* record. Image courtesy of Robert Jelinek of Sabotage Recordings.

club and broadcast the conversations on speakers outside the building. On another occasion, they swapped out the guided-tour audio for an exhibition at a local art museum with audio about various art heists. They also replaced the telephone books in phone booths from Linz, Germany, with ones from Linz, Austria.

But the unplayable record, credited to someone named Matt Winch and titled *Matt Winch Will Not Be Playing Tonight. He is Ill*, was a 12" vinyl disc with no grooves. It came out on a Sabotage sub-label called Craft Records. Jelinek emphasizes that the goal for this record and other Sabotage records was not to create an art record.

"No matter how far you changed technical standards or referred to Stockhausen, Cage, Dada & Co, the focus for me was the expansion of musical habits and not the artistic historization in the White Cube. There was no need and no compulsion to put my artistic ideas back into the art context, because the course of the story did it by itself." Because he did not want to become known as an "art label," these types of concept releases were only done sporadically.

"The record was released at a time when commercialization had begun and the musical hunger for new things was constantly being satisfied," Jelinek explains. "It was intended as a rejection of the continued growth. Not as a standstill, but as a haven of tranquility and an interruption to the tendencies of the time. To illustrate silence, there are no grooves on the record."

He explains that, at that time, record labels would play parts of their records over the phone to record store managers, who would then choose which records to stock. "In the case of Matt Winch, the silence gave rise to a hot discussion about how to sort such a record between club culture and experimental music on the shelf. The dealers were unprepared and skeptical. So we first pressed 150 pieces in the Czech Republic to see what the reactions were. The record was out of stock after two weeks, and our American sales partner, We Never Sleep, wanted more. So we pressed 500 pieces."

Jelinek recalls that he had booking requests for the mysterious Matt Winch, which was actually a pseudonym for Jelinek himself. But Jelinek had borrowed the name from a Chicagoan with whom he had couch-surfed for three months in 1992. "When I had the idea [for the blank record] years later, I remembered Matt because he hated any kind of electronic music. So I took over his name without asking him. Twelve years later, we met again in Paris and I gave him a package with all the releases under his name. I will not forget his facial expression."

If you recall, the goal behind the Winch record was to offer a pause from the relentless commercialization of the electronic music industry. There is an interesting footnote to this story. "The public radio stations are obliged to document every minute on the radio and to report the playlist to the respective state society for author and reproduction rights," Jelinek details. "In Austria and France, some radio presenters decided to indicate the missing seconds and minutes where silence could be heard on the radio, whether by chance, infirmity or error, with Matt Winch's track 'Aquaplaning' in the playlist. This was practiced for a long time and led to a gratifying final invoice [in royalties]. In this sense, Matt Winch was one of the most played Sabotage artists on the radio, even though you couldn't hear anything."

VI.3.6 Anti-Recordings in Other Formats

Just as *Wind Licked Dirt* worked just as well as a tape or CD, many artists have updated the anti-record for more contemporary music formats. Italian noise act Atrax Morgue put out an anti-cassette titled *0000000000000000* in 1995, which was a smashed-up tape nestled in a bed of burnt cotton. In 2009, Gen Ken Montgomery, recording under his moniker Egnekn, put out an empty CD case with the title *Lifeless Guitar Feedback With Themes Of Death, Pornography, Nazism, Etc. Used To Hide Lack Of Ideas*.[39] An outrageously prolific lo-fi acid/techno producer named Sascha Müller, meanwhile, put out a limited-to-four-copy anti-release in 2017, which featured twenty-five original tracks on a hard drive so mangled that any data was irretrievable.[40]

And then there is Kenny Johansson, who runs the imprint Silent Tapes as a sub-label of his Obskyr Records project. Obskyr was the label that did the deluxe reissue of the New Blockaders' 1985 silent cassette *Epater Les Bourgois*, discussed in chapter 6.1, so he was no stranger to antithetical approaches to music. Silent Tapes, which was founded to commemorate the 6th Annual Cassette Store Day, was devoted to anti-recordings. The label's tagline? "Pure Nothingness."

I asked Johansson what interested him in the concept of anti-recordings. "Hmm... tell you this, I would not call it an interest. More like a calling, if you know what I mean? I think that music is boring and bland. There is nothing that speaks to me, and therefore I decided

---

39 There is a funny story behind this one. Around 1994, Montgomery saw an ad in a fanzine requesting submissions for a noise compilation, which specified that they did NOT want "Lifeless guitar feedback with themes of death, pornography, nazism, etc., used to hide lack of ideas." So he recorded a CD-R's worth of music and named it that, then sent it to the label. It was never released. Years later, he decided to reissue the CD-R. He couldn't find it, so he just issued it as an empty CD case, limited to ten copies. Ken Montgomery, "Egnekn: Lifeless Guitar Feedback With Themes Of Death, Pornography, Nazism, Etc. Used To Hide Lack Of Ideas," Generator Sound Art <www.generatorsoundart.org/GL-10.html> [accessed March 19, 2022]

40 "Draft of Sascha Müller – Anti-Data (2017, Anti-Data, All Media)," Discogs <www.discogs.com/release/10499702-Sascha-Müller-Anti-Data> [accessed March 19, 2022]

to reject it. Noise is music but not the music that plays on the radio, mainstream crap, and when you try to make noise more noisier, you get HNW. But if you take it even further, you get silence... and there is my concept, if you cannot make the noise more noisier, do it silent.

"The first anti-record I got was the New Blockaders' *Untitled* anti-LP that came as a bonus with (their debut noise album) *Changez Les Blockeurs*. I loved it from the start, and since then, I was hooked. Today, Richard Rupenus [one half of the New Blockaders] is a close friend and collaborator of mine, and our view of anti-recordings are most similar, we think alike and we create from that."

The idea for Silent Tapes came about in the wake of Johansson's obsession with the possibilities of anti-music. He was producing collages using empty record sleeves as his medium when his friend and bandmate Tony Eriksson proposed releasing tape-deck cleaning cassettes as an album. The idea was to release the tape as *Kopfreinigung Schläger*, credited to their two-man noise act, The New Movement. "I was thrilled, and I approached several labels, and none of them was interested," he recalled. "I then decided that I will start a new label only releasing silent tapes. So it was out of dejection I started the label."

Excited by the project, he told his friend William Rage, who records HNW under the pseudonym Nervous Corps. Nervous Corps' *Nothing's Gonna Change* ended up being the first release on Silent Tapes, and Johansson sees it as the logical extreme of Rage's noise walls—it was a C0 cassette, meaning that there was no actual magnetic tape on it, only a brief bit of the blank plastic leader tape that comes at the start and end of normal tapes.

The New Movement's *Kopfreinigung Schläger* tape, which was Silent Tapes number two, was a response to a controversial one-off release that Johansson and Eriksson had sent out as promo copies. That tape had music on it, but it also contained an evil payload: the tape cartridge was filled with caustic soda and a small ampoule of water. It was rigged up such that, when the tape played, the ampoule broke, and the caustic liquid melted both the magnetic tape and the owner's cassette player. "Tell you this," Johansson told me. "Some who received the destroy-your-deck tape were very angry, and some found it extremely funny."

Around the same time, Silent Tapes' third release came out in the form of the New Blockaders' *Silence(d)*, a truly unplayable work. It featured the deconstructed remnants of a cassette in a Ziploc bag; the magnetic tape itself had been pulled out of the tape, wrapped together in a ball, and surrounded by an orb of rusty barbed wire.

Subsequent releases have approached anti-tapes from a variety of different angles. Anla Courtis' *Tapped Tape* is a cassette wherein the tape has been replaced with sticky tape, which Johansson swears can be played. *A Missed Rendezvous* by Last Rape, the duo of noise icon Richard Ramirez and Sean Matzus, was a recording of a silent tape dubbed at maximum volume. "I was very skeptical to release it at first, but after listening to it several times, I understood what Ramirez and Matzus were up to—and it was to amplify silence and make a wall of silence. And it really works."

Another tape, *Ronees Dreams* by Bookwar, was a dub of an old blank tape found in a defunct Soviet warehouse, manufactured sometime around the time of the USSR's collapse. The Missing Signal's *Banished the Abolished* were old HNW tapes that had been melted to the point of unplayability, then painted. And Johansson's magnum opus, which ended Silent Tapes' run of ten releases, was his limited-to-one edition of *Music Is Pointless*, released as Obskyr. It was a boxed set of ten tapes, all blank. "This was actually a kind of angry thing I did," Johansson told me. "I was so disappointed by having not sold anything in a while, and I saw every release I made as a failure and was very down and under because I lost so much money on pressing LPs. So I decided to make a ten-cassette box and sell it to the highest bidder. It sold but not for very much to a collector who usually buys from me."

Anti-releases have also adapted to the digital age. The 2013 album *Vuoto* by Menthe de Menthe is an unplayable CD. In fact, it is the transparent plastic circle of a CD without any content on it. Menthe de Menthe, whose real name is Riccardo, provides some context on this unusual piece. He explains that, around the time *Vuoto* came out, he used to call himself Sonia Serventi, and that Menthe de Menthe was intended to represent his "woman side." Another alter ego, Bonifacio Serventi, is a male counterpart that he created for another project, named Beheat Gorum de Mentheurd.

Riccardo says that *Vuoto* was intended to conjure a psychological experience. "'Vuoto' means 'empty' in Italian, and it clearly refers to a personal condition of that time," Riccardo tells me. "Something that is terribly common but always somewhat devastating. Actually, 'vuoto' can be felt between persons, or in particular spaces, in every day's life. Since I suffer from major depression and have had an obligatory psychiatric treatment in the past, I think it could describe the 'emptiness' when you're near the threshold."

Riccardo tells me the clear CDs were, in fact, the dividers used as protective bumpers on CD spindles; his pressing plant gave them to him for free. He released ten copies of the disc, intended as a diversion or "funny release" that he distributed for free to his friends and collaborators, juxtaposed against the loud HNW he was recording at the time. "I think one of the most important parts of *Vuoto* was the cover. Gray and urban. Something we experience every day. It's symmetrical, in order to keep a sense of perfection, linked to emptiness to me."

There was also a digital version, produced using Adobe Audition. He told me he set the track to 0 dB within the program, and though the recording is totally silent, it contains bias that moves the stereo's woofers in order to create silence.

Despite the release's novelty, Riccardo says it is one of the most downloaded albums on his Bandcamp page. And yet it has not been as well received by moderators on Discogs, where *Vuoto* was de-listed. Riccardo resents this, pointing out that "silence, in its purest form, was (and still is) one of the most important things in music—just think of 4'33"." Riccardo, who graduated from La Scala's prestigious Academy for the Performing Arts in Milan, believes that anti-music is a part of music itself. For Riccardo, *Vuoto* is also intended as a stand "against the ignorance of the intellectuals and trained or graduated people, academics et cetera," including former La Scala colleagues who discredit pioneering minimalists like Erik Satie and John Cage.

EXTREME MUSIC

VI.3.7 Contemporary Anti-Recordings:
NONE Records, Michael Ridge, and Auris Apothecary

One of the more contemporary faces of anti-records is NONE Records, the brainchild of Douglas Lucas. Lucas is a multimedia artist who currently lives in "an undisclosed location." He recalls discovering unusual records and eventually wanting to release some of them himself. "The first unorthodox record that I ever came across was *Pagan Muzak* by NON, and I bought a first pressing of it after one of my pieces sold in an art exhibition." *Pagan Muzak* is a now-classic record that contains several locked grooves and an extra hole, allowing the owner their choice to rotate the record around its center hole or around a different axis. "I began researching the history of unconventional records and found out about anti-records," Lucas tells me.

"In 2012, I was living in Louisville, Kentucky, and was curating a lot of experimental music shows, including an annual five-day fest called Louisville Experimental Festival, which presented artists from all over the U.S. Some of these artists made very unique handmade packaging to house their recordings on cassette, vinyl, et cetera. That year, I booked a group called Solace Media Corporation (from Cincinnati, Ohio) and they had an anti-45 for sale. The original vinyl was scratched beyond recognition, and the original artwork had been made into a photomontage by the artist. I knew about anti-records, but that was the first one I saw in the flesh. I got it and used it myself during my own experimental turntable performances, thus damaging it more. After that, I started collecting the wonderful anti-releases put out by RRRecords, Auris Apothecary, et cetera. I wanted to encourage more of these kinds of releases, so I thought the best way to do that would be to start a label dedicated to anti-releases exclusively.

"I liked the conundrum of anti-records," he reflects. "They don't fit neatly into any specific category within music or art... I wanted more anti-records to exist, so I decided to produce an exclusive entity for them. I also thought it would be interesting to see the different ways that different artists would respond to a label only for anti-albums. Some approached it from more of a physical perspective, while others from more of a conceptual standpoint."

Interestingly, the first NONE Records release was not a musical object at all. It was a blank book, much like *The Nothing Book*—although Lucas was unfamiliar with that precedent. "The idea for the book by Yoko Molotov and myself came from a conversation we had when she was a guest on an experimental radio program that I used to host," he says. "We were chatting about Fluxus art aesthetics, and somehow the idea came up that we should do a completely blank book with numbered pages and perfect binding (incidentally, the book later entered the collection of the FluxMuseum in Santa Fe, New Mexico). A director of a museum that I sent the book to once asked me what the book is about. I said if you read it, you'll know."

After about a year, Lucas moved to Brooklyn, where he continued to issue his unique anti-records. Thaniel Ion Lee's *Painted* singles were old 45s that were painted by Lee on one side. "The release could be seen as a 'split album' between Thaniel and each original band," Lucas explains. *Wax on Wax* by Jill Lucas was another mutated design.

**Damages' *Underground Music* cassette, after it was exhumed.
Image courtesy of Douglas Lucas.**

"The release is a great example of appropriation," (Douglas) Lucas explains. "I gave her a selection of various LPs, and she used melted crayons and paint to make abstract designs on both sides, totally covering the vinyl and label. She also altered the jacket for each record and usually cut holes in them, so that parts of the record inside could be seen and thus became part of the cover visually. The records can be enjoyed as visual art pieces or as 'playable' records—it is left to the owner's discretion."

Crank Sturgeon put out a tape with a big hole in it, inscrutably named *Dubious Elixir for Dire Retention*. "Crank hand-drilled a hole on one side of each tape, which damaged the related spool, and each cassette came with instructions for playback in this shape. So fun. The cassettes were packaged wrapped in a woodcut print (motif with a hand unspooling a tape) on a page of an Ayn Rand novel."

Lucas' own project, Damages, put out a series of four releases, each limited to an edition of one, meant to represent the four elements. The first one, meant to represent fire, was an LP that was heavily scratched up, then left in direct sunlight for one year, becoming warped to the point of unplayability. The others were a cassette buried in the woods for a full year (representing earth), a tape frozen in a block of ice for a year (water), and a CD hung outside Lucas' apartment window for a year, "exposed to open air" (air).

Lucas' NONE project was even able to involve GX Jupitter-Larsen, reprising his *Shear* release (as the Haters) from 1991. (If you recall, that 'anti-record' was a cotton ball in a box, the owner intended to rub it to produce noise.) *Shear 2014* was a piece of paper with an illustration of a clock face. Text on the back directed its owner to "watch this clock by squeezing it. The time it tells is either a sharp slightness or a thin fluffy pressed."

NONE was a highly specialized label, and its releases were mainly distributed via the label's website, though RRRecords and a NYC shop called Printed Matter did stock some releases. Lucas says that word of his label spread via word of mouth in experimental music circles. "Looking back, I'm surprised by the amount of positive response nationally and internationally there was to the releases, as well as the label itself. I feel that NONE helped to regenerate interest in anti-releases in the 21st century and added great new ones to the genre. Some people who got in touch with me about the label, et cetera, became great friends. It was a lot of fun.

"To my knowledge, there has never been another label dedicated to releasing only anti-records," he says. "NONE was a label of which there were 'none' of, so that's what I decided to call the world's first anti-label."

Like all anti-records, NONE releases have sparked serious debate about whether they count as music. "Almost all of the NONE releases have been deleted from Discogs because some people thought that they can't even be classified as music and voted to have them removed from the site's inventory," Lucas explains. "They started a thread on the site to debate the authenticity of the releases being considered music, which was hilarious as well as interesting."

Then there is Michael Ridge, responsible for the two damaged flexi-discs discussed in the previous chapter. Ridge records music under his own name and under the moniker Zebra Mu, and also runs the record label Quagga Curious Sounds. Many of his releases are conceptual in nature, including a series of anti-records. "Over the years, my anti-record/tape productions usually fit into one of several categories," he explains. "Noise-making instruments, physically altered/modified preexisting records, ephemeral objects with a limited lifespan/plays and unplayable/conceptual art objects."

Copies of his 2014 release *Hole Punched* were just hole-punched circles taken out of flexi-records. At a quarter-inch in diameter, they weren't playable in a simple sense, but they came with instructions telling listeners to glue their piece to a 7" card for playback. "Out of the twenty copies made, one person to my knowledge followed this through," he tells me.

A couple of other releases are interesting because they specify the conditions under which they are intended to be consumed, much like the Haters' infamous *Wind Licked Dirt* LP, the blank LP that is meant to be "played" by rubbing dirt on its surface. Ridge's *Shred of Humanity/Stayin' Alive* was a shred of vinyl gouged out from a copy of a "Stayin' Alive" 45 by the Bee Gees. "Instructions inform listeners to utilize the magnifying glass included to observe their tiny shred of vinyl record whilst humming 'Stayin' Alive,'" Ridge explains. "The original artist and what the record was is conceptually integral to this project; the process of production is perhaps secondary to the music contained on the sliver of vinyl record."

Similarly, his *Cheese Grater Music* was a "small clump of yellow vinyl shavings sourced from attacking a 7-inch yellow vinyl single with a cheese grater. The original

Michael Ridge's *Strawberry Lace* cassette.
The tape has been replaced by strawberry lace.
Image courtesy of Michael Ridge.

vinyl record it was sourced from is not mentioned or is important, rather the color and texture of the vinyl shavings being paramount, which of course resembles grated cheese. Listeners were instructed to simply sprinkle the shavings on their favorite pizza, something I hope no one actually did."

Then there was a 2012 anti-cassette that Ridge produced, toying with the medium itself. "*Strawberry Lace* is one of three anti-cassette projects where the original magnetic tape was removed, then replaced with an alternative material with an exact length of one minute—as if it was still magnetic tape. Strawberry lace sweets were selected for being approximately the same width as magnetic tape, and therefore, with some effort, they could be mounted into a cassette shell. It was also at the time about the most bizarre object I could think of putting into a cassette; very much inspired by Dada artist Marcel Duchamp and the ready-made. A wholly conceptual anti-record, it functions instead as a visual representation of a predetermined amount of time, with the viewer left to perhaps envisage what sound it could potentially produce if played."

Philosophically, Ridge's perspective is akin to Caleb Kelly's notion of "cracked media" and Milan Knížák's concept of creating new art by repurposing the formats of musical reproduction. "The record and cassette tape are mediums utilized for music and sound reproduction," Ridge reflected. "The anti-record/tape in my opinion queries this notion, presenting a myriad of alternative means to interact and consume an artist's work."

Auris Apothecary, the record label responsible for the glue record and 17-inch disc discussed earlier in this book, is another major player in the story of unplayable

Unholy Triforce's *Sandin' Yr Vagina,* with cassettes filled with variably colored sand. Image courtesy of Auris Apothecary.

records, though they might dispute this. Based in Bloomington, a small city centered around Indiana University, Auris Apothecary has been the subject of many feature articles because of their outlandish releases. Originally a collaboration between three musicians named Dante Augustus Scarlatti, Pendra Gon, and Ancient Pine, it is now the sole purview of Scarlatti, who runs the label out of a room in his house.

According to an article by Kevin Warwick for Bandcamp,[41] the label started in 2008 as something akin to concept art: a label putting out music you couldn't hear, because all releases were sold out before you could buy them. A series of relatively straightforward releases followed, each assigned a high rating on the label's "accessibility scale," a metric that refers both to the abstractness of the music and the level of difficulty required to play it. The first release to wade into anti-release territory was Unholy Triforce's charming *Sandin' Yr Vagina.* Sonically, it was a relatively standard-issue noise tape. But would-be listeners had to contend with the fact that the cassette shell was filled with sand. In interviews, Scarlatti marvels at the efforts of those willing to damage their cassette player to play the release. "Even if you clean the cassette out, there will always be these minute grains scratching across the tape head," he notes. He refers to this interactive process (of abrading your tape deck) as "generative," echoing the idea behind Caleb Kelly's "cracked music": the process of creating something new and self-referential through destruction.

"I prefer not to talk about myself," Scarlatti tells me, but he was generously willing to talk about his work, including the significance of producing unambiguously physical media in an increasingly digital world. "When we started over ten years ago, physical media was already well on the decline. While vinyl has steadily increased its dominance over the past decade, streaming has pretty much become the de facto standard way of listening to music for most people. As individuals who enjoy listening to music, it's hard to deny the convenience and ultimate mobility of digital mediums. But as a label, a large part of why we started was to pay homage to the plethora of formats that led us to the present, so we'll continue to publish physical media while still embracing the modern convenience digital distribution allows."

He tells me that *Sandin' Yr Vagina* was a pain to assemble but remains one of his favorite Auris Apothecary records. "It's simple but destructive to the musical content, the

41 Kevin Warwick, "The Auris Apothecary Label Has the 'Very Real Desire to Destroy Everything,'" Bandcamp Daily, March 14, 2017, <daily.bandcamp.com/label-profile/auris-apothecary-feature>

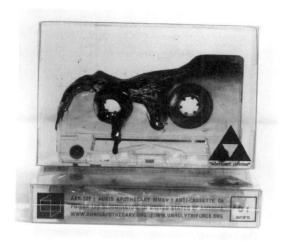

Unholy Triforce's *Siberiliszt Inferno* melted cassette. Image courtesy of Auris Apothecary.

tape player, the listener's personal space, et cetera. The audio content on each side of the tape are polar opposites—nearly silent musique concrète versus unrelenting wall of harsh noise. It requires no deeper meaning in its quest to offend and annoy."

Whereas Auris Apothecary started off as a label whose music "you couldn't actually purchase or hear," this was unsustainably impractical, so they shifted toward quasi-anti-records like *Sandin'*. "Whether or not most listeners are actually going through the steps required or care at all . . . who knows? But technically none of our releases are 'unplayable'—every anti-release is playable with enough work. We methodically design them to be salvageable, despite how they may appear. I think that's something that we view differently from anti-releases of the past—their intention seemed to be focused on destroying the format/object to prevent listening, while our goal is creating an experience that rewards the listener with the audio."

Indeed, this aesthetic of being *challenging to play*, not unplayable, is reflected in several Auris Apothecary releases. An anti-cassette by Mike IX Williams, for example, is completely coated in intricate shards of broken glass—meaning it will damage your hands *and* your cassette player! *Cru|cifict|ion* is a lathe-cut record that has several nails driven through it, which serve the dual purpose of "crucifying" the record and blocking the path of your turntable stylus. And *Some Assembly Required* is a cassette tape that has been taken apart into its components; it is accompanied by instructions on how to put it together.

Then there is the *Siberiliszt Inferno* tape, a cassette that has been partially melted with fire, advertised as being "covered in soot and reeking of burned synthetic chemicals." Scarlatti explains that this release, like others, is technically playable, and that the physical concept is designed to pair with the music. "The name is a reference to Liszt and his piece 'Dante Symphony—Part I, The Inferno,' which is used as a sample, as well as recordings from the alleged 'Siberian Hellhole' urban myth. A company claimed to have drilled so deep, they could hear the sounds of souls screaming out from Hell. Total bullshit, but a fun story nonetheless." Each copy was painstakingly made by holding the cassettes over a candle, tolerating the noxious smoke that resulted.

On the Auris Apothecary website, there is further discussion of the philosophy behind the label's aesthetic. All his releases are subject to two rules. For one, even the most challenging anti-records must be designed with attention to both the audio and visual components. Secondly, all records must technically be playable if enough effort is put into them. "Our anti-releases are some of our most popular, and people legitimately seem to enjoy them, in spite of their purposefully unappealing nature. We've also tried to keep our releases relatively cheap over the years, despite the inordinate amount of labor that goes into crafting them, so admittedly it's only a small gamble for someone if they buy it and think it's pointless, which I'm sure has happened."

VI.3.8 Anti-Recordings: Tying It All Together

The distinctions between silent, damaged, and unplayable records are porous. Although some early silent records emerged from outside the worlds of fine arts and experimental music, most anti-recordings share a continuum with Dada and anti-art. With that said, different artists and producers cite unique motivations for their anti-releases, from analogies to mental illness to comparisons to harsh noise wall to anti-commercial sentiments. It is this conceptual diversity that makes this obscure area so intriguing. Yet, despite the unique ideas underlying them, anti-records rarely occur in a vacuum, and artists tend to acknowledge the influence of similar recordings, frequently naming John Cage, RRRecords, and the Haters' FX Jupitter-Larsen as cornerstones.

As music becomes increasingly digital and as postage becomes more expensive, new waves of artists continue to experiment with anti-records. Music can be disseminated freely online, but anti-music cannot. Although there are examples of digital anti-recordings, most of these works tend to emphasize the method of creating new art by interacting with physical media in unconventional ways.

I end this chapter with a record that could be considered the apotheosis of unplayable records—a record so unplayable, it will destroy your record player if you dare try to play it. In 1989, Rudolf Eb.er released a 7-inch record called *Roto-Tract* under his famous pseudonym, Runzelstirn and Gurgelstock. Instead of vinyl, the circle is a metal grinding wheel designed for use in an industrial grinding machine. Labeled as playable at "0–3000 RPM," at any speed the record will grind your turntable's needle, cartridge, and possibly tone arm.

To some, however, even this record can technically be played. As one online collector describes:

> Back around the time this first came out, I had an old turntable which was no longer useful for playing records, so I used it to play this. It was pure and direct noise, and not only destroyed the needle, but ground up a good portion of the cartridge as well (flecks of which can still be seen in my copy). That fun experience just goes to show that this record is indeed playable and does give one the pleasure of listening to a good noise record. Additionally, as it has no grooves, it will continue to play until your playing arm is totally destroyed or your patience has worn out!

SANDPAPER AND ANTI-RECORDS

Timm Ulrichs' 1968 work *Schleifpapier-Schallplatten* was a series of thirteen sandpaper records, each using a different grade of sandpaper. It was the first in a series of anti-records that experimented with the sandpaper medium, in what would become a tradition. Craig Dworkin's book *No Medium* provides a partial history of these unusual records, which I will augment here with some of my own findings.

Pastzö Power

The French noise group Dustbreeders are rumored to have released a single called "Sandpaper Mantra" in 1989—it was, like Ulrichs' work, a circle of sandpaper with a center hole that threatened to mess up a turntable stylus. In 1992, the German noisecore band Pasztörözött released Pasztö Power, a 7-inch sandpaper circle that they claimed was not sandpaper but instead a one-sided flexi-disc with over three billion songs on it. The legendary electronic music producer Aphex Twin, meanwhile, was known to throw sandpaper records on the turntable during DJ sets. One has even turned up on an online auction site.[1] Most recently, in 2017, a blog called *The Hard Times* satirized noise artists by publishing a piece about a fictional noise group named Antiverb, who had supposedly released a sandpaper 7" called "General Purpose." Musician Jon Lervold then seized upon the opportunity, creating a Bandcamp page for the record, uploading an actual recording he made of sandpaper on a turntable (which unsurprisingly sounds like harsh noise wall), and even staging a photo shoot of the record and its "sixteen-page sandpaper booklet."[2]

Other artists have used sandpaper as part of the packaging for their releases. In 1979, post-punk band the Durutti Column's infamous *The Return of the Durutti Column* was released, which had a sandpaper cover that scratched up abutting records. The punk band Feederz' 1984 album *Ever Feel Like Killing Your Boss?* had sandpaper on its outside cover, as did Illusion of Safety's self-titled 1999 CD. And, in 2018, Michael Ridge self-released a limited-to-six edition called *Grit 1*, under his moniker Norfolk Trotter. It was a floppy disk featuring seven minutes of harsh noise wall that he had recorded by attaching a contact mic to two pieces

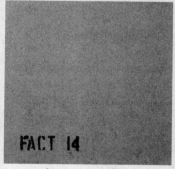

The Return of the Durutti Column

of sandpaper being rubbed against each other. "Each anti-floppy is labeled with coarse sandpaper; standard playback is not recommended as damage to equipment is very likely. A further piece of sandpaper is provided for listeners to rub the floppy disk against to create their own wall."

1 "APHEX TWIN Richard James DJ Set Sandpaper Set with Small Center Hole -- Ltd. 200 - Auction Details," popsike.com - April 2013, <www.popsike.com/APHEX-TWIN-Richard-James-DJ-set-sandpaper-set-with-small-center-hole-ltd-200/161003120854.html>

2 Jon Lervold, "Antiverb - General Purpose," Jon Lervold, May 9, 2017, <jonlervold.com/antiverb-general-purpose/>

THE RRRECORDS ANTI-RECORDS

RRRecords, the pioneering noise label run by Ron Lessard, a.k.a. Emil Beaulieau, was responsible for some of the most iconic anti-records ever produced, including a boom of unplayable discs that came out in 1988. In discussion with Lessard, it was not clear that an exhaustive list of RRRecords anti-records could ever be compiled. Many are not listed on Discogs, including some that were produced in small editions for specific tours. And he can only remember so many of his one-offs. But he did his best to recall as many as he could for me, including some choice details. "I need to emphasize that ALL anti-records are indeed playable—it just requires a record player you don't mind damaging. And actually, you don't even need a record player to play them—you can use contact microphones, table saws or sledgehammers. All it requires is imagination and conviction."

Here is the list as it stands now, excluding anti-records produced for other labels (for example, Emil Beaulieau's *Driven to Extremes* LP on Flykingen Records from 2013 and Emil Beaulieau's *That Old Black Magic* 10" on De Player from 2011):

Billboard Combat, *Metastasis* LP (1988)
Vinyl record covered in paint, cardboard scraps, razors, screws, and tape. 100 copies total.

Due Process, *Do Nothing* LP (1988)
Completely blank vinyl. 100 copies total.

Due Process, *Do Damage* LP (1988)
Vinyl with hand-cut grooves crudely made on a homemade lathe. 100 copies total.

The Haters, *Wind Licked Dirt* LP (1988)
Blank LP with no grooves sold in a jacket with dirt; cover specifies that "THIS RECORD IS PLAYED BY RUBBING DIRT ON IT." 200 copies total.

Do Nothing

Various artists, *Colorado* LP (1988)
A noise compilation in which the A1 track has been scratched over with the words "FUCK ARCHITECTS OFFICE." 100 copies total.

Kapotte Muziek, *Heathen Muzak* (1988)
A 7" record contained within a 12" sleeve, featuring haphazard grooves produced by a homemade lathe and multiple extra holes carved by a drilling machine. 200 copies total.

AMK, *Montage* 10" flexi-disc (1989)
Record made up of different cut-up flexi-discs, assembled together—hence *Montage*. Each copy is unique, and more than 100 were produced.

Honeymoon Production, *Manipulation Muzak* vinyl wad (1988)

Pellet of vinyl intended to be heated and molded into a record by its owner. 100 copies total.

Small Cruel Party/Chop Shop, *Scmaolpl -C-r-u-e-l- Psahrotpy* (1995)

Dubbed "a literal split ten-inch," this is a 10" record that was pressed with Small Party's contribution on one side and Chop Shop's on the other. The record itself was then cut in half and put into a folder, such that the halves could be recombined according to the owner's preference. "Scott (Chop Shop) was a metal worker and he had a small machine shop. He rigged up a vise to hold the records securely and we used a strong cutting blade to slice down the center of the record; we then just snapped them in half. Most ended up having clean cuts. The few that didn't split cleanly were discarded." Unknown edition.

Wicked New England

Emil Beaulieau/Wolf Eyes 7" (2003)

Scratched and painted 7-inch made using old noise records by assorted noise artists. Comes in handmade collage covers and sold at shows during a 2003 tour. 50 copies total.

Emil Beaulieau/Crank Sturgeon/Prurient, *Wicked New England* 7" (2004)

Unplayable singles made for a tour—each copy coated in spray paint and otherwise "abused," with collage covers. Made using old noise records by assorted noise artists. 50 copies total.

Emil Beaulieau/Jessica Rylan/John Wiese, *2005 Tour* LP (2005)

LPs spray-painted and covered in handmade art that was unique for each copy, this was produced to be sold at shows. Made using old noise records by assorted noise artists. 25 copies total.

Emil Beaulieau, *The True Sound of Love* 7" (2005)

A 7-inch single spray painted in different colors of paint for minimal playability. Covers are unique. "This item is an unlimited edition. I keep it in print and make more copies whenever I feel like it."

Nihilist Assault Group, *Untitled* (2005)

Sold at No Fun Fest 2005, this was made using repurposed noise records by assorted artists, which were then spray-painted. "I then made a cassette recording of each 7-inch— each copy of the box contains one (spray-painted) 7-inch and the cassette recording of that particular 7-inch," Lessard explains. The tape and vinyl came in a box. At the time, the Nihilist Assault Group were Ron Lessard (a.k.a. Emil Beaulieau), Richard Rupenus of the New Blockaders, and Dominick Fernow of Prurient. 50 copies total.

Emil Beaulieu, J. Mercado Anti-Record 12" (2006)

Anti-record made by Ron Lessard, but produced in honor of Jadis Mercado, "out of respect for [his] work in the 'Anti-Record' format." Made using an old noise record by an unspecified noise artist. 1 copy total.

Emil Beaulieu, Mr. Beaulieu Goes To Japan 7" (????)

Spray-painted anti-record sold at shows during a tour in Japan. 50 copies total.

Emil Beaulieu/Rubbish, We Are The Professionals double LP boxed set (????)

We Are The Professionals

Lessard with his friend Rubbish, a.k.a. Patrick Cooksey. "It was a boxed set of two anti-records in an edition of 50 copies. I made 50 of the antis and Rubbish made 50 of the antis; each box contained one of each. Mine were simple, just spray paint and then sanded. I wrote on them using white-out (if I remember correctly). Rubbish's were a little more involved, spray paint, silkscreened, and carved/etched using a doweling tool. We split it, 25 copies each—he got 25 copies, I got 25 copies. The contents were the same, but we each designed our own covers." Lessard says his source records were repurposed noise records, whereas he is not sure what vinyl Rubbish used. 50 copies total.

Emil Beaulieu/L'Autopsie A Révélé Que La Mort Était Due À L'Autopsie, Anti-L'Autopsie À La Emil LP (2013)

Split release with the Komma Null label from France. "This is a repurposed LP from the band L'Autopsie, called *Le Souffle De L'Avorton*," Lessard explains. The LPs were painted black with words painted in white. "The covers were all made repurposing the original covers, artwork, and booklets that came with the LP. I also pasted original photographs of myself (Ron Lessard) from various stages of my life, from my childhood, my teens, early adulthood, my military years, et cetera." 25 copies total.

BONUS: "I made a lot of anti-records in editions of one copy only that I used for my live performances as Emil Beaulieu. And now that I think about it, I made more personalized anti-records for various people over the years, just like the J. Mercado one. The only difference is J. Mercado made a Discogs listing for the one I made him, but the other people didn't make a listing for theirs. The most recent one was for a young couple named Autumn and Nick, who live in Ohio but come to my shop once a year when they come to Massachusetts to visit family. Last year, they sent me a mixtape of the records they purchased in my shop, so I made them an anti-record—it was water-themed. The cover was old-timey photos of people frolicking at the beach and cranky old dudes on fishing boats. I called it the Autumn And Nick Swimsuit Edition."

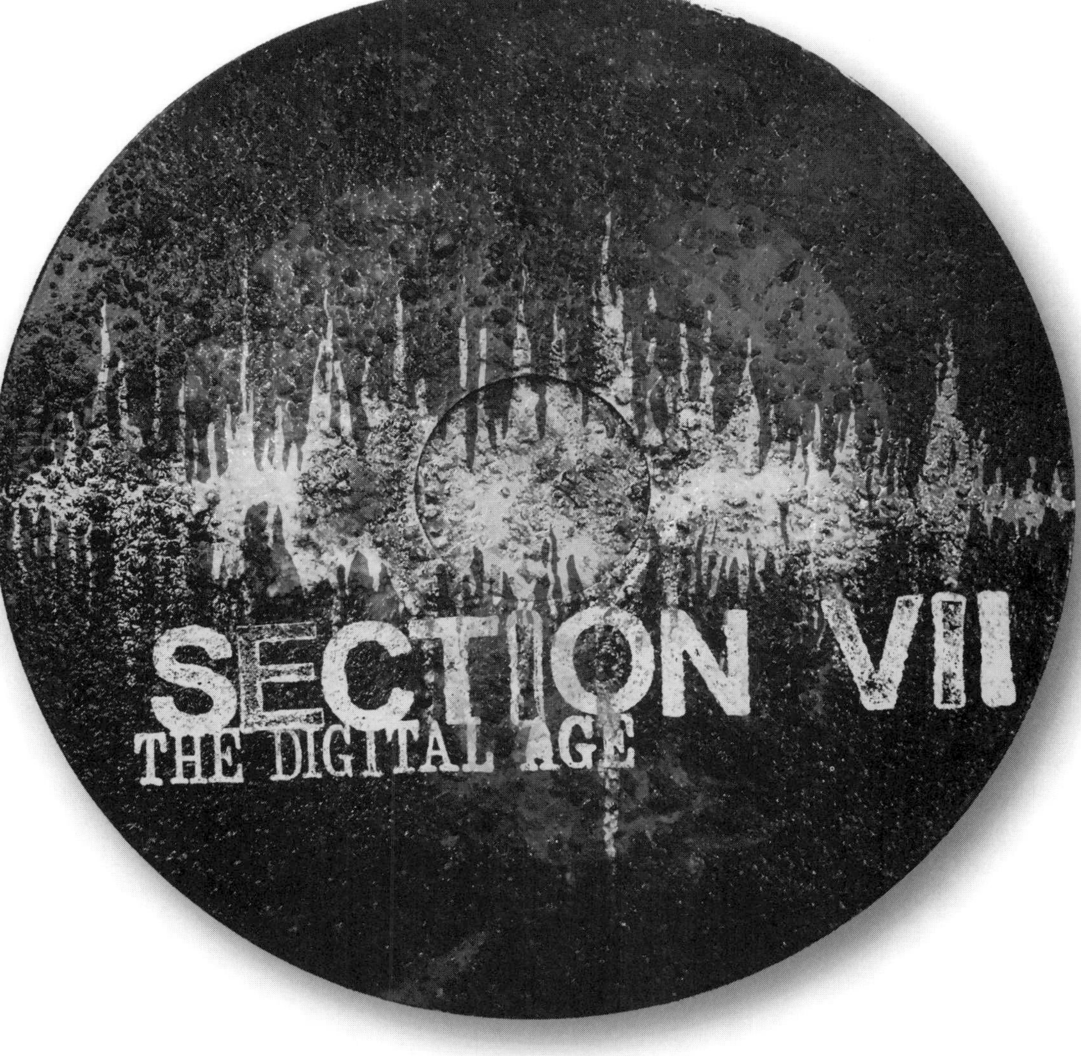
SECTION VII
THE DIGITAL AGE

VII.1 WAVES

Vaporwave is a music genre, propagated and circulated primarily on the internet, whose focus is a nostalgia for the eighties and nineties. Typically, this is achieved by taking samples of music from that era, often the most commercial and gaudy music available: especially synth-heavy pop and smooth jazz. These samples are usually slowed down and lacquered with reverb, the audio imbued with a dreamy quality which evokes the sense of a distantly held memory. In an article for academic journal *Popular Music*, musicologist Laura Glitsos argues that vaporwave takes nostalgia, or *"remembering,"* as the basis for its entire aesthetic. As she puts it, "The pleasure of vaporwave is therefore understood as a pleasure of remembering for the sake of the act of remembering itself."

Simon Chandler, writing for the Bandcamp Daily blog, cobbled together a family tree of vaporwave subgenres, compiling no fewer than ten discrete strains, ranging from the genre's early moments to fresh-off-the-press developments. Some of vaporwave's most intriguing exponents are its hyperspecialized, conceptually pure offshoots, a handful of which warrant discussion in these pages.

VII.1.1 Mallsoft

One of the most compelling subgenres identified in Chandler's family tree is mallsoft, described by Chandler as an attempt to conjure "the imagined space of the suburban shopping mall." Embracing vaporwave's nostalgia for the recent past, mallsoft producers tend to use looped jazz and EZ-listening melodies, but they send these samples deep into the mix, as though they were playing softly into a large, closed expanse. Sometimes they will overlay these compositions with field recordings from actual shopping plazas.

Mallsoft emerged at a time when the popularity of online retail platforms has led to the fading of shopping malls as the main locus of consumerism. The idea of dead malls has become a topic of fascination. On deadmalls.com, a website that shares stories and pictures of defunct and dying malls, you can view endless images of fluorescent-lit hallways walled with shuttered storefronts, all accented in eighties décor. In many cases, mallsoft albums appropriate these interior shots of neon-inflected shopping plazas for their album art.

The "holy trinity" of mallsoft records, as one online commenter puts it,[1] are *Vacant Places* by Hantasi, *Hologram Plaza* by Disconscious, and *Palm Mall* by 猫 シ Corp., though many other albums exist within the subgenre. Some would also include 슈퍼마켓 *Yes! We're Open* by 식료품groceries, a 2014 concept album set in a Korean supermarket.

猫 シ Corp., a.k.a. Cat System Corp., is, despite the Japanese characters in his moniker, a native of the Netherlands named Jornt Elzinga. He also runs a vaporwave record label called Hiraeth. Born in 1989, he has limited personal experience of the eighties and did not even reach teenagerhood until this millennium. In an interview with Bandcamp

---

1 "Completed the Mallsoft Holy Trinity Today," Reddit: Mallsoft, October 9, 2019, <www.reddit.com/r/Mallsoft/comments/dfse86/completed_the_mallsoft_holy_trinity_today/>

Daily,[2] he explains that his father's home videos from the early nineties are a major source of inspiration for him. He started making music in the mid-aughts, ranging "from weird bleeps and beeps to harsh noise walls." In the early 2010s, he started recording dark ambient music, and his oeuvre eventually expanded to include working with samples.

Elzinga tells me via email that *Palm Mall* grew out of an obsession with another mallsoft classic, *Hologram Plaza* by Disconscious. He recalls "the way that [*Hologram Plaza*] worked on me and how other vaporwave became Muzak and/or background music. By accident, I

The cover for 猫 シ Corp.'s *Palm Mall.* Image courtesy of Jornt Elzinga.

created a track for [his record label] Hiraeth called 'Sky Lounge' where I pictured a giant glass platform high above the mountains where rich folks would relax and shop. The reverb created a special feeling and image in my head. Fast forward maybe a couple weeks or months, when I thought the scene could use more mallsoft. So I started to gather some sounds—even got inspiration from a *GTA V* track—and started to create an album dedicated to shopping. I had the idea to place the listener in an actual mall with ambiance and drawn-out sounds."

Palm Mall started off as a "twenty-two-minute long mix of reverb stretched sound," which he submitted to No Problema Tapes. Whereas the final product is known for its background of 'mall ambiance'—actual recordings taken from malls—the original only had a snippet of this ambiance at the beginning. Eventually, Elzinga added a background of mall-based field recordings to the entire twenty-two minutes. He also dotted the recording with samples of corporate advertisements that sound as though they are being broadcast from overhead speakers. The final version of *Palm Mall* features the twenty-two-minute collage as side A; side B is a series of shorter songs that shed the mall ambiance and instead adopt a more traditional vaporwave approach, using looped-and-slowed smooth jazz and synth-pop. Those songs are given mall-esque song titles like "Special Discount," "First Floor, and "I Consume, Therefore I Am" to hammer in the shopping plaza aesthetic.

"I sometimes describe to people that I 'paint' with samples," he explains. "Where an actual painter uses paint, I use samples I find. Recycled sounds from the internet. It's a collage of memories and relics of the past. Because I'm from '89, I grew up on computers and the internet, and therefore I find it interesting how I can re-use sounds found on there.

---

2   Simon Chandler, "The Mall, Nostalgia, and the Loss of Innocence: An Interview With 猫 シ Corp.," Bandcamp Daily, March 8, 2017, <daily.bandcamp.com/features/the-mall-nostalgia-and-the-loss-of-innocence-an-interview-with-corp>

YouTube is an amazing source for that, but also a deep pit... let's just plainly say I use it as a source. The ambiance is cut and paste from a couple mall ambiance videos on YouTube. One of them is very famous for the guy calling out, 'I'm just gonna grab my laptop and sit down here'—which became the Wilhelm scream of mallsoft. Announcements were all taken from eighties and nineties USA and Japanese commercials. But I only use the ones that add to the story; no random commercial makes its way into the concept."

One of the most meticulously crafted parts of the recording is the mall ambiance, which required "cutting, pasting, looping, fading, layering, to create one continuously long loop without cuts. It took about four versions and lots of coffee before that was done. I had to work with only a couple minutes of audio. I tried to have as little as possible recognizable recurring sounds. For example, I don't want to hear the same 'hey, hello' every five minutes that breaks the experience." He then looped synthesizer sounds extensively to "create Muzak."

Palm Mall's cover depicts a three-dimensional interior of some form of commercial plaza. When asked about this, Elzinga told me, "I literally have no idea. I was working with [fellow vaporwave producer] Cvlture on a track and he was excited to do artwork, he found an image of a 3D mall." Years later, he learned the 3D image was intended to be a simulacrum of an office plaza, not a mall.

For Elzinga, "The Mall represents pure utopia. A shiny clean mall in a sunny place called Hiraeth, which is a blend of eighties/nineties USA and Japan." That word, "hiraeth," is a key to understanding his aesthetic. It is a Welsh word that translates roughly to a longing for a place that doesn't exist.[3] "Since I was a kid, I had this idea that one day, you can select a disk with a dream, insert it into a machine, and dream that dream," he tells me. "But what if you want to stay there forever? Why would you resist a *Matrix* system? I sometimes have dreams in which there's a golden sunlight, fuzzy feeling, and pure utopia—I want to stay there forever and not wake up. This gave me the idea of rebuilding a world of our memories, fake or real. I hope I live to see the day where you can actually upload your mind into a machine and play games with friends."

In 2018, Elzinga took this idea of imaginary nostalgia to the next level with the release of *Palm Mall Mars*, set in the distant future:

Today, the year 2199, we celebrate the 50th birthday of Palm Mall Mars. We welcome you with special discounts on luxurious items, grand offers on newly built Ring Worlds and will let you try out the new ARPE! Come visit us and get a 50% discount on your first Poulsen Treatment![4]

Elzinga has also started adding more real-mall content to his music. Whereas *Palm Mall*'s mall sounds come from YouTube, for a later album, ショップ @ ヘルシンキ, a.k.a. *Shop @ Helsinki*, he began sourcing his own mall audio, after an inspiring trip to a Helsinki shopping center called the Forum. He even got his girlfriend, living in Finland, to make recordings at more malls. Soon, he plans to move to Finland to produce music full-time.

---

3 Samantha Kielar, "Hiraeth," Word of the Week, April 2, 2016, <sites.psu.edu/kielarpassionblog2/2016/04/02/hiraeth/>

4 "Palm Mall Mars (Remastered) | 猫 シ Corp.," Bandcamp, February 17, 2020, <catsystemcorp.bandcamp.com/album/palm-mall-mars-remastered>

Reflecting on *Palm Mall* retrospectively, Elzinga remains surprised by the enthusiasm that has grown over his music. "No, I did not think it would be this popular! I did have the idea it would be one of the best, because I strongly felt that the mallsoft it contained was something the scene was looking for. But even back then, I thought 100 tapes would have been more than enough... I do sometimes get a little bit uneasy when people claim that I am the creator of mallsoft... let's be honest, Disconscious started it! If he or she did not make that album, I am not sure if it would be a thing."

Disconscious is the mysterious project responsible for *Hologram Plaza*, a winsome album that sounds like a Muzak medley being piped into a tiled cathedral devoted to capitalism. Little is known about Disconscious as a person; the only concrete hint online is that his Bandcamp page lists San Diego as his location. Apart from *Hologram Plaza*, his only other music output has been a couple of songs on two compilations by a record label called Dream Catalogue. According to one Reddit post, that label's owner, HKE, contacted Disconscious through Bandcamp asking for a submission to the comp; only after three months did he get a response.[5]

What is interesting about *Hologram Plaza* is that it has been deconstructed by fans, most of its sample sources identified on the website WhoSampled.[6] In several cases, the sampled songs, which come from a variety of sources, were recycled wholesale—albeit modified using digital effects. Sampled songs include the synthesized background music to a 1995 Weather Channel broadcast, an obscure Christian fusion band called Koinonia, an eighties Japanese pop record by Naoko Kawai, and the soundtrack to a 1998 children's computer game called *Pajama Sam 2: Thunder and Lightning Aren't so Frightening*. Some have criticized this overreliance on samples, while others have reflected that this is the whole point.[7]

Disconscious was cagey about discussing his identity, though he graciously opened up about his methods and the conceptual background underlying the release. He also confirmed that I should use male pronouns to refer to him.

Disconscious explains that *Hologram Plaza* was not even close to his first musical project. "While I had a number of musical projects before this one, my very first project was quite similar, being purely sample-based," he says. "I had begun it when I was around 11 or 12 years old and had a similar focus on creating odd spaces using samples primarily from the 1960s and 1970s, but I wasn't too keen on effects and plugins and such yet. So it was more like vertically messy plunderphonic mashups with multiple songs stacked on top of each other and odd field recordings mixed in."

In creating those early works, for technical reasons, he had to record the left and right channels individually, combining them imperfectly to form a final stereo sound

5   "Is There Any Information on Disconscious?," Reddit: Vaporwave, October 10, 2016, <www.reddit.com/r/Vaporwave/comments/5c7ajc/is_there_any_information_on_disconscious/>

6   "Disconscious - Samples, Covers and Remixes," WhoSampled <www.whosampled.com/Disconscious/> [accessed March 19, 2022]

7   "Hey Guys, I Wrote an Article on My Findings about Disconscious' Hologram Plaza, and I'd Love to Hear Your Thoughts!," Reddit: Vaporwave, December 18, 2016, <www.reddit.com/r/Vaporwave/comments/5j2hyl/hey_guys_i_wrote_an_article_on_my_findings_about/>

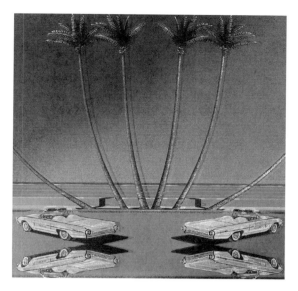

The cover for Disconscious' *Hologram Plaza*. Image courtesy of Disconscious.

that had a "very interesting stereo field." He liked this strange effect and found a way to digitally recreate it for most of the tracks on *Hologram Plaza*.

"I also had a strong fascination with the sort of psychogeographical qualities of malls when I was a kid and wanted to have something like an expressionistic representation of what it's like to be in that kind of a space. It's such an overwhelmingly delirious experience to be in a mall as a kid—the maze-like layout, bright lights and loud people, the smell of stagnant greasy food and intense perfumes, movement, advertisements, colors, all contrasted with the design intention of being a soothing and relaxing environment. It is both safe and contained and boundlessly hostile. That dichotomy between palpable chaos and inherent docility creates this very fever-dream-like quality that I wanted to capture sonically."

Hologram Plaza, then, is Disconscious' attempt to take the commercialized music known as Muzak, intended to blend into the background, and inflect it with a vague uncomfortableness using subtle production techniques. He compares it to "being on the edge of sleep but kept barely awake by some vague sense of something being out of place."

He pulled samples from a variety of contexts. Some were borrowed from his childhood. "I was obsessed with listening to the local smooth jazz radio station before bed as a kid, and there were a few songs they would play that either struck me with wonder or fear in a way music hasn't been able to since, and I always knew I wanted to use those songs in some way." Others were used because they had some quality Disconscious liked, though the goal was for them to be "not so much anachronistic but achronistic, being impossible to place into some kind of historical context."

He subjected his samples to a laborious production process. "Before I started making tracks with any intention for release, I discovered this particular method of chaining alternating delays and reverbs through each other that created this unbalanced acentric echo that seemed to me like a physical representation of a liminal or hypnagogic space, which became the backbone of most of the tracks on the album." In trying to tinge his songs with a subtle darkness, he fought the instinct to just "[throw] noise or dark ambiance into the mix."

Disconscious summarized the goal of converting comfortable music to disquieting sound. "Much of the music I sampled was intended to have an easy, light, or upbeat quality—to sink into the background—and the goal was to imbue the kind of restrained, borderline unconscious dread and fear that lays behind this understanding of being in a space like a mall that exists only to control and manipulate you, but being unable or unwilling to confront it in any meaningful way."

Disconscious was surprised by the way *Hologram Plaza* has resonated with so many listeners. "When I released the album, I expected a couple people making similar music to maybe give it a listen but nothing more. The concept seemed too niche and specific for anyone to be able to relate to it, let alone approach the environment I wanted to create out of it without copious explanation on my part." Yet he is grateful for the attention the record has received, remarking, "The fact that anyone is influenced by it at all is incredibly flattering and feels wholly undeserved."

The decision to keep Disconscious as more or less a one-off was an intentional one. He tells me that he has toyed with the idea of releasing more Disconscious music, tantalizingly alluding to "a number of unreleased tracks from the project collecting digital dust." But don't get your hopes up. "I had said what I wanted to say and showed what I wanted to show, and it felt unceremonious to reach beyond that. Perhaps one day, I'll dust these particular boots off again and fill them in a very different way."

식료품groceries, the artist behind the 슈퍼마켓*Yes! We're Open* supermarket record, is an American artist named Jordan Bortner currently teaching English in Seoul, South Korea. Bortner played viola and percussion in high school and is a self-taught pianist, growing up producing compositions in his bedroom using MIDI. After developing his skills in the contemporary classical vein, including a degree in music composition at the University of North Texas, he eventually shifted to electronic production.

Upon moving to New York in 2013, he started experimenting with recording music under the name Groceries. "My dad called me to talk at some point while he was on a business trip," he explains, via email. "He was at a conference, and he wanted to tell me about how there was this guy there who was playing music, possibly DJing, during this business conference, so there was music while everyone was there walking around, and I replied, '...Like a grocery store?'"

What began as a drone project with a friend of his emerged into a solo endeavor. Around that time, he encountered vaporwave and mallsoft, the latter particularly resonating with him. He tells me that it was the idea that mallsoft was meant to be absorbed passively, akin to music heard while shopping, that drew him to the genre. So he shifted gears toward mallsoft and rebranded to 식료품groceries due to an enthusiasm for Korean culture. "From there, it seemed perfectly natural to make tracks as though each one was an aisle in the store, and each aisle contained things that matched aesthetically with the music, whether physical objects or abstract concepts."

I asked him about his attraction to the grocery store as a theme, and he described the joy of visiting a Korean supermarket with friends. "It's... fun at foreign grocery

The cover for 식료품groceries' 슈퍼마켓Yes! We're Open. Image courtesy of Jordan Bortner.

stores when you can marvel at all the foreign products there, having no idea what they are or what they're for."

Likewise, 슈퍼마켓Yes! We're Open takes the grocery store but makes it somewhat weird. After an introduction, it is separated into nine different "aisles," each one offering different products. Aisles include "Aisle 1 (Earth Tones, Rectangles, and Fake Plants)," "Aisle 5 (Moonlight, Urban Skylines, and Rapid Eye Movement)," and "Aisle 8 (Drink Specials, Warm Evenings, and Rooftop Views)."

"While I was in college, I also got the sense that most of my friends didn't know how to cook," he recalls. "So, even though we would need to go grocery shopping together to buy food for our apartment, it seemed like they really had no frame of reference for what they should be buying while we were there. This led me to imagine how a grocery store can be a big, confusing place, where you feel like you should know what you want, but somehow don't at the same time."

When he set out to work on his album, Bortner was entering new territory. Despite his extensive training in classical composition, he had no experience in creating electronic music, apart from knowing how to use a MIDI sequencer.

"In order to realize what I wanted to make, I had to do so many things that broke my own personal rules for what should be considered 'respectable' art, and it felt really gross and uncomfortable at first," he recounts. "I was searching YouTube for 'most relaxing music for (whatever)' playlists and listening to sappy music with really tacky background images, like overcompressed JPGs of sunsets with gaudy, cursive text overlaid. I would rip the music from YouTube and generate an audio file from Audacity. This whole process felt so unclean, but I carried on. I would listen to the music I found and look for looping points that worked well. Most of the time, I had no idea the name or artist of the music I was working with. I applied effects to the loops I made in a many-years-old crack of Fruity Loops. The whole process felt sloppy. By the end of it all, I assembled the album in one continuous mix and chopped it all up into tracks/aisles."

슈퍼마켓Yes! We're Open was put out digitally via the vaporwave label Dream Catalogue and took a while to catch on, but people eventually took notice. "I was really surprised when David (of Dream Catalogue) let me know that my album was developing a 'cult following.' He showed me one of those 'vaporwave essentials' charts that had my album on it. I was so blown away and humbled that so many people were listening to my album."

Hantasi's *Vacant Places* comes from a different place than these other albums, even though it is grouped within mallsoft. Arriving in 2014, it was seemingly the first mallsoft record ever produced. Yet while other mallsoft records were intended to evoke the experience of walking through a consumer destination, and often made nostalgia their focus, *Vacant Places* was intended to bring up a different set of associations.

Hantasi, who lives in California and whose real name is Alexander Matulionis, is a recently married software developer who became involved in computers long before he began producing music. He taught himself to code in high school, eventually completing a college degree in programming, and links his fascination with mallsoft with the MMORPGs he played as a teenager.

In 2006, he encountered a seminal vaporwave album titled *Contemporary Sapporo*, by the Portland, Oregon producer Ramona Andra Xavier, who was then recording under the alias 情報デスクVIRTUAL, which translates to Virtual Information Desk. Xavier is known best as Vektroid. Matulionis recalls that he initially "kinda hated" *Contemporary Sapporo*, but for some reason, he kept on listening to it, "obsessively," and eventually got to a point where he was *only* listening to it. It was through that process that he discovered the pleasure of immersing himself in the world that a record conjures up, which he likens to the experience of being in the all-encompassing virtual world of an MMORPG.

It was around this time that Matulionis had two different experiences that contributed to *Vacant Places*. For one, he had been visiting some dead malls in his area—or technically malls that were still open, but with only one or two storefronts that still operated. He recalled the experience of wandering these malls, including in a local shopping center known as the Carousel Mall. As he walked through these well-maintained but empty places, he reflected on the "staleness" of vacant commercial settings—that they are, surreally, both clean and empty.

Around the same time, he also started eyeing a local commercial property called Stewart Plaza, which is home to various stores and offices. A square block of tan walls, adobe roofs, and palm trees encircling a parking lot, he refers to it as a "corporate, time-sharey, weird place." Matulionis developed the idea of trying to recreate the aesthetic of this place.

Before this, his only exploits into creating music had involved recording "crappy experimental rock" with a friend who lived down the street. Creating *Vacant Places* was a different beast altogether. He recalls staying up until 1 a.m. searching for "royalty-free music" online, exploring various now-defunct websites that he suspects purchased the rights to big dumps of music to be used for this purpose. These tracks seemed like covers of covers of covers, completely divorced from the origins of their subject matter.

One sample, used on *Vacant Places'* first piece, "Welcome," came from an obscure piano track called "Santiago de Cuba" by German pianist Harry Seegert.

To complete the record, Matulionis looped portions of these royalty-free tracks and subjected them to various modifications—reversing the audio, stretching the sound, adding reverb, and laying down background ambience. When he was satisfied, he named it *Vacant Places* in reference to the feeling of wandering near-defunct malls, naming the tracks after various shopping center features: "Lobby," "Bookstore," "Food Court," "Northwest Plaza." He found an image online to serve as the cover art, a disturbingly dark, blurry interior shot of a mall lobby, replete with escalator. After wrapping up production, burning one hundred copies on CD-R, and posting them online for sale, he recalls not thinking much of it at all. "All right, I guess I made that," he recounted. "I'll probably die and no one will care." He even goes so far as to say that he believes he "absolutely failed" in recreating the experience of conjuring Stewart Plaza's corporate surreal blandness.

It didn't happen overnight, but as time passed, appreciation for *Vacant Places* grew—and increasingly once other mallsoft records appeared, like Disconscious' *Hologram Plaza*, which Matulionis loves but considers aesthetically very different, a "brighter and flashier" beast altogether. In 2016, he produced a cassette version, and in 2019, a vaporwave label called Geometric Lullaby released a vinyl version. Underscoring the fleeting nature of *Vacant Places'* component pieces, when Geometric Lullaby requested a hi-res version of the cover, Matulionis was at a loss. All he had was the image file he used for the CD-R cover, and reverse image searches only turned up websites related to the album. It was only through the label owner's online sleuthing that the original was hunted down, including the name of the actual mall.

Vacant Places indeed has a distinct sound from other mallsoft releases. Its opener, "Welcome," opens with a looped piano melody that sounds like it might have been played in a 1930s banquet hall, but echo effects make it sound like it is being piped into a sinister mall, the melody's senseless repetition adding to the surrealism. Elsewhere, "Restroom" provides the same treatment to some Casio-demo smooth jazz, and "Northwest Plaza" introduces pan flutes into the mix. Though Matulionis at one point felt that the album failed to live up to his vision, to me, it effortlessly captures both sides of the mall experience: on one hand, the environment's schmaltzy consumerism and, on the other, the feeling that Disconscious dubbed "borderline unconscious dread."

VII.1.2 Broken Transmission

Broken transmission is a vaporwave subgenre that, through the use of samples and processing effects, aims to evoke the sound of listening to a radio or television signal that is flittering between stations. To achieve this effect, producers will typically shift between short passages of vintage-sounding audio, as though the listener is channel-surfing. It is also sometimes called signalwave.

One online compiler[8] has argued that this genre began with a ten-minute self-titled cassette by Midnight Television, which was put out by the early vaporwave

---

8   BrothermanTrill, "RYM Ultimate Box Set: Broken Transmission," Rate Your Music <rateyourmusic.com/list/BrothermanTrill/rym-ultimate-box-set-broken-transmission/> [accessed March 19, 2022]

label Beer on the Rug in 2011. This EP comprises seven short songs, each with a brief, looped melodic motif; the combined effect evokes the experience of channel surfing at midnight. Indeed, one sample comes from a 1980 HBO station ID, and another is culled from *Saved by the Bell*. Others, pulled from various disco-funk records, manage to simulate that synthetic as-seen-on-TV aesthetic from the eighties and nineties. This release predates the term *broken transmission*, and its characteristic 2 a.m. vibe has also led to it being cross-categorized under varying stripes of vaporwave, like eccojams and late-night lo-fi. This conceptual overlapping speaks to the nebulous distinctions between genres.

Midnight Television now records under the evocative name Computer Slime. He is a mysterious figure who's now twenty-four years old and studies psychology at the University of Houston. The tracks on the Midnight Television EP were the first he ever produced, while he was still in high school. After posting them on Bandcamp, Beer on the Rug messaged him asking about the EP and arranged to release it on cassette. He says they never paid him.

Midnight Television tells me that there was no unifying concept behind the release when he developed it. Raised in Houston, he cites chopped-and-screwed artist DJ Screw as an important influence. "When I was making the tracks for Midnight Television, however, I lived in Fort Dodge, Iowa," he tells me. "Fort Dodge is a small town with nothing much to do in, full of kids who are nice but cliquish, and like most small towns, Fort Dodge is stuck years in the past—I mean, I literally had a wood-paneled CRT. Plus, it's cold as hell for a kid from Houston. When winter came around, I spent my free time on Last.FM connecting with folks like 骨架的 and Vektroid and discovering far-out tunes," listing the likes of James Ferraro, Daniel Lopatin, and Rangers, among others, as exhilarating discoveries.

When I ask about the inspiration behind his choice of samples, he describes them as incidental discoveries. "Most of the time, it was just stuff I discovered browsing YouTube after class. *Saved by the Bell* was an intentional choice though; that show is awesome."

I was curious about "Channel Surfing," one of the most distinctly 2 a.m.-sounding of the EP's tracks. Even Midnight Television can't recall the specifics. "'Channel Surfing,' if I remember correctly, is from a VHS we were shown in biology. It had such a cool vibe that I had to get my hands on. Unfortunately, I cannot remember the name of the video."

He pieced the record together by ripping the YouTube videos to MP3 using a website, then looping them in Audacity. This was part of several experiments made while "goofing off" using Audacity, inspired by the methods of the artists he discovered on Last.FM. He recalls "making whatever I thought sounded interesting and gave off the hypnagogic, lo-fi, weirdo sound that I was interested in hearing."

Today, he feels somewhat conflicted about the release, telling me that, if he could do it again, he would refine the record and add more tracks. "I'm happy that people enjoy my music. However, I made *Midnight Television* as a means of catharsis and escapism during a difficult time in my childhood—not to be a genre-defining or innovative style.

The cover for Local News' *Channel 8* EP. Image courtesy of Local News.

Vaporwave and broken transmission weren't even terms used to describe music when *Midnight Television* was made. When vaporwave got popular, I actually became really cynical about the whole thing. Today, my opinion is that the style serves a purpose for listeners in the same way it served me. I'm totally down with whatever it's called as long as it helps people find what they're looking for."

Other artists recording music in the broken transmission tradition would become even more explicit about the concept of simulating radio and television signals. *Channel 8*, a short EP by an artist named Local News, runs through nine foggy melodic fragments, none over two minutes. Each track sounds like its own distinct television channel—be it the fluttering harps of "Snow," the smoky jazz of "Tonight's Special Guest," or the EZ-listening Moog orchestra of "Monday Weather Forecast," which sounds as close to a soap opera theme as Weather Channel music.

Local News, who prefers to maintain his anonymity, also records under the name Infinity Frequencies. He has two releases out under the name Local News; the sequel to *Channel 8* is called *Ghost Broadcast* and observes a similar aesthetic. Referring to *Channel 8*, he explains, "The idea for the album is sort of an old ghost broadcast that has been airing since the 1980s."

He tells me that he developed the record in 2011. An enthusiast of old news broadcasts, he collected the audio from a number of these old transmissions, mostly from Japanese sources, and used them to construct *Channel 8*. The goal was to create a kind of musical narrative. "Something cinematic, that told a story," he says.

Since *Channel 8*, the producer behind Local News has put out a well-regarded "computer trilogy" of albums under his other name, Infinity Frequencies. *Computer Death, Computer Decay*, and *Computer Afterlife*, which came out between May 2013 and May 2014, are well-regarded vaporwave records that similarly make extensive use of old Weather Channel broadcasts and Japanese commercials. He tells me that he is planning another Local News release for the future.

VII.1.3 Late-Night Lo-Fi

Another micro-subgenre of vaporwave has come to be termed late-night lo-fi.[9] Typically sourcing samples from smooth jazz and eighties R&B, this genre tends to evoke the urban environment at 2 a.m. as experienced from a penthouse suite. Graphics used on albums often depict cityscapes at night and the types of luxury condominiums featured in films like *American Psycho* and *Wall Street*. Late-night lo-fi's leading auteur was Luxury Elite, often called Lux. She put out a series of canonical records, chief among them her 2015 album *World Class*, which was released on cassette by an experimental label called Crash Symbols. Sources on *World Class* include singles by obscure Euro disco and Italo disco acts like Xalan, L'Affair, and Marco Martina, as well as a track off ABBA member Agnetha Fältskog's 1987 solo album *I Stand Alone*. At other points, she repurposes actual hits. Her album *TV Party* slows and slurs an extended portion of "I Love Your Smile" by Shanice (on "Bubblegum") and much of the sax soloing on "Maneater" by Hall & Oates. On "You Can Sense It," a large chunk of "You Belong to the City" by Glenn Frey is subjected to the late-night lo-fi treatment, including its raunchy saxophone aerobics, the full prechorus, and a good chunk of the chorus.[10]

Lux, who typically brings an enthusiastic and intimate presence on social media without ever divulging any details about her real-life identity, has disappeared from the internet as of late. It is not the first time she's gone blank (she retrospectively attributed a previous hiatus to her laptop breaking down), but my efforts to connect with her via Bandcamp were unsuccessful.

Her record label, named Fortune 500, has also stopped putting out new music. After a string of hotly attended records by several vaporwave producers, it wound down in July 2015 with a final farewell compilation titled *The Music of the Now Age III*. But the Fortune 500 archive persists online and provides a wonderful distillation of the late-night lo-fi aesthetic. An album called *Midnight Love* by a producer named Vector Graphics uses, as its cover, a grainy VHS image of palm trees at twilight. *Empire Building* by Saint Pepsi uses an aerial shot of skyscrapers at night in its visuals. The concept album *Riviera* by Kodak Cameo uses a similar VHS screencap aesthetic, but this time, it pictures the front of a Las Vegas casino; the entire record selects Las Vegas as its focus, with songs like "Caesar's Palace," "The Strip at Midnight," "Mandalay

---

9 "What Are Some of the Best Late Night Lo-Fi Albums?," Reddit: Vaporwave, January 10, 2018, <www.reddit.com/r/Vaporwave/comments/7pdge4/what_are_some_of_the_best_late_night_lofi_albums/>

10 "TV Party | Luxury Elite | Orange Milk Records," Bandcamp, September 13, 2013, <orangemilkrecords.bandcamp.com/album/tv-party/>

Bay," and "Rainforest Café" using eighties samples of variable provenance to evoke the experience of gliding through the Vegas strip.[11]

There are many denizens of late-night lo-fi today, distinguished by an unmistakable audiovisual aesthetic. Several records by a producer named S p o r t 3 0 0 0, who also traffics in other vaporwave subgenres, come adorned in grainy stills of the city at night, and, like Lux and many other artists in this field, he runs his own tape and digital label called Dark Web Recordings. A Virginia-based producer named 死夢VANITY further explores the late-night lo-fi aesthetic with the albums *Evening Bliss* and *Paradise Heights*; 遺却する *p l a z a* is their mallsoft record.

When genres fragment into microscopic subgenres, it is sometimes argued that this level of nano-classification is valueless, or only serves to standardize the music in a way that is antithetical to innovation. In a post on the vaporwave subreddit, one of the major online platforms where vaporwave proliferated, one Redditor argues that these subgenres are useful because they identify strains of ideas that have emerged within the vaporwave genre. Identifying them serves to put words to ideas that are latent in the genre's oftentimes vague blend of inscrutable symbolism and imagery.

One offshoot of that postmodern multimedia aesthetic was the phenomenon of Simpsonswave, which was a trend emerging on online video platforms like Vine and YouTube, in which short clips from *The Simpsons* were slowed, discolored, subjected to VHS-style filters, and set to vaporwave tracks. The same thing was done to clips from *King of the Hill*. Then came a slap-bass-heavy track called SeinWave by a producer named Abelard. Finally, in 2017, a producer going by Costanza released *George*,[12] a full album of vaporwave sprinkled with *Seinfeld* sound bites.

11 "Riviera | Kodak Cameo | Fortune 500," Bandcamp, April 1, 2013, <fortune500.bandcamp.com/album/riviera>
12 "George | Costanza," Bandcamp, June 22, 2017, <cstanza.bandcamp.com/album/george>

VII.2 RINGTONES

In the mid-2000s, ringtones were big business. According to a *New York Times* article from the era, cleverly titled "The Nokia Fugue in G Major," in 2005, the chirpy medium represented a \$5 billion global market and was rapidly growing.[13] Hip-hop music commanded a big part of the market share, at least in the States; an exemplary chart from April 30, 2005 includes 50 Cent's "Candy Shop" at number one, with the rest of the top five split between Lil Jon, two Ludacris tracks, and "Disco Inferno," also by 50 Cent, at number five. The ringtone scene even birthed the monstrosity known as Crazy Frog, an anemic anthropomorphic frog developed in Sweden, originally known as "The Annoying Thing." It scored a preposterous international hit with "Axel F," a remix of Harold Faltermeyer's instrumental theme song from *Beverly Hills Cop*. An animated gummi bear from Germany jockeyed for the same market share. That era was truly peak ringtone. All these glorious digital smears could be purchased with ease—simply a text or click away.

Album art depicting Crazy Frog

The fall of the genre was precipitous. In November 2014, *Billboard* ceased publication of their Hot Ringtones chart—leaving Taylor Swift's "Shake It Off" as the final top dog. Now, most people opt for vibrate mode.[14]

Although many popular ringtones were merely snippets or retools of established hits, there were also several attempts to create original songs. Nokia hired Ryuichi Sakamoto to create original compositions for their new cell phone line. Ringtone provider Zingy commissioned an entire original album by Timbaland intended to be used as ringtones. They Might Be Giants released a few tongue-in-cheek ringtone ditties. And, on the fringes, a few avant-garde artists and labels experimented with the medium.

In November 2001, the British record label Touch, which specializes in experimental electronic music and field recordings, put out *Ringtones*. It was a CD compilation of ninety-nine tracks, featuring 177 ringtones, as prepared by various experimental artists from across the globe. Among the artists were digital avant-superstars like Oren Ambarchi, John Hudak, Fennesz, Mika Vainio, and Ryoji Ikeda. As the liner notes spell out, the idea behind the compilation was to rally against the banal tones then commanding market dominance: "We assume you already agree that the 'cheep cheep' tones of Nokia, Ericsson, and the others leave a lot to be desired."

Ringtones likely came out too early to influence the public arena because, at that time, few phones were calibrated to allow custom ringtones. But the album certainly

---

13 Melena Z. Ryzik, "The Nokia Fugue in G Major," The New York Times, July 10, 2005, <www.nytimes.com/2005/07/10/arts/music/the-nokia-fugue-in-g-major.html>
14 There is a terrific history of the ringtone industry in the first chapter in Sumanth Gopinath's book, Ringtone Dialectic: Economy and Cultural Form (2013), which expertly charts the technological, social, and economic history of ringtones from its very beginnings to its eventual decline: Sumanth Gopinath, The Ringtone Dialectic: Economy and Cultural Form, 1st ed. (Cambridge, MA: MIT Press, 2013).

did stir up a lot of press, some of which centered around one track by actress Regina Lund, who contributed a short recording of a simulated orgasm. As one livid consumer wrote in to the letters section of Britain's *Metro* newspaper:

> I read about the new ring-tone of a woman having an orgasm in Metro (Mon). How do you explain that one to a five-year-old on the bus in the morning? What next? How about a ring-tone of a fart in the toilet or someone being sick? The mind boggles.

On the other hand, Chris Watson's field recordings of animals and Bruce Gilbert's recording of an air raid siren would presage similar sound concepts that appeared on the iPhone's list of presets.

Another innovator was Ringtone Records, the work of Brice Salek, a composer and producer currently living in Spain. He told me that his interest in the intersection between science and art goes back some time. In 1998, while studying at San Francisco State University, he learned how to use computers to create visual art. He would later move to audio production, eventually ditching fine art in favor of music. "I always wanted to be a fine artist but have always had reservations about the fine art industry's support structure as a whole," he explained.

The idea for Ringtone Records hit around 2007, when ringtones were gaining in popularity. "I entered the medium at the moment when polyphonic tones gave way to master tones," he told me. It started as a creative project as opposed to a business, and he initially struggled with some conceptual questions. For one, there were no real standards for ringtones at the time, including how long they should be. He believes he was the one who set the thirty-second standard.

He told me he was one of the first producers to release a ringtone album on iTunes. Possibly the first. "My record keeping at the beginning wasn't very orderly, but I think it was an album titled *Utopia Days* released in June 2007," he recalled. "Then I released a few albums in 2008, and then a bunch in 2012 just wanted to be as creative as possible and keep the semblance of a ringing vibe. At the time, I considered ringtones as a haiku, in a musical format. Only later did I stumble onto the utilitarian practicality of two- and five-second formats for text tones."

Though Salek started out with art in mind, eventually business became the priority. "I started the label in order to get digital distribution, which was hard to come by back then," he reasoned. "The way my label functions is that I list the tracks and let people find them. I use lots of different artist names, and people keep finding them at will."

"Once people started to see that a ringtone album could be on iTunes, the amount of albums quickly grew into a monster of all kinds of garbage material being uploaded." To cope with the flood of these less-than-traditional albums, often of dubious quality, iTunes started taking them down en masse, including Salek's releases. "iTunes would take them down over and over again as they tried to keep their store in order by performing blanket-style sweeps. In iTunes' defense, they just weren't prepared for a new medium like this at the time."

Salek disagrees with the idea that ringtones are reaching their nadir, though he does agree that there has been a decline in using snippets of popular music as ringtones—a phenomenon that never really suited him anyway. He notes that his own novel productions continue to sell, explaining that he can tell what sounds are popular based on which of his works sell. "I'm finding ringtone production in general today is far better than it ever has been," he reflects optimistically.

Though Salek sees himself as separate from the arts world at large, several ringtone-related works have emerged in the fine arts sector. Many of them are described in an excellent scholarly article by Sumanth Gopinath for the *First Monday* journal.[15] *Dialtones: A Telesymphony* was an interactive art installation arranged by Golan Levin, wherein the ringtones of audience members' cell phones were activated in a coordinated fashion. A recording of one performance was released on the Staalplaat label. UK composer Jocelyn Pook wrote *Mobile,* an orchestral work that recontextualized the once-omnipresent Nokia ringtone by embracing it as a melodic motif; this was her effort to neutralize its annoyingness. Meanwhile, British artists Thomson & Craighead, whose focus is on technology and media, sold experimental ringtones through their online store, named *dot-store.*[16] The conceptual pinnacle was a silent ringtone, which raises all sorts of interesting questions—and which, in a pre-block era, sold well to those who wanted to functionally block calls from people they did not want to speak to.

---

15 Sumanth Gopinath, "View of Ringtones, or the Auditory Logic of Globalization | First Monday," First Monday 10, no. 12 (October 2005), <firstmonday.org/article/view/1295/1215>

16 Jon Thomson and Alison Craighead, "Dot-Store's Tone Zone," Thomson & Craighead's Dot-Store <www.ucl.ac.uk/slade/slide/dotstore/pages/tonezonef.html> [accessed March 19, 2022]

VII.3 BLACK MIDI

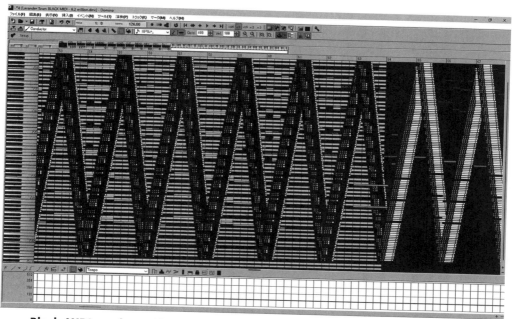

Black MIDI producer Gingeas' remix of the "Lavender Town" theme from the videogame Pokemon Green Beta. Here, the track is visualized in the popular MIDI editing program, Domino. Image courtesy of Gingeas.

Imagine it: You are scrolling around YouTube one day, and you discover a video called "{[Black MIDI]} Bad Apple Rare ASDF Mode 270.65 Million (Total NO LAG)." You open it up and are confronted with a jarring version of a song from a video game soundtrack as millions of little colored blocks fly by on screen.

This is black MIDI. A MIDI file is a computer file that stores music notation. You play it by running it through software that simulates musical instruments playing the notes. Because a computer is doing the performing, you can use it to render songs that humans are incapable of playing—overly complicated notation that historically would have only been possible using a player piano.

Intrepid internet users took this idea to the extreme, programming MIDI files to play as many notes as possible, then recording the results. The practice came to be referred to as black MIDI, because, when you view the notes in standard music notation, it is just a jumbled, black mess.

Despite the complexity and the sheer number of notes, black MIDI producers design their tracks such that, despite their cavernousness, the underlying melodies are discernible. Many black MIDI artists are also gamers, so many, if not most, of the songs available online are covers of computer game theme music. *Bad Apple*, the fourth game in a Japanese game series called *Touhou Project*, has seen its signature song embraced by the community. That game is classified as a *bullet hell* game, so named because the player is responsible for surviving a barrage of thousands of bullets without getting hit. This stimulatory exponentiality is a worthy fit for the thousands of notes per second encountered in black MIDI compositions.

After the initial black MIDI experiments, the scene embarked on an ever-escalating race to see who could produce the version with the most notes. Hitting the four million mark was a celebrated accomplishment, but now folks are well into the hundreds of millions.

Black MIDI production is a young person's game. In an interview for *VICE*, writer Matt Earp hunts down TheTrustedComputer (a.k.a. TTC), a fifteen-year-old gamer and YouTuber who was the first to hit one million notes. In that article, TTC shares some insights into the art form. First, he implores artists to ensure the melody of the song is firmly established in the notation before adorning the background with ambient notes. Second, he points out that MIDI notation can accommodate very short notes—$65,536^{th}$ notes, in fact—and that these micro-notes can be stacked en masse into the background to add to the total tally. But he insists that it is not fair game to use "crash" notes, which means to suddenly have all possible notes play at once. This is done by some folks to quickly inflate the total note number of a track, but TTC considers it jarring and incongruent with the spirit of black MIDI.

Black MIDI is a micro-scene built around a simple concept, and its moment now seems to have passed. Online, there still exists a Wiki directory of key players in the scene, aptly named Impossible Music. There is also an angular math-rock band from London who named themselves after the genre and are experiencing great success, rapidly monopolizing Google results and edging the original black MIDI clan out of circulation.

VII.4 OUTSIDERS

Outsider music is music created by performers operating far outside the conventions of mainstream music. Usually, these artists have not had formal musical training, and in many cases, they grew up sheltered from exposure to popular music, leaving them to make things up as they go along. As a result, outsider music tends to be highly idiosyncratic, abiding by sets of rules and structures that strike most ears as alien.

The reclusive artist Jandek for years circulated his prolific discography of self-recorded and self-released LPs in the back pages of independent music magazines. Each recording was deeply personal and very experimental, skirting traditional song structures and often veering into dissonance. It was never clear whether he was a competent musician choosing to be experimental or someone who didn't know better. He developed a cult following, amplified by the mystery surrounding his identity. Within the past decade, he began staging live performances, yet his sprawling body of self-released work remains a focus of obsession for a core group of fanatics.

The Shaggs, meanwhile, were a trio of sisters from rural New Hampshire who were pushed by their father to attempt a break into the record business. Neither the girls nor their father had any understanding of how pop music was written, so their musical output came across as a highly abnormal simulacrum of pop music—as if someone lived in a cave the first twenty years of their life, then tried to record pop songs based on descriptions of what pop is meant to sound like.

The outsider music pantheon is expansive, and interested parties should consult Irwin Chusid's definitive survey *Songs in the Key of Z*, one of the finest music books ever written. It is a celebration of outsider musicians' amateurism and naïveté, emphasizing their creativity and largely avoiding contempt. But it was published in 2000, and relatively little has since been written about the state of outsider music in the digital age.

Personal computing and the internet have had two distinct effects on outsider music. On one hand, the traditional barriers to music production and distribution have disappeared. While the Shaggs must have paid a miniature fortune for time in a recording studio and the services of a pressing plant, today, anyone can record at home and post their music on streaming platforms. This means that the sheer number of strange musical artifacts has expanded exponentially.

On the other hand, the internet has made popular music much more accessible to the world. Today, nobody grows up sheltered from popular music anymore, so the Shaggs effect is far less likely to occur. Conversely, people can access a diverse library of different music styles, so the digital outsider canon incorporates a far broader set of genres than yesterday's outsiders, who largely coalesced around rock music and crooning.

VII.4.1 R.A.E.D.

Now the subject of a minor online following, Lebanese-Australian rapper R.A.E.D. hit the internet in 2010 with a series of puzzling albums and accompanying YouTube videos. A self-appointed "worldwide phenomenon" with a penchant for bombastic song titles and specious graphic design, R.A.E.D. delivers strangely overdubbed, off-rhythm bars over drum machine presets. His lyrics are repetitious and vague, often enunciated at a blistering pace with idiosyncratic intonation:

> *We don't stop*
> *These girls is so hot*
> *We don't stop*
> *This place is so hot*
> *Tell me what you wanna drink*
> *'Cause you know the next one's on me*
> *Girl, drink it up, have another sip*
> *And let me know what you want for your next drink, girl*
> —(lyrics from "You Gotta Love This City," from *Straight Through*)

After a salvo of ten mixtapes between 2010 and 2013, of which 2010's *Straight Through* might be the best-known or even canonical, things thinned out for a while. Despite his ample web presence, which is largely incoherent, there is a dearth of information about R.A.E.D. himself. According to his Facebook account, R.A.E.D. was born Raed Khalil Melki on February 16, 1978. He attended a couple different high schools, graduating in 1996. He says that he completed a degree in audio engineering at the SAE Institute in 2010. Beyond that, the story descends into hearsay. There are reports he was a drug dealer, and that this is how he financed his BMW. His first track, dated to approximately 2004, was lo-fi but relatively traditional, which led one *Vice* writer to argue that R.A.E.D. "consciously derailed from the conventions of rap music, in search of something original."[17]

And yet there are features to the R.A.E.D. story that don't seem so calculated. It came out at some point that, in 2001, he got in trouble for sending threatening letters to record executive Michael Gudinski, apparently after Gudinski declined to sign him to a record contract. He also, at one point, phoned in a bomb hoax to a local casino, then stayed on the line and performed a freestyle rap for the negotiators.

After he went dark for a while in the late 2010s, fans sorted out that he was serving time in jail, reportedly for stealing tools out of someone's car. But he was released in 2019 and subsequently released his latest opus, *Warping Through*, replete with such telling songs as "I Did It Cause I Could" and "Don't Want This in No Court Room."

R.A.E.D. has also released a slew of music videos, which emphasize his muscly torso and show him surrounded by a small group of friends. He also, improbably, released a feature film called *Still Flowin*, which is an idiosyncratically acted and even more idiosyncratically edited fictionalization of the Michael Gudinski incident. A relatively in-depth review[18] by the *Bad Movie Night Monday* blog reports that the plot was so incomprehensible, they had to consult IMDB for a synopsis. They also note that both

---

17 Mahmood Fazal, "RAED Is a Rapper From the Future," VICE, August 3, 2018, <www.vice.com/en/article/vbpaem/raed-is-a-rapper-from-the-future>
18 Kay, "Still Flowin: The Movie [2014]," Bad Movie Night, September 19, 2017, <badmovienightmonday.blogspot.com/2017/09/still-flowin-movie-2014.html>

the start and the finish of the film feature R.A.E.D.'s bank information, so that you can wire him money.

VII.4.2 Viper

You'll Cowards Don't Even Smoke Crack

You'll Cowards Don't Even Smoke Crack is the name of the 2008 album that brought Viper, a Houston-based rapper, to the attention of the internet. Released on CD with a DIY cover featuring a close-up image of Viper's dopey-eyed face, it became a viral phenomenon, just as much for its glaring grammatical indiscretion as its eccentric and lo-fi interpretation of rap music. Viper has, in interviews, stated it only takes him fifteen to twenty minutes to write a song, in part because he has an extensive backlog of lyrics written in prison.[19] As a consequence, his discography is sprawling; he is said to have put out 333 albums in 2004 alone![20]

He is ambitious in all facets. He is a licensed real estate broker and the owner of at least three businesses (a real estate company, a company that sells "products," and a company that sells "services"). He even runs a website called World Rap Star, intended to compete with WorldStar HipHop but requiring artists to pay far less for exposure.

Viper, whose real name is Lee Carter, was born in El Dorado, Arkansas, but he considers Houston his hometown, having moved there at age six. Growing up in the Hiram Clarke subdivision, he may have been inspired by Big Mello, a local gangsta rapper who rose to prominence in the early nineties, boosting the neighborhood's profile nationally. Viper supposedly started rapping at age nine. In interviews, he mentions that he was in a gang growing up and used to deal crack cocaine, spending time in prison in his younger years. Regardless, he graduated from the University of Houston in 2000, having studied both business and real estate.

Viper seems to hit all the checkboxes for an outsider musician. His music is joyfully divorced from genre convention. He is prolific. He is unafraid to relentlessly promote himself. And though he portrays an image of a hardened drug dealer turned rap impresario, there is a wide-eyed naïveté to his own belief in his endless stream of creative content.

Viper's discography is intimidating to the newcomer, to say the least. It's just mixtape after mixtape, totaling nearly one thousand, many with ridiculous titles:

Put Sum Relish and Musta on It It Ain't Extra 2
Fuck Tha World It Ain't Real I Bend Tha Spoon Wit My Mind 2
Move Ova!! Gimme Dat Bike So I Can Ride It Into Tha Pool
Atomic Bombs and Mutually Assured Destruction Is Fuckin' Stupid II
Muscles

---

19 Jackson Hudgins, "An Interview with VIPER," KRLX: Carleton College, January 24, 2015, <web.archive.org/web/20150709233315/http://www.krlx.org/index.php/130-cisco-hayward-and-david-demark-interview-viper?showall=&start=2>

20 "Our Annual List of the 'Top 333 Albums of 2014' Was Filled Entirely by an Underground Rapper Named Viper.," Rooster Magazine, December 19, 2014, <therooster.com/blog/our-annual-list-top-333-albums-2014-was-filled-entirely-underground-rapper-named-viper>

EXTREME MUSIC

Many of the album covers are just images of models pulled from the internet, often stretched to fit the format. Viper's name and his preposterous titles are laid over the graphics in sans serif fonts. They have all the indications of an MS Paint job.

You'll Cowards Don't Even Smoke Crack is a logical entry point. While there are several versions of it available (including both a "Futuristic Space Age Remix" version and a "Space Age Remix/Screwed and Chopped" version), you are probably best off starting with the original. Lyrically, this album falls within the gangsta rap paradigm. It discusses the various facets of Viper's life as a drug dealer. Some songs address his readiness to shoot someone dead if needed ("I Sell Dope Boy," "Merciless"). Others revel in his profound wealth ("My Money Rolls," "That Baller Out Your Best Side"). The first track is the title track, and it captures what makes Viper great. An oddly flat rhythm frames Viper's oddly deadpan voice, which is characteristically out of step with his passionate treatise on the pleasures of smoking crack cocaine, featuring one-liners like "I'm about to blaze up, 'specially when it's after dinner," and "My coke chopped and screwed 'cause I ball on the block."

VII.4.3 Farrah Abraham

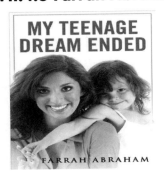

My Teenage Dream Ended

Farrah Abraham's case is a strange one in that she was a celebrity before she was an outsider musician. Born in Nebraska and raised in Iowa, she rose to stardom after appearing on an episode of the MTV reality show *16 and Pregnant*. In that episode, she became pregnant as a teenager and her mother forbade her from having an abortion. Then the father of her child died in a car accident. Her tragic story resonated with viewers, and she was subsequently cast in a full season of *Teen Mom*, another MTV show.

The rest of her career has been spent dwindling between several lower rungs of fame and she has callously been a recurrent target of tabloid magazines. She has starred in several reality television programs, published several books, appeared in low-budget horror films, and even raised eyebrows by featuring in a couple of pornographic movies. But the most unique artifact of her career is her album, *My Teenage Dream Ended*.

MTDE is the perfect distillation of contemporary outsider music. Lyrically, it follows the narrative arc of her high school relationship, unintentional pregnancy, and quest for independence. It finishes with the hopeful "Finally Getting Up from Rock Bottom." From a musical standpoint, however, it is unusual. Modern electronic backing tracks are juxtaposed against Abraham talk-singing in a stream-of-consciousness manner, as on "After Prom":

Waiting for this moment
I'm the king of the world
Trying to find the truth

Crumbles, you will too
Trying to become perfect
Get up a clue

But what lends the record its true strangeness is the way her vocals have been subjected to extreme autotune in an attempt to convert them into songs. *MTDE* takes the tools of modern music production and turns them into the Shaggs.

An interview with Fredrick M. Cuevas,[21] the producer of *My Teenage Dream Ended*, provides some revealing insider information about the album. A mixing engineer by profession, Cuevas met Abraham while doing audio dubbing work for *16 and Pregnant*. After chatting about music for a while, Abraham asked him how he would feel producing an album of her music. He agreed, thinking that he could parlay the experience into further gigs.

Cuevas explains that the album's strange disjunction between music and words, and Abraham's unusual flow, were the result of her choosing to sing her vocal parts without the music playing. In fact, according to Cuevas, her deeply personal lyrics came straight from the pages of her diary. Most of the production work involved Cuevas trying to wrangle Abraham's vocal parts into his instrumental tracks, then sending them to her to sign off on. After an initial single was released via the tabloid magazine *In Touch Weekly*, she self-released the album digitally in 2012. No physical release has occurred, and she has not discussed the record since its release, yet it remains a singular document of pop culture strangeness.

VII.4.4 Al Walser

The 2012 Grammy Award for Best Dance Recording featured, amongst the nominees, such international stars as Skrillex, Avicii, Calvin Harris, and Swedish House Mafia. But the fifth candidate was a song called "I Can't Live Without You" by Al Walser. As music critic Philip Sherburne noted in an article for *Spin* magazine,[22] even after his nomination was announced, Walser's Facebook page only boasted 1,437 likes, and two versions of the song's video had accumulated fewer than 7,000 views combined. Sherburne aptly observed that the track's "clunky rock/trance fusion and low-budget video make Rebecca Black's 'Friday' sound and look cutting-edge in comparison."

Sherburne did some digging and discovered that Walser, who was born in Liechtenstein, had been a member of the exuberant Eurodance franchise called Fun Factory in the mid-nineties and had since moved to Hollywood. He is a relentless self-promoter, having published a book titled *Musicians Make it Big: An Insider Reveals the Secret Path to Break in Today's Music Industry*, and operated both a record label and a music licensing company. It is this blustering faith in his own exceptionalism that Walser shares with a certain breed of outsider artists.

21 Duncan Cooper, "Farrah Abraham's Pop Music Should Make Her an Avant-Garde Icon," The FADER, November 21, 2017, <www.thefader.com/2017/11/21/farrah-abraham-album-producer-interview>

22 Philip Sherburne, "Who the Hell Is Al Walser and How Did He Get an EDM Grammy Nomination?," SPIN, December 6, 2012, <www.spin.com/2012/12/al-walser-edm-grammy-nomination/>

EXTREME MUSIC

It subsequently emerged that Walser had essentially gamed the Grammy nominating system. He released his song days before the Grammy cutoff, then doggedly promoted his song to the Grammy members responsible for voting in nominees. His nomination even withstood the auditing process of Deloitte, which scrutinizes Grammy picks every year to filter out scams. The Grammy organization's vice president of awards, Bill Freimuth, told MTV News: "I'm disappointed to learn that we have a nominee whose music is not embraced by the community from which he comes; that's always hard to hear. That said, I congratulate Mr. Walser as a nominee along with all the other nominees, because he certainly earned his Grammy nomination, whether it was through the power or quality of his music alone, or his ability to market that in a way that appealed to our members."[23]

VII.4.5 Chief Kooffreh

Doctor Viagra Hard Stone

Through YouTube, Spotify, and CDBaby, the Lawrence, Massachusetts-based[24] recording artist Chief Kooffreh has assembled a sprawling body of lo-fi music that is entirely composed of him freestyling repetitive lines over Casio loops. Sometimes his backing is just a drum machine, whereas at other times he adds some keys to the mix. His "BOSTON MASS PEOPLE USA" video, which has amassed eighteen views on YouTube, is a ten-minute loop with an occasional distorted siren thrown into the mix, the Chief speak-singing "Boston, we love you," and other Beantown-themed pleasantries over the top. The video itself is a sprawling collage of images of public figures and handheld footage of different parts of the city. An even more bizarre artifact is called "PRINCESS DIANA ACCIDENT OR MURDERED BY CHIEF KOOFFREH TOP USA MUSIC STAR/CHAIRMAN," parlaying a similar format over twelve minutes.

Not much is known about the Chief, though on his hyperactive and baffling Twitter account, he purports to be a "voting member of the Grammy" and the "Most RECORDED Published Artist in North East of USA." He has also released several songs about the Calabar people of Nigeria; this, combined with the fact that Kooffreh is also the last name of a law professor at the University of Calabar, leads me to suspect he is originally from the same area. One of Chief Kooffreh's other Princess Diana-themed releases was covered[25] in a *Guardian* series on "The 101 strangest records on Spotify," in particular a song called "Tragedy and Dead of Princess Diana England" off an album incongruously named *Doctor Viagra Hard Stone*.

23 James Montgomery, "Exclusive: Al Walser Won't Be Stripped Of His Grammy Nom," MTV, December 10, 2012, <www.mtv.com/news/1698657/al-walser-grammy-nomination-best-dance-music/>

24 "Chief Kooffreh (Chiefkooffreh) on Myspace," MySpace <myspace.com/chiefkooffreh> [accessed March 19, 2022]

25 Rob Fitzpatrick, "The 101 Strangest Records on Spotify: Chief Kooffreh — Tragedy And Dead Of Princess Diana England," The Guardian, September 12, 2012, <www.theguardian.com/music/musicblog/2012/sep/12/chief-kooffreh-tragedy-princess-diana>

VII.4.6 Fallen Vengeance

On January 8, 2012, a video appeared on YouTube titled "Seven Nation Army (Pre-Release) (Complete)," uploaded by a user named FallenVengeance1. Its static background image depicted an eight-person band, each member represented by a different plastic soldier; eventually, this obscure upload accumulated nearly 500,000 views. The audio is a cover of the White Stripes song "Seven Nation Army," as performed by a self-appointed "Teenage screamo band coming to rock your world! hahah." It starts off with the song's iconic bassline, a harbinger of a cataclysmically inept and off-tempo rendition of the song, adapted with hoarse screamo vocals.

The song was the work of Fallen Vengeance, a band of Pennsylvania high school students whose Facebook page cites other screamo bands like Asking Alexandria and Escape the Fate as influences.[26] That adorable page features discussions among the various group members about organizing practice sessions and designing album art. There are also vitriolic debates about which popular songs to cover in screamo style (regarding covering "Lay Me Down" by the Dirty Heads, one member chides another: "Ew, that song sucks, no way to possibly scream an acoustic song it'd be like doing Iris, we'd be hated"). Fallen Vengeance, apparently, sprung from the "long-lost band" Sacrificial Affliction and was started by Brett McCaffrey and Ryan Smalley, each of whose instrument is listed as "screams." Sadly, no Sacrificial Affliction recordings are available online.

Tantalizingly, the members of Fallen Vengeance discuss a five-song EP with an auspicious track list, but it is unclear if the songs were ever recorded, since they only mention rehearsing them:

1. *Who Says Love Can't Be Fake?*
2. *Love Lasts Forever... ... Psh, Nothing Lasts Forever*
3. *OMG! The Boogie Man is Under My Bed*
4. *Interlude*
5. *I Used to Have A Best Friend (But Then He Took An Arrow To The Knee)*

Only the brief "Interlude" is available to be listened to, and it is a gem. Fallen Vengeance's last post came on June 19, 2012, comprising only one word: "#fail". But before their quiet end, there was discussion of a sponsorship from an emo apparel company called Arkaik Clothing and a remarkable trove of band art.

VII.4.7 Girls With Attitude

In April 2000, a group of preteen girls from Montreal, presumably accompanied by one of their parents, uploaded a string of MP3s to the early file-sharing website mp3.com. They went by Girls With Attitude and accompanied their music with a band photo depicting their Photoshop-disembodied heads floating on a preset background. Their complete output comprises five ultra-brief songs with banal titles like "A Fun Time Is A Great Time" and "Don't Judge Me." Their collective vocals do not match the rhythms of the Casio preset rhythms and dinky synths, and nothing is in key.

---

26 "Fallen Vengeance," Facebook <www.facebook.com/fallenvengeance/about/> [accessed March 19, 2022]

Because of their amateurish sound, these songs were disseminated via internet humor sites, a reminder that cruel viral sensations are hardly a new phenomenon. Even *Time* magazine got into the mix, remarking on a GWA song's "extreme awfulness" in a brief 2001 article titled "Bad Music Online."[27] Yet their music has its charms, including the seemingly inadvertent nihilism of their most remarkable track, "There's Nothing in My Dreams." In 2012, the small record label One Kind Favor reissued their "complete recordings" as a twenty-seven-copy edition of lathe-cut singles, presumably on an unauthorized basis.[28]

VII.4.8 Ornaments of Agony

Зовлонгийн Угалзе

This is a Mongolian one-man black metal band in which someone named Albin sings and plays drums, guitars, and keyboards in a highly idiosyncratic fashion.[29] A number of demos have come out since Albin started recording in 2001, but 2007's self-released *Зовлонгийн Угалзе* album seems to be the seminal release.[30] It is a plodding tract of drawn-out bass fuzz, discordant guitar, and tracheotomy-caliber vocals. As a review for the *Coagulopath* website points out, this is an especially sloppy permutation of the funeral doom genre.[31]

VII.4.9 Hekaloth Records

This bizarre Vancouver label advertised itself as "Unlike Anything You've Ever Heard Before" on its basic HTML website, which has long since evaporated from the internet.[32] Their specialty was "orchestral metal that employs epic themes," but the key gimmick was that all the music was entirely made using a guitar synthesizer. "We believe that the guitar synthesizer represents a new frontier in music," their website argued. The apotheosis of the label's bizarreness was the album *Tournament at Constantinople* by Shevalreq. The press release promises "growled vocals accompanied by the sounds of World Music instruments such as Indian tablas and sitars, Chinese erhu violins and zheng zithers, Indonesian gamelan as well as western orchestral instruments." In reality, all said instruments are synthesized using that same guitar synthesizer, typically with a very thin sound surrounded by plenty of negative space. As a result, the half-spoken growl-vocals just hang in the air amongst the repetitive synth lines. It's impossible to make out most of the words, but we're told that the fourteen songs are based on a medieval poem, "Orlando Innamorato," by Matteo Maria Boiardo.

27 Lev Grossman, "Bad Online Music," TIME, May 27, 2001, <content.time.com/time/magazine/article/0,9171,128113,00.html>

28 "Girls With Attitude 7" LATHE CUT | Girls With Attitude | One Kind Favor Vinyl Records," Bandcamp <onekindfavor.bandcamp.com/album/girls-with-attitude-7-lathe-cut> [accessed March 19, 2022]

29 www.last.fm/music/Ornaments+Of+Agony/+wiki

30 "Ornaments Of Agony Biography," Last.fm <www.last.fm/music/Ornaments+Of+Agony/+wiki> [accessed March 19, 2022]

31 "Зовлонгийн Угалз [Zowlongiyn Ugalz] by Ornaments of Agony (Album, Funeral Doom Metal): Reviews, Ratings, Credits, Song List," Rate Your Music <rateyourmusic.com/release/album/ornaments_of_agony/зовлонгийн_угалз__zowlongiyn_ugalz_/> [accessed March 19, 2022]

32 "Hekaloth Records," <web.archive.org/web/20110207182436/http://www.hekaloth.com/> [accessed March 19, 2022]

Other records from the Hekaloth stable include Gluttony's *Collapse of the Roman Republic (Liber Primus)*, which deals with the "events in Roman history between 107 and 70 B.C." and Xynfonica's seventy-minute *A Feast for Famished Ravens*, in which "[s]ix part contrapuctual [*sic*] harmonies juxtaposing strings horns and woodwind sections provide a background for three very long songs based on legends of the Viking age."

Tonetta, as he appears in his *Pressure Zone* video.

VII.4.10 Tonetta[33]

Tonetta is the stage name of a sixtysomething upholsterer from Toronto who has reportedly been a recluse since his wife left him in 1983. Since then, he has shut out popular media and focused on recording songs, using a guitar and an old drum machine. After distributing cassettes locally, someone offered to post his videos to YouTube, and in 2008, his solo performances started to appear on the online streaming platform. These videos reveal him performing idiosyncratic songs like "Be My Concubine" and "Let Me Be Your Drain Tonight" in strange outfits—sometimes just a thong and gimp mask. His isolation from mass media has led to the songs sounding alien and anachronistic. An online following developed, and the label Black Tent Press put out a series of compilations under the name 777.

---

33 Cian Traynor, "Hitler Would Have Loved You: Tonetta Interviewed," The Quietus, December 6, 2011, <thequietus.com/articles/07536-tonetta-interview>

CONCLUSION

CONCLUSION

Are there lessons to be learned from this sprawling examination of music's far reaches? It is difficult to draw connections between such disparate corners. However, it is interesting how certain ideas tend to bunch together, the same concepts attracting individuals from totally different backgrounds. The allure of long-duration music captured the minds of stalwart composer John Cage, underground loft kids Bull of Heaven, and atmospheric ambient producer Robert Rich, among many others. Hardcore kids, digital-age chiptune producers, and opportunistic major labels have all been motivated to put out new music on dead formats like 8-track and floppy disk. Silent and unplayable recordings have been pulled off from all corners: highly theoretical experimental composers, enterprising PR people, underground noise acts— even Sly Stone.

But even *between* these different conceptual extremes, there are convergences. At heart, many extremes share a sense of simplicity, of minimalism. Harsh noise wall represents the apogee of loudness, but at its heart it is highly minimal: unchanging blocks of harsh noise with no structure, melody, or rhythm. Conceptually, this has much in common with the prolonged silences and scant nibs of sound heard on lowercase and *onkyô* recordings, even though the music couldn't look more different on a waveform graph. At heart, any conceptual extreme becomes minimal: as you push further toward the edge, a concept becomes increasingly pure, and there is incrementally less room for variety. Tracks that are millions of years long have no choice but to depend on repetition. Beats become so fast they turn into pure tones. Goregrind music gets limited to microscopically fine variations upon nomenclature from medical textbooks, countless album covers and track listings recycling the same technical jargon and enteric imagery. Even the prodigious work of outsider artists like Chief Kooffreh and Viper, loosened from music convention, ends up paradoxically minimal. Abiding by the surrealists' maxim that art should emerge from the unconscious mind, these artists are something like the abstract expressionists of the music world. Following the shortest possible path from the subconscious to expression, their music typically features an economy of musical devices and depends heavily on repetition—long, repeating loops of sound and repeated lyrical refrains.

Between the extremes, there is another emerging theme: extreme music as a social ritual, as a way to pursue intimacy. Elaborately packaged, handmade editions, such as the ones produced by American Tapes and MSBR Records, allowed experimental music enthusiasts from across the world to come together, trading their personal creations by mail. The idea of unplayable anti-records was similarly taken on by many artists and labels, becoming a rite of passage for some artists, a nod between those in the know. Vaporwave's hyperspecific microgenres become ways for bedroom producers to share in certain emotions, often rooted in a feeling of nostalgia—sometimes for an imagined past. Fast music purveyors established networks of fellow speed-freaks who convened on obscure online message boards to enthuse about their passion. Lathe-cut records, with their myriad permutations—shaped records, small records, bizarre Eulerian records, et cetera—have become the focus of an intricate cottage industry of purveyors and consumers who cherish intimately small-edition productions. This may be the crux of it; all music is about communication, but in the case of conceptually extreme music, it's about the communication of ideas—a shared enthusiasm for strange and whimsical notions.

I will end with a mysterious discovery that occurred recently, a truly unusual set of artifacts that seems to capture several of this book's ideas. In early 2014, a musician named Ben Opie discovered a bizarre record at a Pittsburgh record store: inside a handmade record sleeve was a record made up of pieces of eight other LPs, meticulously assembled and glued together into one 12" disc such that it could be played on a standard turntable. Seeing that it was attributed to a Conglomerate Records of Connellsville, Pennsylvania—a label he had never heard of and could find no record of online—he posted about his find to a local message board for the area, asking if anyone knew anything about it. Nobody did, but an employee of the record store told him that the record was sold to the store by the widow of a local record collector. Even better, Opie learned that the store had a whole pile of other releases from the same mysterious Conglomerate Records: dozens of artifacts released under a variety of different names, all of them unique to Conglomerate from Connellsville, a town in the northwestern corner of the state. These included a half-melted cassette, a tape of the Beatles' *Revolver* played in reverse, an unplayable anti-record with a CD and cassette glued to its surface, a fictional compilation featuring "11 Northwestern Pennsylvania noise bands" (none of which seem to have actually existed), and a release called *One Second* which was simply a loose strip of magnetic tape and shards of a cassette. The true treasure of the collection was an eight-cassette box set containing, among other things, a cassette shell filled with dry macaroni.

Though Opie tells me he has since become convinced he knows who assembled this mysterious discography, which dates to the late eighties based on information on a few of the releases, its origins remain shrouded in mystery. No other copies of any of these releases have shown up, suggesting they were one-offs—though one of the releases bills itself as an edition of fifty. Were these odd items created as a spoof on the noise and experimental music scene of the time? Were they shared with friends, or exhibited at an art gallery? All we can do is guess. But what is certain is that they required a lot of time and effort to produce. That creating them was a meticulous and, dare I say, *extreme* endeavor. The dogged pursuit of a very specific concept.

Indeed, the Conglomerate Records collection touches upon a surprising number of the extreme ideas explored in this book. There are several unplayable anti-records and anti-cassettes. There is a silent tape. There is a cassette adorned with hardcore pornography. Several releases are elaborately packaged, including a tape with a sandpaper cover. There is harsh noise and found sound. An archaic 78 RPM record even makes it into the picture.

That this collection of bizarre releases exists, perhaps as a meta-statement about the fringe music scene, is a testament to the universality of several of these extreme concepts. All the ideas appearing in this book are alive today, meaning their stories are still being told. What the future holds is anyone's guess.

INDEX

A

B

C

D

F

G

U

V

W

X

Y

Z

ACKNOWLEDGEMENTS

Thank you to my partner, Mary, for her love, patience, and support, and for workshopping several parts of this book. Thanks to Mom for her inspiration and counsel. Thanks as well to Christopher Heron and Yvon Poukhovski-Sheremeteyev for their guidance and suggestions along the way.

Thank you to the artists, label owners, collectors, and other folks who generously answered my myriad questions and shared their fascinating stories. Thank you, Mathias Aeschlimann, Arnaud of Sulfuric Diarrhea Records, Matt Bacon, Sean Beard, Tore Honoré Bøe, Jordan Bortner, Keith Brewer, Nathan Brown, Phil Brown, Jerry Cammarata, Spencer Clark, Sylvain Chauveau, Fabrizio De Bon, Ashley Davies, Frans de Waard, Braco Dimitrijević, Disconscious, Michael Dixon, Tim Drage, Rudolf Eb.er, Petter Flaten Eilertsen, Jornt Elzinga, Davide Femia, Curtis Godino, Jordan Gray, Treven Hall, René Heid, Pea Hicks, Zoë Irvine, Robert Jelinek, Neil Jennings, Christopher Jion, Kenny Johansson, Ant Jones, Mike Juliano, Jukka Junttila, GX Jupitter-Larsen, Himeko Katagiri, Neil Keener, Evgenij V. Kharitonov, Freek Kinkelaar, Tuomas Kinnunen, Vincent Koreman, Ron Lessard, Darren Little, Local News, Ivan Loi, Francisco López, Dr. Rainer E. Lotz, Douglas Lucas, Alastair Mabon, Bobby Maggard, Alexander Matulionis, C.V. Mansoor, Liam McGeorge, Sam McKinlay, Sean McMillan, Dr. Ian D. Mellish, Midnight Television/Computer Slime, Paolo Mongardi, Mortlock of Hades Mining Co., Paul Nemeth, Patrick Neve, Kai Nobuko, John Olson, Wolfe Padaver, Romain Perrot, Shaun Phelps, Eric Prykowski, Erik Raddatz, Collin J. Rae, Joe Raimond, Chris Reierson, Kirsten Reynolds, Simon Reynolds, Riccardo of Menthe de Menthe, Robert Rich, Roger Richards, Mark Riddick, Michael Ridge, Martin Ritter, Tony Roberts, René Rondeau, Matt Rue, Richard Rupenus, Brice Salek, Dante Augustus Scarlatti, Harold Schellinx, James Shearman, Julien Skrobek, Jacob Smigel, Skot/Scott Spear, Chris Stowe, Malcolm Tent, Swift Treweeke, William Tyler, Erwin Van Den Bosch, Nicola Vinciguerra, Freda Wallace, Matt Wand, Justin Waters, Mars F. Wellink, James Whitehead, Kyle Willey, Mark Windisch, and Philipp Wolokitin. If I missed you, I apologize profusely—your time and knowledge were greatly appreciated.

Thank you also to those who shared images of their work or items in their collection. Many of these photographs were included in this text, but others were dropped during the formatting process. In addition to the individuals already mentioned above, many of whom provided images, I also want to thank 1000 + Records, Dan Berkman of Jump Jump Music, Emanuele Bonini, Adam David, Henrik Falck, Andy Garza, Peter Huttingerm, Jules at Industrial Strength Records, Ted Malmros, Daniel Menche, Henry Rollins, and Jan van Toorn, Peter William Patrick Wend, and Geir Yven.

An extra thanks to John Olson and Henry Rollins who gave us permission to use the unique packaging of D.L. Savings T.X.'s *Thank You Urine Doll* cassette (American Tapes) within this book's cover art. The packaging was created by Olson and the photo taken by Rollins. (See page 232 for more context.) An extra thanks, as well, to Tim Drage, a.k.a. Cementimental, who provided permission for us to use a page from his harsh noise graphic novel within the cover.

And a big thank you to the Feral House family, who took this from a raw manuscript to the final product you hold in your hands. Thank you to Meg van Huygen for her editing genius, to Ron Kretsch for his design prowess, to Monica Rochester for her skillful behind-the-scenes work, indexing, and connections, and to Christina Ward and Jessica Parfrey for their belief in the book and everything else.